THE VICTORIAN
SCHOOL MANAGER

The Victorian School Manager

A Study in the Management of Education 1800–1902

PETER GORDON

WOBURN PRESS — LONDON

First published 1974 in Great Britain by
WOBURN PRESS
67 Great Russell Street, London WC1B 3BT, England

and in United States of America by
WOBURN PRESS
c/o International Scholarly Book Services, Inc.
P.O. Box 4347, Portland, Oregon 97208

ISBN 0 7130 0125 9

Library of Congress Catalog Card No. 72–90149

Printed in Great Britain by
Clarke, Doble & Brendon Ltd.,
Plymouth

Contents

Illustrations

Acknowledgments

In writing this book, I have been dependent to a very large extent upon a great number of owners of private papers and custodians of records, particularly county and borough archivists. Their willingness to grant permission to use extracts from various documents was readily forthcoming and I would here like to acknowledge my gratitude to those concerned.

For their kind permission to quote from family papers, I have to thank the Marquess of Salisbury (Salisbury Papers); the Duke of Devonshire (Devonshire Papers); Lord Cottisloe (Fremantle Papers); Lord Harrowby (Harrowby Papers); Lord Hampton (Hampton Papers); Lord St. Aldwyn (Hicks Beach Papers); Lord Medway (Cranbrook Papers); Lord Spencer (Althorp Papers); Lord Hambleden (Hambleden Papers); Lord Chilston (Chilston Papers); Captain G. M. Salvin (Salvin Papers); Mr. S. C. Whitbread (Whitbread Papers) and Mr. D. L. Arkwright (Arkwright Papers); and Sir Henry Beresford-Peirse for a quotation from the Robert Hird Diary. I am grateful to Messrs. Routledge & Kegan Paul and the University of Toronto Press for allowing me to quote from Lord Chilston's book *Chief Whip: The Political Life and Times of Aretas Akers-Douglas, 1st Viscount Chilston.*

I would like to express my thanks to the National Trust for permission to make use of the Disraeli Papers at Hughenden Manor, Bucks.; the Trustees of the British Museum (Peel, Cobden, Ripon, Gladstone, Cross, Osborne and Balfour Papers); the Public Record Office (Russell Papers); and the Librarians of the University of Birmingham (Chamberlain Papers) and the University of Sheffield (Mundella Papers).

My thanks are due also to the following for permission to use school managers' minute books, log books and correspondence relating to schools: the Rev. A. J. Comber, Leeds; the Rev. M. J. Ellingsen, High Coniscliffe, Co. Durham; the Rev. R. G. Ellis, Swaffham Prior, Cambs.; the Rev. C. C. Forster, Brafferton, Yorks.; the Rev. J. N. T. Howat, Wheldrake, Yorks.; the Rev. A. F. Lazenby, Houghton-le-Skerne, Co. Durham; the Rev. I. C. Maxwell, Stanhope, Co. Durham; the Rev. H. G. Salisbury, Norham, Northumberland; the Rev. E. O. Sheild, Leeds; the Rev. P. Wright, Tanfield Village, Co. Durham; and many other incumbents whose school records are mentioned in the book.

The unfailing courtesy and helpfulness of the staffs of the county and borough record offices, and university libraries, in tracing relevant materials is here gratefully acknowledged. The list of offices is given at the beginning of the Bibliography. The excellent collection of books on British topography consulted at the London Library deserves a special mention.

For permission to reproduce the illustrations I must thank the following: Bedfordshire County Record Office; Dorset Record Office; Durham County Record Office; Exeter City Library; Greater London Record Office; Lincolnshire Archives Office; Manchester Central Library; the National Portrait Gallery and *Punch*.

I wish to express my gratitude for the advice and assistance of Professor D. V. Donnison, Centre for Environmental Studies, and Professor G. Baron of the London University Institute of Education. Finally, I would like to thank my wife for her constant encouragement and invaluable support during the writing of this book.

Introduction

Graham Balfour, in a lecture delivered in February 1921, first drew attention to the growing importance of the elementary school manager in the system of educational administration during the period with which this study is concerned: "Local administrators of education, other than trustees a hundred years ago, there were none. Indeed it is very curious how imperceptibly that important figure of the latter half of the nineteenth century, the School Manager, steals into existence. In such extracts from the Minutes of the Committee of Council as I have been able to consult, I find no reference to him before the end of 1843, while four years later the 'management clauses' of the committee were the chief battleground between the central authority and those who had local control of the schools as well as, in most cases, the privilege of paying for them."[1]

It has been shown by Professor J. J. Findlay[2] that the term "management" has long been used in text books on education to signify what in other communities is meant by government and organization; that is to say, it indicates the rules devised by the staff for internal government as distinguished from the external control of authority. The word "management" has been used indifferently, to include surveys of curriculum and method and, during the period under review, even class control. In the chapters which follow, the term "management" is used in the sense of a body which exercised control and supervision over the school personnel and organization.

The evolution of systematic school management, as will be shown subsequently, had begun earlier in the century. The use of the term "manager" for those concerned with elementary education clearly indicated their functions. Sir Fred Clarke wrote "that the mass of the English people have never yet evolved genuine schools of their own. Schools have always been provided for them from above, in a form and with a content of studies that suited the ruling interests".[3] Certainly, the concept taken from nineteenth century political economists of the school manager as an employer of labour, found its exemplification in the Revised Code of 1862. Binns has pointed out that this tradition was later imported into the school boards which retained the old terminology and philosophy of the voluntary system. "The members of school boards were men and women trained in the management of voluntary schools. They found themselves still called the managers of their school in the Government Code, and they looked on themselves as the thinking entrepreneurs in a business in which the teachers were the executive hands. The tremendous influence of English social tradition helped to make this assumption easier. The early voluntary managers and members of school boards were 'gentlemen and ladies'. The teachers were not."[4]

This study is an attempt to examine and assess not only the work of the school manager but the changing conception of management especially in response to administrative, political, legal, social and economic pressures. This can be particularly discerned in attempted innovations in forms of management such as local managers under the school boards and the establishment of Voluntary Schools Associations from 1897. Three strands seem to be of particular importance: the political climate in which decisions affecting management were undertaken and which has so far received scant attention from educational historians;[5] the procedures and policies devised by personnel of the Education Department (later, the Board of Education) in dealing with school managers; and, thirdly, the way in which school managers conceived their tasks as compared with what in fact did happen in an era of bureaucratic expansion. To this might be added the need to analyse the social composition of managing committees and the constraints placed upon eligibility.

For the study of the political impact upon management, the correspondence of the leading figures involved in educational issues has been examined. Some indication of the attitudes adopted by members of the Education Department towards questions and principles arising out of day-to-day dealings with managers has been gleaned by reference to the vast collection of policy files of the Department and those for individual schools, both board and voluntary. For the views and activities of the school managers themselves, the most valuable source is to be found in the managers' minute books of these schools. A national survey of these has been undertaken; where they have survived they were largely to be found in either county or local record offices and municipal libraries.

Little attention has been paid in published works to the backgrounds of the three main types of managers considered in this study—the voluntary school, school board and local managers—although the extent to which the same persons were also involved in similar work on other public bodies has been considered by some authors. E. R. Wickham, for example, in a study of Sheffield showed how the same laymen led the town as Commissioners of Police, Overseers of the Poor, officers of the Cutlers' Company and directors of the Gas Company.[6]

Many of the issues which were raised during the period under review have relevance to the present day educational situation. For instance, it will be seen that much attention was focused during the last decade of the century on the question of parental representation on managing bodies, which in turn threw up the issue of the relationship between school and home. The efficiency of the managing body as a viable administrative unit was questioned; this led to experiments in places such as London in different forms of management. In view of recent changes in local government involving the reshaping of administrative areas, it is of interest to observe the adaptations made by school managers in similar situations during the last century. It has recently been argued that there is a need to build up a body of case studies in educational administration from which systematic content can be developed.[7] The evolution of the school manager during the period of this study presents an opportunity for such a contribution.

REFERENCES

1   G. Balfour, "Local Authorities—Their History" in *Educational Administration: Two lectures delivered before the University of Birmingham in February 1921* (1921), p. 9.

2   J. J. Findlay, *The Foundations of Education, Vol. 2, The Practice of Education* (1927), p. 100.

3   F. Clarke, *Education and Social Change* (1940), p. 30.

4   H. B. Binns, *A Centenary of Education 1808–1908* (1908), p. 172.

5   Sir Edward Boyle, a former Minister of Education, has remarked that "nobody could write the history of education without reference to what political parties thought about it." *The Times*, 20 October, 1969.

6   E. R. Wickham, *The Church and People in an Industrial City* (1957), p. 83. See also, W. L. Burn, *The Age of Equipoise* (1964).

7   G. Baron, "The Study of Educational Administration in England" in G. Baron and W. Taylor (eds.) *Educational Administration and the Social Sciences* (1969), p. 13.

1

The Voluntary School Manager—I

THE COMPOSITION OF THE MANAGING BODY

MOTIVES FOR MANAGEMENT

The history of the management of voluntary schools during the nineteenth century centres round a number of issues: for instance, the extent of religious influence in the school committees (Management Clauses 1847–50), the relationship between managers and teachers (Revised Code 1862), the advent of the Education Department in laying down conditions for grant aid, the legal limitations placed upon some by the Charity and Endowed School Commissioners, and the effects of Parliamentary legislation on their organization (the Free Education Act 1891, the Voluntary Schools Act 1897 and later the 1902 Act). There was also, especially after 1870 when the school boards had begun to function, an increasing output of literature on the work of managers; many public figures were also involved directly or indirectly in management and their correspondence gives an idea of some of the attitudes then prevailing towards the management of schools.

A number of fundamental issues, especially that of the ultimate responsibility for control of management, religious or secular, were illustrated in the so-called "Management Clauses" controversy.[1] Four types of management were recommended by the Committee of Council, according to the population of an area. The election period varied between two and four years, and subscribers were to form the electorate.

The reason for the less than full acceptance of the Management Clauses has been given by a number of educational historians.[2] What was of importance henceforth was the increasing lay element in the management boards, or rather, as Kay-Shuttleworth had in mind in drafting the Clauses, to give due place to the three groups of interests in every school: the subscribers, the religious or educational Society with which the school was connected and the Committee of Council as the distributor of national funds.[3]

Kay-Shuttleworth, in offering liberal terms of state aid to voluntary schools, wanted to ensure that the money being given was not used exclusively for religious teaching and held that "the absence of a Committee of Managers is either a sign or a cause of an absence of interest in the school among the influential laity of the neighbourhood". By the mid-nineteenth century the move towards administrative tidiness in legislation covering a whole range of social concerns from chimney sweeps to public health was under way;[4] coupled with this was the motive to assert the claims of the civil power preached by Russell and the Liberals during their periods in office.[5] The increasing lay interest in representation on the bodies which were established as a result of this legislation was clearly seen in the sphere of elementary education.

What was less easy to discern were the motives which induced individuals to take on the often arduous and seldom rewarding work, which could be both time-consuming and expensive. The Committee of Council, realizing this as early as 1853, wrote to Her Majesty's Inspector, Rev. W. J. Kennedy:

"H.M. Inspectors cannot too carefully bear in mind that in the local Managers of schools they have to deal with persons who are voluntarily imposing upon themselves a great deal of trouble and expense for a public object. In communicating, therefore, with such persons it is the duty of public officers to be as courteous and considerate as possible."[6]

For the lay manager, the motives were mixed: partly religious, but partly the chance to exercise authority, if on a limited scale. The work held its own rewards and would on occasions be gratifying. Henry Althans, a British and Foreign School visitor, recording a visit to Borough Road School in 1831 captures some of this flavour:

"On entering the spacious schoolroom for Boys, I was most cordially received by the Master who kindly promised me every assistance to facilitate the attainment of the object I had in view. On ascending the platform, I was highly gratified in beholding FIVE HUNDRED SCHOLARS present, who were all diligently employed in attending to various lessons and directly the Master called 'Halt' the most complete silence prevailed. 'Order is heaven's first law'. . . . I looked with great admiration on the numerous scholars before me, who completely filled all the desks; and the whole of their eyes being directed towards the elevated spot where I was standing caused an indescribable sensation in my mind."[7]

Similarly, the visitor's book of the Plymouth Public Free School, one of the most notable and much visited elementary schools in England, records an entry for 15 November, 1843, by Charles Heare as follows:

"With real pleasure I congratulate myself on contributing to this truly valuable and excellent institution."[8]

However desirable the presence of a secular interest in voluntary management much of the work in fact fell on the shoulders of the clergy. "What are the motives which induce landowners to maintain Denominational schools?", wrote Hicks Beach to the Duke of Devonshire in 1902: "Perhaps a feeling that education ought to be associated with distinctive religion—but certainly a desire to retain the active help of the parson (who is at any rate an educated man)—in managing the school and because he will do it better and more cheaply than the illiterate School Board which is all that an ordinary country parish could produce."[9]

The delicate balance of the social order which might be disturbed by crime and social revolt could, it was believed, be maintained by religious instruction and sound education.[10] Certainly, from the viewpoint of the central authority, the presence of the clergyman was an essential feature of any system of educational administration by virtue of the unique position he held in the parish.

Henry Hobhouse, writing as an Endowed School Commissioner, demonstrated the wide range of the clergyman's activities.

"He is the principal parish officer; he is Chairman of the vestry; he is owner of a freehold property; he is bound by law to be upon the spot; he is either by himself or with others, keeper of the parish records; he is the legal representative of the Church and its appurtenances; and in these respects he is bound to perform, and does perform, duties for all the parishioners, whether they attend his ordinary ministrations or not. By the combined law and practice of the Church, he (often alone in the parish) must have attained a certain amount of intellectual culture, evidenced by a university degree or some like credentials. . . ."[11]

From time to time, during the latter half of the century, the supremacy enjoyed by the clergy, especially in rural districts, was subject to challenge. This came from unexpected quarters: for example, Lord Lyttelton, a fervent churchman and an activist in the Church Reform Association, which wished to effect not change in doctrine but reforms in administration. Lord Sandon, within seven years to be Vice-President for Education, was congratulated by a Burslem working man for a recent public speech at Wolverhampton in which Sandon had said that he hoped the time was not too distant when "the congregation might have the power of choosing from amongst themselves a body of men who should be the Clergyman's advisers and without whose consent great changes in the mode of conducting worship, the management of the schools and the administration of the parish funds should be out of the question".[12]

Montagu Butler, then Headmaster of Harrow, writing to Archbishop Tait upon the introduction of a Bill for Church Reform in

1882, affirmed: "*Some* right must ere long be given to congregations to have a voice in the election of Incumbents; the position of Incumbent, while it must be guarded against caprice or tyranny, ought to fall short of freehold; and that, generally, the congregation who worship in a church *ought* to have more voice than they have now in the regulation of worship."[13]

In practice, however, congregations showed little enthusiasm for schemes in which they were drawn into active participation of church and school affairs. A Warwickshire vicar wrote in 1893: "The plan of such a scheme of representation was drawn up and sent to the Bishop, and except in one unimportant particular, met with his Lordship's full concurrence and sanction. But when I bruited it in the parish I found that the inhabitants had much rather leave everything in the Vicar's hands and I had no reason to think that they were brought to this conclusion by the suspicion that they would lose by acceptance the Englishman's right of grumbling."[14]

The balance between the various interests represents the theme for the rest of this section. The effects of legislative changes and administrative instructions from the Privy Council will highlight the changes in these relationships; but basically, it is a study of the functions of managing bodies and the factors governing or limiting their operations. This will necessarily include a consideration of, for instance, the teaching staff, trustees, the subscribers and inspectors.

TRUSTEES AND MANAGERS

Much confusion was caused during this time by difficulties in defining the relationship between trustees and managers. Before 1839, the constitution of voluntary schools was determined in most cases by the wishes of the founders. In February of that year, the National Society adopted a clause which had to be inserted in the trust deeds of schools wishing to be in union with the Society relating to the government of the school, the selection, appointment and dismissal of teachers and the election of managers by subscribers. Later the other denominations followed, setting out model schemes for insertion in school trusts.

Trustees appointed by the deed were usually the principal officiating minister for the time being of the parish or ecclesiastic district, and the churchwardens. "It is the duty of Trustees," stated a nineteenth-century law manual, "to get in and protect the property entrusted to their charge".[15] This deed of trust contained a conveyance of land with directions as to how the trustees were to be replaced, i.e. in whom the power of appointment of new trustees was vested.

However, it was optional with the promoters whether or not it was to be connected with the Church, and also the choosing of trustees was not necessarily limited to the parish. The filling up of vacancies presented problems. Charles Hunt, a rural dean in Nottinghamshire, set out his position in reply to an invitation to accept a trusteeship of a school.

"I am sadly weighted with Trusteeships already and my Trusteeship of another school involved me in filing a brief in Chancery. However, it all ended well for we were all right in as soon as our opponents saw we were in real earnest they collapsed."

"In this case will the Trustees be simply the legal holders of the property or be also Managers? At Dunham the school is vested in Trustees and there is also a Board of Managers. . . . If the Trustees *are* to be Managers, why have *outsiders*—they would naturally wish to be sleeping partners in the concern and I hope that you and all succeeding Rectors of Weston will always be the best Managers of your own school. . . . As to *myself*, if you make Charles Hunt Trustee and I turn cantankerous, you will have to bear it for my life, but if the Rural Dean for the time being is so and I get *very* troublesome the Bishop if he saw the thing in the same light might topple me over. . . ."[16]

A minimum number of trustees would be stipulated, usually two, but the maximum number was left to the discretion of the other trustees. The trust deed of the Clitheroe National School, Lancashire provided for the filling up of vacancies when the minimum number of trustees existed by vesting the premises in the remaining former trustees and the newly elected or merging trustees jointly. It was unanimously resolved at a meeting of the school managers in July, 1882, that the matter be settled by having the names of the seven existing managers placed in the deed as trustees.[17]

The method of electing trustees in Lancashire differed from that in other parts of England. Jonathan Beswick, a "self-actor-minder" by trade, in his *History of the Village School at Royton,* and himself a trustee, mentions the reluctance of villagers to take on the task of trusteeship of the village school. The division of function between the trustees and the school committee was interesting. In 1846 the latter shouldered the cost of making the repairs to school gates and floor, which was the responsibility of the trustees. "Round up" of members who had a "hereditary right" to trusteeship occurred several times. "When appeals were made to them they showed an indifference to meeting together for the duties of their office. Some declined to admit that they were Trustees. Others had never even seen the school." Since 1885 trustees had been elective and were required to live in the village; more surprisingly the electors were the teachers.[18]

The delineation of functions between the two bodies was often unclear and friction could arise as a result. The trustees of the Sheffield National District Society's Schools were twelve in number, two retiring each year; the gentlemen's committee consisted of twenty-four worthies appointed by the subscribers. In October, 1822, the first sign of trouble appeared. The trustees wrote to the committee disclaiming any intentional disrespect towards them by taking upon themselves the appointment of a new master; a committee, consisting of three to four trustees and an equal number of the gentlemen's committee, met and settled the dispute. Shortly after this, the trustees, in the face of diminishing public interest in the schools, offered to allow twelve of the committee to co-operate with them in their work, upon the understanding that the committee "should also join in pecuniary liabilities connected with the Institution". These advances were rejected by the committee, who left the school "to the uncontrolled direction of the Trustees".[19]

For those bodies of managers and trustees who wished to ascertain the powers given to them by the trust deed, a number of difficulties presented themselves. Often the deed was no longer in existence, although copies of it were occasionally transcribed in managers' minute books. Renewed interest in the activities of trustees followed the 1870 Education Act when the possibility of school boards being established was imminent. The vicar of Birdham, West Sussex, attending a meeting of managers for the school, mentioned this danger to his fellow members and suggested two courses of action:

"First, that you paint the Board in all its horrors and secondly to enquire into the important question of tenure. Whether that Record (which was copied by the Secretary and sent up by him to the Privy Council Office some time ago, and which appears to have satisfied their Lordships, since no further questions were asked on the subject) is really equivalent to a Deed in any legal sense:

"If so, whether the Ownership of the School Premises is so clear, as to enable the Managing Committee to raise money upon them; and if not, whether any new Deed can be drawn up, upon the basis of that contemporary record, which may give the existing committee the ordinary powers, which Owners would possess, either for the above named purpose, or any similar rights. The question appears to be a large one, but I have no doubt that your answer will be ready.

"That the Record is *Law* I hardly expect; (although it may have satisfied the Duke of Richmond, who must be the owner if we are not) but whether new Trustees can be put into a Deed, which is non-existent, that is the puzzle; and pending its solution what are we to be? Owners in fact, but not in law? or owners *de jure* without the rights of ownership?"[20]

One of the main functions of trustees, as has been indicated, was in relation to the trust property, the school and its buildings; financial liability could be contracted on this account. The School Sites Act of 1841 simplified the procedure for donors who wished to give land for a school site. Previously, the fact that the donor may have been a limited owner, for example a tenant for life, meant that he may have been unable to alienate land by way of gift; and secondly there may have been difficulty in finding a recipient who could permanently secure that the land would not be diverted from its purpose. Sections 2 and 6 obviated the first difficulty and Sections 7 and 8 enabled all grants of land and buildings to be made to corporations or trustees, provided that any such grant may be made to the minister of the parish being a corporation, and churchwardens.

Although valid trust deeds did not necessarily have to include Churchmen or local interests, trustees and their heirs could have management of the school, but this became increasingly ill-advised with the need for active management. At Balcombe, Sussex, the trusteeship was originally vested in two ladies, only one of whom survived. The Education Department advised the local cleric to persuade the existing trustee to apply to the Charity Commission for a revised deed. "The existing one," wrote A. T. Cory, at the Department, "is an inconvenient form of settlement which may produce trouble hereafter when the survivor of a number of persons has to be found and it does not permanently provide for that local interest in the school which is most likely to secure its efficient maintenance and Government."[21]

Lord Redesdale, in negotiating for a new trust deed for a school at Winchcomb, Gloucestershire, identified another problem:

> "I believe that the present Vicar of Winchcomb is under a cloud of some sort, which is I suppose the reason for certain arrangements of an unusual character in regard to the appointment of Vicar as *ex-officio* Trustee—I venture to suggest that a temporary present arrangement, should such be necessary, would be more desirable and that the future must be taken on Trust in the usual manner—and suppose any unfortunate circumstances should occur hereafter, I see nothing but litigation and dispute in the terms proposed—it cannot be right to presume that anyone on his appointment as Vicar will be *unfit to become* a Trustee, but who is to determine that anyone (subsequently misbehaving) is *unfit to continue* as Trustee?"[22]

In instances where the trustees and managers were one and the same body, the trustees often felt the need to divest themselves of their managerial functions, either from a sense of the need for wider participation in the school than they themselves could undertake or because of the work involved. At a meeting of parishioners called on 4 April, 1872, at Ardleigh, Essex, it was agreed that the school should be carried on by a committee of the trustees and managers nominated by them. Co-operation with the trustees was to be carried on by joint meetings. But a memorandum drawn up by the Vicar and Churchwardens stated that: "nomination and appointment conferred no *legal* powers on the said Committee in as much as the Trustees alone are the *legal* Managers of the school".[23]

Until the passing of the 1902 Act, the relationship between trustees and managers was an uncertain one. Rarely did the dispute lead to such spectacular proceedings as those at Winchester in 1895.

The rector and churchwardens, the parish authorities of St. Peter Chesil, in Winchester, applied to the Education Department in June, 1893, to claim the trusteeship of the school. One trustee of unknown provenance survived from the time of the original deed in 1844 and no new trustees had been appointed. A local resident, Dr. Earle, had acted as manager for a number of years, receiving the Government grant and paying the school mistress, but had not kept any account books. Earle, it was alleged, had "from time to time on receipt of money mixed them up with his own moneys".[24] The accounts submitted to the Department were audited by a local publican. Matters came to a head when H.M. Inspector reported against the school in 1893 because of its insanitary condition and the school ceased to exist from April of that year. Earle claimed that he had been appointed trustee of the property by the sole survivor but could produce no documents to support this.

In reply, the Education Department stated that they had no power to decide cases of disputed management or to interpret the terms of the trust deed. If the surviving trustee had appointed Earle as trustee, then, if evidence could be produced to support this, he would continue in office. Miller of the Department added: "You will observe that the conveyance being to personal Trustees and not *ex-officio* Trustees, the Rector and Churchwardens have no title to act as Managers in their official capacity."[25]

Two years later, after taking counsel's opinion, which confirmed the rector's view that a manager of the school in no way makes himself a trustee merely by acting as a manager, the vicar and churchwardens were able to obtain a new trust deed, by means of a formal handing over of the previous trust by the Rev. Woodham, the sole surviving trustee, on the 20 April, 1895.

The new trustees requested Earle to hand over the school premises so that the school could claim the Government grant. After a lapse of three months with no reply, the trustees issued an ultimatum, the secretary writing to Earle requiring him to give formal possession of the school buildings within three days.[26] Earle not only refused to hand over the building but threatened to close the school for Church services which had been held in the school during the restoration of the church. This proved to be the final straw; on the last day of the ultimatum the trustees stormed the building and took possession of the premises, but their troubles were not yet over. Eventually, Earle agreed to take £50 in settlement, on threat of prosecution for further interference. Ways and means of settling the claim were discussed and it was decided to endeavour "to collect the amount from friends, two or three of whom had already promised assistance". In spite of their efforts to raise funds, the six new trustees had to contribute £5 each towards the settlement.

Considering the variety of conditions under which trusteeships could be held and the limited functions accorded to trustees under the terms of trust deeds, it is clear that except where they also acted as managers they had little impact on the management of schools. Much depended on situational factors, especially how far the other two elements of management, the managers themselves and the subscribers, exercised their powers. In many cases the distinction between trustees and managers, as has been seen, was a paper one only. During the first part of the century, however, as the provision of schools became more widespread, this distinction became more real; trustees were relieved to be able to hand over their duties to managers, who could be involved in real, day-to-day supervision of the schools. We must now turn to examine the managers themselves.

ELIGIBILITY AND ELECTION OF MANAGERS

The Management Clauses already mentioned made provision for the qualifications required of the body responsible for electing managers.[27] Within the Church of England schools, the committee was to consist of the principal minister, his licensed curate(s) and subscribers. The last named were to be residents having real property to a certain extent in the parish, who had contributed to the school within the current year, and were members of the Church of England. Subscribers could have the number of votes proportionate to their subscription up to the limit of six votes. Before 1902, the number of managers was unlimited.

An alternative method was the one most usually adopted: qualification remained as in the above instance except that election was confined to vacancies occasioned by deaths, resignations, etc. In small country areas, the minister could be the sole manager until the bishop directed the election of a committee of subscribers.

Other denominations followed broadly this same pattern of selecting a committee. The British schools invested the annual chairman with a casting vote where necessary; Wesleyan schools had committees of six managers, two-thirds of whom were to be Wesleyan Methodists elected by 5s. annual subscribers. The model clause for Catholic schools settled after prolonged correspondence with the Committee of Council, invested powers in the priest of the district and six other Roman Catholics. Vacancies were to be filled by the election of the remaining members until the bishop directed that the election should be by subscribers, after which such persons were entitled to vote in proportion to their subscriptions. Undenominational schools, where the Bible was read daily but from which all religious formularies were excluded, had the management of the school vested in a committee annually elected by the subscribers.

A salutary reminder of the actual situation existing, especially in the rural counties, was given by H.M. Inspector, Rev. J. P. Norris, in 1858. Referring to the counties of Chester, Shropshire and Stafford, Norris noted that "in each locality those who are willing to make themselves responsible for the pecuniary maintenance of the school become its *de facto* managers, whatever be its constitution by Trust Deed".

An interesting analysis is given in Norris's Report of the constitution of the management committee of Church of England schools in these counties:

43 per cent Clergymen in concert with a committee.
37 per cent Clergymen alone, the committee being either inactive or not in existence.
9 per cent Clergymen and chief landed proprietors conjointly.
5 per cent Chief landed proprietor or his family.
3 per cent Lay committee.
3 per cent Proprietors of neighbouring Works.[28]

The result of the election was usually a pre-ordained one. Few candidates put themselves forward and close contests were unusual.[29] A typical example was the election at Hurley school in Berkshire, and the record is unusual in giving the voting figures. At the election on 14 January, 1895, four managers were to be chosen from five candidates and this was done by a show of hands. The result was as follows:

Sir G. T. East	8 votes
Mr. Leaver	8 votes
G. Lowe	8 votes
G. Gough	7 votes
A. Lee	3 votes[30]

Assuming that some subscribers had more than one vote each, the total number of votes cast indicates that only a small number of subscribers was present.

Notice of elections of managers did not have to be given previously to the meeting. A ratepayers' meeting which was held at three o'clock in the afternoon at Old Weston, Hunts, on 28 February, 1884, agreed that the committee of management needed to be increased. "The meeting consequently gave place to a meeting of the said school Committee, all seven of whom were present by some good fortune and proceeded to add another five to their number".[31]

Where rules were clearly drawn up by the committee for compiling a register of eligible voters, they were not always scrupulously observed. An instance of this occurred at Burley, Hants. It was settled at the committee meeting of 23 June, 1896, that "the Register of Electors should be made up at the general meeting of subscribers to be held on 9 July at 8.0 p.m.; it appeared that the late secretary had accepted twelve additional subscriptions after the conclusion of the meeting and had thus improperly raised the number of persons entitled to vote at the election of the Committee on 25th July from seventy-three to eighty-five".[32]

The qualities looked for in potential candidates for managers differed from area to area. In a university town such as Cambridge, where school committees included an element of university clerics, nominations for the managers would be closely scrutinized. At Barnwell, one of the oldest suburbs of Cambridge, a school committee was established in 1835: "In the course of the nomination, a question arose as to the expediency of placing any person in the situation of undergraduate on the Committee; and the objection urged at some length by Mr. Hoare, who considered that it might operate prejudically in keeping away some of the Heads and more influential members of the University". It was subsequently agreed that undergraduates would not be eligible.[33]

Managers were normally expected to be subscribers to the school as a condition of eligibility. At a metting of managers at East Farndon School, Northampton, in January, 1888, one of the managers, Mr. W. West, mentioned that a member, Mr. G. Russell, who had held office up to the previous year, had not paid his final subscription. "Mr. W. West wished it to be entered on the Minutes that if Mr. G. Russell were not asked to pay the owing subscription he would give notice of his own intention to quit the Committee at the end of February next and would decline to pay his own subscription for the coming year."[34]

That this should have generated so much heat is not surprising. As will be shown later, the fundamental importance of subscriptions to the continuance of the school made it essential that the managers, in order to induce others to contribute to the school, had to set a good example themselves. Another instance taken from Carnaby School in East Yorkshire, reinforces this point. At a managers' meeting in March, 1890, a suggestion was made that no-one should be eligible for the committee who paid less than 2s. annually towards the school. "The Chairman concluding that the proposal was made partly in reference to the fact that he was not a ratepayer, readily offered to give as much as the highest ratepayer." This offer was accepted and the proposal was withdrawn.[35]

The amount of subscription required for candidature as manager varied, according to what the inhabitants of the district could reasonably afford. As little as 1s. a year would be sufficient in some rural areas,[36] whilst in the wealthier towns the sum of "£1 at least" was sometimes stipulated.[37]

Although the term "manager" was normally used, the office was sometimes disguised by such titles as "Directors", for example, at Lewes British School.[38] Where the trust deed stipulated the constitution of a managing committee, devices were sometimes used to circumvent this requirement. The site of Reach School in Cambridgeshire was conveyed by deed on condition that the vicars of Barnwell and Swaffham Prior and the Vice-Chancellor of Cambridge University should have the control and management of the schools. So that more active day-to-day participation in management could be obtained, the chairman promoted the suggestion of appointing five "Assistant Managers" who would be able to sign the forms and papers of the Education Department as required and carry out the functions of normal managers. It is not recorded whether this proposition was ever challenged.[39]

Managers were eligible to stand for re-election although in fact this was often a mere formality. At a Leicestershire school "Annual Managers" were elected, as possibly the inhabitants were reluctant to commit themselves for a longer period. Difficulties could arise from the existence of two categories of managers on one and the same committee; in this instance at Enderby, Leicestershire, in January, 1898, the vicar announced that he had received a communication from the Manager of Pare's Bank asking that a guarantee should be signed for the overdraft (£500) by the managers and "it was thought best for the annually elected managers not to sign".[40]

During the course of the nineteenth century, there was a growing body of opinion which questioned the election to managing bodies merely by virtue of payment of a subscription. This was no guarantee of fitness to serve, and as has been seen, the system could be abused.

A pamphlet written by a barrister, W. T. Haly, in 1846, argued that after managers had been appointed, there were no general principles laid down by the Privy Council for the removal of inefficient or absentee managers. Haly suggested that complaints of mismanagement might be submitted, in the first instance, to the board of examiners attached to each Normal College; if the complaints came from inspectors, the examiners should inquire and after due investigation make an order. The managers would have the right of appeal to the Committee of the Council. Haly stated that both the Council and the National Society "are, for the most part, satisfied with the list of names sent in with the applications for grants. They never consider, whether that is the best list the parish or district could furnish; never make enquiry whether, from objectionable motives, parties who would be likely to render service to the course of education, have not been omitted from the Committee of Management. The consequence is, that individuals of much influence are frequently found neither lending support nor giving encouragement to schools which they are very well able, and which, under other circumstances, they might be very much inclined to assist".[41]

A full discussion of the role of subscribers as managers occurred in Hampshire at Burley Church of England School, in March, 1895. The Rev. T. Toy, a Dissenting minister, one of the managers at the meeting of 15 March of that year, explained the reasons which had induced both him and the other minister, Rev. H. C. M. Barton, to decline to subscribe to National Schools. For one thing, since the original rules had been drawn up, the school was no longer mainly dependent on subscriptions for its continuance. Thus: "It seemed unreasonable since the granting of Free Education to expect the Managers of a school to contribute not only their time, but also their money, to its support. That education being now so largely supported out of Imperial Funds, he claimed to be already a contributor to the school indirectly if not directly."[42]

The chairman considered that two courses of action were open to them: first, to admit both Mr. Toy and Mr. Barton as members of the committee without subscription, in their roles as ministers of religion, or secondly, to strike out of the rules of the committee relating to managers the clause "who shall be subscribers to the school", leaving it open to all members of the committee henceforward to subscribe or not as they chose.

Most members sympathized with Toy's viewpoint and favoured a fundamental change in the rules, the second course offered by the chairman. Within a week this had been effected: of the two ministers who had resigned, Toy was re-elected by the committee, along with a nominee of the Rev. Barton.[43]

Not all managers showed so great an interest in the conduct of the managers' meetings. Often the minister was left to make decisions in the absence of his fellow managers. A typical entry appears in the managers' book for Brafferton National School, Yorkshire: "The Vicar noted that he had summoned a Meeting of the Committee of Management for July 1860; but that no member so summoned appeared, the Vicar alone appearing".[44] Urgent decisions had to be taken on some occasions and the minister would act on his own initiative. A special meeting of managers of Brinsley National School, Nottinghamshire, was called for 21 July, 1892, to reconsider the furnishing of the new classroom, but was postponed until the following Saturday night at 7 p.m. in order to have fuller details as to lists of furniture, etc. "July 25th. The above citation of Managers was not responded to so no meeting. Under the circumstances the Vicar (on behalf of the Managers) decided to act as he deemed expedient and ordered the necessary furniture for the new classroom—and also the building of a wash-house for the Master's House."[45]

VICAR AS SOLE MANAGER

A large number of schools were carried on by the vicar as sole manager, a condition which many Inspectors deplored. A typical example, taken from the north of England stated: "In nine cases out of ten, all the responsibility of supporting and conducting the school falls upon the clergyman of the parish or district. That nearly in the same proportion the laity, whether owners of the soil or employers of labour, contribute little of their money and less of their time and influence to the right establishment and proper conduct of our elementary schools."[46]

In some instances where subscribers wished to be relieved of this work, the rector became sole manager, especially where he had had previous experience of management. On other occasions, this was achieved by the vicar claiming the right of sole management with the alternative of the school closing down. The managers of Aughton Parochial School, Lancs, petitioned the rector, Rev. W. H. Boulton, in August, 1860, to become "President of the Committee of Managers" on the grounds of "considering that the morals and habits of the rising generation in the Parish require the Counsels and opinions of a Clergy which must necessarily be of much greater nature than the ideas of Laymen in these matters".[47] Later, it was agreed that he should have the sole management of the schools "which includes the appointment and dismissal of Masters and Mistresses, disbursement of the finances and subscriptions and arrangement of all matters connected with the school", a position Boulton held until 1877.

Emergencies arose over matters which forced the vicar to take on sole management. For instance, at Wateringbury Parish School, Kent, the refusal of one of the trustees to sign the Government trust deed in lieu of the original trust deed and the consequent refusal of the Committee of Council to make a grant towards the school, led the seven managers to withdraw their subscriptions; they declined to meet as a committee and left the vicar to carry on the school alone.[48]

Advice on how to cope with the sole management of schools abounds in correspondence between the clergy during the century. "I admit them (the children) at any age when they are stout enough to come," wrote one such Oxfordshire vicar. "I suffer them to go at any age when they can find employment, and to return when their employment is ended . . . I am obliged to bribe the Parents to send their children which many of them are by no means disposed to do. I sell them blankets and coals at an under price. . . . At our weekly meetings for the relief of the poor. . . . I give voice against all applicants who have children running about the streets". The writer added: "I should hope your Curates will not have the same trouble that I have here—But these hints may be of use to them."[49]

We have seen in this section the relations which existed between trustees and managers and also subscribers as managers. It will now be necessary to examine briefly the third strand involved in management: the subscribers themselves.

SUBSCRIBERS

As many sources as possible were tapped by managers for subscription to the schools. The main categories of subscribers can be identified as follows: The *landowners* in the parish,[50] if any, were potentially the most remunerative source, especially when the building of a school was contemplated. The amounts to be subscribed would be determined according to the amount of property held in the parish, the owners paying a proportionate voluntary rate of so much in the pound. At Kirtling, Cambridgeshire, it was hoped that owners of property would pay two-thirds of the £2,190 required and the occupiers one-third, "which is, we believe, the principle upon which the Property Tax is collected". Each owner was informed of the proposed sum to be subscribed, based on the estimated rental of the property as it stood in the Rate Book.[51] In some of the poorer counties the proportion would be lower: rural Herefordshire seems to have been composed of equal proportions of ratepayers and landowners; some owners fixing a ceiling on the total amount to be paid over regardless of "rateable value".[52] The agricultural depression of the 1870s and 1880s led to difficulties and put the burden of subscriptions more heavily on the landowners. An unusual entry of this time appears in respect of Brixworth, an entirely agricultural parish in north-east Northamptonshire, where it was decided "to call upon all except landowners for subscriptions in respect of the year ending 31 October, 1879", which was acted on in consideration of "the present distress".[53]

Before individuals were approached, other large ratepayers were asked to subscribe. The most lucrative source was the *railway companies*. At Aynho, Northamptonshire, a small village dominated by the house[54] belonging to the Cartwrights of Aynhoe Park, the only other substantial ratepayers were the two railway companies whose lines ran across part of the village. "It is altogether inconsistent," complained the rector to E. L. M. Cartwright in 1875, "to expect half of a small parish to do their own heavy share and the other half's also. The Great Western Railway Company will do nothing towards a voluntary measure—the same to be said of the E. and W. Junction."[55] Another company, the London Brighton and South Coast Railway, were willing to pay an assessment of 3d. in the pound to Billingshurst, Sussex, in January, 1894, on condition only that the five largest ratepayers were willing to do the same. Much of the subsequent business of the school managers was taken up with persuading these ratepayers to assist.[56]

In the "railway towns" which had sprung up following the growth of the system from the 1840s onwards, the companies took their responsibilities seriously. At Crewe in 1842, the board of the Grand Junction Railway asked the shareholders to contribute not more than £1,000 towards a church and school for Crewe; to this sum were added some of the directors' fees and part of the Sunday Travelling Fund which consisted of accumulated dividends refused by strict Sabbatarian shareholders.[57]

The Great Western Railway at Swindon built a school in Bristol Street, an area made up of "Company houses", and later a large and improved school in College Street. After the 1870 Act, the Great Western directors favoured the transfer of their schools to the school board and in 1874 were pleased to be "relieved from the charge and responsibility of providing for the educational wants of the District".[58] Subsequently, in 1881 the school board closed down the Bristol Road School and the site was taken over for railway purposes.[59]

Denominational Societies provided subscriptions in much needed cases, as distinct from the Voluntary Schools Associations, which imposed a number of criteria in distributing the official aid grant from 1897 onwards (see Chapter 6). The corresponding manager of the remote Hermitage and Hilfield School, Dorset, stated in February, 1901, that he had written to several societies that usually aided schools in difficulties and had received a favourable reply from the Dorset National School Society saying that if the school could be saved from a board, the Society would make an emergency grant of £10; the remaining £11 needed to square the accounts was donated by two of the managers.[60]

Numerous methods were employed to obtain subscribers. Most parishes had to be content with the contributions of individual subscribers. Naturally, financial support was more readily given by those who were interested in the management of schools both with a view to setting an example to other subscribers and as a qualification for election as managers. Terms were sometimes offered by managers to subscribers: at Plymouth, the managers proposed that those who advanced loans of £21 or £42 "the interest would be made good to them by their discontinuing their subscriptions *untill the principle* so advanced be repaid".[61] The plan was adopted in some places, as at Rocester, Staffs, of holding ratepayers' meetings to confer with the committee of managers on ways of raising funds. Here, the burden of finding the money was put squarely on the shoulders of the ratepayers, with the managers threatening to close the school unless the former body procured the £60 18s. 2d. needed. After a number of joint and separate meetings held during the period January-May, 1881, the ratepayers' committee eventually obtained this amount.[62] Pleas for exemption from payment of subscriptions on the grounds of income tax commitments were sometimes recorded.[63]

The reasoning behind the resolution to apply for subscriptions in a Durham village to "those Persons whose Homes adjoin to the Spot on which the present School House is now standing" was a very sound one: it was proposed to move the school "which from its situation is an object of considerable annoyance to those who live near it to a much better Spot pointed out by the Rector, in the Waste of the Manor".[64] Material loss or gain could result from the payment of subscriptions. An instance of the latter can be illustrated from the rules for the management of Whitwick National Free Schools in Leicestershire: Rule 4 gave subscribers of one and a half guineas the right to send their own children to school on payment of half a guinea for each child per annum; these subscribers were also given an extra vote at elections of managers.[65] On the other hand, liability could be incurred, although legally difficult to enforce, on the closing down of a school. At Chevening, Kent, on

6 April, 1825, at the school committee meeting chaired by Earl Stanhope, it was agreed that the schools erected by the Earl and Countess Stanhope of Chevening should be pulled down, the building stone to be used and divided among the parishes in constructing separate school rooms "and that the Debt which may then be incurred by the Excess of Expenditure above the Receipts shall be defrayed by the subscribers in proportion to the amount of their respective subscriptions".[66]

Most communities depended upon the munificence of a few local individuals for subscriptions. The loss of one such subscriber could be serious in a rural area. An amusing account of such an incident is recorded in a letter dated 3 May, 1870, from the Rev. J. B. Carr, rector of Weston, near Newark, Nottinghamshire, to Lord Manvers,[67] the local landowner. Carr asked Manvers for a subscription towards the new school, as a piece of land suitable for building one had unexpectedly come on the market; and all the parishioners were ready to subscribe. Carr continues: "Since then, the principal man has been what is called 'overtook' i.e. he was brought before the Magistrates—my Father being on the Bench—for being drunk and disorderly and fined—the consequence is I am paying the penalty, for he will neither speak to me nor come to Church—so there is one good subscriber gone to the bad! I have desired my Father in future to remit me a fair compensation for every one of my parishioners he fines."[68]

Subscribers ranged throughout the social scale, from the Queen downwards. Sir James Graham, the Home Secretary under Peel, promising to subscribe £100 to the National Society for the Extension of Education in the Manufacturing Districts, a cause very dear to him,[69] wrote to the Prime Minister in July, 1843, of the anxiety caused by his promise in view of the split which had since taken place in the committee of management. "I trouble you with this matter," he wrote, "that you may be on your Guard with reference to advising the Queen to subscribe and to extending your countenance to these proceedings."[70] Peel's cheerful and brief reply was reassuring: "It will be a great misfortune if anything should be done indicating serious differences among members of the Church in respect of Education. If there be general concord in the Church I mean to subscribe liberally less as a Minister than from connection with the Manufacturing Districts."[71]

Gladstone himself became the centre of public controversy when in August, 1873, at a meeting of the Hawarden School Committee, he spoke in favour of avoiding a school board by raising subscriptions. Of the required sum, £120, half was raised at the meeting.[72] The early fund-raising efforts by the British and Foreign School

Society took the form of holding Dinners addressed by notable authors and speakers of the day. Lord Byron was approached by Samuel Whitbread to address such an audience on behalf of the schools. In his reply, on 20 May, 1814, Byron wrote:

"Ever since I was honoured with your letter I have been trying to nerve myself into attending you and saying something upon the subject of the meeting to whose object I am a sincere friend—but the recollection and the pain which my former attempts at Public Speaking have always occasioned to myself without giving any pleasure to others—must debar me now and ever from all future efforts to express my opinions before a large assembly.

"You will oblige me if you will have the goodness to put down my name as a subscriber to the Institution for 100 guineas and inform me to whom it should be paid."[73]

The collection of the subscriptions was the responsibility of the managers and became one of their chief functions over the years. It will be seen that this work was organized in a variety of ways.

COLLECTION OF SUBSCRIPTIONS

One of the first tasks which was undertaken by a committee of managers after election was to issue a circular requesting subscriptions. Usually, a member of the committee was delegated to prepare the necessary circular letter: shortly after the Rev. George Crabbe, the author of *The Borough*, arrived in Trowbridge, Wiltshire, he was made responsible for drawing up such a circular.[74]

Two methods of collecting were employed: either the managers divided up the work between themselves or a paid collector was engaged.

Where the work was undertaken by the managers, it was often done on grounds of economy. The statement of the rector of Friern Barnet Church, the Rev. R. Morris, to the new managers of the Parochial Schools on 18 September, 1880, and the discussion which followed, gives some idea of the problems which collection of subscriptions involved. The schools had expanded in a few years from 80 to 400 pupils "till both the expenses and the requirements of keeping up the supplies and even the correspondence and account keeping and etc. had become very considerable, so that there was a plain necessity for more persons to be interested in maintaining the machinery". One major difficulty was the maintenance of the level of income of the schools with the frequent loss of subscribers in consequence of removal and other reasons:

C

"Indeed my principal object in making this statement is to show the need of Managers and other friends looking out habitually for fresh annual subscribers. This at first may sound difficult—but if each Manager in the course of the year, could enlist four or five persons to become subscribers of a guinea or a larger number for half that amount the difficulty would be materially lessened, if not quite removed.

"At all events I must express decidedly that I cannot any longer be the only person who is supposed to have the responsibility of keeping up the subscriptions, and I earnestly trust the Managing Committee will make a decided effort for the same object."[75]

In the discussion which followed this, the levying of a voluntary school rate was mooted, but was rejected on the grounds that the parish already had a church rate. Finally, several of the managers undertook to make application from house to house for annual subscriptions.[76]

Paid collectors became increasingly common during the later part of the century. In a number of instances it proved to be an uneconomic proposition. Sometimes for purely personal reasons the work reverted to the managers. Submitting his resignation to the committee, Mr. W. B. Dunsthorne, the collector for Cheshunt British School, Herts, wrote:

"Gentlemen,
Having experienced great difficulty in collecting subscriptions for the above School and having found that many persons subscribed to the school through the influence of the late Mr. Paul (one of the managers) and as a matter of business with him, I beg to suggest that some influential members of the Committee take this important position of Collector, and I think that the subscription list would be greatly increased thereby."[77]

Often the collector was the school teacher, as at Feltham. The managers of the Windlesham National School, Surrey, laid down the conditions for this work, which also included keeping of the accounts. "Resolved—that the Master be provided with a book, in which to make entries of the subscribers' names and subscriptions and to get receipts and expenses of the school. Agreed—that with a view to simplifying the school accounts the master be requested to collect at once the subscriptions for the current year and that in future the subscriptions and donations be collected for the current year in January."[78]

The manager of Rickinghall Inferior School in East Suffolk employed rate collectors for gathering subscriptions "but we considered that too great a tax on our Revenue, as we had to pay them liberally for their labours—so my Curate and I undertook the task and even then we had to pay for Assessment Information. After a time the Collectors gave this information free of charge."[79]

Matters were simplified when an inhabitant of the parish collected, especially one with a fair amount of leisure time.[80]

A unique case of a manager acting as a paid collector occurred at Sandhurst,[81] a small rural hamlet in Gloucestershire. At a meeting of the National School committee, the collection of subscriptions was discussed. During the course of the meeting,

> "Mr. Trueman, who was both Collector and a Manager, agreed to retire from the management and continue the office of Treasurer and Collector.
> "The Chairman thanked Mr. Trueman for his action in this matter and said he would gladly himself give (and he believed others would too) something *each half year* in addition to his voluntary rate to add something to the very small sum allowed by the Education Department to the collector for his delicate and arduous work."[82]

Commission on the collection of subscriptions varied widely over the country. In Cheshire 2½ per cent was offered,[83] in Middlesex 5 per cent.[84] The onerous nature of the work made it necessary to offer attractive terms. It was decided at St. John's National School, Potters Bar, Middlesex, in January, 1900, that the collector should be paid 5 per cent on the money collected by him rather than the then existing practice of a definite sum. By July of the same year "it was thought advisable to offer a Commission of 10 per cent to a suitable person for the collection of sums under a guinea, other amounts to be collected by the Treasurer".[85] Extremely generous terms were offered to the teacher-collector at Chapel Allerton, Leeds, in May, 1882, where the committee resolved that his remuneration should be "5 per cent on all subscriptions received, an additional fee of 5 per cent on each new subscription obtained by him and a fee of 2½ per cent on each donation obtained by him. The remuneration on any single subscription or donation not to exceed 10s. 6d."[86]

In large towns, substantial amounts of money were involved in the collections, so it is surprising that there are so few recorded items in managers' minute books, such as that for St. Mary's National School, Stafford, which appointed a collector with a 10 per cent commission "also that Capt. Salt and E. Lloyd, Esq. be appointed as a Committee to superintend the collector".[87]

OFFICERS OF COMMITTEE

Apart from the key role of chairman, the posts of secretary and treasurer were of complementary importance. The chairman was usually the correspondent[88] for the school, the nexus through which all correspondence, forms, etc., to and from outside bodies flowed. The secretary usually received an honorarium for his work; at Old

Weston School, Huntingdon, the secretary/treasurer received £2 per annum for the following duties:

"1. To keep all the school accounts and pay all the bills and salaries.
 2. To collect any voluntary rate as authorised from time to time.
 3. To enforce any rules laid down by Managers with reference to cleaning the school, lighting of fires and providing of fuel.
 4. To summon regular quarterly meetings of the Managers on or about each quarter day."[89]

Deficits were often left to the treasurer to make good out of his own pocket. Sometimes the vicar, because of the uncertain state of the funds, felt that he could not let other persons take up the responsibilities of their maintenance and undertook the office of treasurer as well as secretary for this purpose.[90] On the other hand, where the vicar was regarded by the rest of the committee with hostility, the taking over of all the management offices was opposed. At West Mersea Church of England School, the managers on 11 November, 1887, asked the vicar to resign from the treasurership, "stating that if he did not do so there would probably be a considerable falling off of subscribers".[91]

One country vicar, Rev. G. W. Hales, exasperated at the Department's enquiry as to why the signature of the correspondent on the school forms for the current year differed from the previous one, replied, "Mr. James was away from home and there was some little difficulty in obtaining other Managers' signatures, and the Rev. Geo. Hales being Chairman, Manager and Correspondent Manager, it was thought sufficient to sign as he did. Mr. James is often abroad—imagine the delay and difficulty involved if an inviolable rule be made that the manager who signed the last Form should, of necessity, sign the following one! It would be rather awkward in case of death! or even if Mr. James had sailed for Timbuctoo!"[92]

Schoolmasters sometimes acted as secretary, although the Education Department would not recognize this a part of their duties. At Brixworth, Northamptonshire, the teacher/secretary's salary was increased by £5 a year to cover this work.[93]

Ignorance of basic procedures by some secretaries is shown by the first entry in the managers' minute book for 1868 of Enderby National School, Leicestershire. "The Vicar laid before the Managers the fact that the minutes of the meetings had hitherto been placed in the Log Book of the school and that hence their business was invariably known to the Master of the school. He thought that this might not always be convenient or be for the good of the School." As a result, a minute book was obtained.[94]

The treasurer's job was a fairly straightforward one except where negotiations with the Education Department and banking companies were involved. H.M.I. Mr. King, the Chief Inspector for the West Central Division, expressed in his General Report for 1895 his concern for the burden placed on the average treasurer, especially in rural areas.

"One office requires special provision, that of Treasurer; the chancellor of the exchequer ought never to be an executive officer; he has to meet incessant demands for school material, salaries and the rest; he has to consider where he shall find the necessary funds and then keep a strict account of them. Could the managers order what was necessary for the school and then send the bill to an independent treasurer, who must provide the necessary funds, the relief would be welcome and the schools might benefit by the change."[95]

The main qualification for such a post was some standing in the community and, equally important, honesty. In spite of this, cases of default were fairly common although representing a very small proportion of the total number. At the Huntingdonshire school mentioned above the treasurer defaulted with £62 9s. 8d., leaving the school in debt for the current year to the extent of £41 1s. 7d.[96] The treasurer at Tewkesbury British School procured tradesmen to lay a new floor of the schoolroom for £150 and absconded before payment with a legacy given to the school of £50.[97]

The accounts were to be audited by an independent person with one or other of the qualifications set out in Article 85 (d) of the Code except "in cases where no person so qualified is available".[98] Until 1898, there was no guarantee that the auditor was a responsible person. To carry out these functions, the auditor did not have to visit the school; but the Education Department informed the chairman of a rural Sussex school that "the fact that no person possessing the required qualifications resides in the neighbourhood is not sufficient to exempt the school from the ordinary operation of the rule".[99] This was not always easy to secure in a small parish. The Rev. J. J. Blandford, H.M.I., entered the following into the log book of a rural Derbyshire school: "Will not be able to accept the statement of Income and Expenditure for the current year unless H.M.I. in his next report expresses himself satisfied with the manner in which the accounts have been kept and unless they are duly audited by some responsible person other than the Treasurer and Schoolmaster."[100]

MEETINGS OF COMMITTEES

Managers' meetings opened with a prayer, often especially composed by the chairman. One has been preserved at the beginning of a Sussex school minute book; besides referring to the need for wisdom in their deliberations it was hoped "that teachers with all needful gifts will open the hearts of the children to receive instruction with a willing and teachable spirit".[101] The meetings themselves were held usually in the school room, the rectory or sometimes in the free library, where one existed. As late as 1903, however, at the last meeting before the committee was reconstituted, the head teacher of a Kent school was called before the managers to apologize for writing to the chairman "I wish to state that we object to have any more Committee Meetings held in our house".[102]

Attendance at meetings, as has been noted earlier, varied. Not many committees could have enforced the rules of the Sheffield National District Society School meetings, laid down in 1813, which stipulated a fine of a 1s. for non-attendance, provided two days' notice be given of such meetings.[103] Seven years later the rule had been slightly relaxed, "medical gentlemen and Gentlemen ten miles from home to be exempt".[104]

Meetings were held mainly in the evenings or weekends; where the body was small and mainly clerical in composition, the afternoons were convenient. Rural areas, however, were chiefly governed by seasonal requirements. The chairman of the Duntisbourne Abbots National School, Gloucestershire, Captain Burke, the principal landowner of the village of some 285 people, thanked the meeting for coming in the afternoon "to their own disadvantage whilst harvest operations were in full swing and thus saving him the necessity of coming out at night".[105]

Rules of procedure for meetings were not universally drawn up. A Wiltshire school placed at the head of its rules the resolution "That no question of importance can be decided at meetings of Managers unless it has appeared on the Agenda Paper".[106] Many incidents arose out of complaints that action had been taken without the knowledge of interested managers. The rector of Sheepy Magna National School, Leicestershire, was asked to explain his reason for speaking to the school master about dismissing the monitress without first having the authority from the managers to take such a step. The rector admitted that no formal motion had been placed on the agenda for the previous meeting, but that the matter had been discussed at it. After a heated argument with a member of the committee the rector, who was both chairman and correspondent, stormed out of the meeting, resigning his position as correspondent.[107]

If a manager accused other members of unfair or underhand dealings, the committee was not empowered either to force an apology or to insist upon the resignation of that manager. In one instance, the chairman stated that "in his opinion, to ignore his (the offending manager's) presence at future meetings would be an illegal act on the part of the Chairman".[108]

Such heated discussions could lead to strange results. At an extraordinary meeting of managers of Crooke School at Shevington, a mining village near Wigan, Lancashire, one manager, Mr. Hill, objected to a colleague sitting on the committee on account of his absence on seven successive occasions. At a meeting a week later (3 December, 1883), Messrs. Downham and Aspinall withdrew from the room, "the latter voluntarily and the former because Mr. Hill objected to his presence in as much as he was said to be indirectly receiving profit from the Board in the stipend of his daughter as monitress in the Infant School".[109]

Even more dramatic was a meeting of the West Mersea Church of England managers, held on 1 November, 1887, which resulted in total disruption.

"The Chairman called upon Mr. Thorpe to read the minutes of last meeting. Before he did so Mr. Green interposed and enquired by what right Mr. Farman was present. Mr. Farman replied, he attended as Mr. Musselwhite's legal adviser, and refused to withdraw unless everyone who was not a member of the school committee withdrew also.

"As no one withdrew Mr. Farman insisted on his right to be present, and thereupon the meeting broke up, Mr. M. explaining that he did not propose to come to the school-room again, for the purpose of taking the chair unless some business was to be transacted."[110]

FUNCTIONS OF MANAGERS

(a) Contemporary written advice

A wide range of functions had to be carried out by a manager in addition to the responsibility for financing the school. Advice on the constitution of managing committees abounded in the handbooks of the period. The Rev. H. W. Bellairs, H.M.I., in *The Church and the School: or Hints on Clerical Life*, published in 1868, wrote: "In School Management enlist as much lay agency as possible. For this, call a meeting of the respectable parishioners. . . . If you can, induce the parish to rate itself voluntarily. If not, propose a Finance Committee, of which make the most substantial man the Treasurer, accepting yourself the office of Chairman."[111]

The two departments of managers' work, according to another contemporary writer, were those which could be conducted without personal visitation to the school and the other which necessarily involved personal intercourse with school teachers and scholars. The first included attention to the appointment and removal of teachers, the proper equipment of schools and regulation and remission of fees, and "require[d] business habits, administrative ability and the capacity for working harmoniously with other managers in the general management of the school". The second involved "the frequent visitation to the school and personal superintendence of business during school hours and encouraging teachers and children in their work[112] [which] requires some amount of educational tact, interest in school work and love for detail and even to superintending the business of the school in its minutest particulars".[113] To this should be added their attendance at H.M. Inspectors' examinations of the scholars. The biographer of John Allen, one of the three Inspectors appointed by Lord John Russell in 1839, tells how "when he inspected the schools in the parish where Lord Palmerston lived, Lord P. stood in his long blue coat with brass buttons, listening attentively all through the inspection and at the end thanked him for the pains he had taken".[114]

Most of the manuals for managers were written by H.M. Inspectors or ex-H.M. Inspectors. Hugh R. Rice-Wiggin and A. P. Graves, in *The Elementary School Manager*, warned that "care should be taken to distribute duties, as far as possible, with due regard to any special tastes and capacities of the individual managers. For example, those with a taste for figures might well undertake the chief supervision of the registers or the keeping of the accounts. Lady Managers should take under their special care the musical instruction of the whole school and the general supervision of the girls and infants departments. . . . Managers with special knowledge of science or languages might encourage and supervise the instruction in 'specific subjects'."[115]

H.M.I. Mr. J. R. Blakiston, drawing on twenty-five years' experience, mentioned the need for thorough supervision of the schools. "They will depute one of their body to inspect the school daily and inquire into absenteeism, insure and test accuracy of registration, enforce cleanliness and tidiness, give advice and encouragement to their teachers. Such Managers would no more leave everything to teachers than would the colonel of the regiment leave all to its adjutant and subalterns."[116]

How far these counsels of perfection were adopted depended to a great extent upon the nature and constitution of the managing committees themselves. In reply to criticism of the irregularity in the conduct of the school committee, the rector and chairman of King's Stanley School, Gloucestershire, cited the minute book, which showed that from 1870 to 1886 only six such meetings were held on special occasions. "He urged that this continued demand for Committee Meetings seriously increased the already arduous labours of the Working Managers" and threatened to "give up an office which in no way increases my privileges in connection with the school and seriously enhances my cares".[117]

(b) General

The constant theme running through the voluntary school managers' activities was that of keeping the school solvent. Attempts to secure loans or overdrafts from banks were often made in anticipation of the following year's grant and/or subscriptions. But as voluntary schools did not represent a good risk, banking houses were not eager to accept managers as clients; managers themselves were equally loth to contract a debt which would have to be incurred on the bank's own terms. An account of such a transaction by the Shepshed British Schools, Leicestershire, makes interesting reading. At the managers' meeting of 25 July, 1876, the

> "Treasurer and Secretary Reported that they went to Bank on 19th as requested at last meeting but failed to open an account with Nottingham and Nottinghamshire. But went to Messrs. Middletons & Co. and was successful. Mr. Marshall the Manager gave them a notice which is as follows: 'We hereby agree to be responsible to you for any cash you may advance for the Shepshed British School and we engage to repay the same when called upon to do so.'
>
> "Mr. Marshall told them that if the Committee would sign and return that to them with copy of the Resolution passed to declare who must sign cheques we could have what money we wanted—Mr. Bott Bought a cheque book.
>
> "Agreed that all the Committee sign the note to Messrs. Middleton . . . that all cheques be authorised by Committee."[118]

Within two months the bank had asked the managers to settle the account. Two of the managers immediately resigned.

Favourable terms were sometimes obtainable. A Northamptonshire school which owed a £100 on buildings in July, 1897, deputed one of the managers to interview the bank manager in Northampton "and offer him the Managers of the school, or the Vicar, Churchwardens and Overseers as Security for an advance of £250". The bank manager reported that "he could not take the Managers as Officials as security for an advance but required their names".[119]

A legal decision in 1890 further increased the possible financial commitments of managers. In the case of *Crisp* v. *Thomas*, the plaintiff was a scholar in St. Michael's Church School, Woodford Green, Essex. The defendant was vicar of the parish, an *ex officio* trustee of the school, and one of the committee of management. The plaintiff sought to recover damages for injuries inflicted by the fall of a blackboard alleged to have been insufficiently secured on its easel by a pupil teacher, who was one of a staff appointed by the committee of management, but not otherwise under its control. It was held that there was no evidence of negligence, but that if there had been the defendant, as one of the committee of management, would have been liable.[120]

The most frequent contact with the law came through charges of assault brought by parents against the clergy as a result of their administering corporal punishment. These cases were usually leniently treated by the bench. In Shropshire, after being discovered by the vicar in a public house, one boy was beaten with a walking stick until it was broken, and he displayed bruises on his legs to the extent of four or five inches. In summing up the case "the bench certainly thought the boy had been guilty of gross misbehaviour, and to show that they felt Mr. B. was justified in acting as he had done, they would only fine him 6d. and 17s. 4d. costs".[121]

Routine tasks undertaken by managers covered every aspect of school life. A typical example is taken from Reach School Log Book, Cambridgeshire: "Mr. Don Mason and Mr. Arthur Wells staid a considerable time on Monday Morning after the other Managers had gone and assisted in entering the names etc. of the children."[122] The ordering of equipment sometimes became the work of a sub-committee (as at Taunton), "to whom shall be submitted from time to time, lists, prepared by the Master and Mistress, of such articles as they may require for their respective school, the sub-committee to write to Tradesmen in the Town to tender for supplying the same".[123]

Children's treats came within the province of the managers' work. In some instances, the treat occupied a greater part of the school year in its organization. The managers of Romford British School in 1864 made a street-by-street collection for subscriptions and with the money provided dinner for eighty-six children. They also persuaded a local brewery to donate nine gallons of beer.[124]

"The Penny Dinner" movement which was originated by Sir Henry Peech at Rousdon in Devon in 1876[125] was taken up, though not always with enthusiasm, by managers. A cottage next to the school was provided by one of the committee of Kingston St. Mary School, Somerset, in 1886 for providing penny dinners, and a Penny Dinner Committee was established to supervise. This endeavour collapsed the following year when, after a proposal was approved "that free dinners be given to a limited number instead of the penny dinners open to all" the task of selecting children proved too difficult for the committee.[126]

This chapter has been concerned with the relationship which existed between the managers and the local community from which the trustees, managers and subscribers were drawn. It will now be necessary to examine another set of constraints which affected the internal management of schools; these included the Education Department, Her Majesty's Inspector, the landowner, his agent and the clergy, individual owners of schools, and of course the teachers themselves.

REFERENCES

1 Full details are to be found in Minutes of the Committee of Council, 1846, BPP. 1847 XLV and Correspondence, &c., respecting the Management Clauses, 1848–9, BPP. 1849 XLII.
2 See for instance J. W. Adamson, *English Education 1789–1902* (1964), pp. 129–30, C. Birchenough, *History of Elementary Education* (1925), pp. 90–2, S. J. Curtis, *History of Education in Great Britain* (1965), pp. 243–4.
3 F. Smith, *The Life and Work of Sir James Kay-Shuttleworth* (1923), p. 187.
4 J. Bartlet Bremner, "Laissez Faire in 19th Century Britain" in *Journal of Economic History*, Supp. VIII (1948), pp. 70–3 for many examples.
5 H. J. Burgess, *Enterprise in Education* (1958), p. 146. The attitude adopted by denominations on this question varied. As early as 1816 a certain amount of indignation was aroused at the Wesleyan Conference by the ruling that ministers should seek to get themselves elected on managing committees. R. F. Mathews, *Methodism and the Education of the People 1791–1831* (1949), p. 122.
6 *Grants under Minutes 1846. Copies of letters selected from old Letter Books 1847–1858*, p. 306 (Department of Education and Science Library).
7 *A Compendious Report of the Order of Proceedings and Actual Operations in the Central School of the British and Foreign Society Borough Road, 1831* (Borough Road College of Education Collection, Isleworth, Middlesex).
8 Plymouth Public Free School, Visitors' Report Book, 1837–95, 15 November, 1843 (Plymouth Public Library).
9 Hicks Beach to Devonshire, 3 February, 1902, Ed 24/19 (Public Record Office).
10 See for example James Hole, Chapter 6: "On the Relation between Education and Crime" in *The Working Classes of Leeds: an Essay on the present State of Education in Leeds and the Best means of Improving it*, (1863), pp. 88–95.
Harold Silver has pointed out that early nineteenth-century educational circles elaborated the theme of the schoolmaster being as essential a property of life and property as the policeman; the choice was between building more schools or more prisons. H. Silver, *The Concept of Popular Education* (1965), pp. 208–9.
11 First Report of Endowed School Commission to the Committee of Council on Education 1872, BPP. XXIV Appendix.
12 "A Poor Man out of a Situation" to Sandon, 8 October, 1867, Harrowby MSS, Vol. LII, ff. 4–5 (Sandon Hall, Staffs.).
13 Butler to Tait, 9 March, 1882, Gladstone MSS, B.M. Add. MS. 44308, f. 198.
14 Edward Miller, "Confessions of a Village Tyrant" in *Nineteenth Century*, December, 1893, p. 959.

15 L. S. Bristowe and W. I. Cook (eds) *The Law of Charities and Mortmain: Tudor's Charitable Trusts* 3rd edn, (1889), p. 230.
16 Charles Hunt to the Rev. J. B. Carr, 16 June, 1870, Weston Parish, Manvers MSS, SBX 69/18/2 (Nottinghamshire C.R.O.).
17 Clitheroe National School, Managers' Minute Book, 1839–1903, 28 July, 1882. PR 2003 (Lancashire R.O.).
18 Jonathan Beswick, *History of the Village School, Royton* (1922), pp. 24–5.
19 Sheffield National District Society, Minute Book, Committee Meeting 19 November, 1822. (Sheffield City Library, Department of Local History and Archives).
20 Rev. J. W. Miller, Birdham, Manhood School, Correspondence 1855–1953, 2 and 3 September, 1874, Par 23/25/4 (West Sussex R.O.).
21 Balcombe School. Papers relating to School, 1869–1914. A. T. Cory to Rev. R. G. Mead, 29 November, 1869. 234/25/2 (East Sussex R.O.).
22 Gretton National School, Winchcomb. Correspondence 1861–7. Lord Redesdale to W. Mackgill, 19 December, 1863. P 368 SC 2/6 (Gloucestershire R.O.).
23 Ardleigh National Schools. Draft Memorandum. 31 May, 1875. D/P 263/28/14 (Essex R.O.).
24 St. Peter's Schools, Chesil, Winchester. Case for the Opinion of Counsel. 7 February, 1895. Shelf 27 Box 10 (Winchester City R.O.).
25 *Ibid.* Papers relating to Disputed Management of School and Ownership of Site. 4 July, 1893.
26 St. Peter's Schools, Chesil, Winchester. Minute Book of New School Trustees, 1895–1911. 4 October, 1895. Shelf 27 Box 10 (Winchester City R.O.).
27 An important decision was made by the Lord President of the Council in 1847 arising out of a query from the Liskeard Local Board of Education, Cornwall. The Board claimed that the description of the qualifications of managers of Church of England schools should be more closely defined and suggested that the word "Communicants" be added. The Department in reply objected to the adoption of the term on the grounds "that the word appears to revive the risk that the Holy Sacrament would be subject to desecration by those who had no better motive for partaking it than that of qualifying for a secular office". *Grants under Minutes 1846, op cit.* 25 November, 1847, p. 40.
28 Committee of Council on Education. Report of Rev. J. P. Norris for 1858 on Church of England Schools in Chester, Salop and Stafford. BPP. 1859 XXI, p. 99.
29 One writer commented on such apathy in the following terms:
"How often does it occur in the establishment of a new school, that after the novelty is worn off, and the patrons and supporters have been arduous in their endeavour, as they generally are, to 'give it a fair start', that lukewarmness succeeds the boiling heat before manifested, and that icy coldness follows on till the thermometer of the original enthusiasm is down to zero. Thus schools are left, perhaps entirely, or to the active benevolence and energetic humanity of some single member of the committee, who too often in return for the good he would do, is looked upon with jealousy, and is compelled after years of heart-yearnings for the good of his race, to retire in sorrow and disgust." "The British and Foreign Schools Society. Its Principles. Its Schools. Its Capabilities and Its Defects" in *The Educational Magazine*, May, 1838.
30 Hurley School. Minutes of Management Committee, 1894–1907. 14 January, 1895. D/P72/25/4 (Berkshire R.O.).

Another reason for the informal method of voting was probably linked with the level of educational attainment in a community. At Burwash, Sussex, in 1868, a manager of the village school, a farmer, signed his name in the minute book with a cross. J. Goodwin. *Burwash and the Sussex Weald* (n.d.), p. 156.

31 Old Weston School. Minute Book, 1884–1901. 28 February, 1884. Acc. 346 ddx 62 (Huntingdonshire C.R.O.).

32 Burley Church of England School. Managers' Minute Book "D", 1894–6. 20 August, 1896. 48M68 (Hampshire R.O.).

33 Barnwell National School. Committee Minutes, 1835–48. 10 and 17 July, 14 August, 1835 (Cambridgeshire and Isle of Ely C.R.O.).

34 East Farndon Managers' Minute Book, 1879–1905. 19 January, 1888. No. 73 (Northamptonshire R.O.).

35 Carnaby, Managers' Minute Book, 1879–1902. 14 March, 1890 (East Riding C.R.O.).

36 Burley Church of England School, Managers' Minute Book "D", 1894–6. 23 June, 1896. 48M68 (Hampshire R.O.).

37 St. Silas Hunslet (Leeds) National School, Managers' Minutes, 1890–8. 24 September, 1902. Ref. 65 (Leeds City Libraries, Archives Dept.).

38 Lewes British School, St. John Sub Castro, Managers' Minute Book, 1884–93. 9 July, 1884. E412/1 (E. Sussex R.O.).

39 Reach National School, Minute Book, 1876–1903. 22 February, 1900 (Cambridgeshire and Isle of Ely C.R.O.)

40 Enderby National School, Managers' Minutes, 1868–1901. 18 January, 1898. E/MB/B/101/1 (Leicestershire R.O.).

41 W. T. Haly, *Education: Showing What is Done, What is Not Done, What we can Do. What we must Do, to Educate the People.* (1846), pp. 92–3.

42 Burley Church of England School, Managers' Minute Book "D", 1894–6. 15 March 1895. 48M68 (Hampshire R.O.).

43 *Ibid.,* 23 March, 1895.

44 Brafferton National School, Minutes of Managing Committee, 1861–71. 11 June 1861. PR BRA 43/3 (Borthwick Institute of Historical Research, York).

45 Brinsley National School, Managers' Minute Book, 1892–1904. 25 July, 1892. SBX 51/1 (Nottinghamshire R.O.).

46 Committee of Council on Education. Report of Rev. F. Watkins for 1845 on the Northern District. BPP. 1846 XXXII, p. 180.

47 Aughton Parochial School, Managers' Minute Book, 1835–1901. 3 August, 1860. SMA V4/1 (Lancashire R.O.).

48 Wateringbury National School, Managers' Minute Book, 1843–75. 1854 (no date), Wateringbury Parish Records. P385/25/4 (Kent Archives Office).

49 Rev. W. Wood to the Bishop of Oxford, 10 December, 1814. Wheatley Parish Records, 1813–58. MSS D. D. Par. Wheatley b.18 (Bodleian Library, Oxford).

50 The proposition that educational progress before 1870 depended more on the efforts of the greater gentry than any other category is demonstrated in a case study of Hertfordshire. J. S. Hurt, "Landowners, Farmers and Clergy and the Financing of Rural Education Before 1870", in *Journal of Educational Administration and History* Vol. 1, No. 1, December, 1968, pp. 10–12.

51 Kirtling School, Copy to Landowners about the Parish School, undated but probably early 1850's. Kirtland Parish Records. P101/25/14 (Cambridgeshire R.O.).

52 Upper Sapey School, Minutes of Committee of Management, 1872-1927. 26 March, 1872. Parish Records (Herefordshire C.R.O.).

At Frodsham, Cheshire, in 1874, the landlords had promised to pay a 6d. rate for their property, but the Marquess of Cholmondley, the largest owner of the district, had promised only 3d. It was resolved by the managers "that the Vicar be requested to write to the Marquess of Cholmondley, stating that it is the general opinion that it would be difficult, if not impossible, to collect the 6d. rate from the Tenants, unless the landlords paid an equal sum." Frodsham National School, Managers' Minute Book, 1836–90, 5 June, 1874. P8/15/1 (Cheshire R.O.).

53 Brixworth Church of England School, Managers' Minute Book, 1873–97, 2 December, 1879, Parish Records. No. 91 (Northamptonshire R.O.).
It was not only the agricultural distress which affected landowners. Commenting on the decision of the Anstead Brook and Chiddingfold schools to join the Voluntary Schools Association in 1897, the local vicar wrote to the Rural Dean "this school is in a necessitous condition. It was not always so. Built at the cost, and on the property, of Mr Stewart Hodgson, it was always liberally supported by him. But after his misfortune as one of the members of the Insolvency of the Great House of Baring Brothers, he could only contribute a portion of his former donation. The school has gradually fallen into debt". Chiddingfold Church of England School, Managers' Minutes, 1894–1910. 14 May, 1897 (Surrey R.O.).

54 N. Pevsner, *Buildings of England: Northamptonshire* (1961), pp. 88–90.

55 Rev. Dr. W. Wilson to E. L. M. Cartwright, 5 January, 1875. Cartwright of Aynho MSS. C(A) 7445 (Northamptonshire R.O.).

56 Billinghurst National School, Minute Book 1893–1903, 6 January and 5 February, 1894. E2 1/1/1 (West Sussex R.O.).
At Southampton, it was the generosity of the London and S.W. Railway Co. in donating £25 to a local church school which made possible the continuation of the Aid Grant to the school as voluntary subscriptions locally had declined. Millbrook and Redbridge Parochial Schools, Managers' Minute Book, 1897–1903. PR 10/18/1 (Southampton R.O.).

57 W. H. Chaloner, *The Social and Economic Development of Crewe, 1780–1923*. (1950), p. 61.

58 F. G. Saunders, Secretary G.W.R. London Terminus to Clerk of Swindon School Board, 10 June, 1879. Swindon, Ed. 16/323 (P.R.O.).

59 L. V. Grinsell (ed.) *Studies in the History of Swindon* (1950), p. 111.

60 Hermitage and Hilfield School, Managers' Minute Book, 1899–1903, 9 February, 1901. P61/SC/1 (Dorset R.O.).

61 Plymouth Public School, Committee Minute Book, 1809–28, 13 September, 1814 (Plymouth Public Library).

62 Rocester National School, Managers' Minute Book, 1873–91, 20 January–12 May, 1881. D/925/8/1 (Staffordshire R.O.).
Similarly in order to avoid a school board at Teddington, Middlesex, in 1879, the funds needed to continue the so-called Teddington Public School were raised by a ratepayers' committee. *Victoria County History, Middlesex II* (1962), p. 81.

63 King's Stanley National School, Managers' Minute Book, 1870–1920, 25 January, 1889. P190. SC. 1/1 (Gloucestershire R.O.).

64 Haughton-le-Skerne Church Day School Minute Book, 1814–16, 24 January, 1815. EP/No. S.27 (Durham C.R.O.).

65 Whitwick National Free Schools Trustees Minute Book, 1819–1851, 24 November, 1819, E/MB/B/354/1 (Leicestershire R.O.).
In a like manner, a subscription of a pound at a Durham school entitled every subscriber to send one scholar free or four scholars at the rate of $2\frac{1}{4}$d. per week for each scholar, and so on in proportion for any larger or smaller

sums. Coniscliffe Day School, Managers' Minute Book, 1829–48, 11 August, 1829. EP/C.12 (Durham C.R.O.).

66 Chevening National School, Minute Book, 1817–25, 6 April, 1825. Parish Records. P88/25/9 (Kent Archives Office).

67 Sidney William Herbert Manvers, 1825–1900; Tory M.P. for South Nottinghamshire, 1852–60; *The Complete Peerage*, Vol. 7 (1932).

68 Rev. J. B. Carr to Lord Manvers, 3 May, 1870. Manvers MSS. SBX 69/14/5 (Nottinghamshire R.O.).

69 Graham's Bill had been withdrawn in the face of bitter Church opposition a fortnight earlier on 15 June. J. T. Ward, *Sir James Graham* (1967), pp. 195–7.

70 Graham to Peel, 8 July, 1843, Peel MSS., B.M., Add. MS. 40448 f. 346.

71 *Ibid.* Peel to Graham, 10 July, 1843, f. 348.

72 See, for example, the account in *The Times*, 18 August, 1875, and Gladstone to W. E. Forster 21 August, 1873, Gladstone MSS. BM. Add. MSS, 44157. f. 81.

73 Lord Byron to Whitbread, 22 May, 1814, Whitbread MSS., correspondence, 1764–1815, 5727 (Bedfordshire C.R.O.).

74 Trowbridge District Society for the Education of Children in Trowbridge, Minute Book, 1812–47, 2 February, 1815. 206/23 (Wiltshire R.O.).

75 Friern Barnet Parochial Schools, Committee Minute Book, 1854–97, 18 September, 1880. DRO. 12 I. G/3/3. (Greater London R.O. hereinafter G.L.R.O. [Middlesex]).

76 *Ibid.* 6 May, 1881.

77 Cheshunt British School for Boys and Girls, School Correspondence, 1867–1903, 4 December, 1867. H. Ed. 2 5/1 (Hertfordshire C.R.O.).

78 Windlesham National School, Committee Minute Book, 1864–72, 1 July, 1865 (Surrey R.O.).

79 Rev. G. Hales to G. R. Wilson. Rickinghall Inferior National School Minute Book, 1883–1903, 26 February, 1900. FB122/12/1 (Ipswich and East Suffolk R.O.).

80 Stroud National School, Committee of Managers' Minute Book, 1849–1900, 23 January, 1880. C/ES. 150 B/3/1 (Kent Archives Office).

81 The population in 1891 was 438. Edward Trueman, the holder of these two posts, is listed as a Machinist in Kelly's *Gloucestershire* (1897).

82 Sandhurst National School, Managers' Minute Book, 1896–1901, 2 November, 1901. P281. SC1/2 (Gloucestershire R.O.).

83 Frodsham National School, Minute Book 1836–90, 5 June, 1874. P 8/15/1 (Cheshire R.O.).

84 Feltham National Schools, Committee Minutes, 1848–78, 25 August, 1860. Acc. 563 (G.L.R.O. [Middlesex]).

85 Potters Bar—St. John's National School, Managers' Minute Book, 1890–1903, 16 January and 24 July, 1900. MCC/E.PB.1 (Middlesex R.O.).

86 Chapel Allerton (Leeds) Parochial School, Managers' Minute Book, 1873–1909, 26 May, 1882. Ref. 180 (Leeds City Libraries, Archives Department).

87 Stafford St. Mary's National School, Managers' Minute Book, 1854–95, 12 June, 1862. D 834/10/2/2 (Staffordshire R.O.).

88 Correspondents, although invariably the clergymen of the parish, did not necessarily have to be managers. W. F. Norris, *Elementary Schools* (1904), p. 93.

89 Old Weston School, Minute Book, 1884–1901, 25 February, 1899. ACO. 346 dd X62 (Huntingdonshire C.R.O.).

90 Friern Barnet, Cromwell Road School, Managers' Minute Book, 1868–82, 13 March, 1868. DRO. 12. I/G3/1 (G.L.R.O. [Middlesex]).

91 West Mersea Church of England School, Managers' Minute Book, 1887–93, 11 November, 1887. B/MM 17 (Essex R.O.).

92 Boyton School, Minute Book, 1872–95, 22 March 1894. FC 163/M2/1 (Ipswich and East Suffolk R.O.).

93 Brixworth Church of England School, Managers' Minute Book, 1873–97, 8 December, 1896, Parish Records, No. 91 (Northamptonshire R.O.).

94 Enderby National School, Managers' Minute Book, 1868–1901, 27 January, 1868. E/MB/B/101/1 (Leicestershire R.O.).

95 Committee of Council on Education, General Report of Mr. King for 1895, BPP. 1895–1896, XXVI, p. 98.

96 Old Weston School, Minute Book, 1884–1901, 14 October, 1897. Acc. 346 dd62 (Huntingdonshire C.R.O.).

97 Tewkesbury British School Society, Minute Book, 1850–97. 1856 (n.d.) S329 (Gloucestershire R.O.).

98 See A. W. Newton, *The English Elementary School. Some Elementary Facts about it* (1919), pp. 43–5, for examples of dishonesty recorded by a former H.M.I.

99 Kidford National School. Correspondence 1898–1901, 1 June, 1898. E116/8/11 (W. Sussex R.O.).

100 Brackenfield National School, Log Book, 1865–99, June, 1870. 83/C/EF 1 (Derbyshire R.O.).

101 Amberley, Houghton and North Stoke Schools, Managers' Minute Book, 1897–1903. Par 3/25/4 (W. Sussex R.O.).

102 St. Margaret's National School, Yalding, Managers' Minute Book, 1891–1903, July, 1903. P 408 B/25/2 (Kent Archives Office).

103 Sheffield National District Society, Trustees' Minute Book, 1813–22. 8 December, 1820. (Sheffield City Library, Department of Local History and Archives).

104 *Ibid.*, 24 May, 1813.

105 Duntisbourne Abbots National School, Minute Book, 1893–1902, 8 May, 1894. P 122 SC 1/1 (Gloucestershire R.O.).

106 Collingbourne Ducis National School, Minute Book, 1858–1904, 19 November, 1903. 665/18 (Wiltshire R.O.).

107 Sheepy Magna National School, Managers' Minute Book, 1874–1924, 26 March and 12 April, 1901. E/MB/B/286/1 (Leicestershire R.O.).

108 Chiddingfold Church of England School, Managers' Minute Book, 1894–1910, 9 July, 1890 (Surrey R.O.).

109 Shevington, Crooke School, Managers' Minute Book, 1881–86, 3 December, 1883. SBS 6 (Lancashire R.O.).

110 West Mersea Church of England School, Managers' Minute Book, 1887–93. E/MM 17 (Essex R.O.).

111 H. W. Bellairs, *The Church and the School: or Hints on Clerical Life* (1868), pp. 112–13.

112 A popular manual for managers postulated the principle of perpetual employment: "Every child in the school should be engaged at some useful employment, at every moment of the entire day. To solve the problem of perpetual employment is one of the objects of every system of organisation." P. W. Joyce, *A Handbook of School Management* (1867), p. 26.

113 Thomas More, *The Education Brief on Behalf of Voluntary Schools* (1890), pp. 73–4.

114 A. O. Allen, *John Allen and his Friends* (1922), p. 98.

115 H. R. Rice-Wiggin and A. F. Graves, *The School Manager* (1880), p. 13.

116 J. R. Blakiston, *The Teacher: Hints on School Management* (1879), p. vi.

117 King's Stanley National School, Managers' Minute Book, 1870–1920, 25 January, 1889, p. 190. SC1/1 (Gloucestershire R.O.).
118 Shepshed British Schools, Committee Minutes, 1875–84, 25 July, 1876. E/MB/B/289/2 (Leicestershire R.O.).
119 Brixworth Church of England School, Managers' Minutes, 1873–97, 13 July, 1897, Ref. 91; and Managers' Minutes, 1897–1904, 6 August, 1897, Ref. 92 (Northamptonshire R.O.).
120 *Law Times*, 62 Rep. 810 (1890).
121 *The Schoolmaster.* 1 May, 1884.
122 Reach National School, Log Book, 1863–1903, 27 March, 1876. P150/25/4 (Cambridgeshire C.R.O.).
123 Taunton Central National School, Managers' Minute Book, 1874–91, 28 March, 1881 (Somerset R.O.).
124 Romford British School, Managers' Minute Book, 1851–72, 5 September, 1864. E/MM 40 (Essex R.O.).
     Recalling his childhood experiences of the mid-1850s, a Lancashire author commented on the fact that "everything was celebrated with beer. Beer was taken into the field for Sunday School children to drink at the Whitsuntide festivities. When Queen Victoria and Prince Albert were married the school children marched in procession through the village and afterwards, in their own schools, they were regaled with cheese and bread and ale". P. Holland, *Recollections of 'Old' Swinton, Lancashire* (1914), p. 55.
125 R. R. Sellman, *Devon Village Schools in the 19th Century* (1967), p. 139.
126 Kingston St. Mary Parish School, Managers' Minute Book, 1871–88, 26 January, 1888. 18/7/1 (Somerset R.O.).

D

2

The Voluntary School Manager—II

HIS FUNCTIONS AND RELATIONSHIPS WITH OTHERS

MANAGERS AND TEACHERS

Naturally, the main function of the managers was in connection with the appointment, supervision and dismissal of teachers. Some of the problems which arose from the teacher/manager relationship clearly illustrate the basic issues involved in management.

The appointment of teaching staff was a frequent and often non-productive task. Supply and demand fluctuated throughout the century and between urban and rural parts. Advertisements for the posts appeared in the educational and Church journals, varying in the qualities and the qualifications expected of the applicants. One advertisement for a school in Kingsbridge, Devon, in *The School-master* in April, 1887, read as follows:

> "CERTIFICATED MASTER wanted immediately for mixed school (very nice children) in wholly agricultural parish. Must have efficient female relative for infants and sewing. Both must be High Church and un-varying communicants. Sunday School twice for both. Average attendance about 71. Passes last year 96 per cent. Testimonials, reports and parchment endorsements must be of the highest order. Harmonium in church and care of choir under the Rector. *No* man self-willed or otherwise Radical need apply. Salary about £90 for both."[1]

Many of the candidates, upon applying, were seen by the managers, who undertook to visit them in the schools where they were already teaching. Sometimes, the journey was a substantial one. The managers of the Staines, Middlesex, National Boys' School resolved in April, 1870, that "the Rev. N. D. Tyssen be requested to go down, at the expense of the School Fund, to Shepton Mallet to see Miss Ellis and the Clergymen of the Parish and to report to the Managers at their next meeting".[2] This involved a round journey of some 230 miles.

As a general rule, the further away the school was situated from a town, the less easy would it be to obtain assistants, especially women. Mr. Hepple, the corresponding manager of such a school at Cap-heaton, Northumberland, had written no fewer than 52 letters to school mistresses and others, besides advertising in four newspapers without success. Hepple recorded his efforts in the managers' minute book:

"I wrote to Miss Lowes and found her agreeable to come until the beginning of September, 1901, when she had to go to College. She left then but in the meantime I advertised for another teacher but received no applications. I got the names of several parties who wanted situations as Schoolteachers and wrote to several of them, but had some excuse for not coming—too far from Station—salary too small and etc.—until I wrote to Mrs. Lee. She appeared anxious to come and having a first-class reference, I wrote to ask her to come to Capheaton. That was the last we saw of Mrs. Lee. Few days after I heard an unsatisfactory account of her and in consequence I cancelled the engagements. After all the trouble writing we are no further forward and we are still without an Assistant."[3]

References were taken up and forgeries, when detected, summarily dealt with. The vicar of Gerrards Cross, Buckinghamshire, on checking a new assistant teacher's testimonial discovered an alteration; at the instigation of the vicar, the teacher was brought before the Beaconsfield magistrates, fined and instantly dismissed from his post by the managers.[4]

Life in a rural school could however sometimes be a very pleasant one for a teacher. In a diary kept during the years 1864 and 1865 by Albert Brett, assistant schoolmaster of Puddleton British School, the changing seasons, visits to Salisbury Cathedral and studying for examinations are all recorded. On Boxing Day, 1864, he mentions: "In the evening went to N. Sparks (presumably Nathaniel Sparks, Violin Maker) and met Thomas Hardy. Spent a pleasant evening."[5] There were, however, some difficulties, such as dealing with the older boys; and during the three weeks in April to May, 1865, Brett was inspected by Mr. Milnes, the British and Foreign Society Inspector once and Dr. Morrell,[6] H.M. Inspector, twice.

Subsequent relationships between managers and teachers hinged to a large extent on the terms of appointment, especially in security of tenure and pecuniary arrangements. An educational writer in 1855 put forward a strong case for the schoolmaster's greater independence from the managers.

"The very name of *schoolmaster* and *schoolmistress* indicates that the teacher is, in all the internal arrangements and in all the daily working of the school, the manager. . . . True, the master is the servant of the managers, he is engaged by them to perform certain duties; but he is supposed to be competent to their performance, or he would not be engaged. We claim only that for the teacher, which every gentleman concedes without questioning to his lowest menial. Who ever heard of a

1875

At a meeting of the School
Managers on July 1st
Present.   Lord St. John
Rev? R. Young
Rev? J. J. Slick
Rev? I. Cook
Mr. Hawk
Mr. Bellow
Mr. Sam? Baancco

It was agreed by 5 to 2
that the Diocesan Inspector
should visit Really School
this year, for the purpose
of examining the children in
religious knowledge – Messrs
Banks & Cook, alone being
opposed to it.
The following Scheme to regulate

the fees paid by the children
was submitted to the Managers
by Mr. Pearson
Farmers of over 200 acres or
persons of independent & about
Equal means 8 each per week.
Farmers of from 100 to 200
acres, 4 each per week.
Small farmers 2 Each.
Shopkeepers 3 each
Shopkeepers having other
businesses 4 Each.
Tradesmen & Policemen 2 Each
Workmen 2 Each.
Carriers 2 Each.
Labourers 1 Each.
Half time Scholars to pay the
same weekly fee as they would
if whole timers –

1. MINUTES OF A SCHOOL MANAGER'S MEETING   A proposal to fix fees according to ability to pay, 1875
Bedford County Record Office

gentleman telling his cook how to do the work of the kitchen? Or where, we would like to know, is the competent cook who would not resign rather than submit to such interference? Let the same be conceded to the teacher and we are satisfied."[7]

With the issue of the Revised Code in 1862, following the publication of the Newcastle Commission's Report, grants payable to certificated teachers were abolished: for this, grants to children were substituted, dependent upon individual examination by H.M. Inspector coupled with the fulfilment of a minimum number of attendances. Payments to teachers direct by the Privy Council ended and thenceforth all payments were made to the managers.

Robert Lowe, Vice-President of the Committee of Council on Education, who instigated the Revised Code, himself indicated how this move put the teacher in the position of the servant of the manager rather than of the State, as previously. "It will probably be said," wrote Lowe to Lord Brougham in 1863, "that a Grant resting on examinations will bear hard on schools where contributions are scarce and population are stubborn and barbarous. My answer is that the hardship is also a stimulus and that if the grant will often be reduced, so may the expenditure be. We for the first time put it in the hands of the managers to make what bargain they please with Pupil Teachers and Teachers and no longer as before offer a bounty in the employment of male in preference to female labour."[8] A year later, a further advantage of the system was put forward. "The system of examination has also the effect of discouraging the undue multiplication of schools, for the unit of payment is no longer the school but the child and it is therefore in the interests of the Managers to have as many children in one school as possible."[9]

Few managers or teachers relished the change.[10] John Grote, then Professor of Moral Philosophy at Cambridge, Vicar of Trumpington, and a manager of many years' experience, in a pamphlet directed against the Code, expressed the belief that it would lead to a deterioration in the relationships between teachers and managers, the latter already being looked on "as savage taskmasters only anxious to get out of the poor schoolmaster the most work for the least pay, utterly careless of *his* health and interests".[11]

Another manager summed up the situation as follows: "The plan for making over to the managers a grant apparently largely determined by conditions over which they have no or little control and then paring it down by twelve or fourteen fines, deductions, penalties and abatements, is admirably suited to deprive the Government of every trace of sympathy or kindness and to turn it into a series of petty wrongs and affronts leading to endless complaints and ceaseless irritations."[12]

25

WEDNESDAY, the 27th JULY, 1887.

PRESENT:—

THE REV. J. R. DIGGLE, M.A. (*Chairman for the day*).

MR. E. BARNES,   REV. R. RHODES BRISTOW, M.A.
MR. EDRIC BAYLEY,   MR. J. W. SHARP.

STATEMENT OF MR. W. WINNETT, A MANAGER OF THE "PULTENEY" SCHOOL.

MR. W. WINNETT, in answer to questions put to him, replied to the following effect:—

Managers.

I have been a Manager for four years. I do not think it would be an improvement upon the present system of electing Managers for the parents of the children attending the Board's Schools to elect representatives on the Committee of Managers. I consider that when there is a vacancy in the Managers' Committee the Committee itself should fill up the vacancy, the Divisional member sitting with the Committee and simply having a vote with the Managers. What I mean is, that a Divisional member should not be able to say " I have got a friend of mine whom I wish to be put on the Committee," but should, for the purposes of electing a Manager, be in the same position as an ordinary member of the Committee, or, in other words, that the Divisional Member should not have a right of veto. I consider it would be very irritating to the Managers if they had to submit, whenever there was a vacancy, the names of say three candidates to the Divisional members if they had the power of veto. We know persons living in the neighbourhood of our Schools who might be proud to get on the Committee of Managers. I do not think there is any danger of our Managers forming themselves into a ' close corporation.' I lay a very great stress upon the supreme veto resting with the Board. The Committee of Managers should have power to elect persons to vacancies in their own body. If the Board see any unwise election made, they could put their veto upon it. Such a power can only safely be vested in the Board. The Board should, if I may so speak, exercise a "liberal despotism" over the election of Managers. I think that the Board should, when a new group is formed, allow the local men who had already been engaged in educational work in the neighbourhood to have a voice in the selection of suitable persons for the Committee of Managers. I consider it to be an absolutely necessary qualification for the position of a Manager that any person nominated should be able to visit the Schools in the day time, as, in my opinion, the visiting of the Schools is one of the chief duties of a Manager. I think that Managers should be selected from those ladies or gentlemen who are known to take an interest in educational matters. I should prefer to see Managers elected from ladies and gentlemen of leisure who have been actually connected with Schools. Perhaps, however, persons engaged in the City might, in cases where they are otherwise qualified, and like School management, be elected as Managers. I have often heard of persons being elected as Managers who had no qualifications whatever for the position.

Teachers (Appointment of)

There is a little difficulty which sometimes causes a great deal of irritation to the Managers. The Managers, while considered competent to carry out the instructions of the Board, are not thought capable of themselves choosing a teacher. A short time ago we wanted an Assistant Mistress. We went thoroughly into the matter, examined the candidates,

D

7. THE ELECTION OF MANAGERS

Evidence given before the Special Committee of the School Board for London on the mode of election and the powers of managers in December, 1887

Greater London Record Office

APPOINTMENT OF TEACHERS

The terms of appointments[13] varied according to the finances and standing of the school. Engagements for six months with reconsideration of the position at the end of that time were not unknown.[14] At the Binchester Colliery School, Durham, the master recorded in the log book for 4 March, 1887: "Received notice from R. Robinson Esq., Manager, that in future, arrears of school pence to be paid by master."[15] A schoolmaster at Uxbridge British School, Middlesex, complained in the log book that he had to pay for the boys' exercise books. "In some of the schools about here they are found by the Managers."[16] The managers of Vowchurch School, Herefordshire, decided that they would not engage pupil teachers unless the teacher agreed to pay half salary and give tuition gratis.[17]

A contract drawn up between the schoolmaster and the managers at Purbright, Surrey, bound the former to carry out "to the best of his abilities" the respective duties of organist and choirmaster of the parish church and of the National School as master and to provide a competent sewing mistress. For a total salary of £100 per annum, "the schoolmaster E. L. Wilkinson, also agrees to conduct the Sunday School and during the winter nights a school for Young Men, and to render active aid to the Parish Priest in such matters as Public Readings, Reading Room, Cottage Gardeners' Society, Guilds and Entertainments".[18] In writing a letter of recommendation for the chairman of a school committee, the rector of a Yorkshire parish where the teacher then held an appointment praised his manner, accomplishments and beliefs very highly. "In only one way might Mr. Wild be improved," added the vicar, "and that is in *looking up a scholar* when absent. He has acknowledged this to me and he is I believe wishful to improve."[19]

To attract teachers to posts, it was often necessary to hold out some inducement. Writing in 1838 to the vicar of a neighbouring parish, the Rev. J. Landon of Aymestry, Herefordshire, stated: "I have always had it in view to keep the Appointments of Parish Clerk, Sexton and Schoolmaster united in the same person. Because, I think it would be the means, your only means, of providing a decent, permanent subsistence for a respectable and efficient School Master at Aymestry. I have many years experience of the Advantages of such a Union of Offices here. With you it would also remove the difficulty of finding any salary for the Clerk and the apprehension of adding needy inhabitants to the Village."[20]

Some managers encouraged the teachers to apply for the holding of additional posts. One of the conditions made for the teacher at Kingston St. Mary School, Somerset, accepting the post of parish

34.

Copy of letter referred to in previous page 33.

School Board Offices. Exeter
16th May 1881.

To the Exeter School Board,
Gentlemen,

As the warm weather approaches we are desirous to call your attention to a request made by a Teacher, Miss Hutchings, that she may be granted a bedstead similar to that in the S. Sidwells School for the use of the Infants under her care. Some of the children attending the New Town School are under 3 years of age and become extremely drowsy in the afternoons one having slipped off a bench when slumbering and hurt itself last Summer. As it is generally considered that in order to ensure a healthy development of the mental and physical powers, much sleep is required in early years, we venture respectfully to request that the Exeter School Board will grant such a boon, as a resting place for the little ones as we feel assured that it would prove a valuable addition to the resources of the New Town Infants School.

The numbers attending this School are so large and at the same time so young that space cannot conveniently be found for laying the children on the floor.

Signed, on behalf of the Ladies Committee
Beatrice Temple.

8. THE WORK OF A LADIES' COMMITTEE
An example of the growing concern for the welfare of young children, 1881

Exeter City Record Office

clerk was that "he must appoint a thoroughly suitable person to sit with the school children and see to their behaviour during Divine Service".[21] On the other hand at Uxbridge, the master was dismissed upon accepting this post part-time on the grounds "that it is likely to take him at times from the duties at the school and that the duties of that office are incompatible with his proper attention to his school duties".[22]

In spite of the managers' insistence on the devotion of the master's full time to the school and the Department's Code, Article 85e, which reinforced this, where the opportunity arose a number of other occupations were followed. As late as 1897 a report that the master "abstain in future from taking a prominent position in politics—and that it is advisable in the opinion of the Managers that he be recommended to discontinue his coal agency" was made by a Nottinghamshire school committee.[23] A complaint by the committee of the Plymouth Free School concerning the schoolmaster's entry into business "as a butcher and his occasionally attending distant markets for the purpose of buying Cattle", added that there was "slaughtering of Sheep on the premises occupied by these schools".[24] Mr. Lawrence, the master of Birdham Manhood National School in Sussex from 1837 to 1872, was the official postman. "The mail was delivered in Chichester by the coach from London. The carrier brought the letters out from Chichester in the morning and presumably they were sorted out at the school."[25]

A number of enterprising schoolmasters became leading members of the local community, having a stake in a number of different interests. Richard Cookson of Goosnargh in Lancashire, was one such person. He was headmaster of the school from 1832 to 1873 and became in addition Registrar of Births and Deaths for the Broughton Division of the Preston Union, and responsible for the ten-yearly Census, ran a farm and became an author.[26] In one of his books on the parish he mentions the salaries offered to the masters were "so very small that first-rate scholars cannot be obtained".[27] In Cookson's papers, there is a memorial signed by the schoolmasters of Goosnargh appealing to the trustees for an increase in salary.

"Your memorialists hope they will not be altogether overlooked, for as they are now situated in their present schools, they consider themselves, if you will allow the expression, to be somewhat like men with fine coats upon their backs and empty bellies."

The three extra benefits formerly available to the masters had, they complained, virtually ceased:

"The *Cockpenny* had dwindled to the sum of £1 9s. 2d. and about one third of the scholars absent themselves on that day. The *Annual Banquet* formerly intended for the Masters was no longer held because of shortage of funds. . . . That the *Fire Money* previous to last year had almost dwindled away, when the Masters made a stand and drilled and teased the children until most of them paid something, but it was found very unpleasant and almost as ill as begging for it."[28]

After 1870, the managers competed with the school boards in the appointment of teachers, but even before this managers were responsive to the needs of the locality. This can be seen in an examination of the rise of the plaiting industry in the South Midlands during the nineteenth century. The boom in the straw hat industry which centred around Luton and Bedford, created a demand for plaiting schools where children could learn the art of plaiting and at the same time receive rudimentary forms of education. By 1867, the Chief Constable of Buckinghamshire had estimated that there were about 600 schools with an attendance of between 10,000 and 73,000 children starting from the age of four and leaving at ten for the sewing rooms.[29] Parents provided the straw and sold the articles and the teacher saw that the plait was made up. Earnings were high during the boom years and any pretence at education was often dropped. The moral character of many of the mistresses, unqualified except in plaiting,[30] was doubtful, punishment was common, and the conditions under which the children obtained their instruction deplorable.

"A slow or lazy child was probably sent to a school where the discipline was stronger, for the mistress who got the most out of the children was the most patronised. Sarah Meagher, aged seven said: 'If I do 5, Mother says I am a good girl. She doesn't hit me; the mistress does sometimes'. Closer questioning revealed that her '5' meant 5 yards of plait in the morning, another 5 in the afternoon and 5 more in the evening, and with an extra yard at lunch time and another at tea time."[31]

The effect of the plaiting boom was to raise the wages of both agricultural labourers and domestic servants[32] and for children to leave school early. Confronted with the severe opposition of the plaiting schools, it seems from the fragmentary records which have survived on this topic, that the managers were torn between abolishing plaiting in their schools and on the other hand facing up realistically to the situation of employing a plaiting master or mistress in order to attract children;[33] in the end, the latter expedient seems to have been more generally adopted.

At Billington National School in Bedfordshire, there appears in the account book for 1864 the following memorandum:

"A plaiting Teacher was engaged to attend to the plaiting, light the fires and clean the school. She agreed to do this for 2s. 6d. per week and entered on her duties February 22nd, 1864. She resigned the situation assigning as a reason that the Salary was too small. Caroline Shannon was then engaged at the same salary but it was agreed to pay her sixpence per week for lighting the fire."[34]

In the log book at Langford School, Bedfordshire, in the heart of the plaiting country, the mistress notes with satisfaction on 1 September, 1869, "Several children have given up plaiting in school", and by the following March it was abolished. A week later, a teacher was engaged to teach sewing three times a week. No indication of the course of events during the next few years can be gleaned from the log book, except that attendances were steadily dropping. Certainly by the 1890s, the managers must have bowed to the inevitable, for on 29 July, 1895, the school was taught as two classes, the "mistress having gone to Luton to receive a prize in connection with the plaiting class".[35] By the end of the century, however, the industry had died away owing to foreign competition.

DISMISSAL OF TEACHERS

Just as managers were responsible for the appointment of teachers, so they had the power to dismiss them where necessary. This power was widely used. Inefficiency, real or alleged, detected by the visit of H.M. Inspectors, was the primary cause; falling attendances and the inability to work smoothly with the managers were equally important ones.

Not all dismissals generated friction. By some miscalculation on the part of the managers at Romford British School, the master, Mr. T. Matheson, had been engaged, but being under the age of 22, the Committee of Council's regulations rendered him ineligible for the Government examination. This made it necessary for him to leave at Christmas, but the committee informed him that they were perfectly satisfied with the way in which he was conducting the school and that they should be sorry to lose him. Mr. Matheson, for his part, "thanked the Committee for the kind way in which they had spoken of him—regretted his youth—and retired".[36]

Strict moral propriety was regarded as a prerequisite for any person holding the post of schoolmaster; a transgression of it was severely dealt with. Drunkenness was one of these. At a managers' meeting at Handforth Church of England School, Cheshire, it was reported that the schoolmaster "had been frequently seen in a drunken condition and that between the hours of six and seven o'clock this Monday evening he had been seen leaving the Greyhound Public House in the village in a state of inebriation and was followed from there to his lodgings by a number of children hooting him and on being sent for by the Committee a reply was sent that he had gone to bed".[37] He was instantly dismissed.

Scandal was the most serious offence of all.

In Thomas Hardy's novel, *Jude The Obscure*, Phillitson, the schoolmaster of Shaston, had condoned his wife's behaviour in going away with Jude. The chairman of managers came to the school to verify the facts; later, after being interviewed by the committee of managers, Phillitson was dismissed. They insisted "that the private eccentricities of a teacher came quite within their sphere of control as it touched the morals of those he taught".[38]

Masters holding doubtful theological views were suspect in Church schools. Appeal on this ground lay to the bishop of the diocese, who treated the cases as far as possible on their merits. The Lord Bishop of Gloucester, replying to an appeal regarding such a schoolmaster by John Sayers, patron of the living of Arlington, replied:

> "It seems to me that the prejudice against the schoolmaster has originated from his not agreeing with some sectarian notions on the subject of infant Baptism. But the Teacher of the National School, if a believer in the Doctrines of the Prayer Book, is not expected to pass any further Theological Examinations and it is most undesirable to have a polemical controversy on the Instruction of Watermen and Labourers. But however this may be the man must have justice—and must not be punished without discussing punishment."[39]

In exceptional cases a teacher could resort to litigation against the managers attempting to dismiss him. The managers of Chapel Allerton School, Leeds, found themselves involved in such proceedings in connection with the master, Mr. Wick. It had been hoped to improve the school finances by obtaining better results at annual examination and more seriously, because of the master's lack of efficiency, it was noted, "many good Church people preferred to send their children to the Board schools". One difficulty in the way of effecting his dismissal was that the master had been elected by the ratepayers for life, and on 19 March, 1891, Wick told the managers that he refused to resign unless assured of a pension. On 1 June, the vicar reported that Wick had secured a writ and notice of a motion against six managers for an interim injunction to restrain them from removing or purporting to remove the plaintiff from his office as headmaster of the school. One of the managers, Mr. Middleton, was a solicitor and his firm was retained to represent the committee of management, now the defendants in the action. In the subsequent proceedings (*Wick* v. *Maud*) in which the master was successful, the plaintiff's costs paid out by the treasurer amounted to £68 4s. 0d. in addition to the £162 for the remainder of the master's contract. The solicitor's costs for the action were another £90 1s. 6d. but Mr. Middleton, to the great relief of the managers, magnanimously offered to settle the bill for £50.[40]

With the growing power of the National Union of Teachers,[41] teachers became readier to challenge allegations of inefficiency. The headmasters of the Taunton Church Schools petitioned the schools committee on the occasion of the annual report to subscribers. This contained extracts from the reports of both Diocesan and H.M. Inspectors. They protested:

"In many instances such action has had a serious effect upon a teacher's reputation, without any power of self defence. We beg to point out also that the Managers themselves from the knowledge of the teacher and his or her work and influence on the school, acquired by constant intercourse during the year, can, in their annual report to the subscribers, fairly give a more just report of the condition of the school than can be formed by one or two official visits, of an inspector."[42]

Considering the conditions under which many of the teachers worked, it is surprising how infrequently teachers and managers came into conflict. Daily visits by managers,[43] visits by the housekeeper from the lord's house to inspect the children,[44] and schools open to "all persons desirous of inspecting or visiting the same" were not uncommon;[45] on 5 March, 1875, the school at Bradford-on-Avon, Wiltshire, was visited by nineteen people and ministers.[46] Few managers were as considerate as the committee of the Buckingham National School, which set out in its rules:

"That no stranger be permitted to visit the school unless he be accompanied by, or produce a written order from, a member of the Committee—And as the frequent introduction of strangers is found to interrupt the regular business of the school and distract the attention of the children, it is earnestly hoped that no member of the Committee will recommend any Visitor with whom he is not personally acquainted or who wishes to see the School from motives of curiosity only."[47]

The right to examine scholars was reserved to managers. Thomas Wright, master of Falkingham School, Lincolnshire, recorded in his diary for 30 April, 1853:

"Monstrous! A meeting of the inhabitants at six o'clock this evening in the Vestry Room to take into consideration the lost state of the Free School. Monstrous! . . . The Managers came to a Resolution all of them to examine the Free Scholars—*not at my school* but privately at their own homes or somewhere and Report to the Trustees their opinion thereon."

This must have been carried out, for Wright mentions briefly on 7 May, "The Blockheads' Committee met at six and adjourned to the Greyhound to examine the progress of some who had left school seven years".[48]

Perhaps it is not surprising that many teachers left for more amenable occupations. Entry into the Church, setting up as a stationer and taking up duties as a school attendance officer, the last "forsaking teaching as he could not stand the monotony of the work"[49] are recorded. For many it was a point of no return. An application by the master at Riseley National School, Bedfordshire, to the managers, "for leave to try his success of a business which he had made arrangements to undertake on account of ill-health which he considers to be the result of his school work and if it should not succeed to return at the end of one year to resume his duties as master" was unanimously rejected.[50]

THE SCHOOL MISTRESS

So far in this section, reference has been made to the school master and managers; in many instances the situations were equally applicable to school mistresses,[51] although a number of different issues arose in connection with the employment of women.

The question of how far single rather than married teachers should be employed was almost invariably answered by managers in favouring the former rather than the latter category. This issue was pertinent to both board and voluntary schools, with the difference that the comparative geographical isolation of many church schools involved the managers in finding them suitable accommodation; and having once supplied this, ensuring that the mistress did not leave her post too quickly.

A memorial from the mistresses employed by the Bristol School Board, in May, 1882, asking the Board to reconsider its recent decision not to employ married mistresses and urging the Board to treat each case on its merits, gave rise to a debate on the principles involved in employing women as teachers. Many members voiced the opinion that after a woman was married she should stay at home to look after her children. "If England is to hold her own," cried one speaker, "it must be through the good influence in the future of the mothers upon the rising generation".[52] The unreliability of married women teachers in consequence of maternal duties was also emphasized. Finally, a curiously-worded resolution allowing "Head Teachers to marry to any extent they might think proper" was passed in spite of the final speaker's belief that such a system would make for improvident marriages and make the married mistress's life a "complete slavery".[53] A mistress of a Sussex school requested the managers to continue her employment after her marriage, on the grounds that "we should stay at home with my parents so that domestic may not interfere with scholastic duties"; the managers decided that this was not desirable, and terminated her engagement.[54] Some managers, however, were prepared to continue the mistress's employment until such time as she obtained her Parchment Certificate.[55]

Finding suitable accommodation presented problems to the committee. The Rev. Bellairs in his manual had advised managers:

"If you take for mistress an unmarried young woman, make arrangements before engaging her that she will not live alone. Many Managers are very careless in this and unfortunate scandals occur."[56]

In rural Dorset, the mistress could hold out for her own terms against the managers. At Affpuddle, near Dorchester, the mistress demanded a shed in the garden of the house where she was lodged for preparation of work and accounts and marking of registers, etc., failing which she threatened to resign. The rector in considering the request reflected, in a letter to a colleague, that such resignation "would be a great misfortune for the school, as it is very difficult in these days to get a mistress of her experience and efficiency for a small village school. Besides this, I do not at present see where we would obtain lodgings for her with a comfortable *private* situation."[57] After the elaborate arrangements of renting a cottage, buying furniture, etc., had been undertaken, the mistress of a Gloucestershire village school begged leave to change "on account of preferring to walk to and from her school".[58] A sign of the changing times was the resolution of the managers of Edburton School in Sussex, in 1892, to change the custom of boarding the teacher with a villager for 2s. 6d. per week: henceforth the mistress was to find her own lodgings, and given a £6 allowance.[59]

A want of respect from the school mistress towards the managers, which would not have been tolerated from a master, was often noted.

"Visited the school this morning when I felt most annoyed by the mistress repeating to me the observation made on several occasions previously that we ought to have had a twelve months' Grant from the Education Department, as other parishes which she happened to know have done.

"I have to complain of remarks being made (in reply to my own) most improper and disrespectful—from the mistress of a school to a Manager and Clergyman in the presence of her scholars."[60]

On the other hand, the managers sometimes took advantage of the mistresses by giving them duties to perform which were outside their

official terms of reference, such as the distribution of parish magazines from house to house,[61] acting as caretaker because of the
difficulty of finding a suitable person for the work and instructing
privately the rector's children.[62]

A bigger problem for the managers resulted from mistresses
teaching in mixed schools. H.M.I. Rev. J. J. Blandford, in his report
for 1882 which was afterwards separately printed and was widely
distributed to managers,[63] based his disapproval of such an arrangement on social, moral and educational grounds.[64] Where a girl
pupil teacher was apprenticed to a master, the managers of a Somerset school resolved, "a female relation should be present when the
private instruction was given her".[65] Many were unable to enforce
discipline, especially when confronted with a class consisting
entirely of boys. Managers found themselves personally involved as
the result of such a situation. At Reading New Town Boys' School,
the managers recorded in the minute book:

> "The new assistant called in great trouble on Mr. Grisby (Manager) at
> his house last evening, stating that she could not manage her class at all,
> and that in the absence of the Head Master she was so worried that she
> was afraid she might have brain fever. Miss S. complained that she had
> no idea that she was coming from an Infants School to a class of 4th
> Standard boys, and she did not feel that she could go again the next day.
> After a lengthy conversation in which she was strongly advised to try
> again and do her best, Miss S. decided to be at her place as usual."

In spite of encouragement, the mistress continued to hold the
opinion that "she cannot be equal to the work and requirements of
Standard IV boys, as the jump is so great from Infants . . ." and she
was eventually allowed to resign.[66]

Whatever steps the committees took to ameliorate the conditions
of the mistresses in a more than usually lonely life, they fought a
losing battle to retain their services for lengthy periods of time.
Resignation to this situation was well expressed by the managers of a
small Nottinghamshire village school when they recorded:

> "After about six months' service Miss Langham resigned her post of
> mistress of the school together with her sister, Miss Alice Langham, on
> account of ill-health—or a desire to be married—we know not which."[67]

The plight of women teachers was summed up by H.M.I. Mr.
Brodie in 1894.

> "Forlorn indeed is the lot of the young mistress in some of these out-
> lying rural nooks. They have perhaps been pupil teachers in towns, and
> then trained in some college, and accustomed to social intercourse.
> Suddenly they are moved off to distant, secluded spots, where there is
> little or no society and find themselves at the outset of their careers

To,

Mr. Thomas Harvey of Spettisbury in the County of Dorset.—

I am directed by the Trustees of Bishop Hill and Dr. Roper's Charities to give you Notice as the Master of Spettisbury and Charlton Marshall School part of the said Charities that at the Meeting held by them at the Greyhound Inn in Blandford Forum in the said County of Dorset on Wednesday the twelfth day of March Instant to take into consideration the alleged charge against you for recently intermarrying with Mrs. Rowman the wife of Samuel Rowman the said Trustees, after hearing what you had to allege in your defence and it appearing from your own Statement that you knew that the said Samuel Rowman was living so recently as three years since and that you had never received any account of his death and had no reason to allege for believing him to be dead, unanimously resolved and determined that on account of the said offence and for other acts of misconduct you were an unfit Person to be continued in the office of Master of the said School and that you should be removed therefrom And I give you further notice that I was at the said Meeting further directed by the said Trustees to require and I do hereby accordingly require you to yield and deliver up to the said Trustees the School House at Spettisbury aforesaid with the Garden outhouses and Premises thereto belonging on or before the sixth day of April next— Witness my hand the thirteenth day of March 1834—

Septimus Smith
Steward of the said Charities—

2. THE DISMISSAL OF A SCHOOL-MASTER 1834
The private life of a teacher was often the concern of the managers.

Dorset County Record Office

3. ANGELA BURDETT-COUTTS (1814–1906)

confronted with all the hard circumstances of school life, ill at ease, and with circumstances far from encouraging. It is not surprising that many of these teachers become restless and mere birds of passage. The marvel and the honour is that a few of them do so well and bravely against wind and tide."[68]

LANDOWNERS AND CLERGY

The extent to which landowners and the officiating minister of the parish worked harmoniously together affected the chances of the establishment and smooth management of the school. Earlier in the nineteenth and indeed throughout the previous century the parson and the landowner could meet on common ground. Writing in February, 1887, to Sir Richard Cross,[69] then Home Secretary and at the time in charge of a Bill connected with the sale of glebes, a rector, Rev. A. W. Williams, outlined the relationship that once existed.

"The parson who held a large Glebe was, by virtue of that circumstance, admitted to the fellowship and the privilege of a select and exclusive body. He gained a certain advantage from this. It added to his importance and to his influence, brought him into relation with his fellow gentry and enabled him to keep in practical sympathy with the secular affairs of his parishioners."[70]

With the reduced prices of agricultural produce and high cost of labour, the vicar's possession of land as a means of wealth as distinct from an outward symbol of status had become drastically reduced; nevertheless there was a bond between the gentry and the parson. The Rev. T. Mozley, rector of Cholderton, Wiltshire, wrote in his reminiscences (1885) that "the ignorance of farmers is even sadder and more positively obstructive of free social intercourse than the ignorance of their labourers. They choose to know nothing except farming, horseflesh and game. One of the results of this ignorance is that it creates a want of sympathy between the classes. . . . From the day a boy enters a public school, to the wine or supper party he gives to his friends on passing his final examination at the university, he hears the blunders and stupidities of the poor country folk treated as good jokes, and as demonstrably the vast superiority of the Clergy and Gentry."[71]

In many instances too, the Church's connection with property strengthened this bond. For instance, in 1873, clerical landowners in East Yorkshire included the Rev. R. M. Taylor with 1,258 acres and Archdeacon Long with 1,286 acres. Nominations to livings were used to provide sinecures for younger sons, deprived by primogeniture of any large share of their family inheritance.[72]

E

This bond had been weakened but not severed as the clergy struggled to maintain their financial position. When, for example, the Rev. Thomas R. Terry, Rector of East Ilsley, Berkshire, late Fellow and Tutor of Magdalen College, Oxford, and Chairman of the East Ilsley School Board, was directed by the Education Department in December, 1897, to proceed against the local landowner, Mr. Francis Stevens, the Rev. Terry was averse to instituting legal proceedings "as this would cause very serious ill-will and much personal feeling in this small village"; he resigned the chairmanship and clerkship rather than be the cause of any such embarrassment.[73]

Where a school was to be built, it was natural for the parson to assume that the local gentry would be willing either to lease or give a site of land for this purpose. Increasingly, after 1870, owners attached conditions to the leasing of school land. John Walter, M.P., and chief proprietor of *The Times*,[74] lent to the parish of Finchampstead, Berkshire, the school buildings and the maintenance of them at his sole expense, rent free, "so long as the school expenses are defrayed without the aid of a School Board".[75]

The Vicar of Aynho, Northamptonshire, went so far as to make enquiries about a suitable plot of the land belonging to the lord of the manor, W. C. Cartwright, and engaged a surveyor who "fixed upon the piece in your hands". Cartwright rejected the vicar's presumptuous request. The vicar wrote again, adopting an attitude of pained surprise, noting that "the application to you in the name of the Chapter had issued in no favourable result. I am extremely sorry for this but I am the furthest possible from a disposition to interfere with your undoubted right, or to suggest an arrangement which, though in my judgment, permanently beneficial to our neighbours, would interfere with your wishes". The rector announced that the only alternative would be for him to sell off a piece of his own garden near the vicarage.[76]

Even less sympathetic to the plans of the clergy were the gentry who concerned themselves with estate management and were active in political life. The sixth Lord Monson of Lincolnshire (1796–1862), a notable and outspoken Liberal, took the opportunity of remonstrating with one of his incumbents, the Rev. W. James, who complained that the increased number of children in his school had led him to use the vicarage to give lessons, "to the detriment of my furniture and the annoyance of my servants". Pointing out that the vicar had freely chosen to accept the living, Monson mentioned that he was not altogether happy with James's attitude.

"You very gently and deliberately hinted of a 'clerical *otium cum dignitate*' combined with a pretty increasing balance at one's bankers and then you then add 'neither as yet can I see much *prospect of either*'. I regret this for I have a strong opinion that it is the duty of a Clergyman to save for the decline of life. I even wish that a life assurance in proportion to the profits of the benefice were obligatory. A despotic idea and therefore no doubt unpopular."[77]

Sometimes the cleric was dependent on the assistance of a landowner of a different religious persuasion from his own. In Catholic Lancashire, this was especially the case. In the Church Returns of Schools, 1837 to Easter Day 1838, for Blackburn, appears the entry from the vicar: "No return from this school, in consequence of a prohibition from an opulent landed proprietor (a Papist) who contributes something annually to its support. The schoolmaster is a Protestant."[78]

Such a situation would give rise to an uneasy alliance between the landlord and parson.

Gerard Salvin (1804–70), the seventeenth successive Lord of Croxdale in Durham (one of the oldest English Catholic families, which produced the notable architect Anthony Salvin), inherited from his father a school room which had been built at Sunderland Bridge, near to the family home. The Rev. H. Chayter, the local Church of England minister, had traditionally paid a small quit rent for the building, selected the master and had superintendence of the school. The accommodation was for all the children of the parish, the majority being Church of England; the Catholic children read only the Authorized Version of the Bible and no attempt was to be made to force the Prayer Book or the Catechism on them. With the growing population of the village and the dilapidated state of the school room, Salvin was approached to sell the site so that rebuilding might take place. After a long exchange of letters between the parties, Salvin refused to sanction the scheme on the ground that "the only object and purpose is a sectarian feeling towards the owners of the present school".[79]

Outright hostility could occur when both parties were completely out of sympathy with each other. At King's Stanley National School, Gloucestershire, the Rev. Arthur Jennings, M.A., of Jesus College, Cambridge, was chairman of managers of the school. Also on the committee was Sir William Henry Marling, D.L., J.P., of Stanley Park, a local industrialist, one of the lords of the manor and joint chief landowner, who had already built one school in a neighbouring parish.[80] The rector, an independent-minded and a somewhat oversensitive person, had had a number of brushes with Marling since accepting the living some five years previously. Matters came to a head at a committee meeting convened at the special request of Sir W. H. Marling in January, 1889.

Jennings notes at the beginning, "Sir W. Marling's deportment on this occasion was such that the Chairman had to remind him that he (the Chairman) was not a Stanley Mill employé". The only other member present was Mr. George Hague, proprietor of the Red Lion public house and virtually a spectator at the meeting. Jennings threatened to resign if his position as working manager was further interfered with. Financially the school was sound, thanks to "applications by himself to his own family. Whether he should continue to make such appeals to external liberality on behalf of a school which ought to be adequately supported by the rich of its own Parish would be a matter for future consideration". [81] Jennings anticipated further trouble from Marling who had in a number of ways cast aspersions on his (Jennings) conduct of affairs. The rector had insisted on the school's H.M. Inspector auditing the accounts for the past year "by comparison with each and every voucher" and he had drawn up a written statement of the financial and educational status of the school for the next meeting on Thursday, 4 April. However, the day before the meeting, as Jennings noted triumphantly, "Sir William Marling thought proper to resign his place on the Committee". Jennings was thus left in sole charge. Three years later, in 1892, the smouldering animosity still remained. At the annual meeting of 1891-2, Jennings reported, after noting the palpable improvement in the work of the school and the "Excellent" grant gained in the annual examination, "The Management had no annoyance from Sir William Marling other than some delays of subscriptions which the Rector treated as before". [82]

How far the landowners acted on their own initiative or upon the advice of their agents is not always clear, but the agents' ability to influence decisions relating to schools is borne out in a number of instances.

AGENTS

The position of the local agent, although at times an uncomfortable one, gave the occupier of that post a unique oversight of the day-to-day activities of the estates and in the parishes. Involvement in local politics and religion, as well as the engagement of suitable tenants for the land, public houses, etc., gave him access to inside information which would be of great value in advising his master. Nowhere was this more true than in regard to education; at the same time the agent's own views coloured his interpretation of the situation and this was apparent in his assessments and reports.

Thomas Finlay, a Scotsman, was one of the two sub-agents in charge of the Grimsthorpe and Lindsey Coast estates of Lord

Willoughby d'Eresby; the estates which were scattered over Lincoln-shire, Perthshire and North Wales, were under the overall superin-tendence of the chief agent, Mr. Lewis Kennedy, to whom Finlay reported, writing as many as three or four letters a day. The need for promoting education as an antidote to debauchery and ignorance was emphasized by Finlay. Attempts to revitalize parish school education was therefore made:

"As long as Governments have not the power to institute a broad system of education it must be sectarian—I know of no Parish but Welton where Churchmen and Dissenters meet on equal terms at one school.
"I asked Mr. Mawe of Partney (a leading Wesleyan) why he could not join the Rector as to the new school as both called themselves *Liberal*—his Answer was that he went to the Rector, offered him Money and Assistance, providing the Children of the Dissenters were allowed to accompany their parents to Chapil on Sunday, but this was deneyd. After all perhaps this loss of principle and competition is the best way to advance the Cause of education!"[83]

When asked for his opinion on the siting of the school house, he wrote:

"I must say that the present site of the school is the best you can get for the *convenience of the children* as it is in the centre of the town. The Vicar complains of an open sewer not far off, but that would be easily turned over. I am altogether opposed to the Rev. M. Turner's views. What I believe he wishes is a school house for show as well as use."[84]

A further clash with the Rev. Turner, a High Churchman, with humble aims in education, well displays the grandiose views of the agent who, judging from his correspondence, had received only a scant education himself. Writing to Kennedy a little later, he men-tioned that he had had some further conversation with the vicar about a site for the school house.

"We must give up all vulgar notions about the Children and their Parents. . . . The children are to be trained for India and the Colonies and not to the ignoble office of servants to Tradespeople or Farmers."[85]

The authority of the agent was strengthened by his continuity in office to successive lords of the manor.[86] A manuscript auto-biography of Robert Hird, a shoemaker of Bedale, Yorkshire, written in old age, gives an example of this. In his preface, Hird stated:

"The year 1839 brought a great change in Bedale; by the death of Lady Throgmorton, Lady of the Manor of the Stapyltons Estate and also by the death of her successor, Thomas Stapylton, Esquire of the Grove, Richmond, whose son, Myles, then came to the estate; and in the Month of January, 1840, the change was severely felt. His agent stretched the cords of his power, to that length that every tenant was on the rack and not a few gave up their land."[87]

The agent to the Duke of Manchester, Peter Purves, in thanking the Duke on 4 September, 1843, for his kindness in continuing him in his position which he had held under the previous Duke mentioned the engagement of a teacher who had applied to him for the post at the school then being built. It seems that all the decisions connected with the schools rested with Purves, including fixing the scale of fees for boys (1d. a week), visiting the school and advising the Duke on subscriptions to be given to the schools on his estates.

> "I gave the Rev. Mr. Eastbrooke, the Vicar of St. Ives to understand," wrote Purves to his master, "that I thought you ought not to be called upon for anything further. My opinion is that the middle classes in St. Ives with the exception of a few individuals have contributed in a very niggardly manner—and I do think that the Vicar's first call for the deficit ought to be upon his parishioners."[88]

In this section, the importance of the relationships existing between the vicar and landowner, and the latter and agent, has been explored. No reference has so far been made to individuals or organizations who both established and managed schools. These will now be considered.

INDIVIDUAL OWNERS/MANAGERS

Many instances were to be found of individuals with both money and administrative capacity who, for a variety of reasons, wished to conduct a school under their own supervision. One such reason could be the intense dislike of the local rector;[89] in remote areas such as at Whitehaven, Cumberland, where Lord Lonsdale established a school, the agent wrote to the Education Department informing them that Lonsdale did not wish to appoint managers, "indeed there are none in the locality";[90] occasionally the motive was philanthropic,[91] but usually it arose out of a strong sense of individualism where working with others in a committee would not have been congenial.

Not all acted as impetuously as Mr. Ashe, the local squire of Langley Burrell, Wiltshire, where the Rev. F. Kilvert was incumbent. The latter wrote in his diary on 11 November, 1874:

> "Mr. Ashe came angrily to Miss Bland the school mistress and ordered her always to keep all three windows and the door of the schoolroom open during schooltime, except in very cold weather when one window

might be shut. He said in a fierce determined way, 'This is my school and I will have my word attended to. If you don't do as I tell you, Miss Bland, instead of being your friend I'll be your enemy'."[92]

Under such conditions the school was unlikely to flourish. A graphic account of the relationships between the vicar, teacher and the sole proprietor exists in the letters of Miss Rose Knowles, a school mistress of Thorpe Malsor, near Kettering,[93] Northamptonshire, in 1888. Thorpe Malsor Hall was the seat of the Rev. C. H. Maunsell and his wife; the rector since 1876 was the Rev. M. J. Connelly, and the living was in the gift of Maunsell. The teacher in a letter to her mother on 13 June, 1888, wrote of the death of the rector, "I expect there will be no living here if she gets a clergyman like her. They will be always interfering. She is very pleased." Three days later: "Mrs. M. has had a paper put on the Church door to say he is only clerk not Rector. They say that is because he was in debt when he died. She heaps every indignity she can on him." Mrs. Maunsell managed the school, her husband holding a benefice in Brighton. There had already been a number of disputes over various matters between herself and the schoolmistress. Miss Knowles had earlier written to her mother advising the postponement of a visit to Milton Malsor, "You had better wait till she (Mrs. M.) comes back. She generally sacks somebody when she comes and as I have been here longest it will be very likely me." A week after the rector's death, Mrs. Maunsell sent for her. "I wished her good morning when I went in", wrote Miss Knowles, "she never spoke so I knew there was something up. She layed my money down then said there were going to be a great many changes here. She wished to give me two months notice from today. I thanked her and asked her if she would please write me out a Testimonial. She said yes and that ended it. She did look savage."[94]

In an isolated part of the country, the owner-manager could occasionally set up deliberately as a rival to the local church school. At Langton Matravers in Dorset, Mrs. Frances Serrell, who held most of the land in the area, believing herself as a person best qualified to manage a school in the village, established one near to the existing Church school. She was a member of the Bankes family, formerly owners of Purbeck Castle, and granddaughter of Lord Eldon, the Lord Chancellor;[95] her husband died shortly after their marriage and her income was considerable.

The rector, who was chairman of managers of the day school, the Rev. E. F. Trotman, was not a strong character although he attempted to challenge the encroachment by Mrs. Serrell and appealed to the Education Department. The H.M.I., Mr. W. F. Tregarthen, reported to the Department on Mrs. Serrell's attitude.

"Mrs. S., who devotes all her time and income to educating the people of this Parish (whether judiciously or not is another question) will brook no interference from local magnates and I have already asked the help of many influential persons in the District, as well as tried myself, to smooth over the differences between her and the Rector, without effect."[96]

One of the problems was whether a school maintained by a private individual and which could be discontinued by her at any moment could be said to provide effectually for the public education of the district. It exercised the mind of the officials of the Education Department how, under the circumstances, to deal with the shortage of school accommodation which had arisen in the parish. Trotman wrote desperately to the Department on the 2 August, 1872:

"It is a critical moment with us. Your Lordships' decision may confer a lasting benefit on this place, or may do a permanent injury. I therefore implore you to pause in carrying out what seems to be the present project of allowing all to Mrs. Serrell, in decided opposition to the Managers of the National School room and Ratepayers of substance. If only the Education Act is brought to bear here, it provides in the School Board just what we want."[97]

The Department then proceeded to build up an enormous file of correspondence containing charge and countercharge from the two parties. At one point, over a year later in September, 1873, it seemed as if some sensible division of responsibility could be effected by letting Mrs. Serrell make provision for girls and infants, and the boys to be in the National School, but this plan also failed.[98] The last entry in the Education Department file, written after the failure of the plan, simply reads: "I do not see what more we can do. Send F.N. (Final Notice) and let them fight it out among themselves."[99]

The solution came about by a fortunate series of events. The rector died and was succeeded by the Rev. Lester Lester, owner of the Manor of Langton Matravers, who was even richer and more influential than Mrs. Serrell. One day when she wrote asking him to prevent a working-class parishioner from holding open-air religious meetings, he played his trump-card by writing a sermon against Mrs. Serrell, printing and distributing it beforehand, then reading it from his pulpit at morning and evening service. It ruined her influence. Later, she offered to become school correspondent for the infants department of the re-united schools and not to interfere with the remainder. This plan continued until her death in 1889, aged sixty-one.[100]

Baroness Angela Georgina Burdett-Coutts (1814–1906), an educational philanthropist and friend of the Duke of Wellington and Charles Dickens,[101] provides a rare example of an individual who experimented in restructuring the rural schools system in many parts of the country. The unevenness of educational provision outside the urban areas had concerned educational reformers from the early part of the century. Burdett-Coutts established the "grouped school system" in order to overcome this difficulty. She wrote: "The principle of this plan consists in the schoolmaster being the ambulatory centre of unity to a group of schools carried on under his superintendence, according to local resources and capabilities; and its main advantage consists in the elasticity with which the plan can be adapted to varying circumstances."[102]

The system was first tried out with a group of five schools near Torquay, by the Rev. Reginald H. Barnes, vicar of Heavitree, near Exeter. The ambulatory master's work was to visit the schools, classify the children and remodel the time table. Weekly visits to the schools were to be made, where he set work for the coming week, pointing out how this was to be done. The master set topics, corrected grammar and instructed the children in singing and other subjects. In Barnes's district, the children were to be examined quarterly at Torquay by an Inspector for purposes of grant aid. One journal at least commented that it did not "look very practical that the children of one school should be invited to come to meet H.M.I. once a quarter *by sea*".[103]

The ambulatory schoolmaster was the key person, for the teachers were often uneducated local persons. At sixteen Devonshire schools in 1865 under this system the following information on the teachers can be gathered: six were labourers' wives, two tradesmen's wives, one farmer's wife, six spinsters and one widow, and the remaining two schools were taught by the Master "assisted by a Spinster".[104]

An interesting feature of the scheme was that each group of schools had its own constitution and form of management.

> "In one case a layman is the chief Manager, in another the Rector of the Living, in another the Trustees of the School property, in another a lady maintains the School. In eight more, the Clergymen are the Chief Managers. And in the remainder, there is every possible combination of Landowners, Churchwardens, Ladies and Clergymen and yet these schools in their several groups which they maintain are harmonious corporations."[105]

The novelty of "mixed" management did not go unchallenged by denominational interests. A correspondent wrote indignantly to *The School Guardian*:

> "The result will be to withdraw the education of the poor more and more from the hands of the clergy, and thereby to loosen if possible the Church's hold on the labouring population. There is no reason whatever

why the main principle of the scheme should not be adopted by Diocesan Boards and applied to the formation of educational districts, the parochial clergy being ex-officio members of the local board, and having the sole management of all that concerns the moral and religious conduct of the district school; but the local board being otherwise responsible for the management of affairs common to the whole district."[106]

A Minute of the Committee of Council on Education on 8 February, 1864, made it possible for small schools in poor parishes to be placed under Government inspection and thus receive a grant,[107] and this was incorporated into the Revised Code of 1865. The scheme, it was remarked, "would use up all the untrained teaching force which now lies idle in the country, and would enable many a clever lad who has no great hankering for the spade or the plough, to follow a more congenial as well as more intellectual occupation".[108]

Reactions to the scheme were soon forthcoming. The Rev. J. Fraser, giving evidence before the 1865 Select Committee on Education, was convinced that Miss Burdett-Coutts's plan was quite impracticable as a general measure, and stated: "I shall be very much surprised if six groups are formed in all England."[109] Rev. H. W. Bellairs, H.M.I., also reported unfavourably on the experiment in Oxfordshire.[110] In spite of the misgivings voiced by witnesses, the Committee in their draft Report praised this system; they recommended that the plan should be adopted along with an alternative one which combined a number of small parishes of a district by establishing one good central school.[111] By 1868, grants were being earned by groups of schools in Devon, Carlisle, Oxford, Norwich and Yorkshire.

With the passing of the 1870 Education Act and the requirement that school boards should be formed in all cases where the voluntary system was insufficient, the impetus of the group system faltered. Attempts to combat the changing circumstances proved abortive. "You ask me," wrote the Rev. Harry Baber, vicar of Ramsbury, Wiltshire, to Burdett-Coutts, "to look at a question coming before me in my own parish where I have a School Board. Here the School Board has built three excellent schools. Thus ample accommodation is provided for all the Children of the Parish. But besides this there are three small private adventure schools in the Parish. Would it be worthwhile to try to associate them and put a good master to improve them? I know the three old women who help these Schools. One can read a little. The other two are thoroughly ignorant women."[112] The growing encouragement by the Education Department for certificated teachers caused further hardships for group schools. A general manager of a group of five schools at Nunburnholme, a remote village in East Yorkshire, complained of this trend in

February, 1875. Baroness Burdett-Coutts had herself paid in this instance the salary of a certificated master who had been engaged.

> "Even if suitable masters could ever be found in sufficient numbers, in very numerous instances there are not funds to be obtained for the higher salaries which certificated masters would naturally claim, at least not without a very heavy tax on the ratepayers."[113]

Although the Scotch Code for 1875 offered grants to small schools grouped together, the effect of the English Code of that year was strongly to discourage the system in England. In January, a deputation headed by Roebuck and Mundella on behalf of the main school boards of England saw Sandon, the Vice-President of the Education Department, on the difficulties experienced by school boards in enforcing bye-laws, especially with reference to dame and other private adventure schools.[114] In order to eliminate a number of these schools, the 1875 Code did not recognize as a school a group of rooms of which not one was contiguous with the others. This requirement fell heavily on grouped schools, most of which were situated in small cottages.

Burdett-Coutts now attempted to bring pressure to bear on her political friends to alter this ruling. She wrote to Montagu Corry, Disraeli's secretary, the Duke of Bedford, Lord Granville and Lord Hampton and sent emissaries to interview Sandon, a relative of hers. In her letter to Corry she stated:

> "I have been so much struck with the results and *re*-impressed with the advantages of this system that I am determined to put the papers into print. I am quite sure that there is a sort of apprehension that the system will be called re-actionary. I venture before its final rejection in England that the subject should receive consideration."[115]

The day before the Code became law, Richmond, the Lord President, rejected Burdett-Coutts's request, claiming that the new Code "offers large grants for small schools, and though the English Code does not contain the Article in the Scotch Code which you sent me, I believe it will work as favourably for the small schools as the old grouping system".[116]

This was virtually the end of this interesting experiment which filled a gap in the existing educational provision and introduced the most liberal form of school management yet devised up to that time. After the system's demise, Burdett-Coutts returned to her many other philanthropic activities in the educational fields, which included the Ragged School movement, the founding of higher grade elementary schools and an interest in the training of teachers.[117]

One other category of owner-managers of schools was that connected with industrial concerns. Robert Owen, undoubtedly an individualist, was an early example.[118] Also worthy of mention was the school at Burley-in-Wharfedale, Yorkshire, which W. E. Forster and his partners established for part-timers in their works. Forster was an active manager "quietly watching the whole operation of the school, making himself master not only of the methods of teaching, but of the system of organisation under which the school was carried on".[119]

The Abram Colliery Schools at Bickershaw near Wigan, Lancashire, was a typical example of the owners of the works being responsible for the running of schools. The Bickershaw schools were erected in 1882, a few hundred yards eastwards of Bickershaw Hall, by Messrs. Hughes and Johnson, the proprietors of the Abram Coal Company who worked the mines under the Bickershaw Estate.[120] A. E. Johnson became the sole manager and visited the school regularly, urging the children to make regular attendances.[121]

The Rev. F. P. B. N. Hutton, senior chaplain to Messrs. John Bagnall and Sons, Ironworks, at West Bromwich, Staffordshire, stated in his report for 1864:

> "that experience (so far as your school is concerned) shows that the fear of a good English education proving detrimental to the interests of Employers, by preventing the Boys thus educated from entering the Ironworks and Collieries, is altogether groundless; from an investigation which I made in 1860 it was shown that out of every hundred Boys who leave the school on the completion of their education, eighty become engaged in the various Ironworks and Collieries of the District".[122]

In the overwhelming majority of works' schools, the management was vested in the owners or their agents. An unusually enlightened system prevailed at the Elswick Ordnance and Engine Works, Newcastle-on-Tyne, in 1869. There, the company provided at their own cost buildings for schools and a mechanics institute. A tax on wages of a penny in the pound was levied on the men entitling them to use the facilities without further cost. The management of the schools and institute was entrusted to committees jointly appointed by masters and men and the system worked well.[123]

THE INFLUENCE OF THE EDUCATION DEPARTMENT: TRANSFER OF SCHOOLS

The operation of the voluntary schools system alongside the board schools after 1870 in many cases resulted in a competition in which the voluntary schools were inevitably the losers. Many were forced to close down, but a great number took advantage of Section 23 of the Act enabling the schools to be transferred to the board. Reactions of voluntary schools committees and managers to such a suggestion when mooted were mixed, but some of the legislative, judicial, financial and local pressures which finally determined whether or not schools were transferred, give an interesting insight into the operations and attitudes of managers after 1870.

Section 23 of the Act set out the conditions under which transfers could be arranged. Briefly, it provided that in the first instance, a resolution must be passed by the majority of the committee of management at a meeting; in addition, a meeting of all the annual subscribers was to be called and a two-thirds majority in favour of transfer was necessary before further action could be taken. The Section did not attempt to define an "annual subscriber"—for example, whether one subscription was sufficient, if members in arrears were eligible, or at what point a person could subscribe in order to qualify for attendance at the meeting.

No payment of rent beyond that charged upon, or reserved out of the premises by the original lease, and no other valuable consideration except an undertaking to insure and keep the premises in repair, and to keep down or redeem charges on the same, would be sanctioned by the Education Department.[124]

Where there were trustees who were not also managers, notice had to be given to them; their observations and objections were to be sent by the clerk of the school board to the Education Department, together with those of the school managers and the school board.

Other parties who contributed to the establishment of the schools could also make objections and representations to the Education Department. This was to take into account the various societies such as the National Society, British and Foreign Society, the Wesleyan Education Committee and Catholic Poor School Committee who would make representations.

The arrangement provided for the absolute conveyance to the school board of all the interest in the school-house possessed by the managers, but did not preclude the managers having use of the school for certain parts of the week by arrangement with the board, nor indeed in continuing to participate in managing the school. The school board were not able to undertake to pay any consideration other than a strictly nominal one of five shillings nor could the board take over any existing debts or interest on existing debts. Similarly, the board was not responsible for any current expense incurred by the school managers up to the time of transfer. For fittings, fixtures and furniture, books and apparatus of the school, unless private property, no valuable consideration was to be given.

One ray of hope for managers however remained. Under Section 24 of the Act, under certain conditions the school board could re-transfer the school to the managers on a proposal of two-thirds of the members of the board. The Education Department's consent was necessary first but this was not given unless the Department were satisfied that any money expended on the school out of a loan raised by the school board had been, or would be on the completion of the re-transfer, repaid to the board.[125]

Much turned on the willingness or otherwise of managers to consent to the transfer. Where there was a dispute as to the legality of the appointment of managers who could bring about the transfer to a school board, this, as in *Re Burnham National School* (1873), had to be decided in the Court of Equity. The dispute concerned two clergymen, both managers and joint rectors of the parish of Burnham, Buckinghamshire, Dr. Bates and Rev. G. G. Hayter, of whom the latter took the more active part in management.

In August, 1871, the schoolmaster resigned and the rectors were unable to agree on the appointment of a new master; in consequence the school was closed. Three months later, the parish elected a school board of which Rev. Hayter was one of the members. It was not surprising, therefore, that shortly after this, when the school board applied to the voluntary school managers for the school to be transferred to the board, Rev. Hayter agreed and Dr. Bates refused.

In July, 1872, eight landowners of the parish, five of whom were members of the school board, presented a memorial that three additional trustees should be appointed in order to break the deadlock. The following April, the Charity Commissioners appointed three additional trustees, including Mr. Blyth, the chairman of the school board. At a meeting of the trustees convened shortly afterwards, the resolution was passed by a four to one majority that the school should be transferred.[126] Dr. Bates thereupon took the case to law. In his judgment, Sir George Jessel, M.R., stated that the trust deed of the school simply stipulated that the trustees should be members of the Church of England; the appointment of additional trustees was accordingly valid, and the resolution to transfer the school could be acted upon.[127]

The religious societies concerned with education also became involved in the transfer of schools. The vicar of Emmanuel parish, Camberwell, was, by 1871, the only remaining manager of a Church school; a meeting of subscribers was subsequently called on 12 February, 1872, under the direction of the vicar, and a resolution was carried proposing the transfer of the school to the London School Board. The National Society who had made a grant of £220 in 1867 towards its establishment had provided in the trust deed as was customary, that the school should be "always in union with and conducted according to the principles and in furtherance of the ends and designs of the National Society". The deed contained no power of disposing of the school site by way of alienation; the Society therefore appealed to the Education Department objecting to the transfer, but this was overruled and the transfer executed. It provided for setting apart a portion of time on two days a week when the school might be used for religious teaching.

When the Society brought the case to Court in 1874, the view was put that "a Society no more than a Trustee or Manager (as in the Burnham case) should have the power of obstructing the working of the Act by vetoing a transfer". Whilst having sympathy with the Society (and by implication the other Societies) in the alienation of schools largely built with its own funds, the Vice-Chancellor, Sir R. Malins, pointed out that the procedures of appeal to the Education Department, made available by Section 23, were fair, and he was not prepared to say that "it would have been wise that such a power of vetoing which would have been a very formidable one, should have existed".[128]

The upholding of administrative procedures under Section 23 by judicial decisions in Equity secured the strict adherence to the terms of transfer. A further case in the same year, 1874 (*School Board for London* v. *Faulconer*),[129] reinforced school board powers in this respect. In 1873, the Flint Street schools, in London, had been transferred to the school board by their managers, who at the same time assigned to the school board by deed the endowment so far as they could lawfully assign the same. The trustees of the charity estate refused to pay to the school board the amount of the endowment on the grounds that the poor inhabitants of the locality would be deprived of their benefits if such payments continued to be made. The Court found for the school board on the assurance that the funds would be applied to the benefit of that particular school; thus the principle that endowments could be transferred to a school board was established.

Difficulties arose as in *Re Poplar and Blackwall Free School*, 1878,[130] where the existing charity school was transferred to the London School Board and a new scheme had to be prepared for the regulation of the charity funds. Jessel, M.R., in his ruling stated that "Application of the fund to the general purposes of the school is objectionable because that is really a grant in aid of rates and not strictly for the benefit of the school". He suggested that it could be used for the advancement of learning in the school, for instance in establishing scholarships and exhibitions.

In one more case (*Gurney and other* v. *West Ham School Board*) concerning the transfer of annuities from a school to a school board in March, 1891, it was decided that where the conditions of bequest requiring religious instruction continued to be fulfilled, the school board was entitled to the benefit of the annuity.[131]

Reactions of managers to possible transfer ranged from a bowing to the inevitable to last-ditch stands to preserve the school. The ambivalent attitude of Rev. J. Dunne, a member of the Buckingham School Board and also manager of the Gawcett School which was about to be transferred to the school board was interesting. At an earlier meeting of the board the rector had agreed upon the transfer. By the time of the following meeting in February, 1872, he had changed his mind. "He was by no means willing," it was reported later, "that any act of his should be binding on his successor; he was simply the custodian of the property for his own time".[132]

The ambiguity of the wording of Section 23 relating to the necessity of a two-thirds majority of subscribers before transfer could be considered by the Education Department, inevitably led to difficulties in practice. In addition, trustees were often difficult to trace. The solicitors acting for the Tanfield (Durham) National School managers in preparing the necessary papers for submission to the Education Department in connection with transfer on the 2 February, 1893, reiterated the need for the subscribers' as well as the committee's consent to the proposal.

John Arkless, the correspondent, summoned a meeting of annual subscribers after first obtaining the managers' assent to transfer.

> "I subsequently summoned a meeting of the annual subscribers to have the Resolution confirmed," he replied on 2 March, 1893, "but as only one of them attended, no meeting was held. I brought the matter before the Education Department and asked their advice as to what should be done, but got no assistance whatever."

Arkless asked the solicitors,

> "The meeting of subscribers having been properly convened and they having failed to attend to protest against the Managers' proposals, could this not be considered assenting thereto? as I am afraid it will be almost impossible to get them to attend a meeting."

After advising the correspondent to convene another meeting, only one subscriber attended: the Education Department had also advised the committee's solicitor on 15 March that "if one subscriber only attends a meeting duly summoned, the consent of him will be sufficient". Unfortunately for Arkless the subscriber left without any meeting actually being officially declared held; accordingly a further meeting had to be convened to obtain at least one subscriber's assent.[133]

Where a serious divergence of opinion on the wisdom of transfer occurred between the principal subscriber and the rector, as at Rus-

wasted on comparatively trivial
details, & the ordinary working of
the School so entirely cast aside
that the inspector cannot form
any opinion respecting either the
general character of the instruction
or discipline.

25. The managers are led to look upon
the inspection as merely a scheme
for raising money, and on the
inspector as a necessary evil or
nuisance, invented by government
to enhance the value of the cash.

26. The Code has lowered the character
of School Reading Books throughout
the country, such as are required
for the upper classes.

27. The children, according to some
inspectors, are not so well taught as
formerly. The sympathy with stupidity
displayed by the government in taking
the part of dunces against the teachers,
even if it has possibly improved the
dunces has certainly to the same

[marginal note, written vertically] This entry is not correct and ought not to have been made. The managers are pleased with Inspector's Praise of —

4. EFFECTS OF THE REVISED CODE OF 1862
A strong criticism by the schoolmaster in the log book, with the manager's
marginal note protesting at the entry 1865.

Lincoln Archives Committee

5. ROXETH HILL SCHOOL, HARROW-ON-THE-HILL, MIDDLESEX

hall, Walsall, the composition of the meeting convened to arrive at a decision was not always entirely made up of subscribers. Lord Hatherton had ordered a meeting to be held on 2 November, 1876, consisting of parishioners not limited to subscribers, to give their opinion, claiming that "as it was a public matter the parishioners must be consulted".

"Of the nine persons present besides myself," wrote the rector after the meeting, "only one—my warden—had subscribed. The gentleman who proposed the refusal had promised £50 but paid not a penny. I had to pay that deficiency myself. The seconder had given nothing; his father gave £20 when I proposed building the new school. . . . Two others present were brothers of the above, two others gave nothing. One was a recent parishioner and only one (whose father gave) had any right to have voted: had his father been at home, it would not have occurred I feel sure. Thus, the only two subscribers—myself and the warden, were in favour of the plan."[134]

Where transfer took place, clergy who had provided furniture, etc., out of their own pockets expected to be reimbursed for it. The vicar of Kingsbury, Middlesex, the Rev. F. F. Spiers, writing to the clerk of the school board regarding an inventory of fittings included in the transfer, protested:

"I am informed they are valued at £14 and which the Board will have to *pay him for*. . . . The Board surely cannot be so unreasonable as to expect me to make them a present of these things. They have already driven a very close bargain—and further concessions on my part are out of the question."[135]

It was not only the unsuccessful schools which managers were obliged to transfer. This is borne out by tracing the transfer of one such school, Roxeth Hill National School, Harrow. Matthew Arnold, then the H.M. Inspector for the school, reported shortly before negotiations took place for the transfer: "This school continues to be one of the best taught and governed Elementary Schools which I know", and upon his last inspection in 1875: "I take leave with regret of a school which for general soundness of the work and for the success with which the intelligence of the boys is reached has very few superiors."[136] In spite of this, a number of events had undermined the school's position. In Dr. Vaughan's first year as head of Harrow School, at only twenty-nine years of age, he sympathized with the Harrow residents' grievance that the school had developed into a national institution without attracting local boys; he therefore at his own expense had cleared the stables and wash-houses near the school. This became the "English Form", giving an education on less classical lines than that obtainable at the public school itself. Some

F

of the boys from the Roxeth School went on to the English Form and its management committee complained in December, 1875, that boys who had attended Roxeth for most of the year left for the English Form shortly before the annual inspection, thus causing a loss of grant.

After the passing of the 1870 Act, one of the many Harrow School masters who had contributed to the upkeep of the National School, E. E. Bowen, wrote to the managers stating his intention to withdraw his subscriptions in order to compel the parish to set up a school board; the letter was also published in the local paper and many other subscribers followed his example.[137] In the board elections which ensued, Bowen, standing as an Anti-Clericalist and a Progressive candidate, was elected along with the vicar of Harrow.

The final blow came when the Education Department had required, among other works, additions to the girls' school to be made in 1873 and 1876. Optimistically the managers borrowed £1,300 on their personal security, intending to pay off the loan as had been done on previous occasions. The managers' chairman, the Rev. F. Hayward Joyce, the vicar of Harrow, stated that "if a School Board were eventually established, it was hoped either to transfer the debt to the School Board or to extinguish it gradually by leasing the premises at a rent".

The school board was finally established in December, 1877, but having no schools of its own wished to take possession of the Roxeth buildings. Now the managers agreed on condition that the debt was taken over in exchange for the school. Cumin, the Secretary of the Education Department, writing to the managers said that it was "quite impossible to comply with the proposals of the Managers. I am to point out that ever since 1872 my Lords have informally declined to sanction either a sale or an arrangement of transfer under Section 23 in which more than a nominal rent has been paid. Any exception to this rule which has been acted upon during so many years would not only contradict an established practice but would act unfairly towards those Managers whose schools have already been transferred to the School Board".[138]

Dr. Montagu Butler, who succeeded Vaughan as head master in 1860, and an *ex officio* manager of the Roxeth Schools, wrote to Joyce offering him advice on the course to pursue.

"It seems clear that we cannot suggest any means by which either the School Board or any other body can legally compel the Parish to provide the money for paying the debt. On the other hand it cannot, I feel sure, be the wish of the Managers to put the Parish to the great expense of building a fresh school and if that were possible to produce in the market the existing schools."[139]

Butler's plan was to make over the schools at once to the school board and at the same time put out a statement to parishioners making clear the circumstances under which the debt was contracted.

> "I cannot believe that the mass of Parishioners would wish to leave the burthen of the debt on the shoulders of a few gentlemen who guaranteed payment. It seems to me far better to make over the schools *at once without conditions* and to take our chance of recovering the money."

Butler's advice was taken: £600 was collected from the parishioners, £286 was raised from the sale of furniture and books and a debtor waived a claim for £200. For the remaining £200 the managers applied to the Education Department for a loan and the school was transferred to the school board later that year.

The history of this transfer illustrates the liabilities which could be incurred by managers at the time when it became necessary to transfer. Dealing with the question, the Cross Commission echoed the sentiments of the Buckingham school manager quoted previously who regarded himself only as the custodian of the property for his own generation of parishioners. The effect of the provision of Section 23 according to the Commission "was to set aside almost entirely the influence of the trustees and founders of the school and place its fate at any given moment in the hands of the Managers for the time being, who are an uncertain and changing body and may never have contributed towards the erection of the schools". The Commission recognized the friction caused and the grievances created by the working of Section 23; it recommended that, in any fresh educational legislation, no transfer of a school held under trust should take place without the consent of a majority of the trustees.

A suggestion by the vicar of Eastbourne in 1896 that voluntary schools should be empowered to borrow for building funds on the same basis as board schools was rejected by Kekewich, the Secretary of the Department:

> "Who," he asked Fitzroy, "is to lend the money? The State alone could do it, but if it did, it has no guarantee for efficient management or for the continuance of the interest or for repayment of the principal."[140]

By the 1902 Act, the matter was disposed of in a brief sub-section.[141] Much ill-feeling has been generated amongst voluntary school managers, particularly over the operation of the 23rd Section. What it did make clear was the tangible responsibilities and possible consequences involved in undertaking school management.

MANAGERS AND H.M. INSPECTORS

"The eyes and ears of the Department", Her Majesty's Inspectors, came in contact with the managers most frequently with the inspection of their schools. As the chief link between the central authority and the managers they were handicapped, as Leese has pointed out,[142] by the dictatorial tone of the office in its dealings with managers; as representatives carrying out the policy of the Department the Inspectors were inevitably identified with it.

From 1840 to 1870, denominational inspection was a separate function, the appointment of Inspectors being approved by the Bishop. The early Inspectors, because of the uncertainty of their position, were tentative in their approach and genuinely anxious to help the teachers rather than simply to inspect. To persuade managers to continue in their endeavours was an important function also. One of the first Inspectors to be appointed, H. S. Tremenheere (1839–43), writing later about his work in British and Foreign Society schools, stated:

"I was here engaged on a work which I knew would be watched with the greatest jealousy and suspicion on the part of the Patrons and School Managers of all the schools. Accordingly, I took unusual precautions that I should not be open to contradiction as to any of the conclusions that I might come to in my Report. Before I left a School I asked each Master or Mistress to read the notes I had made of what I had seen and heard; and begged for any correction that they might wish to submit to me."[143]

The changing nature of the work following the issue of the Department's Codes and Minutes, especially after the Revised Code Instructions of 1862 drove a wedge between the interest of the teachers and the managers, with the Inspector uneasily in between the two parties. One Lincolnshire teacher wrote in his log book shortly after the introduction of the New Code:

"The teachers have been defrauded. The time of Inspectors is wasted on comparatively trivial details; the ordinary working of the school is so entirely cast aside that the Inspector cannot form any opinion respecting either the general character or discipline. The Managers are led to look upon the inspection as merely a scheme for raising money, and on the Inspector as a necessary evil or a nuisance invented by Government to enhance the value of the cash."

The managers hurriedly wrote in the margin:

"This entry is not correct and ought not to have been made. The Managers are thankful for Government Inspection."[144]

This was unfair to many Inspectors who wrote freely in the published reports and articles[145] of their dislike of the system; in addition as a body they were not consulted before the passing of important educational measures, as was made clear by witnesses before the 1865 Select Committee on Education.

More often than not, the managers looked to the Inspectors as a source of help—settling disputes between managers (seen earlier at King's Stanley School, Gloucestershire), and sometimes between managers and parents.[146] They recommended suitable teachers[147] and suggested means of overcoming difficulties and amending defects.[148] Some Inspectors, such as T. G. Rooper, in charge of the Bradford District in the 1870s, believed on the other hand that too many of the managers' functions were expected to be performed by Inspectors. "The managers ought to be kept up to the mark; they expect the inspector to improve their schools and they ought to do it themselves."[149]

The lack of interest by managers in the work of Inspectors was a constant cry of the latter body in their annual reports. An experienced Inspector of almost forty years' standing, the Rev. D. J. Stewart, complained to the Cross Commission that the only member of the committee he usually saw at inspections was the correspondent.[150] Certainly this could be accounted for in British and Wesleyan schools where, as C. H. Alderson stated, "the gentlemen who usually form a Committee are liable to have their time so fully employed by business as to leave little opportunity for them to do more than attend the formal meetings of school business".[151] Matthew Arnold noted the same phenomenon but, unlike Alderson, believed that "the condition of comparative independence in which teachers are left is not without its advantages. They form and pursue their own plans with entire security and conscientiousness; and occupy in the eyes of their scholars, and of the parents of their scholars, a position of undivided dignity and authority".[152]

On the other hand, those managers who refused to accept inspection although the school was in receipt of a grant could be chastised by the publication in full of the correspondence between themselves and the Department.[153]

Where managers bemoaned the unsteady financial basis of their schools, they were often urged to look to themselves to provide the answer. The Rev. H. W. Bellairs recommended:

"that a little trouble on the part of the Managers would tend to remove this evil, by inducing such persons to send their own children to the National School at a higher payment than that charged to labourers and so contributing to its support."[154]

Although, as has been seen, the Inspector could be used by managers as an instrument for removing teachers from their posts, the former's advice was not invariably followed. The managers of Staines National Boys' School in Middlesex convened a special meeting in October, 1864, at which the secretary "was requested to communicate to Mr. Lane (Boys' Master) in writing the continued confidence of the Committee in his teaching and their non-concurrence in much of the Inspector's Report".[155] Similarly, where the Report of H.M. Inspector was of an unsatisfactory nature, some committees, like the one at Norham, Northumberland, in 1870, decided not to issue it to the subscribers for that year.[156]

Despite such incidents, the general tendency after the setting up of school boards was towards closer co-operation with Inspectors, especially as many of them were sympathetic towards the voluntary system. H.M. Inspector Mr. P. Grave's well-known co-operation with the Huddersfield voluntary managers is an instance of this. An account of his work in the north of England was given before the Cross Commission:

> "Some of the Managers of Voluntary Schools came to me when I went to the district and said that their schools were in a very defective condition and that they found it very hard to work against the school boards; and they suggested to me that it might be possible not to be so rigorous in my examinations of their schools. I said that of course was quite out of the question. Then they asked me what counsel I could give them; and my advice to them was to take a leaf out of the book of the Board. 'If you find it difficult to maintain your schools profitably, form a sort of day school association and appoint an inspector of your own who will visit your schools periodically, as the Board's master does'. . . . The result of it was that a day school association was formed and has been working there for the last five or six years with success."[157]

A competent Inspector was chosen and the movement spread to other towns, such as Rochester and Sheffield.[158]

The changing concept of management resulting from the 1880 Mundella Code, especially the encouragement to introduce a wider range of subjects, put a heavier burden on managers,[159] which they were happy to share with the Inspectors. Also, with the growing complexity of the Codes which, according to one Inspector "put a distinct premium on real dishonesty and on something approaching cruelty",[160] H.M. Inspectors frequently held meetings with teachers and managers to explain their ramifications.[161] Co-operation was on the whole successful. In his final Report before retiring in 1882, E. M. Sneyd-Kynnersley was able to write:

> "The Managers of the schools may claim a parting word. Our relations have been, and are I rejoice to say, most cordial. Looking through the

long list of over 250 Departments, I can find only ten that have complained of their report in the past five years, and a few of these complaints were entirely frivolous."[162]

Two important administrative changes in the last decade of the century had further consequences for both parties. Between 1890 and 1894 "payment by results" came to an end; the virtual guarantee of a Government grant allowed the managers to become independent in their dealings with members of the Inspectorate.

Further, with the introduction of "visits without notice" system, the close relationship which had existed between managers and Inspectors ceased. Graves, in his autobiography, showed that the change was for the good.

The Inspector visited the schools without notice, dropping in with none of the "field-day fuss" that accompanied the old annual inspection. He saw the school in its normal state and not in an unnatural condition of fear and anxiety and because the school had not been tuned up for a special effort, he would be better able to discover its strong and weak points. But something was lost by this system:

"I missed the opportunity which the old fixed inspection gave me of making or renewing acquaintance with the Managers, and conferring with them about the interests of their schools. Under the new plan it was quite a chance whether one met any Manager in the school and if one sent for the school Manager who lived nearest, the chances were that he would be out."[163]

Managers were especially unhappy over this loss of contact and misunderstandings could arise because of the secondhand nature of reports of what occurred during the "surprise visit" between H.M. Inspectors and teachers. Moreover, the teacher as the spokesman for the school was in a vulnerable position. In the chaplain's report of 4 October, 1899, to the St. Nicholas Memorial Girls' School, Brighton (an elementary school), an account of such a surprise visit was given:

"There followed H.M.I. Mr. Danby's visit in the afternoon of Friday, April 14, so late that it was impossible to apprise the Chaplain. This was indeed a surprise. What he *said* in approval is summarised in Miss Rowe's note handed in, but what he *wrote* in the Log Book was as follows. . . ."

The Vicar then read out some of the critical remarks entered by the Inspector.

"Why should he threaten us in this way with ruin, for certain mere trifles? . . . I determined to write to the Department and ascertain our true position. The answer is simply in general terms and is no absolute solution. The question still remains, are we to be thus screwed down? If so, the whole management of the secular arrangements of the school passes into the hands of a Government Inspector, who aggravates this result by using the mistress to tell the Managers what he means and the Log Book as the place for the inscribing of threats."[164]

Successive Codes reinforced this new situation between Inspectors and managers to the increasing exclusion of the latter. J. H. Arkwright, manager of a Herefordshire school, felt moved to write a protest on 18 February, 1900, to Dr. Williams, the school's H.M. Inspector, on this topic:

"I want to draw your attention to what I am bound to call a very serious result of the new code as it has happened to me, viz. that I never see you or know till afterwards what you and my schoolmaster are doing at the school! I hoped to have a voice in the new Time table and often told Noakes (the schoolmaster) that I should like to have less drawing and more needlework. He explained that it was impossible and that we should lose grant. Some months after I found that both these things had been done by you and him without me or the other Managers and I have not even a copy of the Time table for myself as I have always had for at least 30 years.

"I am perfectly estranged from the school and feel no longer a Manager. All I know of the school is through Mr. Wale the Diocesan Examiner.

"Having greeted the new Code as intended to give Managers a chance of making improvements with the Inspector, I find that it has simply banished the Manager, putting the Master in his shoes. Several Managers who have spoken to me lately fully agree that it is much to be regretted."[165]

Certainly, greater freedom was given, on the one hand, to the teacher from 1895. E. A. G. Holmes, who doubted the wisdom of the new policy, wrote later:

"Having for thirty three years deprived the teacher of almost every vestige of freedom the Department suddenly reversed its policy and gave them in generous measure the boon which it had long withheld; coupled with the centralizing of all major administrative decisions affecting school management, it diminished the authority of the Voluntary School Manager."[166]

On the other hand, the new system threw increasing responsibilities on managers as it now became more necessary for them to ensure that the progress of the children was tested.

For the remaining few years of the nineteenth century, the voluntary school managers were occupied with financial and administrative arrangements arising from the Voluntary Schools Act of 1897. Of greater consequence, however, had been the growth of the school board system, which posed further difficulties. Some of these will now be considered.

REFERENCES

1   *The Schoolmaster*, 4 April, 1887.
2   Staines National Boys' School, Managers' Minute Book, 1857–71, 29 April, 1870. DRO. 2.J1/1 (G.L.R.O. [Middlesex]).
3   Capheaton Voluntary School, Managers' Minute Book, 1895–1904, 11 November, 1901. CES24/1 (Northumberland R.O.).
4   Gerrards Cross National School, Managers' Minute Book, 1879–1952, 16 November, 1881. E/MB/83/1. (Buckinghamshire R.O.).
5   Diary of Albert Brett, 1864–5. D255. (Dorset R.O.).
6   Diary of Albert Brett, 1864–5, 13 and 21 April and 16 May, 1865. D255 (Dorset R.O.).
7   "The Schoolmaster's Relations to the School Managers" in *The School and the Teacher* Vol. 2, 1855, p. 4.
8   Lowe to Brougham, 1 October, 1863. Brougham MSS (University College, London). See also A. Briggs, "Robert Lowe and the Fear of Democracy" in *Victorian People* (1955), pp. 263–6, for an account of Lowe's educational philosophy.
9   Lowe to Brougham. Undated but 1864. Brougham MSS.
10 A number of protest meetings against the Code were held in Halifax in February, 1862 at one of which the masters and managers of the town's many National Schools attended. J. L. Hanson, *A History of Education in Halifax during the Nineteenth Century* M.Ed. Thesis, Leeds University, (1940), p. 155.
11 J. Grote, *A Few Words on the New Educational Code and the Report of the Educational Commissioners* (1862), p. 6.
12 The Rev. T. R. Birks, *The Revised Code: What Would It Do and What Should Be Done With It?* (1862), p. 30.
    One school manager wrote at the time: "Managers of schools . . . to whom the working of the educational system is a labour of love, disbelieve almost with one consent in the possibility of deriving any advantages from the new Code." *National Elementary Education and the new Code. By a School Manager* (1861), p. 13. Education Miscellanies, Vol. 8, 1861–2. (Department of Education and Science Library).
13 Travelling expenses were rarely paid to candidates. "A Miss Besley having asked the managers to pay her fares from Essex it was resolved that Mr. Savage should inform her that the managers did not pay fares." Mansfield St. Peter's Church of England School, Managers' Minute Book, 1873–94, 10 October, 1900. SBX 4/2 (Nottinghamshire R.O.).
14 Reach National School Minute Book, 1876–1903, 5 March, 1877 (Cambridgeshire C.R.O.).
    In addition, there was a clause in a standard agreement offered to teachers by Church managers whereby the former could be turned out at a week's notice after undertaking by way of bond to hand over £100 if he refused to vacate the premises. C. K. Francis Brown, *The Church's part in Education, 1833–1941* (1942), p. 11.
15 Binchester Colliery Log Book, 1877–1902, 4 March, 1887. E/SW (Durham C.R.O.).
16 Uxbridge British School Log Book, 1863–78, 2 May, 1873, MCC/E (Uxbridge). (G.L.R.O. [Middx]).
17 Vowchurch Church of England School Managers' Minute Book, 1874–1902, 26 January, 1876 (Herefordshire C.R.O.).

18   Purbright National School, Correspondence, 1872–99, 22 April, 1872 (Surrey R.O.).
As late as 1904 it was likely that when a vacancy occurred, "the willingness to rent the school house or to undertake outside duties might be allowed to outweigh teaching or other qualifications". "Those Good Old Days", by T. O. Willson, *Times Education Supplement*, 24 November, 1967.

19   Wheldrake School, Correspondence and Papers, 23 July, 1880, PR. WHEL. 81 (Borwthick Institute of Historical Research, York).

20   Aymestry Parish Records, II, 12 March, 1838 (Herefordshire C.R.O.); cf. Committee of Council on Education, Report of Rev. F. C. Cook on Eastern Districts, January, 1845. "In more than one school I have inspected persons invariably incompetent to teach are kept in the situation of school-master by committees who fear that, being qualified for no other occupation, they will become chargeable on the parish if dismissed." BPP. 1846. XXXII.

21   Kingston St. Mary Parish School Managers' Minute Book, 1871–8, 29 January, 1875, 18/7/1 (Somerset R.O.).

22   Uxbridge British School Managers' Minute Book, 1834–1900, 6 December, 1848, E. Mx. 2/2 (G.L.R.O. [Middx]).

23   Sutton Bonington School Minute Book, 1879–1926, 9 May, 1897, SRX 72/85 (Nottinghamshire R.O.).

24   Plymouth Public School Committee Minute Book, 1809–25, 20 May, 1817 (Plymouth City Library, Archives Department).

25   Birdham National School, 1817–1967; F. Morgan MSS., E23/19/2 (W. Sussex R.O.).

26   Lancashire Record Office Report for 1962, p. 17 ff.

27   R. Cookson, *Goosnargh: Past and Present* (1888), p. 285.

28   Memorial of the School masters of Goosnargh, 17 November, 1844. Cookson of Goosnargh MSS. D. HHI (Lancashire R.O.).

29   BPP 1867–8 XVII Appendix Pt. 2 p. 547.

30   A deposition given by a Plaiting Master regarding a former pupil on trial at Bedford has survived. Some estimate of the master's qualification for teaching can be arrived at by a study of the document: "I have known James Johnson from a Child and he Came to my Scould to plat and larn to Read and he left my scould four year ago and was a steady and carefull Lad and allways payd. Grate a tenchon to is Worke and i Near see aney indecency in Him." Deposition of Lannach Almond, Plaiting Master. Bedford Quarter Session Rolls, 1834–5. Petitions 1835/532–3 (Bedfordshire C.R.O.).

31   J. G. Dony, *A History of the Straw Hat Industry* (1942), p. 74.

32   M. F. S. George, "A Straw Hat for Victoria" in *The Bedfordshire Magazine* Vol. 3. No. 21. Summer 1952, p. 203.

33   The Rev. C. J. Robinson, who during the years 1855 to 1865 lived in a straw plaiting district as parochial clergyman, diocesan inspector of schools and later as H.M.I., gave a vivid account in his Reports of the effects of the plaiting industry in Buckinghamshire and Bedfordshire in the 1860s. "Is the standard (of education) to be brought down to fit in with the demands of straw plaiting?" he asked. "It is difficult to escape the inevitable consequence that school must preserve its integral position for education, and not for plaiting." Committee of Council on Education. BPP 1866 XXVII, pp. 181–182.

34   Billington National School, Account Book, 1863–1939, 22 February, 1864. S.D. 9714/5 (Bedfordshire C.R.O.).

35   Langford School, Log Book, 1869–1902, S.D.2081/1 (Bedfordshire C.R.O.). A full-scale study of the effects of the plaiting industry on education in the

Home Counties during the nineteenth century would yield much interesting information.

36 Romford British School, Managers' Minute Book, 1851–72, 2 October, 1868. E/MM/40 (Essex R.O.).

37 Handforth National School, Minutes of School Management Committee, 1889–1904, 17 June, 1889. P10/7/5 (Cheshire R.O.).

38 Thomas Hardy, *Jude the Obscure* (1951 edn.), pp. 296–9. See also H. S. Duffin, *Thomas Hardy—A Study of the Wessex Novels* (1962), pp. 247–8.

39 Letters to Master and Mistress of School at Arlingham, 1852–5, 7 April, 1855. Gloucester Diocesan Archives, S1/1 (Gloucester City Library, Archives Department).

40 Chapel Allerton National School, Managers' Minute Book, 1873–1909, 14 December, 1891. No. 180 (Leeds City Libraries, Archives Department).

41 This of course was only in the latter part of the century. The first President of the National Union of Teachers, J. J. Graves (1832–1903), was Master of Lamport and Hanging Houghton Endowed School situated in rural Northamptonshire. Graves remained at the school for over fifty years, taking on the usual extra tasks which fell to the lot of a village schoolmaster. M. Seaborne & G. Isham, A Victorian School Master: John James Graves in *Northamptonshire Past and Present* Vol. 4, Nos. 1 and 2, 1966–7 and 1967–8.

42 Taunton Central National School, Minute Book, 1874–91, 20 January, 1890 (Somerset R.O.).

43 Basingstoke British School, Managers' Minute Book, 1840–3, 1 February, 1841. 8 M62/35 (Hampshire R.O.).

44 Croft and Yarpole National School, Log Book, 1867–92, 28 February, 1873 (Herefordshire C.R.O.).

45 Chevening Parish School, Regulations for the National School, 1817. Chevening Parish Records, 1817–25, P88/25/9 (Kent Archives Office).

46 Bradford-on-Avon, British Undenominational School, Log Book, 1863–1901, 5 March, 1875 (Wiltshire R.O.).

47 Buckingham National School, Minutes of Meetings of Committee, 1818–34, 3 October, 1818. E/MB/29/8 (Buckinghamshire R.O.).

48 Diary of William Wright MSS. D/WRI (Lincoln Public Library).

49 *Lincoln Chronicle* 21 January, 1950.

50 Riseley National School, Managers' Minute Book, 1871–90, 31 January, 1882. SP. 2812/1 (Bedfordshire C.R.O.).

51 The 1861 Census found that 72·5 per cent of teachers were women. It was the only occupation to which the Census awarded professional status except midwifery. W. J. Reader, *Professional Men*, (1966), p. 172.

52 Bristol School Board. Report of Meetings of School Board: Married Female Teachers. MSS. Minutes. 27 May, 1887. MB/B6 (Bristol Archives Office).

53 *Ibid.*

54 Lewes British School, St. John Sub Castro, Managers' Minute Book, 1884–93, 8 May, 1884. E412/1 (E. Sussex R.O.).

55 Belper National School, School Minutes 1871–1903, 28 September, 1871 (Derbyshire R.O.).

56 *Church and School*, *op. cit.*, p. 120.

57 Affpuddle. Letter from Rev. H. Williams, Vicar of Affpuddle, to the squire concerning Village School Mistress, 16 November, 1898. D29/R22 (Dorset R.O.).

58 Coln Rogers and Coln St. Dennis United Schools, Managers' Minute Book, 1875–1905, January, 1891. P95. SC2/1 (Gloucestershire C.R.O.).

59 F. A. Howe, *A Chronicle of Edburton and Fulking* (1958), p. 38.

60 Inglesham School, Log Book, 1873–93, 31 August, 1877 (Wiltshire R.O.).

61 Reach National School, Log Book, 1863–1903, 2 March, 1877. P150/25/4 (Cambridgeshire C.R.O.).

62 Stapleton National School, Managers' Minute Book, 1895–1903, 29 July, 1903. 883/71/Stapleton Psh. (Salop R.O.).

63 The pamphlet was headed: *Mixed Schools and Good Manners.* Copies are to be found in Managers' Minute Books in many parts of the country, e.g. Toton School, SBX 56/1 (Nottinghamshire C.R.O.).

64 In 1879, Lord George Hamilton, as Vice-President, had ruled in the case of Elkington Street Board School on the employment of Female Teachers in Mixed Schools. At first the appointment was refused in accordance with a precedent in the Secretary's Minute Book, 1872–88, p. 199 (now lost), but as a result of "pressure and remonstrance" from the Board this rule was modified at Sandford's instructions. Under the new terms, arising from a requested appointment by the Huddersfield Board, the Department conceded on condition that "more than ordinary supervision than is ordinarily practicable or probable be exercised by the Managers and the Managers would be responsible for such appointments thereafter". Sandford to Huddersfield School Board, 4 June, 1880 Ed 16/365 Huddersfield P.R.O. See also Report of Committee of Council on Education for year 1880, PPP. 1881 XXXII, p. 143.

65 Kingston St. Mary Parish School, Managers' Minute Book, 1871–88, 29 January, 1875. 18/7/1 (Somerset R.O.).

66 Reading New Town School, Management Sub Committee Minute Book, 1889–1905, 9 and 14 January, 1890. RSB/MC/52 (Reading Corporation Archives Department).

67 Hoveringham Public Unsectarian Schools, Managers' Minute Book, 1874–1923. 1882 (n.d.) SBX 22/1 (Nottinghamshire C.R.O.).

68 BPP 1895, XXVII, p. 5.

69 Richard A. Cross, Conservative M.P., S.W. Lancs; Home Secretary 1874–80 and 1885–6; Secretary for India 1886–92. Created Viscount Cross, 1886.

70 A. Williams Wynn to R. A. Cross, 1 February, 1887, Cross MSS., B.M. Add MSS. 51276, f. 130–2 (British Museum).
As late as 1856 the Rev. H. E. F. Vallency, a Fellow of King's College, Cambridge, on taking the living at St. Helen's, Lancs, could write to the leading local landowner in the following terms: "You will pardon me, I trust, for what I am going to say for I must speak out very plainly. You are beyond question my wealthiest Parishioner and what is the amount I receive from you as your annual subscription for the support of our Schools? Merely five pounds! . . . If I obtain the land from you, I shall not look for any further assistance from you for the building fund: if you are still indisposed to give it, I must tell you that I conceive I have every right to look to you for a subscription of £100; less than this I do not expect from you. . . ." T. C. Barker and J. R. Harris, *A Merseyside Town in the Industrial Revolution, St. Helen's, 1750–1900* (1959), p. 389.

71 Rev. T. Mozley, *Reminiscences Chiefly of Towns, Villages and Schools* Vol. 2 (1885), pp. 276–7.

72 J. T. Ward, *East Yorkshire Landed Estates in the 19th Century* (1967), pp. 8–9.

73 East Ilsley School Board, Minutes 1891–8, 3 January, 1898. C/EB/5/1 (Berkshire R.O.).

74 John Walter (1818–94). Conservative M.P. for Nottingham 1847–59, Berkshire 1859–65 and 1868–85. See W. Lyon, *Chronicles of Finchampstead*

(1895). Walter himself was an *ex officio* manager and nominated one of the three other managers.

75 Finchampstead Church of England School, Minutes of Committee Meetings, 1871–7, 27 November, 1871. C/EM (Berkshire R.O.).

76 Cartwright of Aynho MSS., 5 October, 1851. C(A) 7429 (Northamptonshire C.R.O.).

77 Monson MSS., 15 February, 1862. Mon. 25/13/10/14/19 (Lincolnshire Archives Committee).

78 Blackburn, Minutes of the National and Sunday Schools, 1829–43. PR/1551 (Lancashire R.O.).

79 Salvin MSS., Gerard Salvin to Rev. H. Chayter, 7 July, 1850. For full details see Letters from various correspondents relating to religious teachings of Catholic Children at Sunderland Bridge Elementary School, 1849–55, D/Sa/C220, 1–20 (Durham C.R.O.).

80 Kelly's *Gloucestershire and Bristol* (1899), p. 587 gives the population of King's Stanley as 2,217.

81 King's Stanley National School, Managers' Minute Book, 1870–1920, 25 January and 4 April, 1889, p. 190 SC. 1/1 (Gloucestershire C.R.O.).

82 *Ibid.* Annual Report, 1891–2.

83 Ancaster MSS. 3 Anc. 7/23/73/51, 2 October, 1857. T. Finlay to L. Kennedy (Lincolnshire Archives Committee).

84 Ancaster MSS. 3 Anc. 7/23/73/62 (n.d.).

85 *Ibid.* 3 Anc. 7/23/73/63 (n.d., but probably October, 1857).

86 The relationships between landowner and agent are explored in Mrs. Gaskell's *Wives and Daughters* (1969 edn), p. 37.

87 The Life, Birth, Parentage and Consanguinity of Robert Hird, Shoemaker, Bedale, b. 17 October, 1868. Autobiography. Robert Hird Diary MSS. Preface. ZBA 27 (North Riding C.R.O.).

88 Manchester MSS. Letters to the Duke of Manchester from Mr. Peter Purves, his Agent, 1840–6. Bundle No. 13, 30 July, 1844. Kimbolton dd. M. 57 (Huntingdonshire C.R.O.).

89 See, for example, O. Chadwick, *Victorian Miniature: a study of squire and parson in a little Victorian village* (1960) especially pp. 79, 144–5.

90 D. J. F. MacLeod to Education Department, 2 May, 1879. Ed. 16/35 Whitehaven (P.R.O.).

91 A typical case is given in Rex C. Russell, *A History of Elementary Schools and Adult Education in Nettleton and Caister, Pt. 1, 1800–1875* (1960), pp. 12–14. At Nettleton, Sir Culling Eardley Smith founded and subsequently managed the school himself.

92 Wm. Plomer (ed.) *Kilvert's Diary* Vol. 3, 1874–9 (1960), p. 111.

93 The population was 138 in 1881. *Kelly's Directory of Northamptonshire* (1885), p. 475.

94 Letters of Rose Knowles, School Mistress of Thorpe Malsor, 1882–1906. Found in Kettering Board of Guardians Records. 27 June, 1888. YE. 5541. Acc. 19 Box X2385 (Northamptonshire C.R.O.).

95 J. Hutchins, *The History and Antiquities of Dorset* (1861), p. 633.

96 Langton Matravers National School, 1 June, 1872. Ed. 21/4167 (P.R.O.).

97 Langton Matravers: Papers 1870–3 re School. P92/SC.1 (Dorset R.O.).

98 *Op. cit.* 18 September, 1873.

99 19 September, 1873. Ed. 21/4167 (P.R.O.).

100 Mrs. Serrell held daily services opposite the Church, employing a brass band to drown the harmonium. She also conducted the services herself and gave sermons. Before she died, Mrs. Serrell gave orders that she should not be buried with her husband.

I am grateful for additional information supplied by Mr. R. J. Saville of Langton Matravers, who has made a study of education in the parish.

101 See C. B. Patterson, *Burdett-Coutts and the Victorians* (1953), pp. 65–177, and J. Butt and K. Tillotson, *Dickens at Work* (1957); Janet Dunbar, *The Early Victorian Woman* (1953), pp. 166–8.

102 *The Times*, 19 January, 1865.

103 *School Guardian*, 11 January, 1865.

104 Memorandum on Grouping Schools in Devonshire for Teaching Purposes, *c.* 1865. Burdett-Coutts MSS., 1387, f. 55 (Lambeth Palace Library).

105 *Ibid.*
Nevertheless, as a friend of hers made clear, Burdett-Coutts was anxious not to hand over elementary education to the control of a secular body which might result in the exclusion of definite religious teaching in the schools. She determined from the outset to work with, and not in opposition to, the Committee of Council on Education. C. C. Osborne MSS., B.M. Add. MS. 46406 B, f. 39–40 (British Museum).

106 *School Guardian*, 18 January, 1865.

107 Code Articles 135–41 sanctioned the union of small schools, two to six in number, of which no one had within 1½ miles a population of more than 500. Each group was to be under a certificated master or mistress who had been trained for two years at a Normal School.

108 *The Educational Times*, 5 March, 1865.

109 The Select Committee on the Committee of Council on Education, BPP. 1865 VI, Q. 3991.

110 Committee of Council on Education Report on Oxfordshire Church of England Schools for 1868, BPP. 1868–9 XX, p. 30.

111 Select Committee, *op. cit.*, Draft Report, 5 July, 1866, BPP. 1866 VII, p. xiv.

112 Burdett-Coutts MSS., 1387, 10 March, 1875, f. 158 (Lambeth Palace Library).

113 Rev. F. O. Morris to Burdett-Coutts, 16 February, 1875. *The Group System of Schools and its Results briefly stated* (1875), p. 37.

114 *The Times*, 30 January, 1875.

115 Burdett-Coutts to Corry, 1 April, 1875, Hughenden MSS., Box 123 B/XXI/C/537 (Hughenden Manor, Bucks.).

116 Duke of Richmond to Lord Hampton, 4 May, 1875, Burdett-Coutts MSS. 1387, f. 256 (Lambeth Palace Library).

117 One of her interests was the introduction into teacher-training of new elements into the curriculum. She was responsible for the teaching of Domestic Economy to all students, and the teaching of "Common Things," in order "to produce a feminist and domestic effect on the minds of the female teachers". Burdett-Coutts to Brougham, 16 June, 1856, Brougham MSS. (University College, London).

118 Owen regarded the New Lanark system of education as a chance to put into practice many of his own ideas. "After trying the influence of these laws of nature for some years on a mixed population of 500 persons in Manchester with considerable success, I obtained in 1799 *the sole direction* of a population which gradually increased to 2,500 men, women and children situated at New Lanark in Scotland". Robert Owen to Lord Brougham, 14 August, 1844, On the Origins of Infant Schools, Brougham MSS.

119 T. Wemyss Reid, *Life of W. E. Forster*, Vol. 1 (1888), p. 441.

120 J. Leyland, *Memorials of Abram* (1882).

121 Abram Colliery School, Bickershaw, Wigan, Log Book, 1882–1907, 19 May, 1892, SMA 1/1 (Lancashire R.O.).

122 F. P. B. N. Hutton, *Report of the Church, Schools, etc. in connection with Messrs. John Bagnall and Sons' Ironworks, Golden Hill, West Bromwich* (1864), p. 9.
Frederick Engels cast a sceptical eye on these activities. "No doubt the mill-owner has provided a school . . . but he uses it to inculcate strict obedience in the children's minds." F. Engels, *The Condition of the Working Class in England* (translated by W. O. Henderson and W. H. Chaloner) (1958), p. 211.

123 Rev. H. W. Holland, *Proposed National Arrangements for Primary Education* (1870), p. 127.

124 Minutes of the Education Department, 17 July, 1871, Resolution 1.

125 W. E. Forster refused to sanction the device of a voluntary school offering to be discontinued on condition that a school board should be called into existence. Forster to P. Cumin, 22 February, 1872, Ilkeston Ed. 16/43 (P.R.O.).
Re-transfer from the school board was not easily achieved. A notorious example at the time was that of the parish of Smeeth in Kent, which handed over to a board a school previously under voluntary management. After a year's trial, the previous managers were able to show the unnecessary expense of a school board and obtained the agreement of the board to re-transfer the school back. The board, left with no school, dissolved itself. The parish was astonished to learn from the Education Department that they must elect a new board at the end of three years unless section 41 of the 1876 Act applied. "D.C.L.", *The Education Craze and its Results* (1878), p. 59.
Besides Smeeth, there were in 1876 three other boards which had no school and no site: Sutton Courtney, Berkshire; Tadmarton, Oxfordshire, and Heybridge, Essex.
Forster to Sandon, 21 July, 1876, Harrowby MSS. Vol. LII, f. 381 (Sandon Hall, Staffs.).

126 This was a fairly common occurrence. See for example, P. Lucas, *Heathfield Memorials* (1910), p. 6, and Heathfield School Board, Minute Book, 1875–87, 27 July and 24 August, 1875. 372/1/1 (E. Sussex R.O.).

127 Law Reports Equity, 241–51. Vol. XVII (1873).

128 Law Reports. *National Society* v. *School Board for London*. Equity, 608–21, Vol. XVIII (1874).

129 Law Reports, 8 Chancery, 571 (1874).

130 Law Reports, 8 Chancery, 541 (1878).

131 Fuller details of the legal aspects of transfer are to be found in the following: W. W. Mackenzie, *A Treatise on the Elementary Education Acts, 1870–1891* (1892), T. A. Organ, *The Law Relating to Schools and Teachers* (1900), and *Owen's Education Acts Manual 1870–1919* (1920). 21st edn.

132 *Buckinghamshire Express*, 6 February, 1872.

133 Tanfield National Schools, Correspondence and Papers, 1891–4, 22 February to 23 March, 1893, EP/Ta 82 (Durham C.R.O.).

134 Rev. F. G. Littlecot to Lord Hatherton, 6 November, 1876, re Rushall Butts School, Hatherton MSS. D260/M/F/5/137 (Staffordshire C.R.O.).

135 Rev. F. F. Spiers to Mr. Tootell, 14 January, 1876, Kingsbury, The Hyde School, Misc. Papers, 1875–91. MCC/E (Kingsbury). (G.L.R.O. [Middx]).

136 Quoted in M. Harris, *Roxeth School in the 19th Century—from Parish to Board School* (n.d.) MSS., F.2c, p. 4 (Harrow Local Collection, Harrow Public Library).

137 E. E. Bowen, the poet *par excellence* of Harrow and of school life in general, was responsible for the words of many of the Harrow songs,

including "Forty years on". E. D. W. Chaplin, *The Book of Harrow* (1948), p. 76. He wrote to J. W. Cunningham, the treasurer at this time, demonstrating that Sec. 23 placed the burden of any outstanding debt not on the school but upon the managers personally. 7 November, 1877, Roxeth Hill School, Minute Book, 1864–78. DRO.3. J/2/4 (G.L.R.O. [Middx]).

138   P. Cumin to J. W. Cunningham, 11 January, 1878. Roxeth Hill School, Minute Book, 1864–78, DRO.3. J/2/4 (G.L.R.O. [Middx]).
Cumin had been appointed to the Department because of his legal knowledge, to deal with the immense complexities arising out of the transfer of schools. Anon, *Patrick Cumin, Secretary of the Education Department: A Sketch*, pp. 12–13.

139   9 February, 1878, Roxeth Hill School, *supra.*

140   Memorial to Education Department by Rev. H. B. Ottley, Vicar of Eastbourne, Kekewich to Fitzroy, 2 February, 1896. Ed. 10/12 (P.R.O.).

141   Section 8 (3).

142   J. Leese, *Personalities and Power in English Education* (1950), p. 98.

143   E. L. & O. P. Edmonds, *I Was There: the Memoirs of H. S. Tremenheere* (1965), p. 44.

144   Louth Wesleyan School, Log Book, 1863–93, 7 June, 1865 (Lincolnshire Archives Committee).

145   Frederick Meyrick, for instance, published an article in the *Quarterly Review*, January, 1860, attacking the Code. F. Meyrick, *Memories of Life at Oxford, and Experiences in Italy, Greece, Turkey, Germany, Spain and Elsewhere* (1905), p. 218.

146   At a Committee meeting of the Elsworth National School, Cambridgeshire, some parents attended to complain of the punishment given to their children for absenteeism and enquired if the school master was entitled to do this. The Rector wrote to H.M. Inspector, F. W. H. Myers, for guidance. In reply Myers dismissed the complaint as "frivolous, so far as regards punishments for absence from school, which are distinctly necessary in some cases" and reminded them that "Schoolmasters do not punish children so severely as *parents* frequently do". On hearing the contents of the letter the parents expressed themselves quite satisfied to leave punishment in the hands of the Master. Elsworth National School, Log Book, 1863–97, 14–18 May, 1889 (Cambridgeshire C.R.O.).

147   E. M. Sneyd-Kynnersley, *H.M.I.—Some Passages in the Life of one of H.M. Inspectors of Schools* (1908), p. 167.
At Goosnargh and Threlfalls School, Lancashire, the Managers, on dismissing the master in April, 1899, resolved "that the Correspondent ask H.M.I. Mr. Iles to kindly submit names of 6 persons suitable for appointment as masters for the Managers to choose from". Minute Book, 1879–97, 29 April, 1899. SM GO 1/1 (Lancashire R.O.).

148   D. R. Fearon, *School Inspection* (1876), p. 2.

149   R. G. Tatton, *Selected Writings of Thomas Godolphin Rooper, M.A., late H.M.I.* (1907), p. lxi.

150   *Cross*, Evidence, Q. 3154.

151   Committee of Council on Education. Report on British, Wesleyan and other Denominational Schools for 1858. BPP. 1859, XXI, p. 177.

152   M. Arnold, *Reports on Elementary Schools, 1852–1882*. General Report for the year 1858 (1889), p. 75.

153   See for instance the correspondence between H.M.I. Rev. J. J. Blandford and Rev. T. F. Salmon of Scalford, Melton Mowbray. Committee of Council on Education. Report on Nottinghamshire, Leicestershire and Derbyshire for 1857. BPP. 1857–8, XLV, pp. 365–9.

154 Committee of Council on Education. Report on South Midlands, 1849. BPP. 1850, XLIII.
155 Staines National Boys' School, Managers' Minute Book, 1857–71, 21 October, 1864. DRO 2 J1/1 (Middlesex R.O.).
156 Norham Free Mixed School, Managers' Minute Book, 1878–1900, 10 March, 1870. PNO 20 (Northumberland R.O.).
157 *Cross*, Evidence, Q. 57,260.
158 Committee of Council on Education. Report on the Huddersfield District for 1881. BPP. 1882 XXIII, p. 303.
159 See, for example, S. Buxton, *Overpressure and Elementary Education* (1885), Ch. VII Managers, pp. 78–91.
160 A. W. Newton, *op. cit.*, p. 20.
161 E. Farndon School, Managers' Minute Book, 1879–1905, 2 December, 1883, Ref. 73 (Northamptonshire C.R.O.).
162 Committee of Council on Education. Report on the Schools in the Chester District for 1882, BPP. 1883 XXV, p. 375.
163 A. P. Graves, *To Return to All That: An Autobiography* (1930), pp. 258–9.
164 Brighton, St. Nicholas Memorial Girls' School, Minutes of Managers' Meetings, 1855–1911. E. 255 (B) 1/1 (E. Sussex R.O.).
165 J. H. Arkwright to H.M.I. Dr. Williams, 18 February, 1900. Arkwright MSS. A63/IV/HB/521 (Herefordshire C.R.O.).
166 E. A. G. Holmes, *What Is and What Might Be* (1911), p. 111.

3

School Board
Administration and Management

BEFORE 1870

A number of individuals put forward plans to establish systems of schools with innovatory forms of management based on defined areas before the Education Act of 1870 set up the school board system. Some of the factors responsible for their limited success were the lack of any suitable existing administrative unit, the monopoly of education by the two main Societies—National and British and Foreign, the suspicion of secular education, the hatred of rates, the fear of State interference with such systems and the fact that the need for educational reform coincided with national economic distress, war and political upheaval.

The number of members who voted on Whitbread's Bill in 1808, fifty-five in all, indicates the interest taken in educational reform at the time. Perhaps the inclusion of proposals to alter the assessment for rates was responsible for some of the opposition; it did at least move the Archbishop of Canterbury to circularize the bishops, asking them to find out from the clergy in each diocese the number of schools in which the poor were taught to read.[1] The prevailing ethos favoured the approach of Joseph Fox who told Whitbread that he wished "for a moral resuscitation for so indeed it would be, if it were possible to please the *whole rising* generation of the Nations of Europe under a system of Education which would form them to habits of subordination and morality and Scriptural knowledge".[2]

Like Whitbread, Lord Brougham[3] was associated with Lancaster's experiments and commended the cheapness of the system for educating large numbers of the poor. This was borne out by his move which established a Parliamentary Committee to enquire into "the Education of the Lower Orders in the Metropolis" in 1818. His 1820 Bills, which included provisions for the compulsory building, government and maintenance of parish schools, were in many respects like Whitbread's, and met with a similar fate.[4]

Brougham during the rest of his long life, searched for a unit which would be appropriate for educational administration. In 1837 Lord

John Russell, who had been responsible for the passing of the Municipal Corporations Act two years previously, begged him "to consider the whole constitution of Parish Vestries and Union Boards and I think you will come to the conclusion that the Union Boards, though unimportant, will form the best machinery you can employ".[5] Brougham's thinking had moved on and in a new Bill he planned for the extension of education to be facilitated by the new town councils, where there were municipal corporations, and the county councils, for which a Bill was before Parliament. "If it shall be rejected, those powers must be given to other local authorities; the addition is obviously necessary in order to provide for those towns where there are no Municipal Corporations and for country districts".[6]

Russell was impatient to proceed with the work and on a different footing to Brougham. He wrote later to Brougham,

"I do not at all want to take the matter of Education out of your hands but it is time that something should be done upon it. I was for a session Chairman of a Committee of the House of Commons where your evidence, or rather statement, is printed. It does not appear to me that you have contemplated making education general, as I think it ought to be—indeed when in office you made a speech rather relying upon the voluntary societies than proposing interference by the State."[7]

In a memorandum which Russell drew up for Brougham shortly afterwards in October, 1837, he asked the outstanding question,

"Can the Bill be kept clear of the fierce dispute between the three parties (formerly two) into which the promoters of education are divided—the Church of England system men—the British and Foreign Schools system men and to separate religious instruction systems men? I fear that and suspect that each party will try to get a clause into the Bill, to give the balance on its own side."[8]

Russell agreed with Brougham that the question should be avoided in the Bill.

J. A. Roebuck, who had recently been unseated at Bath, largely on account of the exclusion of all religious instruction apart from a reading from the Bible in the model school he had founded there,[9] believed that in addition to Church fury with the proposed measure, "the humble will see that this new scheme is a subterfuge, a means of avoiding the ballot, upon which the popular mind is more and more intent".[10] Brougham, meanwhile, had interested Sir James Graham, then Peel's Home Secretary, in a scheme for national education[11] with at least three hours' education a day in carefully inspected schools; to ensure the success of the measure, children under eight years of age would be prohibited from employment in the textile industries.[12] Local rates and pupils' pence with Government grants would be used to finance the schools and they would be controlled by seven "trustees"—the church priest, churchwardens, two industrialists and two ratepayers nominated by the magistrates. When the Bill ran into trouble Russell suggested that ratepayers should be accepted on the board; this was a step forward, especially as at least four trustees were to be elected by £10 ratepayers.[13] The Bill failed because of opposition by the Dissenters. Graham remarked bitterly shortly before this occurrence:

> "It is quite clear that the Pusey Tendencies of the Established Church have operated painfully on the Wesleyans and are converting them rapidly into Enemies. I am afraid that the time for conciliating them has passed away and they will be committed in hostility to the progress of the Bill."[14]

W. L. Burn has shown that the political fluctuations of the period 1852–9 created conditions which made dramatic legislative action unlikely; that because of the defects in the administrative structure, implementation of policies was difficult and this led to the encouragement of private individuals and societies to take the initiative rather than the establishment of new Governmental agencies.[15] In addition, the quality of the elected representatives at local level was an unknown factor. On the other hand, from the time of the Crimean War onwards, the reform of public administration was inevitable. The problem for the rising middle class was that of wresting the initiative from the landowners, who largely dominated the political system, without condemning private property.[16] In education the parochial interference by the State in setting up the Committee of Privy Council in 1839, and throughout the 1840s in making grants to schools on certain conditions, paved the way for wider reforms, though not without stiff opposition. The attempts to promote educational legislation in the 1850s which provided for elected authorities with rating powers and the basis of the moral and religious instruction in the schools became a matter of difficulty.

Although the attacks on the various schemes were manifestly directed against the diluted religious instruction offered, or worse, entirely secular education, the opposition was based on a more fundamental objection. The fear was of a national secular system of education based upon the representative principle.[17] As Adams wrote:

> "The fight at this time was not so much respecting details as upon the principles of management. On the one side, the Church, the Wesleyans, the Voluntaryists, and the Roman Catholics were contending for the management by the Church or congregation—on the other hand those who looked to education for political and social advantages were striving to secure local representation."[18]

W. J. Fox's Bill of 1850[19] called into opposition these forces, with its provisions by the Committee of the Privy Council for the creation of educational committees in deficient parishes with powers to levy school rates. "It will seem to most (persons)," wrote a barrister to Lord John Russell in an open letter on the Bill, "that a single Educational Local Committee composed of men of all religious persuasions could never act harmoniously together; that such a heterogeneous body could never agree upon a common plan of education; that it ought not to be entrusted with the powers of levying a rate."[20]

The Lancashire Public School Association, later the National Association, formed in Manchester in 1847, aimed at non-sectarian education maintained by local rates and controlled by locally elected committees. It has a formidable list of supporters, including Cobden, James Hole and Samuel Smiles of Leeds, Benjamin Heywood and Dr. McKerrow.[21] By 1851 the plan put forward by the Association would, if adopted, have had little connection with the Committee of Council; each county was to have its own educational system complete in itself. The ratepayers, assembled in public meeting, were to elect district school committees who were to conduct the management of schools and in certain cases to be the County Board, a body which they elected. By 1852 the County Boards had disappeared in the Association's plan and a Board of Education, appointed by the Queen, took its place. The Board would have divided the whole country into school districts, the ratepayers in each district to elect a school committee as in the previous plan. Annual elections were contemplated, one half of the committee going out of office each year. These committees could levy rates to any amount on the poor rate assessment and could be entailed upon the ratepayers of a district for twenty years to come. As a counter to this secular system the Manchester Church Education Society came into being, consisting of local clergy and laymen with a programme for dealing with Manchester and Salford only. A proposed Bill was drawn up which would have enabled the two towns to create a free education system, maintained out of the local rates, but with religious teaching as an essential part of the curriculum and the retention of management in the hands of the clergy.[22] The administration of this scheme would have been complex: two school districts were to be formed out of the two boroughs and three adjoining townships, and a district school committee appointed for each. In one district the committee was to be wholly elected by the town council out of their own body: in the other, partly by the town council and partly by the ratepayers of the three townships. The qualification for a committee-man elected by the ratepayers was that he should be rated at £30 a year and not be in holy orders. The town council was to levy a rate not exceeding

6d. in the pound annually. This plan received the support of Kay-Shuttleworth; the energetic committee included the Rev. Charles Richson as secretary and later president of the Manchester Statistical Society, Oliver Heywood and Thomas Bazley.[23]

Despite the hard words which were exchanged between the two associations, there were many important points of common agreement—free education, local rating and the establishment of new schools where needed and of admission of all children irrespective of religious belief.[24] Although the most influential members of both committees were anxious to support local educational rating, the Bill put forward by the Manchester and Salford Committee failed in 1852. A petition against it by the Manchester Town Council led to a Select Committee being established; the Bill was delayed under a different Administration and finally dropped.

The levying of rates as a method of financing education was never popular at any time during this period. Edwin Waugh, the Secretary of the then Lancashire Public Schools Association, was given the task of canvassing for signatures in support of the Association's scheme and persuading the residents to join the movement. This involved door-to-door enquiries, stopping passers-by in Piccadilly and the High Street and visiting the business premises in the City.

"A fine cluster in Messrs. Wood & Westhead's Counting House and Warehouse," Waugh recorded on the 20 April, 1848. "The principal was an Irishman. He stepped from the desk towards me laughing and said: 'Is it repale? We never sign anything except repale o' the Union'."

Waugh was convinced that the plan would be welcomed by the middle and working classes:

"I have found it so in counting-houses and in warehouses, in front shops and especially in workshops and even in the inhuman cellar-dwellings of the very poor, some of which I visited in Shudehill. Everywhere I have found it received by the great majority with pleasure and friendliness, and chiefly on the score of its unsectarian and secular character, and on account of the popular nature of the management proposed."

But the work was not always so pleasant.

"The most frequent objection, however, is on the grounds of taxation, and this objection springs almost invariably among those *occupiers* of property who have so much occasion to complain of the unequal pressure of taxation—They admire the plan.

"But I have often been amused as I have watched them reading the Petition, and prepared myself to meet the coming storm—They read the first clause. 'That's good!' They 'quite agree' with that—They read the second slowly—and 'that's good' also. They then take the pen which I offer to them at this stage of the proceedings, and begin to read the third clause, and at the words 'local rates' down goes the pen and a furious dispute is taken up. 'More rates! Do you think there isn't rates enow?' Then follows a volley of red-hot invective against government, unjust laws and unequal taxation."[25]

A Free Schools Bill drawn up by Milner Gibson, Cobden and Headlam introduced by the National Public Schools Association in early 1853 clashed with one introduced on behalf of the Aberdeen Coalition Ministry in February of that year whilst the Manchester and Salford Committee were still sitting. In many ways, it anticipated the 1870 Act; corporate towns were, under certain circumstances, empowered to set up school committees—town councils[26] in boroughs and churchwardens in vestries and parishes. These could levy an education rate and although the Bible was to be read in the schools, a conscience clause would operate to protect children attending denominational schools. The borough school committees were to work under the supervision of the Committee of Council on Education which would provide for inspection of assisted schools.[27] Milner-Gibson, the promoter of the National Public Schools Association Bill, doubted whether two-thirds of a town council would be found to agree to teach all forms of religion in their respective towns and to support such teaching out of the rates.[28]

In June, 1853, a deputation headed by Milner Gibson waited on Russell to voice some objections to his Bill. Absalom Watkin of Manchester emphasized the necessity for local control. "We object to all centralization as dangerous to civil liberty and at variance with constitutional principles." Edward Swaine assured Russell that the voluntaryists "however divided they may be on the Education Question all alike object to everything that looks like an approach to the State Endowment of all religions". Dr. Smiles of Leeds mentioned that the schools connected with mechanics institutes which were under secular instruction only, although excluded from receiving aid as a result, were a model to be followed.[29] The Executive Council of the Association after the Bill's failure called it an ill-digested and most imperfect measure.[30]

The movement virtually ceased to exist after 1856. Cobden, a Vice-President of the Association, analysed in a letter the reasons for the failure of the movement and prophesied accurately the successor to Manchester in this work:

"There is no remedy for what has occurred at Manchester believe me. A place like Birmingham and the neighbourhood is much more suited for democratic movements as there the ranks of society are more gradually blended. Masters and men work at the same benches and there are no great capitalists employing thousands of men, and perhaps not on speaking terms with a score of them."[31]

The initiative during the rest of the decade, when the main principles of a system of national education were for the first time marked out, rested between two statesmen of different political persuasions but alike in their independence of thought on educational questions, both offending their respective parties in doing so: they were Lord John Russell and Sir John Pakington.

Russell,[32] the Liberal Prime Minister from 1846 to 1852, had been, as was seen earlier, concerned with introducing education measures. A semi-jocular self-portrait written in 1854 emerges from the following.

> "Lord John Russell has been so long leader of the House of Commons that like Sir Robert Walpole he may at any time fall before the public lassitude. Many of his opinions are old-fashioned and out of date. He has offended some out of his zeal for Parliamentary reform, others because private interests have not received the attention they thought their due."[33]

Pakington,[34] later first Lord Hampton, was a Conservative who had briefly been in Lord Derby's first administration of 1852 (February to December) as Secretary of War and Colonies. His utterances had occasionally caused his party some embarrassment and Disraeli's biographer mentions that the latter breathed a sigh of relief when, after thirty-six years in Parliament, Pakington was defeated at the 1874 election.[35]

A month after Russell's Bill had failed in the Commons in February, 1853, Pakington introduced his own, which met with the strong approval of the National Public Schools Association. Like their own Bill, Pakington's had provided for free schools, the formation of school districts for school committees popularly constituted and elected, to be maintained equally from local and Parliamentary funds. It differed in that for the most part, schools were to be in connection with the Church of England and the teachers to be members of the Church.

Edward Stanley, 14th Earl of Derby, told Brougham in December, 1853,

> "Next year *must* give us a good Education Bill, whoever is in power; the people mean to have it and Parliament cannot refuse it".[36]

This forecast proved to be correct. Russell's Assistant Secretary at the Education Department warned him some months later that Pakington was about to put forward a proposal for the Commons.[37] This was a fact. With the Conservatives in opposition, Pakington had discussed with Derby and Disraeli after the failure of the Manchester and Salford Bill, the possibility of a further Bill and, although encouraged to do so, Pakington had not found the time to proceed. The matter was now becoming urgent. "I know, accidentally and in confidence", he told Disraeli, "that *Lord John Russell is preparing a Bill*—that mysterious paragraph in the Queen's speech about which he made jokes means—*Education*". Pakington felt that, despite the Crimean War which was then raging, there was widespread interest in the subject. There was a lack of sympathy with his views within the party; he doubted whether J. W. Henley, John Manners and himself would ever agree to his plan; Cobden and Adderley would be likely to move for a system of national education. In the course of his long letter, Pakington volunteered, in order not to embarrass his colleagues and to produce swift action, to become an independent M.P. and introduce his Bill, the outline of which was almost settled.[38]

He told Cobden that the Bill "will be introduced with a singleness of purpose", on his part. It would extend the provisions of the Manchester and Salford Bill and Russell's Bill of 1853 and adopt the principle of administration by the Poor Law Unions as units outside the towns.[39]

Derby approved the plan after a long discussion, but new events temporarily overshadowed the progress of the measure. "Thursday, 25 January, 1855, busy in preparing for Education speech this evening," Pakington recorded. "Lord Derby sent for me about point in Bill—advised me not to go on—he thought affairs so critical that he had considered how to form government—House of Commons—heard that *Lord John had* RESIGNED!—all notions given up."[40]

This had come about because of the disastrous handling of the war against Russia in the Crimea which Russell and Palmerston had pressed for in 1853. Lord John Russell, an advocate of a vigorous prosecution of hostilities, told the pacifist Prime Minister Aberdeen that "my colleagues however differed from me and concurred with you. I remain responsible for all that has taken place up to this time for the Crimea except the choice of its commander (Lord Raglan)." Roebuck moved for an enquiry into the conduct of the war on 23 January, 1855; "as it involved a censure against the War Department," wrote Russell to Aberdeen, "my only course is to hand in my resignation".[41] This led to the downfall of the Aberdeen Government and education matters were temporarily put aside.[42]

Meanwhile, Derby who had the problem of trying to form, unsuccessfully, a new government, advised Pakington to send to all colleagues in the Commons, a copy of his draft Bill and invite their impartial considerations of it.[43]

Apart from Members of Parliament, Pakington invited comments from a wide spectrum of interests, religious and educational as well as political. Many of the letters to Pakington were concerned with the nature of the management of the schools proposed. As the Act was to be a permissive one, ratepayers would elect an education board annually; the board was to be given the power to provide schools, superintend education in the district, regulate the rate expenditure and to exercise generally the functions entrusted to them by the Act.

"A compulsory rate," the Rev. J. J. Blandford, H.M.I., remarked, "is the only mode of breaching the present want of Education and all that I am anxious for is that it should be administered by persons capable of appreciating the value of education."[44]

J. C. Colquhon, writing from Chartwell, Kent, was concerned

"that the managers of the schools to be elected under the Bill would be the Ratepayers of the district. That the Ratepayers are a good body and possess such powers I do not think the country will be of opinion. But this is clear that those who now manage schools and to whom we owe the large and various system of education we have, will not like to see themselves thus thrown aside. The feature of our Education that schools are now managed by earnest men, Lay or Clerical, Church or Dissenting, and that into the management of these schools, their life and earnestness passes—and your Bill would substitute for these a body of men of whom we have ample illustrations, in the Corporations, Town Councils, and in Scotland at least, Police Commissioners (for these are elected by Ratepayers) and a more vulgar, selfish, overbearing set of fellows are not to be found between the North Sea and the Channel."[45]

The Rev. J. S. Hodgson commented:

"From personal observation I have known so much jobbing to take place in Poor Law Union Boards, that I should be very loath to see them entrusted with the choice of Schoolmaster or management of School funds."[46]

John Bright gloomily concluded that the project would be shipwrecked on the very same rock on which all former schemes had been destroyed—the religious portion of the Bill.[47]

Palmerston's government was formed on 7 February, 1855. To avoid defeat, Palmerston set up a Committee of Enquiry[48] and Pakington was nominated for this distasteful work. From 23 February, when the Committee first met, until the evidence had finished being taken on 15 May, Pakington was involved in the hearings on four or five days of the week. In between embarrassing interviews with generals (Pakington informed one that he would have to be dismissed) and Committee meetings, his educational measure was put down for 16 March. Pakington noted in his diary on that day:

"Sebastopol Commission—till 2 p.m. home then to dinner. At 5 made education speech and motion—spoke two and three-quarter hours—very successful.

"Great compliments all day about Education speech and plan."

Few members on the Conservative benches were happy about the Bill. The second reading was sabotaged by Henley who, according to Pakington, moved an amendment in a speech of three and a quarter hours[49] and thus led to the debate being adjourned. Disraeli refused further time for Pakington and it was not until 14 June that the debate took place, Pakington hurrying across from the Sebastopol Commission who were considering their Report.

"I spoke in reply to Henley", wrote Pakington, "and made good speech—but not with usual success. I *read* too much."[50]

The Commons were too preoccupied with foreign affairs: this virtually spelt the end and the Bill was dropped.

"They have been lulled into false security by knowing that Parliament is Liberal and Committee of Council active", wrote Pakington to Brougham, the following year.

"The money is only given where it is *least* wanted—to the really poor districts *nothing* is given—all this needs correction and I hope Your Lordship will agree with me in the demand that the Committee of Council shall be *recognised* as a *Department* and be represented in Parliament and act under proper Parliamentary responsibility."[51]

Russell drew up a list of resolutions for presentation in the House in April, 1856, which included, as its first head, the expediency of extending, revising and consolidating the Minutes of the Committee of Council on Education. A bold plan for administering education was postulated in the other resolutions: the dividing of England and Wales into eighty-five divisions,[52] each division being under an Inspector and with sub-divisions under Sub-Inspectors; that Quarter Sessions should have the power to grant applications for a school rate to be levied in any parish or school district not adequately supplied with schools; and a conscience clause allowed. Looking ahead to Sandon's Act of 1876, employers of children between eleven and fourteen years of age would be required to pay a rate to be fixed for the instruction of such children and to furnish quarterly certificates of the attendance of the children at school.[53]

Having suffered at the hands of the House, Pakington appreciated that the object in view transcended party differences. He wrote to Russell shortly before the debate on the resolutions, suggesting a number of amendments:

"I believe that it is only by cordial co-operation between those Gentlemen on both sides of the House who share the views which your Lordship and I entertain in common that we shall be able to resist successfully the combination between the Ultra Church Party on my side and the Ultra Voluntary Party on yours.

"I do not wish therefore to endanger your resolutions by pressing small points of difference.

"I would also beg leave to submit to you whether it will not be better to let the new rate system be worked between the central Board and the local Committees, than to call in the aid of the Courts of Quarter Sessions—I fear that part of the plan will be unpopular without being effective."[54]

In his reply, Russell agreed that he was apprehensive about conferring on the Committee of Council a power of ordering a rate.

"It is a matter for deliberation; we must avoid the cry against centralization, and at the same time endeavour to provide an effective machinery.

"I am told there will be much local objection to clubbing parishes together; yet in many cases no school committee capable of reading and writing could be formed in a single Parish—on this subject I shall expect your personal assistance."[55]

Pakington spoke up for Russell in the debates in the House. The irascible Henley,[56] as usual, opposed.

The following day:

"Lord John told me he gave up *seven Resolutions*—pith of plan! he had better given up all! he opened adjourned debate and hoped to stop discussion but he failed—A Division on even first resolution (i.e. relative to the Minutes of the Council) was forced—painful scene— more passion than reason."[57]

Both Pakington and Russell could claim that the opposition to their education measures arose out of misunderstanding of the means by which their objectives could be achieved. Russell's plan to give more authority to the Committee of Council on Education was a device to ensure administrative efficiency in the supervision of the proposed local committees. It was misinterpreted by Churchmen as a check to private benevolence and a threat to Church schools.

Even more strange was the accusation levelled by his own Party at Pakington, that as far as religious instruction was concerned, as Lord Robert Cecil said on the introduction of Pakington's 1855 Bill, he regarded it as a secular system in disguise.[58] Stafford Northcote, who only three years previously had been responsible with Sir Charles Trevelyan for effecting reforms in the Civil Service, regarded

Pakington's secular views as standing in the way of the introduction of a system of local administration in education.[59]

Possibly the fact that the Lancashire Public Schools Association had found many points of agreement in Pakington's Bills with their own coupled with his readiness to address meetings in Manchester gave this impression. Pakington, however, strenuously supported religious teaching in schools; a clause appeared to this effect in his final Bill of 1857, although making provision for the withdrawal of children whose parents objected to their instructions in distinctive religious formularies.

> "In the last part of your letter to me", he replied to Cobden, "you call upon me for a difficult task when you ask me to remove the prejudice of the Clergy with respect to the secular system—how am I to set about it? I don't approve of it myself. . . . When I saw the class of children in that secular school at Manchester I could not help thinking, 'If they do not read the Bible here, where will they read it?' The answer of course would be 'In the Sunday school'. My rejoinder would be 'that is not true with regard to all and where it is true it is not enough."[60]

Pakington was responsible for the setting up of the Newcastle Commission in 1858 to enquire into the state of popular education throughout the country. The Commission was unwilling to contemplate more than partial parochial rating. Although the Report admitted that "where the object is felt to be of immediate local interest and advantage, the ratepayers are the proper persons to pay for and superintend the matter",[61] nevertheless, there was little experience from the management of workhouse schools to point to their taking such an interest.[62]

The Report argued that:

> "trained teachers would be regarded by 'careless observers' as conceited, above their work, insubordinate and dissatisfied with their position. This makes it necessary that the management of schools should be in the hands of persons who feel a genuine interest in the subject, are willing to bear with disappointments and shortcomings in the hopes of ultimately attaining a satisfactory result and are ready to try experiments and adopt suggestions for increasing the efficiency of the school."[63]

Subscribers who took a lively interest were the obvious body.

A compromise solution was arrived at which took into account the recognition of local interest which local payment and management would secure. Assistance to schools was to be of two kinds: partly by the Committee of Council for schools fulfilling conditions on adequate provision of educational facilities, and partly by the examination of each child under seven years in the school by inspectors of a county or borough board of education, the latter to be elected by the Court of Quarter Sessions or in boroughs by the town council. The only function of this body was to distribute the funds from the county or borough rate to schools.[64]

Although a number of the recommendations were incorporated in the New Code issued by Lowe in July, 1861, by February the following year the celebrated Revised Code changed the nature of many of them. Pakington remained unconvinced that the two main issues had been dealt with, namely the plight of small parishes and the absence of any organized local agency to assist and guide the Central Department. District boards were essential to assist in the distribution of the central grant and provide a network for small parishes where there were difficulties in forming a school committee.[65] This proposal foreshadowed in the case of Church schools the Voluntary Schools Associations after 1897.

Pakington's last major educational effort was in accepting the chairmanship of the Select Committee appointed to enquire into the constitution of the Committee of Council on Education and the best mode of extending the benefits of Government inspection and the Parliamentary grant to schools at present unassisted by the State.[66] Pakington's draft report gives clear evidence of his usual inventiveness and wide grasp of the educational needs of the country. Like so many of his other projects, it was not brought to completion. Both the first and second Committees in 1865 and 1866 suffered two changes of Government[67] during their two years of existence and in spite of Pakington's request that the Committee should be appointed for a further year, this never came about.

"Mr. Forster joined me as I left the House last evening", Pakington, at this time First Lord of the Admiralty in Disraeli's Government, told the Prime Minister in February, 1868. "I asked if he expected any Debate on Education this evening. He intended himself to make a short statement, the principal object of which would be to say on behalf of Mr. Bruce whether or not to introduce his Bill."[68]

Bruce, a former Vice-President under the Liberal Government, had been impressed with Pakington's proposals for education and, with his encouragement, adopted them in a Bill in 1867. The movement towards the establishment of a more permanent structure of educational authorities was reinforced by the findings of the Taunton Commission which reported in 1868; they recommended that provincial boards be set up for secondary education, as in Pakington's proposals. Joseph Chamberlain had already drafted his manifesto for the National Education League in 1867;[69] with Gladstone in office from 1868, and the passing of the Reform Bill, an Education Act was inevitable.

Pakington's activities in connection with education have not so far received their true recognition. His extremely flexible attitude on political and religious questions[70] made his views attractive, if not entirely acceptable, to those educational interests concerned with reform;[71] many of his ideas were incorporated into legislation subsequently enacted during the rest of the century.

The main issue in all discussions relating to the management of a national system of elementary education during the middle portion of the nineteenth century had turned on the nature of the administrative unit to carry out this function and the nature of the representation of ratepayers and other interests on such a committee. In no instance were these difficult questions resolved; in many cases they were, for a variety of reasons, never posed. We shall examine the nature of the school boards as a unit of management created by the 1870 Act.

SCHOOL BOARD ADMINISTRATION FROM 1870

The administration of the Act was given to the school boards[72] who could either manage the schools as a board or delegate the powers to local bodies of managers. From 1870, therefore, including those of the voluntary schools there were three different classes of managers. The voluntary school managers have been dealt with in Chapter 1 and local managers in Chapter 4.

In considering the nature of the boards it is important to bear in mind the constraints placed upon them by the administrative decisions of the Education Department. Such decisions were formulated as the result of experience and the policy files of the Department show the processes which led to the creation of such precedents. Perhaps this is most clearly demonstrated in looking at the relationship between the town councils, the school boards and the Education Department.

ELECTION AND DISSOLUTION OF BOARDS

The boards, set up to fill the gaps left by the voluntary system, could be established in a number of ways. After allowing six months for sufficient accommodation to be provided, the Department could send a requisition ordering a board for a district (Section 10). If a school board failed to comply with the requisition within twelve months, it would be regarded as being in default (Section 11). An alternative was for the electors of a school district or council or borough, being ratepayers,[73] to apply direct to the Department for a board (Section 12): ratepayers alone constituted the electorate.

The number of members of the board varied between five and fifteen, depending on the decision of the Department. Election was to be by ratepayers and members held office for three years[74] (Section 31(1)). Disqualification arose from a board member accepting, or gaining profit in connection with his official work, or absence from meetings of the school board for six months. Finally the Department could declare a school board in default after enquiry and could appoint a new board or individual members in their place (Section 63).

One of the early difficulties encountered was the filling of casual vacancies on the board. The Liverpool School Board claimed in 1872 that the costs to the borough of supplying a casual vacancy amounted to £525 3s. 3d. in addition to the candidate's own expenses of between £500 and £600, with only a year before the next election was due.[75] Similarly the Department ordered that two vacancies were to be filled at Birmingham at a cost of £1,000 although the result would not have affected the balance of the parties.[76]

Legal advice had been taken by the Department as a result of the Salford School Board's resolutions made on 22 October, 1874. The Board determined not to fill up a casual vacancy until the next election; meanwhile the number of members would remain at fourteen. Mr. W. G. Lumley, the Department's Counsel and later the Solicitor-General, advised on the expediency rather than the competency of the Department to allow this.

Disallowing the Board's resolution the theoretical situation was postulated by Lumley of a school board consisting of fifteen members, seven of one party (x) and eight of another (y) with a majority on the board:

"Party (y) having the majority, elect a Chairman of their own and give the Vice-Chairman to one of party (x). The Vice-Chairman acts as Chairman in the absence of the Chairman. The Chairman dies, Party (x) (minority) having now the casting vote, pass a Resolution reducing the number of members to 14—thus wishing to retain the power of a majority for the remaining term of office of the Board." [76a]

The scale of five to fifteen members had been carefully considered and was fixed at an odd number to prevent difficulties arising from the balance of parties. By the Third Schedule of the 1876 Education Act casual vacancies were allowed to be filled by the remaining members of the board at a specially convened meeting.[77]

No hard and fast rules were operated by the Department in approving the number of members on a board. In 1894 the Boston School Board, Lincolnshire (which had a population of just over 14,000), requested eleven members for its first Board. The usual ratio laid down by the Department was seven members for between five and fifteen thousand people, but Newport Pagnell in Buckinghamshire had been allowed to have nine members with a population of only 3,788.[78]

The Third Schedule of the Act governing the proceedings of school board meetings fixed a quorum at not less than three members (later raised to four), with not fewer than nine members in the case of London. Much ingenuity was shown by the Department in handling cases where, for one reason or another, a board might be in default if the members refused to work together. A member of the Low Leyton, Essex Board was, according to the local newspaper, "so afflicted at times as to lose all control of himself and all memory of what he has done while under the influence of this affliction".[79] Although not specifically mentioned, the affliction was repeated drunkenness at board meetings; five of the nine board members complained to the Department of the bad effect in the parish, and particularly on his (the offending member's) position as employer of the school teachers. If the five resigned, as they wished to, he and his three supporters (a working blacksmith, a working cobbler and huckster) would have constituted a quorum.

Two previous similar cases had occurred. The Department had decided in the instance of a member convicted of assault at Stourbridge, Worcestershire, where the other five members represented that the moral character of the member prevented their working with him and resigned, to nominate the five members for a new board. At Walthamstow[80] five out of the seven members resigned because of the obstructiveness of one of the others; here, the Department ordered a fresh election.[81] Neither of these cases exactly fitted the Low Leyton case. George Miller, Senior Examiner in the Education Department, hit upon what he called "a most manifestly and confessedly special expedient for the purpose of practically getting rid of Mr. B.": the number required for a quorum was raised to five instead of four and now allowing the five members to resign left Mr. B. with less than a quorum.[82]

Where the Department suspected that the majority of a board wished to use the device of resignation for selfish reasons in order to make the board in default, they were dealt with sharply. The Rev. Charles Patterson, curate of the parish of Stoke Green, Warwickshire, was elected at the head of the poll as one of the five school board members to, in his own words, "more especially watch the financial affairs of the Board". He proved conclusively that the clerk and the schoolmaster were in league but the other four members resigned, leaving Patterson alone.

H

"I am uncertain", wrote Sykes to Cumin, the Secretary of the Education Department, "whether Mr. Patterson deserves to be applauded for his vigilance or censured for a troublesome activity."

Mundella, to whom the case finally went, sent off a characteristically blunt reply to the members, refusing their request:

"It is difficult to understand how four members out of a Board consisting of five only should be powerless of acting in unison to protect themselves from any inconvenience resulting from the opposition, however distasteful to them, of a single colleague."[83]

Where the Department used their powers to nominate new members to a board, dissolving an existing board for not having performed their duties under Section 66 of the Act, difficulties could be encountered. This threat was used particularly where the board refused or neglected to supply extra school accommodation. The Willesden School Board in a celebrated case in 1885 were guilty of this misdemeanour[84] and after taking the advice of the Law Officers, who recommended caution, Cumin declared the Board in default. In an exasperated Minute, Cumin wrote,

"It is not competent for the Department to discuss the expediency or inexpediency of what the Law Officers have declared to be the law. It would be stultifying ourselves to do anything now but enforce the requisition. I saw Mr. Campbell, the H.M.I. and explained to him that *we had no option* but to appoint members of the School Board."

Miller enquired from Cumin as to the number of members needed.

"If it is desired to inflict a severe punishment upon the Parish of Willesden, this would be better done by the appointment of a *large* number of members than the minimum (five)."

It was also desirable to know whether

"he should make any proposals *about payment* in the first place, or confine himself to the simple enquiry whether the people are prepared to serve. The people will not be easy to find, and the negotiations will be somewhat delicate."[85]

Campbell for his part made enquiries but was unable to find a sufficient number of influential people for the work.[86] In the event, the Department was saved from the task of imposing a board.

The Department was limited in the methods it could employ to make recalcitrant boards fulfil their obligations. Unorthodox and ingenious suggestions for doing this were eschewed.[87] H.M.I. Mr. T. G. Rooper, Inspector for the Bradford Division, had threatened the Idle School Board that the Department would exercise the powers conferred upon it by Section 27 of the 1876 Elementary Education

Act, whereby a board could be declared in default after inquiry for not enforcing school attendance. Much of the apathy displayed by the members arose from causes which Rooper thus described:

"The Denominationalists particularly object to a Board and the others objected to carrying out the compulsory clauses in order, as they thought, to fill denominational schools, it being the case that there were no Board Schools."[88]

For their part, the board claimed that the migratory working class population of the district and the outbreak of scarlet fever and other epidemics had been responsible for poor attendance. "They (the Board) respectfully but firmly decline to be catechised," wrote the Clerk of the Board to the Department and called for an impartial enquiry. Rooper, who was no slavish adherer to the rigid rule and who refused to be strangled by red tape,[89] suggested to the Department that instead of declaring the Board in default,

"some kind of historical recapitulation of the flagrant and persistent neglect of the Idle School Board would, *if published in the local paper* have a good effect in disarming criticism and allaying that hostility to authority which is rather popular in Airedale (remember the Keighley Martyrs and the Antivaccinationists)."[90]

Lindsell, a Junior Examiner in the Department, condemned the idea:

"such a course appears highly undesirable and one which a public department could under no circumstances adopt."

Miller, the Assistant Secretary, agreed, adding:

"moreover, *who* is to get the letter into the local papers? Surely Mr. Rooper does not think the Idle Board will do it?"[91]

Finally, enquiry by Lindsell settled the matter amicably.

TOWN COUNCILS AND SCHOOL BOARDS

In many towns there was a state of uneasy co-existence between the town council and the school board. Where the majority party was of the same political and denominational colour relationships were easier; on the other hand this could lead to a call for the dissolution of the board, if the Church majority prevailed. Other factors contributed to the uneasy relationships. Except for London, the different systems of voting—ballot in municipal and cumulative in board elections—led to confusion on the part of the voters.[92] The *ad hoc* principle did not accord with the spread of the representative principle in most types of civic and national committees; and the fact that the town councils were originally intended to be the educational authorities when the 1870 Act was first drawn up made in many instances for rivalry rather than co-operation.[93]

Where town councils took the initiative under Section 12 of the 1870 Act to ascertain from the ratepayers whether a school board was desirable, no stipulation was made as to what constituted a majority decision by the ratepayers. A poll at Cannock, Staffordshire, in January, 1874, resulted in a vote of 485 out of the 1,769 ratepayers in the town who were eligible and by a majority of nine (247 to 238) voted for a board. Discretionary powers rested with the Department of granting a requisition. Since the poll, Viscount Sandon had taken over the office of Vice-President from W. E. Forster and a protest from the clergy of Cannock indicated that the poll had been won by the Dissenters.[94]

"As you are aware", wrote Cumin to Sandon, "it has hitherto been *where a poll has been taken* to act in accordance with result thereof."[95]

Sandon's decision on this case became an important precedent for the future.

"When you are allowing a meeting of Ratepayers to impose upon a locality for all time such an important institution as a School Board, I think it is not desirable that a mere majority of an uncertain number of Ratepayers should decide the question . . . we should lay down a general rule where a Poll has been demanded, requiring that a certain proportion of ratepayers should have polled and possibly requiring also that more than a mere majority (say two-thirds) should be in favour of a School Board before we issue the irrevocable order."[96]

A town council, however, could make a resolution in favour of a board by obtaining the agreement of the majority of the council members.[97] A year after the Cannock decision, the Winchester Town Council met in February, 1875, and voted fifteen against five in favour of a board to supervise school attendance rather than on the ground of a shortage of school accommodation. A meeting of more than 1,000 citizens out of the population of 16,366 met after this and unanimously passed a resolution against a board. When the council met again in March, the original resolution was confirmed fourteen against nine. Richmond, the Lord President, concluded that

"they (the Department) would not at present be justified in agreeing an order for the election of a School Board."

Sandon, approving the reply, could only give as his reason "that the minority in the Council against a School Board has considerably increased".[98]

Many years later in a similar case, Kekewich mentioned that under

Section 12(1) neither the ratepayers nor the inhabitants had any *locus standi*.

> "Notwithstanding Lord Sandon's minute in the Winchester case, I hardly think that we ought to make our decision in a Borough practically depend on the action of the Ratepayers thereby really giving them under the section the same position in a Borough as they have in a Parish, and which apparently they were not intended to occupy in a Borough."[99]

The case for a school board at Heywood, Lancashire, illustrates the political considerations underlying educational policy at the time. In June, 1895, just before the Liberal Government left office, the closing of the Hopwood United Methodist School was announced and this would have created a deficiency in school accommodation. In response to a request from the town council, Acland, the Vice-President, approved an order for the election of a board in June, but on 16 August, with a change of Government, the matter was deferred "until after the municipal elections to be held in November".[100] The decision to defer an order was, it was claimed, without precedent[101] and the town council protested that as it was undesirable for the election to turn entirely on the question of a school board, a poll of ratepayers should be taken. This was done, resulting in a narrow majority against a school board.[102]

No further action was taken and in the November elections the anti-school board party gained only two seats and in the following year's elections gained little more representation. The town council therefore renewed their application for the school board order to be implemented. Gorst and Devonshire, ignoring the results of the two elections, both reiterated the belief that the council was acting in opposition to the general opinion of the ratepayers as shown in the poll. Questioned in Parliament, Gorst did not move his ground.

If, on the other hand, a town council wished to dissolve a board, Section 41 of Sandon's Act 1876 stipulated that a two-thirds majority of a council would be sufficient, providing that the board had no schools under its control and that there was sufficient school accommodation for the district. Stockport School Board, formed on 1 December, 1870, along with Liverpool and Bootle, was the first to have its bye-laws sanctioned.[103] It had no schools of its own. The council, by thirty-one to thirteen votes in May, 1879, hoped to dissolve the board. Lord George Hamilton, who had succeeded Sandon as Vice-President in 1879, minuted,

> "As we are in no way bound by the Act to consult the Board as to whether or not they concur in their proposed dissolution, I think it would be a rather dangerous precedent to establish."[104]

The town was well supplied with Church schools of all denominations and the Board passed a resolution in favour of its own dissolution by six votes to three. One of the defeated amendments displayed some antipathy towards the town council:

> "That while in the election of School Boards the legislature have carefully provided for the representation of minorities and have left the election of suitable persons for the work, to the intelligence of the constituencies, there is no such provision in the municipal election Acts, and there is no guarantee that an unscrupulous majority in a Town Council, appointing a School Attendance Committee, would have any regard for either of these principles."[105]

Certainly, after 1876, by dissolving the school board, the school attendance committee as part of the council would have eliminated other interests in education. Stalybridge, sharing with Stockport the distinction of having no board schools, followed suit in attempting to get rid of its school board. The grounds given for this were that, besides there being enough accommodation available, there would be from September, 1879, in the coming fourteen months, three if not more elections within the borough:

> "the Municipal Election in November, a School Board Election in January, a Municipal Election in November of next year besides the possibility of a Parliamentary Election."

A school attendance committee appointed in the board's place would avoid "the cost, excitement and ill-feeling attending one of such Elections".[106]

A petition from the Stalybridge Reform Club, a Liberal organisation, protested at the statements made at meetings by the Conservative leader of the council, Councillor Napoleon Ives, that the "Board Elections had generated personal unpleasantness, ill-feeling and hatred and class set against class, turmoil, and religious ill-feeling".[107] Sandford drew up in two columns the cases for and against dissolution; on balance, he favoured retaining the board.

> "At Stockport they agreed (by a majority) with the proposal to dissolve themselves. I think that great weight ought to be given to this consideration."[108]

In addition, the board administered an endowment for scholarships for intending pupil-teachers. Hamilton anxiously replied to Sandford:

> "I think we must not stress too much the difficulty of providing for the accommodation of an endowment vested in the School Board, otherwise

any individual member of a School Board could permanently prevent its abolition by handing over to it a small educational endowment."[109]

The distinction between these two cases was that at Stockport the board was dissolved because by a majority of six to three it supported the town council. At Stalybridge, on the other hand, the Department did not dissolve, not because of the opposition of the school board but because the municipal election took away the two-thirds majority in favour of dissolution.

A third variation on this theme occurred in 1889, again in Cheshire. The Macclesfield School Board, elected in October, 1886, after a heavy poll, consisted of one working man, three Nonconformists, four Churchmen and one Roman Catholic, a fairly representative board.[110] In June, 1889, the town council voted for its dissolution on the grounds that election costs would be saved, amounting to two-fifths of a penny of the rates. After a meeting of the school board, whose chairman was a Churchman, a petition was sent to the Department praying for its continuation on the ground that no ratepayers had made representations against the board and that it was functioning efficiently.[111] In August, the Department agreed that the board should continue and that new elections should shortly be held.[112]

The unsatisfactory nature of the relationship of the town council with the school board lay partly in the financial arrangements of the 1870 Act. Under Section 54, the board served a precept on the council as the rating authority: in case of default by the council, the board could appoint an officer to levy the rate to meet their expenses (Section 56). This latter course was resorted to on a number of occasions by school boards, especially in the early years of their existence.[113]

It was a logical conclusion after the Technical Instruction Act of 1889 which allowed local authorities to levy a rate for technical education,[114] that town councils should attempt to become educational authorities for elementary and secondary education in their own right. The Warrington Council introduced a private Bill into the House of Lords in March, 1902, after encouragement by the ratepayers, to enable them to exercise certain powers of a school board and to borrow money for the provision of schools. The Bill was an attempt to avoid a Final Notice from the Department ordering a school board. It was not a propitious time to introduce such a measure, with the debate on the Education Bill then approaching its climax. The Lord Chairman of Committees refused the Bill on the grounds that it "dealt with questions which could only be dealt with by general legislation".[115]

SCHOOL BOARD AND VOLUNTARY SCHOOL MANAGERS

The relative efficiency of the manager under the two systems was a constant source of debate. After hearing the witnesses on the subject, the Cross Commission declared that the honours were evenly divided.

"It would be impossible to deny the superiority of the management of the School Board in dispensing the money of the ratepayers. If however, we look for the closest supervision of the school and the most effective sympathy between managers and teachers, or between managers and scholars, we should feel, on the whole, bound to pronounce in favour of the efficiency of voluntary school management."[116]

The Report also condemned the unwholesome, if natural, rivalry which existed between the two systems and exhorted managers to work closer together if possible.

Co-operation was practised in some matters, especially with regard to school attendance and co-ordination of holiday periods. The Liverpool School Board took the lead in this matter.

"In January, 1875, soon after the opening of their first school, a meeting was convened of all managers of public elementary schools in the city under the presidency of the Mayor; a committee was subsequently set up to ensure uniformity of admittance procedures in the school."[117]

At a slightly earlier date, 1873, the Newcastle-under-Lyme Board requested the Department to sanction bye-laws, which had been framed after conferring with the voluntary school managers of the town,

"so that attendances could be checked and capricious removal from school to school obviated and also save the capitation grant which in such instances is lost."[118]

The bye-law would have provided that before a parent could remove his child from a school, it was necessary that 250 attendances had been made there.

Cumin believed that such a bye-law would be *extra vires* and asked Sandford to consult Forster on the matter. Whilst sympathizing with the intentions of the managers, the Department mentioned that a refusal to admit a child under such rules would be regarded as a violation of Article 17a of the New Code which stated that "No child is refused admission to the school on other than reasonable grounds". Any protest from a parent to the Department would have to be dealt with by the Department on its merits.[119]

Co-operation could be secured by means other than formal concordats. H.M.I. Rev. J. J. Blandford gave the Department the reason for the harmonious working together of the Derby School Board and voluntary schools in the town. This was

"in great measure due to the determination of the Board to build their schools as far away as they can from existing schools; as a matter of fact they interfere very little with each other."[120]

Unfortunately, the framing of the Education Acts provided little in the way of encouragement for the two bodies to work together; in their interpretation of the statutes, the Department for the most part rigidly adhered to the letter of the Acts.

Some formal co-operation was statutorily provided by the 1876 Education Act (Section 7), which imposed on school boards the duty to report to the Department any infraction of Section 7 of the 1870 Act relating to the conduct of all public elementary schools in their districts. Shortly after the former Act came into operation, the Luton School Board requested the Department to supply them with copies of the Inspectors' reports on the voluntary schools, "as the Board are very anxious to compare the several figures and facts named therein with the reports upon the Board Schools".[121]

Searching for precedents in this matter it was discovered that Mr. Sykes had refused to supply the Aberdare School Board with such reports in 1874, but in February, 1875, the Oxford School Board were supplied with these details, "on receipt of 5/-". White put the matter to Cumin for a decision, who stated that the Department should continue to refuse such requests, but "if they can get copies of the Reports from the Managers of the Voluntary Schools they may do so".[122]

NON-COOPERATION BETWEEN SCHOOL MANAGERS

Archdeacon Denison, the celebrated incumbent of East Brent, whose bitter opposition to the Management Clauses and subsequent extravagant opinions on the evils of the Committee of Council on Education isolated him from his church colleagues, wrote to Lord Lyttelton[123] in 1875:

"Last autumn I was standing with Woodard[124] at Old Shoreham. He said, 'There's our new School Board house.' 'Please,' say I, 'let me get away from it. Don't you know what the definition of a School Board House is?' 'No,' says he. 'Well then,' says I, 'I'll tell you: It's a place where all the gargoyles are turned inwards.' He was greatly pleased and laughed considerably."[125]

Not all the clergy adopted such an attitude, but nevertheless the Education Department was called upon frequently to arbitrate in disputes between the board and voluntary school managers over a wide range of issues. In Stanhope, Durham, the school board appointed a school attendance officer whose salary depended on the number of children attending the board schools. The board admitted that it would be preferable for the bonus to depend rather on the average increase in all the public elementary schools of the township, but visiting all the schools for information would be too time-consuming for the officer.[126]

Naturally, it was the voluntary school manager who was usually the more aggrieved party.[127] A petition in March, 1882, to Earl Spencer and A. J. Mundella from the managers of all the voluntary and denominational elementary day schools in Bradford, protested that the school premises of the borough had been rated. A petition in the previous November had shown that nearly half the children in Bradford were in voluntary schools and not on the rates. The school board rate was now over 9d. in the pound, with a yearly expenditure of £28,000.

> "We wish to point out that one of the consequences of the newly improved rate is that the Voluntary Schools are now assessed for School Board purposes. We are therefore not only supporting our own schools without aid from the local rates but at the same time compelled to pay rates for the building and maintenance of the Board Schools but our School Buildings themselves are now rated for School Board purposes."[128]

This added to the already existing disadvantage of the voluntary schools following the 1876 Act, which allowed school boards to remit fees in its own schools but did not empower them to pay fees on behalf of children attending voluntary schools. For voluntary schools only the Guardians could do this; in order to avoid this distasteful procedure, many parents transferred their children to board schools.

The deliberate siting of board schools near to existing voluntary ones was another source of irritation. A new board school had been built "not more than 80 yards from our St. Stephen's School" in Hull and the board were charging lower fees than officially recognized in order to induce children to leave the voluntary school.[129] Bad feeling could also be aroused over the methods employed by a board to obtain information on the existing school accommodation, which the Department required under Sections 19 and 23 of the 1870 Act. It was usual to obtain a return from the school managers, but at Carlisle, the managers of Christ Church School protested about a visit by the board members "without first asking permission from the Managers and without even giving notice of their intention. . . . Teachers and Books were examined as though the Returns made by the Managers were not to be trusted."[130]

Especially in cathedral towns, where voluntary schools were strong, efforts at co-operation with the school board, who were on the defensive, failed. For example, the Bishop of Norwich's efforts to co-ordinate with the board's schools such matters as school attendance, admissions, payment of fees and school accommodation were dismissed out of hand by the board.[131]

Although there were a number of areas of possible disagreement between the two types of management as so far indicated, by far the most important and fundamental matter was that of making good the deficiencies of accommodation, the *raison d'être* of the boards.

Boards were initially to engage a competent person to inspect and report on the character and efficiency of all the elementary schools in the borough which were not under Government inspection. A number of towns requested that an H.M.I. should carry out this work. In the case of Leicester, which was to act as a precedent, the reply of Forster was "My Lords will be glad in the first instance, to have the report of the Board".[132]

In an interesting letter from Riversdale Walrond, Private Secretary to Gorst, the Vice-President, in answer to an enquiry on this point by Lord Stanley of Alderley, he replied, after consultation with Kekewich:

"(1) The practice of the Education Department has been, since 1874, at any rate, to treat a School Board as having the prior right of supplying any deficiency which may exist in the school supply of its district. The enclosed memorandum by Sir George Kekewich explains the reason for this practice.

"(2) So far as he can discover, this practice is not based upon a decision of a Court of Law, or upon a decision of the Law Officers; but he would point out that the cases where the Department have refused grants to Voluntary Schools in such circumstances as being 'unnecessary' have been yearly published in the Blue Book.

"(3) That in some cases, the Department have overridden the objections of the School Board and have given grants to Voluntary Schools, which appeared to them to supply the deficiency in an adequate manner.

"This being so, Sir John considers that each case should be judged on its merits: and that grants given to Voluntary Schools in School Board districts *if in the opinion of the Education Department* the Voluntary Schools would meet the educational needs of the district better than a Board School."[133]

Thus it can be seen that no hard and fast rule for the supply of accommodation was laid down by the Department, a policy which caused an enormous amount of work for the Department's staff and a sense of grievance on the part of managers because of the apparent lack of consistency in the Department's policy.

Where the Department listened sympathetically to both school board and voluntary parties in an attempt to smooth out differences it was soon realized that the Department was placed in an intolerable position. The struggle which ensued between church and chapel at Luton and the school boards elected from 1874 onwards, gained national notoriety. The nine seats for the first board were contested by the "Prayer Book Five" and the "Bible Five". Four members were elected from each party, the vicar of the town, James O'Neill, using his casting vote to give the church party a majority. Both parties were publicly committed to either building or suppressing the building of schools.[134]

Sandon, on becoming Vice-President in 1874, ordered that "as an experiment to be tried in the first instance" the Department would correspond officially with the Luton Board's opponents. Cumin, from the beginning, had doubted the expediency of this experiment. After a year's exhaustive and fruitless correspondence, White suggested by December, 1875, "that it would appear to me to prove the experiment a failure". From that time onwards, the opponents were informed, all proposals "must be laid not before this Department, but before your Board, the only body representative of all the ratepayers, and legally authorised to make proposals on their behalf to the Education Department".[135]

Unnecessary expense was incurred and rivalry resulted by board and voluntary schools providing accommodation in the hope of attracting pupils away from each other. The determined fight by the voluntary school managers in Wednesbury, Staffordshire, to compete with the school board resulted in the schools between 1883 and 1901 having about 1,000 more places than the number of children in actual attendance, just as in the board schools the average attendance was always below the accommodation provided.[136]

Up to the late 1890s the Education Department were called upon to decide on a number of different cases where potential or actual deficiencies might exist. The Willesden School Board, formed in 1882 in consequence of the closing of a Wesleyan school, consisted of eight Churchmen and one Dissenter.[137] It had fought a long battle with the Department, maintaining that the voluntary schools in the district had adequately provided for the need. To this the Department did not agree and issued a requisition to the Board to provide accommodation within twelve months. The Board politely but firmly refused to comply with it and the Department were obliged to take counsel's opinion on the legality of the Board's action, which had hitherto been unchallenged in such matters.

At length, the Department had to appeal to the managers of the Church schools to transfer their boys' school to the Board as a means of saving the Board from default, but met with a refusal. Fortunately, the Department's face was saved only by the Board admitting eventually that the recent growth of population in the area justified the building of a new school.[138]

Towards the end of the century, the Church of England party especially, with the backing of the National Society, had adopted a more positive role in the battle to preserve their schools as far as possible.

The city of Salisbury provides an example of the strength of the church authorities towards the close of the century in resisting possible school board encroachment on the provisions of school places. A school board had been elected as early as 1871 following a visit to the city by Henry Fawcett, who had lectured on the Education Question.[139] As the city was well provided with Church, Roman Catholic, British and a Free School for the very poor, no action needed to be taken by the board.

In November, 1888, the premises of the Scots Lane British School were condemned by the Inspector. Together with those of the Fisherton British School, the managers gave notice that they did not intend to rebuild and that both the schools would be closed. This was in order to force the hand of the school board to build schools and the school board election of February, 1889, was fought on this issue. Of the seven members returned, four were Churchmen, polling a slightly larger total than the three voluntaryists.[140]

Meanwhile, the Salisbury Church Day School Association had been formed in April, 1888, for the purpose of supplying the deficiencies of school accommodation arising from the closing of voluntary schools as in such an instance as this. As the Department had given only until August, 1889, to supply the accommodation, it seemed unlikely that the Association would be able to satisfy their requirements, and it was believed that the school board would be called upon to provide it. Instead, after a meeting of the Association at the end of April, 1889, it was announced that they would supply the 1,121 places needed at a cost of about £11,100. A week later the Kilburn Sisterhood, an order of nuns operating under the auspices of the Church Extension Society,[141] offered to build a school for the Association, and this was accepted. In addition, the Bishop of Salisbury as President offered to build and maintain at his own expense a higher grade elementary school for 200 boys, which would provide a link between the voluntary schools and the grammar schools of the city. Funds were to be raised by subscription.

The Department accepted the Sisterhood's offer although insisting that a guarantee of maintenance should be first given by the Association. "I hardly know," wrote the Bishop, "why our City has been chosen for what appears to be a novel exercise of the Department's unquestionably great authority."[142]

Meanwhile, the opposition forces had been gathering and memorialized the Department on the count that "by the majority of one vote the Board proposed to relegate the responsibility of Elementary Education of the City to the managers of six different schools".[143]

Mundella, as President of the British and Foreign Schools Society and former Vice-President of the Education Department, led a deputation to see Lord Cranbrook. His case rested on the belief that "never had a School Board been permitted to force upon the community schools which were not acceptable to a very large proportion of the community". Cranbrook, the Lord President, denied this and stated that the Law Officers had decided on its legality. Mundella's second objection was that the children of Dissenters would be taught in schools with whose creeds, catechisms and formularies they did not agree.

> "In a similar case, when he was Vice-President of the Education Department, he was advised by Sir Francis Sandford that it was his duty to insist upon the School Board providing a school by which the parents of children secured freedom of choice."[144]

Mundella's challenge was taken up by the Bishop of Salisbury, an irascible and dogmatic High Churchman. He asked Mundella with touching naïveté:

> "I notice that you describe yourself as appearing as 'President of the British and Foreign Schools'—But I confess I am at a loss to understand how those proposed by Voluntary Schools or yourself as their President come forward simply to advocate Board Schools. Are we to understand that these schools have as a body commissioned you to announce their retirement, wherever possible, in favour of the Board Schools? The answer to this question will be of interest to the Managers of all Voluntary Schools throughout the country. It is painful to be driven to conclude that many of those, whose fathers had religious principles and who fought and suffered for them, should be willing and often eager now to hand over the consciences of their children to be subjected to the training of a colourless and ratepayers' religion. . . ."[145]

Hart-Dyke, Cranbrook's Vice-President, was absent from his office when the deputation was received. He wrote to Cranbrook on the bishop's attitude. The latter had been incensed by a demand from the Department to guarantee maintenance of the school, which requirement he considered to be *ultra vires*. "It is impossible to watch all correspondence leaving the Department," wrote Hart-Dyke, "but I hope you will be able to satisfy the Bishop that his scheme will be accepted". Hart-Dyke had written a strong letter to Mr. Hulse, Conservative M.P. for Salisbury, to show to the Bishop in an attempt to smooth matters over.[146]

By August, only a small part of the total subscription required had been raised and further extensions of time were granted by the Department for fulfilling the requirements. Eventually these efforts were successful.

Much of the difficulty experienced by the Department in making decisions to determine which bodies should provide deficiencies in accommodation stemmed from the highly complex interpretations of the sections of the 1870 Act. Lacking flexibility in procedures, the Department administered the provisions in the light of experience and expediency and in doing so, caused offence to both board and voluntary managers.

RURAL SCHOOL BOARDS

T. J. Macnamara,[147] who campaigned strongly for an extension of the areas of rural school boards, maintained that the greatest single error on the part of the framers of the 1870 Act was that outside the boroughs, the parish was made the unit of school board administration. Inefficiency and expenditure of money had been caused by the "unnecessarily multiplied miniature pieces of administrative machinery". In a pamphlet on the matter, Macnamara demonstrated that in some of the smaller parishes, for example, in Wield, Hampshire, the board spent all its grant on administration; at Mallerstang in Westmorland, the seventeen children in average attendance were served by a school board of five elected members and a paid clerk.[148]

Soon after the Act was passed, administrators of large school boards were aware of the anomaly of the small unit. As early as 1874, William Rathbone of Liverpool had discussed with the chairman of the board, Christopher Bushell, the proposition "that instead of having specially elected School Boards in small towns and rural districts which excite alarm and opposition, it would be far better to have a united, local administrative body of importance which should combine parochial, sanitary and Educational work and by the importance which would be thus given to such a body get the best men of the locality to serve upon it".[149]

Rural boards were not taken up with the same enthusiasm as was manifested in the urban centres. A year after the 1870 Act had come into effect, it was calculated that over a half of the largest towns (twenty-seven out of fifty-two) in England and Wales had boards; of the rural counties, five—Dorset, Herefordshire, Huntingdonshire,

Rutland and Shropshire—had none, and there were seven counties with one each, three with two and nine with three boards. Four of the largest agricultural counties, Lincolnshire, Norfolk, Suffolk and Essex, could boast of only sixteen boards between them. The influence of the Church in rural areas was given as the main cause.[150]

For the most part, the rural school boards consisted of farmers. A typical board existed at Carlton Husthwaite,[151] a small village four miles north of Easingwold in the North Riding of Yorkshire; in 1880, of the five board members, four were farmers and one was listed as an "Agent for Manure". Replying to the Department's threat to withhold the payment of the grant for the previous year because of an insufficient number of meetings of the school, it was explained that

"The School being in an entirely agricultural district, it becomes a necessity to give what is termed harvest holiday as the principal part of the children assist in securing the crops, and if the school was open during the harvest the children would not attend and even if summoned the magistrate would not commit."[152]

This situation led to some bizarre happenings at board meetings. The Vicar of Long Sutton, Lincolnshire, sent an account to the Education Department of a typical board meeting in his parish.

"One member of the Board was threatened by the Chairman (a farmer) and the Clerk's clerk with a summons. 'All right', said he, 'but while you are getting a summons for me you get four summonses out against the Chairman for illegally employing four children'. The clerk is reported to have said, 'We must protect the Chairman!' and so the matter was dropped. There is not a farmer in the parish", the Rector concluded, "who is intellectually or otherwise fit for the work of Manager."[153]

It was a fact that the parson was often one of the few members of a rural board who was interested primarily in the welfare of the school children. Writing a few years later of his experiences on the St. Mary Bourne School Board (in Hampshire), the Rev. G. H. Aitken stated,

"The Board was composed, before I joined it, entirely of farmers and small shopkeepers. Their idea was to spend not a penny that could be avoided. Before I left I persuaded them to pass a resolution in favour of lighting the school with oil lamps and also in favour of getting an additional teacher who was sorely needed. Both these resolutions were rescinded at the first meeting after I left the parish and for all I know the school works on still in darkness through the winter afternoons."[154]

James Hawker, a one-time poacher without schooling who turned to village politics and got elected on to his village school board at

Oadby, in Leicestershire, was an untypical but colourful member. His election to the board was not due to his administrative capacity. One of the members of the board was a temperance advocate and his unwanted lectures at the working men's club made him unpopular.

Hawker's account of his election and subsequent service on the board is astonishingly candid.

> "They determined to get their own back on the School Board Election. They drove this man out and put me in, a Duty I was unfit to Fulfil. This shows you what stuff the Oadby men are made of. They won't be sat on . . . I remained on the School Board for six years—simply Because I see no chance of getting off it."[155]

Before the advent of school boards, parish affairs were conducted by the select vestry, a sort of parish council consisting of the vicar and churchwardens, the overseers of the poor and other persons appointed by general vestry of all the ratepayers, and meeting usually in the church vestry or the vicarage. Rarely did any but the most important ratepayers of the village attend, for the meetings were held during the day. With the passing of the Parochial Rate Assessment Act in 1869, every *bona fide* householder was given the right to vote at the annual vestry meeting when the churchwardens and overseers were appointed. This concession was taken up by Joseph Arch from 1872 when the National Union of Agricultural Labourers of England and Wales was formed, the labourers being urged to assert their right to a share in the parish government. An attempt by George Dix, at Swanton Morley in Norfolk, to be elected as churchwarden in 1875, led to his being driven out of the vestry although his candidature had been supported by sixty labourers and sixteen tradesmen at the meeting. The remedy lay in serving on the school board; Dix was elected from the same year.[156] On the whole, however, the agricultural labourers' interest in school management was very limited, with far more concern being shown towards the defence of educational and charitable endowments.

The apathy of the villagers towards the work of the board made for discouragement where the board wished to effect improvements. At Bratton Fleming in Devonshire, it was reported at a meeting of the Board "that some of the people living in the lower part of the village were strongly opposed to a tap being placed in the playground. Mr. Yendell considered that the Board would not be justified in going to the expense and no motion was brought forward on the subject". Nine years later, in 1899, the matter had still not been settled.[157]

Such conditions were unlikely to produce either good schools or well-qualified teachers. Elsing, a small village in mid-Norfolk, saw

I

four principal teachers come and go during the school year 1894–5. The reasons for this were stated in the log book: 13 August, 1894: "Last night Board meeting held. Ordered to keep the school open no matter how few present. This morning three children present, the children of the Clerk to the Board." On the charge of the actions of the board being regarded by the people as "acts of undiluted tyranny", the chairman, the Rev. J. J. Valpy wrote in the log book a vituperative three-page piece on the failings of the master. The last of these teachers in that year remarked in the log book:

"It does not require much brain to kick a fellow that is bordering destitution. It may have been dishonest to come here so poor but as soon as Mr. Rix (School Board Clerk) found out I was not stylish enough in my domestic arrangements he knew he could insult me with impunity."[158]

The Education Department listened to protests from many aggrieved parties but were unable to move against such boards. Correspondence flowed between the Department and Runham Vauxhall, a parish which had been almost entirely swallowed up by Great Yarmouth under an Act of Parliament, confirming a Provisional Order of the Local Government Board of 1890. The part of the parish left outside the borough had some thirty inhabitants, ten ratepayers and only two children (infants) living within the parish. "Unfortunately", wrote Miller to Kekewich in April, 1890, "there is a School Board for the Parish and the Triennial Election is due on the 8th May. We have in vain endeavoured to induce the Board to meet and to obtain a Resolution in favour of Dissolution from the Ratepayers under Section 41 of the 1876 Elementary Education Act."[159] Ten years later, the Board was still in office. The anomaly of the small board remained until the passing of the 1902 Act.

FINANCIAL CONSTRAINTS

(a) District Auditor

School boards accounts, balanced twice each year in March and September, came under the scrutiny of the district auditor who, throughout the boards' existence, proved a powerful constraint to experimentation and innovation. He was employed by the Poor Law Board, audited their accounts and operated in the school boards' areas which fell within the district for poor relief. The school board paid his fees.

Section 60, Subsection 6 of the 1870 Act gave the auditor power to allow or disallow items in the accounts and to charge the school board, or any member or officer with any sum. Appeals could be made by aggrieved members to the Local Government Board; any ratepayer of the school district might attend the audit and could object to the account.

The Nottingham School Board[160] became involved in a series of decisions by the district auditor in 1889 and 1890. At one of these audits, sums of £60 and £28 10s., representing expenditure on a piano and gymnastic apparatus respectively, were disallowed on the grounds that "being the first cost, were not expenses for the annual maintenance of the school" and the School Board, a progressive one in its methods, challenged the surcharge.

One of the reasons advanced for the refusal to allow expenditure on physical apparatus was that the appliances—eight swings, horizontal trapeze, parallel bars, climbing ladders and ropes—"were, in truth and fact for amusement and recreation only". A significant and direct reference to poor law children indicated clearly the criteria adopted by the auditor:

"The School Board or School Managers do not stand in *loco parentis* as Guardians of the Poor do in respect of pauper children and were not under any legal obligation to provide for the physical and muscular development of the children attending the Board Schools."[161]

Contending that

"inasmuch as a school which does not provide for the suitable recreation of its scholars cannot be considered to have made intelligent provision for so combining play with work",

the clerk to the board remarked with heavy sarcasm that

"if the Auditor be right in his contention that any expenditure 'for amusement and recreation only' may not be allowed it would seem that to be consistent he must also disallow as illegal the whole cost of school playgrounds."[162]

Hodgson noted significantly to Kekewich on this,

"I think the tendency of opinion as to the educational effect of play will shortly lead to a change of the official view as to School Boards."[163]

More contentious was the disallowance and surcharge on two school board members, Rev. J. Hirst Hollowell and C. L. Rothera, for the purchase of "one skin covered Rocking Horse". Not only, did Hollowell maintain, was it useful in assisting "to carry out the Kindergarten spirit of giving instruction in the form of directed play" along with small tea services, dolls, balls and skipping ropes but "the article surcharged being properly modelled and skin-covered serves as an excellent model for the object lessons".[164] This seemed rather too much for even the Department. Hodgson believed that although "the contention that the Rocking Horse is an 'object'

is new and ingenious, I think £2 5s. is a heavy price for an object".
Kekewich agreed: "We must draw the line somewhere. If we passed
a Rocking Horse, I don't see why swings should not be put up in
the School Rooms or Battledore and Shuttlecock paid for or any
other game."[165]

A request by a board to allow temperance lectures to be given by
a Band of Hope Union official was treated with grave suspicion by
the Department. The nearest precedent which could be found related
to a disallowance of grants for swimming. John White remembered a
case he had dealt with himself "where some Brewer challenged the
legality of a payment made to such a lecturer by the York School
Board in 1891".[166] Miller solemnly stated that the payment for the
suggested lecturers should be advised against, "unless we also permitted pro-alcoholic lectures".[167]

Where a clerk to a board had, as at Dudley, Worcestershire,
muddled the accounts over a number of years, thus making auditing
almost impossible, the auditors exercised their powers. In July,
1888, the auditor wrote to the board, pointing out that no further
grants would be paid to them unless steps were taken for the accounts
to be kept in a satisfactory manner.[168] A full-scale investigation was
carried out by the auditor, who then admonished the board at a meeting for their laxity in supervising the clerk and for retaining his services.

> "The School Board appeared to be divided", wrote W. F. Fry the
> auditor, "on the appointment of an additional officer to keep the
> accounts punctually and accurately. In view of the triennial election now
> imminent, it was undesirable that the unsatisfactory keeping of the
> Board's accounts should be made public."[169]

Not only was expenditure on schools questioned, but the activities
of board members and permanent staff acting in their official capacities came under scrutiny. Conferences of school board clerks had
been held since 1873, but for some reason the auditor for Huddersfield decided six years later to challenge the expenses incurred by the
clerk in attending the 1879 Birmingham Conference; no other
instance had been brought previously to the Department's attention,
but here the clerk had requested the Local Government Board to do
so. Lindsell of the Department considered the conferences to be of
great value and, as in a previous instance where the auditor had disallowed the purchase of *The School Board Chronicle* by boards,
told the Local Government Board that the Conference "was almost
indispensable for the due conduct of business".[170]

Mundella recommended that "this trifling expenditure" be
allowed, although Sandford, who was no friend of the school boards,
did not favour this course.

"I doubt if the L.G.B. would sanction a charge for a Conference of Poor Law Union Clerks", he wrote to Mundella, "or that it is expedient to allow these gentlemen, however able and successful, to become as in some cases they aim at becoming, the Masters of their Boards."[171]

In 1897, the School Board Conference Act [172] provided for expenses incurred in relation to school board conferences and thus took the matter out of the auditor's hands.[173]

This did not, however, prevent the auditor from surcharging the Liverpool School Board £39 18s. in September, 1899, for consulting Counsel to prepare a Voluntary Schools (Amendment) Bill in order to modify the 1897 Voluntary Schools Act; and from surcharging four school board members £5 4s. 6d. arising out of an interview on the matter by the clerk to the board with Sir George Kekewich, Secretary of the Education Department.[174]

Apart from some modification in procedures under the District Auditors Act of 1879, the supremacy of the auditors' decisions, which were more appropriate to poor relief than to educational expenditure, continued to be unchallenged by the Department. The long-term effects of such decisions could be seen at the turn of the century in the decision of T. E. B. Cockerton, the London auditor, to disallow the board's expenditure on higher grade schools. This ultimately led to the collapse of the school board system.

(b) Fees in Schools

Undoubtedly, one of the prime causes of poor attendance was the fact that education, even after becoming compulsory in 1880, was not made free until 1891.

Sandford replied to a question from Spencer in 1881, "Do we make grants to schools which are *free*?" in the following terms:

"*Yes* to Voluntary Schools, without question. But there are not many of them. The only thing we look at in their case is whether the scholars do or do not pay more than 9d. per week.

"A fee *must* be charged in Board Schools—unless on the score of the poverty of any district, we allow a free Board School.

"There are none such—though a good many Penny Schools have been passed.

"The right of questioning the scale of fees in Board Schools is a troublesome one, but it is now imposed upon us by the interest of the Ratepayers."[175]

The earliest and fullest debate on the issues involved in establishing an equitable scale of fees involved the Norwich School Board between the years 1874 and 1881. At a meeting of the board in June, 1874, it was resolved that from the following September, subject to the consent of the Education Department, fees were to be one farthing a week in all board schools. The board, giving its reasons, pointed out that the 1870 Act fixed only the maximum payment of fees (9d.), and not a minimum, leaving to each board a discretion to prescribe a suitable fee (Section 17). In addition, a free school for children whose parents were unable to pay a farthing a week was to be built on the grounds that

> "the low wages of artisans and labourers employed in the district of Norwich as compared with the wages paid in other large towns and the exceptionally heavy rates pressing upon the city, affect the question of school fees".[176]

Naturally the Department, under Cumin's instructions, refused to sanction such a suggestion. With the return of a Conservative Administration in 1874, pledged to support the continuance of voluntary schools, a low scale of fees for board schools would hardly be allowed. As the clerk to the board wrote to the Department "the opinion is general that the higher fee is exacted, not in the interests of Public Education, but to preserve other schools from wholesome competition".[177] The Department's solution favoured a graduated fee of not less than 2d. with powers to remit in necessitous cases, as provided for in Section 17.

In March, 1875, a new school at Crooke Place was to be opened and it was decided by the board to use this as an occasion on which to test the Department's resolution on fees. On 15 February the school board fixed on a penny fee. Cumin's terse notes in reply to the board's voluminous letters were sufficient evidence of the line to be taken by the Department:

> "Their Lordships letter of the 9th inst. was sufficiently explicit on the point in question. They trust that your Board may have been able to come to a decision without any further communication from this Department."[178]

And in July, 1875,

> "The Education Department having on the 24th ult. finally refused to sanction the proposed fee of 1d. in your Board Schools, it remains for the Board to propose another fee. Should they decline to do this, their Lordships will be prepared to take such steps as the Act requires to secure the provision of the requisite school accommodation."[179]

One of the members of the school board, J. H. Tillett, who was also Liberal M.P. for Norwich and an active member of the National Education League and the Liberation Society,[180] moved:

> "that a Sub-Committee be appointed to consider the present position of the Board as opposed to the Education Department and the question

of school fees—to collect information—to take (if necessary) Counsel's opinion and to report on the subject."[181]

What followed was a sample survey of national wages, which for its date was remarkably sophisticated. (It was at this time that the Board asked the Department to define the expression "social class" as used in one of their letters.) Returns of assessment were obtained from the Poor Law Guardians, showing the gross rental of the houses in each parish and dividing them into above and below £10; then the average rental for each ward was calculated. In addition, the sub-committee enquired into the comparative wages of the working classes in Norwich and in London, Birmingham, Sheffield, Leicester and Bristol, and into some trades in Manchester, Newcastle, Leeds and Liverpool, taking particularly stonemasons, bricklayers, carpenters, tailors and labourers. The survey showed both variable need from ward to ward of the town and the comparatively low wages of artisans in the town itself.[182]

Some two years later, the Norwich Board pressed the Education Department to institute its own inquiry into the situation, as the Department had refused to receive any deputation from the town.[183] At first the Department claimed that they had no legal power to institute a special enquiry into the educational requirements of the various districts of the city.[184] It later relented, sending two senior Inspectors, H.M.I.s Mr. J. A. Stokes and Francis Synge, to take evidence and report (16 January, 1878).

Their conclusions went a long way to meet the demands of the Norwich Board. Of the seven groups of schools in the city which were surveyed, all except one were allowed to charge a 1d. fee, with only one school having a graduated fee up to 3d. Tillett, now the chairman of the board, whilst still favouring free education, indicated that the board would concur in the compromise solution suggested. Cumin told Sandon, "I do not see how the Department can do anything now but endorse the conclusions of the Report".[185] Sandon agreed, stating that "our principle as to School Board fees has thus been fully maintained. I should at once allow their scale of fees".[186]

Special categories of children were treated more sympathetically by the Department. As to the suggestion of a lower scale of fees for children under seven than for those over that age, made by the clerk to the Wolverhampton Board, Forster wrote to Ripon:

"This is an important case. We ought not to refuse our consent to a scale of fees under eight without good reason but I think we should both refuse to sanction discouragement to proficiency and an encouragement of one of the greatest practical evils with which School Boards will have to deal, viz: the non-attendance of the elder children."[187]

Throughout the period, the Department refused school boards' requests for the establishment of free schools, as at Norwich and Hull,[188] stipulating rather a remission of fees under Section 17 of the Act. Further complications arose, however, with the repeal of the troublesome Section 25 of the 1870 Act, when it was replaced by Section 10 of the 1876 Act. The latter transferred the responsibility from school boards to the Guardians of the parish to pay up to 3d. a week for the children whose parents, not being paupers, were unable to afford the fees.[189]

Although many boards resolved to continue to remit the fees in their own schools, for the rest it was left to the discretion of the Guardians whether or not to pay the fees of parents who applied. At Maidstone, which had no board schools of its own, several parents were refused payment by the Guardians, with the result that a number of children were absent from school. The clerk to the school board selected an unemployed journeyman printer with two children to bring before the magistrates as a test case; the magistrates adjourned the case and referred the matter back to the board, who sent the correspondence on to the Guardians but without success. With considerable reluctance the magistrate convicted, "but," wrote the clerk to the Department, "gave me to understand that they thought Anderson was unable to pay the school fees".[190] Sandon, the author of the clause, remarked,

> "This is clearly a case in which we cannot interfere. It was the intention of Parliament to put the responsibility upon the Guardians of deciding respecting the ability of parents to pay school fees."[191]

A memorial from the school board to the Department in December, 1877, spelled out the anomalies of the payment of fees being a Guardian rather than a school board decision. Although the school district comprised at least half the population and rateable value of the Union, only six of the twenty-four Guardians were from the district and the magistrates of the borough were totally unrepresented.

The fortnightly meetings of the Guardians were at the Union workhouse some two miles from the town hall, which made for difficulties of access. It was left to the discretion of the relieving officer whether the case was brought before the Guardians. Proceedings by the Guardians were slow, taking on an average four to six weeks before a favourable decision was implemented. The board had learned from the school attendance officer that during November, 1877, no fewer than 111 children were absent from school from such causes, although there was no shortage of accommodation in the schools. There was some truth in the memorialists' complaint,

"That the objects of the Boards of Guardians and of the School Boards are completely diverse, the first desire of the Boards of Guardians being to save the rates whilst the education of children is the work and object of a School Board."[192]

What was equally pernicious was the provision of Section 3 of the 1870 Act. This laid down the conditions under which relief was to be given, and was made more explicit by Section 40 of the 1876 Act. This later Act forbade relief to be given by Guardians to the parent of any child above five who had not reached Standard Three of the Code of that year, and made it a condition that the child was in attendance at a public elementary school.

During the drafting of the 1880 Act, Earl Spencer wrote to T. J. Dodson of the Local Government Board which supervised the work of Boards of Guardians:

"The enclosed Memo will explain the alteration which will be proposed in the Education Bill which we want to introduce. It seems hard that when once a child has earned either by his attainments or attendance the right to his full-time for labour he should be driven back in order that his father may receive outdoor relief in an emergency."[193]

Dodson agreed with Spencer that the proposed amendment was expedient; this referred to Section 5 of the Act, which finally divorced out-door relief from school attainment.

A growing number of people interested in education joined in the debate on the desirability or otherwise of free education after 1870, as a third and necessary element alongside the universal and compulsory aspects of schooling.[194] A school board member for Leyton, Essex, wrote to Mundella in 1881:

"The feeling is largely extending in the towns even among Conservatives that the education up to the Third Standard should be made free as well as compulsory. Cannot the present Liberal Government carry a measure to effect this desirable result? It would be regarded by all Members of School Boards as a perfect Godsend owing to the difficulty of getting many children of the poor into the schools."[195]

Mundella, whose approach to this question at the time was a cautious one,[196] expressed sympathy with the sentiments of the writer in a Minute on the Department file: "It is becoming, in my general opinion—I am afraid—that unless this last *case* is *met* somehow—the feeling will spread."[197] Politically, however, it would have been an inexpedient move and economically an irresponsible one. Such details did not prevent Chamberlain from taking the matter up as part of his 1885 election theme.

Chamberlain asked Mundella to meet him to discuss future tactics. "We shall sweep the country with Free Education and Allotments— The Tories will be smashed and the Whigs will be extinguished."[198] Mundella, campaigning in London, was less optimistic. He cautioned Chamberlain:

> "It is a fact that some of my best supporters who are radical on other questions are not yet convinced about *'Free Schools'*—And I shall have to put all my powers of reasoning and persuasion to satisfy them. The truth of the matter is only just beginning to be thought over and discussed and the rate payers in the large towns are so poor just now that they are frightened out of their wits at the prospect of increased demands for education.
>
> "I have seen some of the candidates in the London School Board who are advocates of Free Education. I am told that *not one of them* not even our friend Lyulph Stanley, has had the courage to mention it in their addresses. What is true of London is certainly true of Sheffield and many other large towns. Do you wonder therefore that the less advanced section of our party are somewhat shy of the proposal?"[199]

Mundella's assessment proved correct. A Conservative Government was returned and except for two short breaks, remained in office for the next seven years. Meanwhile, Chamberlain left the Liberals in the following year after the Home Rule split, and the impetus of the free education campaign faltered, not to be regained for another four years until the Free Education Act of 1891 became operative.

REFERENCES

1 R. Fulford, *Samuel Whitbread—a Study in Opposition* (1967), p. 180.
2 Fox to Whitbread, 18 October, 1814, Whitbread MSS., Acc 2483, WI/3734.
3 Henry Peter, Baron Broughton and Vaux (1778–1868), M.P. for Camelford 1810–12, for Winchelsea 1815–30. Created Baron and appointed Lord Chancellor in 1830. Established the Society for the Diffusion of Useful Knowledge 1825 and the University of London, 1828.
4 Chester F. New, *The Life of Lord Brougham to 1830* (1961), pp. 328–31. Brougham wrote bitterly after the Bill's failure "I do most earnestly deprecate those men taking the field now, against education when they said so little before. Can any man oppose this who made hardly any resistance to the same sum raised for new churches." 31 July, 1820. Brougham to W. Smith, M.P. Brougham MSS. (University College, London).
5 Russell to Brougham, 10 April, 1837, Brougham MSS. Of this period, G. M. Young has written, "There was the Imperial Government, there were the boroughs. But between Whitehall and the people at large there were, except for the Poor Law Unions, no administrative links or gradations." G. M. Young, *Portrait of an Age; Early Victorian England, 1830–1865* Vol. 1. (1934), p. 465.
6 Brougham to M. Mornier, 29 March, 1837, Brougham MSS.

7 Russell to Brougham, 15 August, 1837, Brougham MSS.

8 *Ibid.*, 2 October, 1837.
Melbourne, then Prime Minister, made difficulties for the Bill. His biographer has written: "Not only did he disbelieve in educational schemes as such but he rightly thought that they always raised trouble with the Church." Lord David Cecil, *Lord M.* (1954), p. 344.

9 R. E. Leader, *Life and Letters of John Arthur Roebuck* (1897). p. 341.

10 Roebuck to Brougham, 9 August, 1837, Brougham MSS.

11 J. T. Ward, *op. cit.*, pp. 194–5.

12 The Second Report of the Commission on the Employment of Children, Trades and Manufacturers, 1834, BPP. XIII, had demonstrated the lack of educational facilities for such children. See sections 15–18, and 20–22.

13 J. L. and B. Hammond, *The Age of the Chartists, 1832–1854* (1930), p. 186.

14 Graham to Peel, 13 April, 1843. Peel MSS., B.M. Add. MS. 40448 f. 269.
See also J. T. Ward, "A Lost Opportunity in Education: 1843" in *Researches and Studies*, No. 20, October, 1959, pp. 40–51.

15 W. L. Burn, *op. cit.*, pp. 217–8.
An alternative theory put forward to account for the lull in reform between the years 1850–60 was that of "the anodyne of prosperity in all ranks of society" during this decade. G. Kitson Clark, *The Making of Victorian England* (1962), p. 45.

16 An examination of those problems can be found in "Social Research and Social Policy", O. R. McGregor in *British Journal of Sociology*, Vol. 3, No. 2, June, 1957, pp. 146–57.

17 Voluntaryists were aware of the consequences of a national system of education from the then recent events in New South Wales, Australia. E. J. Payne, "The Management of Schools in New South Wales (1848–1866). Local Initiative Suppressed" in *The Journal of Educational Administration*, Vol. 5, No. 1, May, 1968, pp. 69–85.
For the position of managers in Ireland at this time, an interesting account is to be found in D. H. Akenson, *The Irish Education Experiment. The National System of Education in the Nineteenth Century* (1970), pp. 151–5.

18 F. Adams, *History of the Elementary School Contest in England* (1882), p. 157.

19 W. J. Fox (1786–1864). Bank clerk, Norwich, became a priest in 1817. Later, a Radical orator, active in Anti-Corn Law League matters. M.P. for Oldham, 1847–52 and again from 1853 onwards. For an account of his educational work, see R. and E. Garnett, *The Life of W. J. Fox: Public Teacher and Social Reformer* (1910), pp. 300–6.

20 J. Beldam, *A Letter to the Rt. Hon. Lord John Russell on National Education* (1850), p. 5.

21 T. S. Ashton, *Economic and Social Investigations in Manchester, 1833–1933* (1934), p. 64.

22 Minutes of Evidence taken before the Select Committee on Manchester and Salford Education, BPP. 1852 XI. Rev. C. Richson, Q. 633, 29 April, 1852, and W. Entwhistle, Q. 676, 3 May, 1852.

23 A full account of the movement is contained in S. E. Maltby, *Manchester and the Movement for National Elementary Education, 1800-1870* (1918), Ch. 7, pp. 82–94.

24 For the American influence on the Manchester movement see D. K. Jones, "Lancashire, The American Common School and the Religious Problem in British Education in the 19th Century" in *British Journal of Educational Studies*, Vol. XV, No. 3, October, 1967, pp. 292–306, and

P. N. Farrar, "Massachusetts and the Movement for National Elementary Education in England and Wales in the 19th Century", *ibid.*, Vol. XIV, No. 1, November, 1965. Also, correspondence between Temple and Chamberlain on the Massachusetts Schools, February to March, 1867. Chamberlain MSS., Domestic Politics III, Education, 1867–1900 (Birmingham University Library).

25 Edwin Waugh's Journal, 6 October, 1847–13 May, 1851, Lancashire Public Schools Association MSS. F.379 4272 L.1. (Manchester Central Library, Archive Department).

26 Richson dismissed this proposal on the grounds that "there are town councils to whom this would no doubt be acceptable, but there are others who consider their duties already so onerous that the prospect of an additional burthen would probably be a very serious impediment to the introduction of the proposed measure". Rev. C. Richson, *Education: the Government Measure shown to be susceptible of Improvement on its own Principles* (1853), p. 8.

27 J. B. Conacher, *The Aberdeen Coalition, 1852–1855, A Study in Mid-Nineteenth Century Politics* (1968), p. 111.

28 *Hansard*, Vol. CXXV, 3rd Series, House of Commons, 4 April, 1853, Col. 552.

29 Minutes of L.P.S.A., 1851–62, 6 June, 1853, *supra*.

30 8th Annual Report of L.P.S.A., n.d., but 1855, *ibid.*

31 Cobden to Vaughan, 23 May, 1857, Cobden MSS., B.M. Add. MS. 43669, f. 147.

32 Lord John Russell, Earl Russell 1861, (1792–1878), Prime Minister 1846–52, 1865–6. Introduced first Reform Bill. Leader of the Whigs under Melbourne, 1834, Colonial Secretary 1839, Foreign Secretary 1852, President of the Council 1854. *D.N.B.*

33 Memorandum 18 October, 1854. Russell MSS. 30/22/11/E. (Public Record Office).

34 Sir John Somerset Pakington, 1st Lord Hampton (1799–1880). M.P. for Droitwich, 1837–74. Baronet 1846. Secretary for War and Colonies under Derby 1852. Twice First Lord of the Admiralty under Derby in 1858 and 1866, Secretary for War in Disraeli's Ministry 1867–8, Baron Hampton, 1874.

35 R. Blake. *Disraeli*, (1966), p. 539.
Sir Henry Ponsonby, Private Secretary to Queen Victoria, recorded the following conversation which took place between the Queen and Disraeli at Osborne in February, 1874, on the formation of the new Government: "The Queen seemed satisfied with Mr. Disraeli's proposed Cabinet. 'What about Sir J. Pakington?' she asked. 'Providence has interposed,' replied Disraeli thankfully. (He was thrown out of Parliament.) 'But he is to be made a Peer'." Memorandum, 17 February, 1874. A. Ponsonby, *Henry Ponsonby, Queen Victoria's Private Secretary* (1942), p. 174.

36 14th Earl of Derby to Russell, 24 December, 1853, Brougham MSS.

37 H. Chester to Russell, 19 September, 1854, Russell MSS., 30/22/11/E (P.R.O.).

38 Pakington to Disraeli, 7 January, 1855, Hughenden MSS., Box 107/XX/P/18.

39 Pakington to Cobden, 12 January, 1855, Cobden MSS., B.M. Add. MS. 43669, f.3. In his reply, Cobden warned Pakington that "no educational measure will work which does not separate dogmatic religious teaching so far from secular instruction as to allow the rates to be devoted solely to the payment for the latter", *ibid.*, 13 January, 1855, f.8.

40 "Diaries of un-named persons for 1856" (but definitely Pakington's), Hampton MSS., Ref: 705:349 BA 3835/2 (Worcestershire R.O.).
41 Russell to Aberdeen, 8 and 27 January, 1855, Russell MSS., 30/22/12A. Russell to Aberdeen, 23 January, 1855, Aberdeen MSS., B.M. Add MS. 43068, f. 274–9.
42 Pakington noted in his Diary for 26 January, 1855: "H. of C. Ld. John Russell made explanation much to his discredit: he had unseated his colleagues."
43 Pakington to Disraeli, 26 January, 1855, Hughenden MSS., Box 107/XX/P/30.
44 Blandford to Pakington, 24 January, 1855, Hampton MSS., Political Correspondence Education Bill, 1854–5. 705:349 BA 4752, M/P/54 (Worcestershire R.O.).
45 Colquhon to Pakington, 20 January, 1855, *ibid.*, M/P/49.
46 Hodgson to Pakington, 25 January, 1855, *ibid.*, M/P/61.
47 Bright to Pakington, 1 February, 1855, Hampton MSS. Political Correspondence Education Bill 1854–5. 705:349 BA 4732. M/P/58 (Worcestershire R.O.).
48 Brougham commented on this decision after a conversation with Palmerston that "the Country is more insane upon the subject than even the House". Brougham to unknown correspondent. 19 February, 1855, Brougham MSS.
49 Diary, 2 May, 1855, Hampton MSS.
50 Diary, 11 June, 1855, *ibid.*
51 Pakington to Brougham, 8 March, 1856, Brougham MSS.
52 Russell's original draft for the Resolutions, dated March, 1856, named twenty-five divisions. Russell MSS. 30/22/13B.
53 *Ibid.*
54 Pakington to Russell, 25 March, 1856, Hampton MSS. M/P/59.
55 Russell to Pakington, 26 March, 1856, Hampton MSS. M/P/60.
56 A witness of the Debate which ended in a heavy defeat for Russell (260 votes to 158) said of Henley: "He is unquestionably the artful and true exponent of British prejudice; and the leader of the objective or Tory as opposed to the subjective or Whig School." Lord R. Grosvenor to Russell, 12 March, 1856, Russell MSS. 30/22/13B.
   One of Henley's arguments against the Bill was that it would involve the combination of parishes into district committees "which would sever the clergyman of those parishes from the school. They could not have four clergymen, perhaps with different views on education, combining in a district committee for the management of a school." (Col. 783). For details of the full Debate, *Hansard*, Vol. CXLI, 3rd Series, House of Commons, Cols. 779–959, 10–11 April, 1856.
57 Diary, 10–11 April, 1856, Hampton MSS.
58 *Hansard*, 3rd Series, Vol. XXVII, Col. 685.
59 Northcote to Pakington, Christmas Day, 1856, Iddesleigh MSS., B.M. Add. MS. 50022, f. 248.
60 Pakington to Cobden, 9 December, 1856, Cobden MSS., B.M. Add. MS. 43669, f. 70.
61 Report of the Commission on the state of popular education in England, 1861, Vol. 1, Chapter 6, p. 302, BPP 1861, XXI, Pt. 1.
62 The charges made against workhouse schools were fair but arose out of the special nature and quality of management required of those participating in the work. See Transactions for October, 1854, in Norwich Boys' Home and Workhouse School Committee Minute Book, 1847–55. MS. 4356 (Norfolk and Norwich R.O.).

63 Nassau Senior, one of the members of the Commission, suggested the managers of rate-supported schools should consist of all ministers of religion, if rated; the Inspector who would preside over the district whether ratepayer or not; one inhabitant elected by the ratepayers; one inhabitant appointed by Petty Sessions or Borough Magistrates; and one inhabitant to be appointed by the Inspector. *Suggestions on Popular Education* (1861), pp. 57–8.

He also suggested to Brougham for further investigation a number of issues not taken up by the Commission, including the length of the school day and the position of children in the unregulated trades. 1 July, 1861. Brougham MSS.

64 W. F. Connell, *The Educational Thought and Influence of Matthew Arnold* (1950), p. 110.

65 Pakington to Disraeli, 10 April, 1862, Hughenden MSS., Box 107, B/XX/P/67. Pakington however did not attempt to determine either the composition of the District Boards or their area.

66 Select Committee appointed to enquire into the Constitution of the Committee of Council on Education. BPP 1865, VI and 1866, VII.

67 In the General Election, July 1865, Palmerston was re-elected with a Whig-Liberal majority. Russell succeeded on Palmerston's death in October, and in June 1866, a fortnight before the Select Committee met for the last time, Lord Derby replaced him at the head of a Conservative Administration.

68 Pakington to Disraeli, 15 February, 1868, Hughendon MSS., Box 107, BXX/P/93.

69 See the draft in Chamberlain's own hand amongst his papers. The title is given as "National Society for the Promotion of Universal Compulsory Education" and noted "Education 1867—Beginning of *National* Educational League. Programme by J. C." Chamberlain MSS., JC 6/3/2/24.

70 M. Cowling, *1867, Disraeli, Gladstone and Revolution: The Passing of the Second Reform Bill* (1967), p. 358.

71 He expressed his disappointment at the provisions contained in the 1870 Bill. It was not comprehensive enough and an opportunity to reorganize the Education Department was lost. Pakington spoke for many when he stated "I do not think any man understands the constitution of the present Department." *Hansard*, Vol. CIC, 3rd Series, House of Commons, Col. 483, 17 February, 1870.

Pakington was never popular with his own party. See W. Jeans, *Parliamentary Reminiscences, 1863–1886*, (1912), pp. 43–4. For a kindlier and more objective assessment of Pakington's character and achievements, see H. W. Lucy, *Men and Manner in Parliament* (1919), pp. 232–3.

72 The school board system was based on the American pattern which had long been in existence. Reformers from Roebuck onwards had held it up as a model to be copied. W. H. G. Armytage, *The American Influence on English Education* (1967), p. 17. It has been shown recently in an astringent study that, in the State of Massachusetts at least, disillusion with the system began to set in in the 1860's, just as it was about to be established in England. M. B. Katz, *The Irony of Early School Reform in Mid 19th Century Massachusetts* (1968), p. 213 ff.

73 One of the few exceptions to this rule seems to have been policemen. No authoritative decision was taken by the Education Department on their eligibility to vote. In London, they were not refused voting papers, but at Birmingham, the chief superintendent issued an order to the following effect: "The police are not eligible to vote for a School Board; if they do,

they are liable to a penalty of £10". T. Preston, *The School Board Guide and Teachers' Manual* (1871), p. 171.

74 A number of criticisms were directed at this method. An Inspector commented after thirteen years' experience: "The annual election of a few members would secure a certain number of gentlemen used to the work being always upon the board, whereas now, when entirely new blood is imported into the work, much time is lost, while the various members are acquiring a knowledge of the ordinary routine work". Report of Mr. F. Wilkinson for 1883. BPP. 1884 XXIV, p. 454.

75 Town Clerk to Cumin, 21 February, 1872, Liverpool, Ed.16/166 (P.R.O.). A similar complaint had been received from Wolverhampton.

76 *Birmingham Daily Post*, 5 November, 1874.

76a Lumley to Sandford, 26 October, 1874. Salford, Ed. 16/185 (P.R.O.). All Ed. 16 School Board files are deposited at the Public Record Office.

77 Within a year of this concession, no fewer than 800 casual vacancies had been filled in this manner. Committee of Council on Education. Reports for 1877. BPP. 1878 XXVIII, p. xxiii.

78 N. Gibbs to J. White, 10 March, 1894. Boston, Ed. 16/196.

79 *Leyton Express and Independent*, 27 June, 1885.

80 Miller to Cumin, 26 January, 1885. Walthamstow, Ed. 16/77. For the background to the case, see *Walthamstow Express*, 17 January, 1885.

81 At Bolton, Lancashire, eleven of the thirteen members refused to serve with another member, Mr. J. Bleakley, who had continually obstructed business. The Department were prepared, under S.32 surprisingly, to re-appoint all the 11 members under a new Board. Hart Dyke to Kekewich, 21 June, 1892. Bolton Ed. 16/160.

The incredible scenes which occurred at meetings of the Bolton School Board, culminating in Bleakley's appeal to the Commons can be followed in the *Bolton Chronicle* and *Bolton Weekly Guardian*, 12 and 19 March and 20 May, 1892.

The Bolton case was used as a precedent for others: at Scarborough, Yorkshire, in February 1893, Mr. Enderby Jackson, who headed the poll, was the only member not renominated by the Department because of alleged dishonesty in Board transactions. Trench to Gibbs, 6 March, 1893. Scarborough, Ed. 16/338. *Scarborough Mercury*, 12 February, 1893.

82 Miller to Sandford, 2 July, 1885, Low Leyton. Ed. 16/80.

83 Mundella to J. Gulson, Chairman, 14 January, 1881. Coventry, Ed. 16/318.

84 "I warned them of the necessity of keeping up a boys' school in the locality and of the risks they ran by not giving it proper support", wrote H.M.I. Mr. J. A. Willis in his Report for 1882. BBP. 1883, XXV, p. 470.

85 Miller to Cumin, 22 January, 1885; Cumin to Miller, 27 February, 1885; Campbell to Cumin, 28 February, 1885. Willesden, Ed. 16/217.

86 F. C. Hodgson to Kekewich, 24 September, 1894. Blackburn, Ed. 16/157.

87 It should also be noted that with great caution the Department had always refused to answer general questions relating to the various codes and hypothetical questions relating to possible future action of school boards. F. T. Palgrave to Sandford, 21 April, 1880, Chesterfield, Ed. 16/41.

88 Rooper's Report, 10 December, 1886, Idle School Board, Ed. 16/357, Pt. 2.

89 R. G. Tatton, *op. cit.*, p. xlvii.

90 Rooper's Report, 3 January, 1887, *supra*.

91 Miller to Lindsell, 7 January, 1887, *ibid*.

92 An illustration of this difficulty is provided in the 1873 Birmingham School Board elections. "A great number of voting papers were made invalid. The voter in many cases had begun to make a cross and then wrote

a figure over it, so that the number intended could not be ascertained. This was no doubt the result of the mode of marking the papers at the municipal elections at which crosses and not figures are placed opposite the names of the candidates." *Birmingham Morning Post*, 19 November, 1873.

About 20 years later this confusion still existed in Birmingham. Letter from Vicar of Edgbaston to Education Department, 12 November, 1891, Ed. 9/22.

93   Charles Dilke was responsible for an amendment in the Commons on 4 July, 1870, which brought this about. *Hansard*, 3rd Series, Vol. CCII, House of Commons, 1870, Cols. 1399–1414 and R. Jenkins, *Sir Charles Dilke: a Victorian Tragedy* (1958), p. 8.

W. E. Forster wrote to Lord Ripon on the previous day, "I am inclined to think the House certainly dislikes the Town Councils and presumably prefers the Minority vote, but it is a great change to make in a hurry". 3 July, 1870, Ripon MSS., B.M. Add. MS. 43536, f. 245.

94   Francis Adams wrote rather unkindly upon Lord Sandon's succession to the Education Office "Whitehall was crowded by clerical wire-pullers and friars of all colours and the Department was interviewed and memorialized without cessation. A clerical minority unable to carry its policy on a School Board had nothing to do in order to frustrate the majority but to hold a private meeting, and pass resolutions and forward them to the Department. The wishes of the representatives of the ratepayers were coolly ignored." Adams, *op. cit.*, p. 312.

95   Cumin to Sandford, 12 March, 1874, Cannock, Ed. 16/265.

96   28 March, 1874, Cannock, Ed. 16/265.

97   This did not lead to its automatic acceptance. At Rotherham, by means of a well organized opposition, the Town Council's proposals to the Department in 1872 for a Board did not bear fruit until 1875. Rotherham, Ed. 16/369. *Sheffield and Rotherham Independent*, 18 and 22 March, 1875, and *Rotherham and Masbro' Advertiser*, 20 March, 1875.

98   Richmond to Sandon and Sandon to Richmond, 8 April, 1875. Winchester, Ed. 16/97.

99   Kekewich to Gorst, 29 July, 1895. Heywood, Ed. 16/139.

100   Heywood Education Assn. to Gorst, 17 February, 1897, *ibid.*

101   This in fact was not true. Forster had quashed an order at Rawdon, Yorkshire, in 1872 as had Hart-Dyke at Chadderton, Lancashire, in 1891. J. Knott to A. H. D. Acland, 28 August, 1892. Chadderton, Ed. 16/148.

102   Memo. on the Heywood Case between July 1895 and 18 February, 1897, E. K. C. Chambers, February 1897. Heywood, *supra*.

Acland had little sympathy with recalcitrant town councils. Writing to his father of the plight of the "labouring people" in 1888, he attacked the ruling elements in town councils, who "have no belief that you can gradually educate even very ignorant people by making them feel their responsibility". . . . A. H. D. Acland to Sir T. D. Acland, 4 November, 1888, 51/12/1, (Exeter City R.O.).

103   Stockport School Board. General Report from 1 December, 1870, to 1 November, 1873, p. 3.

104   Hamilton to Sandford, 5 July, 1879. Stockport, Ed. 16/26.

105   Stockport School Board, Adjourned Meeting Resolutions 14 July, 1879. Stockport, *supra*. Committee of Council on Education, Report for 1879. Stockport School Board: Reasons for Assent to Dissolution, BPP. 1880 XXII, p. 94.

106   S. Buckley, Town Clerk to Education Department, 3 September, 1879. Stalybridge, Ed. 16/22.

107 Petition of Stalybridge Reform Club, 25 November, 1879. Stalybridge, Ed. 16/22.

Serious disturbances on such occasions were always a real possibility. The Clerk to the West Ham School Board wrote to the Department on 6 March, 1871, before the elections for the first Board: "I have reason to apprehend, both from the Class of Electors, and from the precedents of neighbouring school districts, that the proceedings will be of somewhat an uproarious nature and I think that it is highly desirable for all parties concerned that there should be a strong force of Police at the various polling places." Cumin visited the Home Office after receiving this letter and "a sufficient force of Police" was provided for the occasion. Cumin to Forster, 7 March, 1871. West Ham Ed. 16/83.

108 Memorandum 25 November, 1879, Stalybridge, *ibid.*

109 Hamilton to Sandford, 5 December, 1879, *ibid.* There would have been no difficulty, however, as the Charity Commissioner could have nominated another body, e.g. The Official Trustees of Charities, with the administration of the trust in the hands of the school attendance committee of the borough.

110 Hodgson to Cumin, 24 August, 1889, Macclesfield, Ed. 16/20.

111 *Macclesfield Courier and Herald*, 17 August, 1889.

112 Cumin to Hodgson, 29 August, 1889, Macclesfield, *supra.*

113 As at Sunderland, Swansea, Rochdale and Birmingham, where a *mandamus* was granted against the authority in each case. *The Education Acts—Owen's Manual*, 12th edn (1876), pp. 161–2.

114 See P. W. Musgrave, *Society and Education in England since 1800* (1968), p. 68.

115 L. Whittle, Clerk to the School Board to Education Department, 3 March, 1902, Warrington, Ed. 16/189.

116 *Cross Commission*, Final Report, Chapter III, School Management, p. 69.

117 S. Booth to Education Department, 6 February, 1886, Liverpool, Ed. 16/169.

118 10 May, 1873, Newcastle-under-Lyme, Ed. 16/262.

119 Sandford to School Board, 25 May, 1873, Newcastle-under-Lyme, Ed. 16/262.

By 1878, the Department's attitude had shifted more towards the boards' point of view. A meeting of school board and voluntary managers at Ordsall, near East Retford, Nottinghamshire, in October, 1878, under the chairmanship of an H.M.I., agreed not to allow pupils to enter schools until after the Annual Examination. "I think", wrote Cumin to Sandford, "the Board should be supported in this case. But the case might, if it were taken up by some M.P., become notorious. Still, I should risk it". 26 November, 1878, East Retford, Ed. 16/240.

120 Blandford to Sandford, 29 April, 1879, Derby, Ed. 16/44. See also *Derbyshire Advertiser and Journal*, 25 April, 1879.

121 C. Bell, Clerk to the Board to Education Department, 13 December, 1876. Luton, Ed. 16/3.

122 J. White to Cumin, 20 December, 1876; Cumin to Sandford, 21 December, 1876, *ibid.*

123 George William, 4th Baron Lyttelton of Frankley (1817–76), Gladstone's brother-in-law. Principal, Queen's College, Birmingham, 1845. Member of Public Schools Inquiry Commission 1861. He reluctantly accepted the post of Chief Commissioner in 1869 to administer the Endowed Schools Act of that year (see correspondence with Gladstone on this point 15 and 17 June, 1869. Gladstone MSS., B.M. Add. MS. 44240, f. 97–9). Subject to fits of melancholia, Lyttelton committed suicide in 1876.

K

124   Nathaniel Woodard held views similar to those of Denison in the field of secondary education. Woodard anticipated that the coming of State intervention would lead to unbridled denominationalism. He hoped to restore the position of the Church in education by establishing a system of moderately-feed Church schools; Lancing, Hurstpierpoint and later Ardingly were the outcome. Sir J. Otter, *Life of Nathaniel Woodard* (1925). For an evaluation of Woodard's achievement see B. Heeney, *Mission to the Middle Classes: The Woodard Schools, 1848–1891* (1969), Ch. 7, pp. 182–7.

125   G. A. Denison to Lyttelton, 30 July, 1875, Hagley MSS. Unclassified Correspondence, f. 57 (Worcestershire R.O.).

126   J. Thompson, Chairman, Stanhope School Board to Education Department, 27 September, 1878. Stanhope Parish E.P. St. 40 (Durham C.R.O.).

127   One grievance voiced by voluntary school managers was the high cost of school board administration. In London in 1894, the salaries of the officers of the School Board was £59,629 3s. 4d. with 390,000 in attendance. "The voluntary school managers do the same work for their 177,000 scholars without receiving one penny of public money or remuneration for their services." Rev. W. F. Brown, *Our School Boards. A Contrast between the Expenditure of Board Schools and Voluntary Schools* (1895), p. 6.

128   Bradford, Ed. 16/357.

129   Managers of St. Stephen's School, Hull, to Education Department, 10 August, 1875. Hull, Ed. 16/333.

130   Carlisle, Ed. 16/37. Forster had agreed in an earlier instance that even local Inspectors appointed by a board would be unable to enter voluntary schools in order to verify returns unless with the previous permission of the school managers. Forster to Sandford, 22 March, 1871, Nottingham Ed. 16/243.

131   John T. Norwich to W. H. Cozens-Hardy, Clerk to the Board, 19 and 24 March, 1876. Norwich, Ed. 16/226.

132   25 January, 1871, Gateshead, Ed. 16/68.

133   T. R. Walrond to P. McDonnell, 14 December, 1895, Salisbury MSS. (Christ Church, Oxford).

134   A fuller account is given in J. Dyer, F. Stygall and J. Dony, *The Story of Luton* (1964), pp. 154–6.

135   White to Cumin, 20 December, 1875. Luton, Ed. 16/3.

136   J. F. Ede, *History of Wednesbury*, (1962), p. 350.

137   *School Board Chronicle*, 14 June, 1890.

138   Willesden, Ed. 16/217. Hodgson, commenting on the case some years later, used it to illustrate the awkward position the Department sometimes found itself in. Here, it would have had to establish a Board of outsiders to establish an unnecessary school, while the Department refused annual grant to the school that was full and popular on the ground that *it* was unnecessary. Hodgson to Kekewich, 29 April, 1894. Blackburn, Ed. 16/157.

139   H. Shortt, *City of Salisbury* (1957), pp. 112–13.

140   Result of Election, Salisbury School Board, 1899.

Churchmen		Voluntaryists	
C. H. Radcliffe, Solicitor	2225	J. Phillips, Baker	2365
E. M. Thwaites, Clergyman	2147	H. Brown, Bookseller	2249
W. M. Hannick, Gentleman	2008	J. Saunders, House Painter	1620
E. F. Pye-Smith, Solicitor	1381		

School Board of Salisbury Minute Book, 1888–93, 20 February, 1889 (Wiltshire R.O.).

141   Dr. Cruickshank has claimed that the challenge of the Sisterhood, both at Salisbury and York, was greatly exaggerated by the opponents of de-

nominational schools. M. Cruickshank, *Church and State in English Education* (1963), p. 49.

142 Bishop of Salisbury to Chairman of School Board, 25 June, 1889. School Board of Salisbury Minute Book, 1888–93 (Wiltshire R.O.).

143 Memorial of Ratepayers of the City of Salisbury to Education Department, June 1889. Salisbury, Ed. 16/322.

144 This was with reference to the Rothwell School Board, Northamptonshire. See *School Board Chronicle*, 28 November, 1889.

145 John Sarum, Bishop of Salisbury to Mundella, 28 November, 1889. Mundella MSS., Box 9, (Sheffield University Library).

146 Hart-Dyke to Cranbrook, 18 October, 1889, Cranbrook MSS., HA 43. T 501/63 (Ipswich and E. Suffolk R.O.).

147 1861–1931. Trained at Borough Road. School teacher at Exeter, Huddersfield and Bristol. M.P. 1900–24. Vice-President of the N.U.T., 1895. Editor of *The Schoolmaster* 1892–7. J. E. Roscoe, *Dictionary of Educationists* (1913), p. 82.

148 *The School Board System in the Villages* (1895), pp. 8–9.

149 William Rathbone to W. H. Smith, 2 March, 1874. Hambleden MSS. PS 4/18 (W. H. Smith and Son).

150 *National Education League on the Working and Defects of the Elementary Education Act* (1871), pp. 6–7. National Education League Papers 1869–75. 68340 (Birmingham City Reference Library).
John Morley, then Editor of the *Fortnightly*, wrote scathingly of the predominance of the clergy on rural boards: "It is precisely in these districts that our present educational policy takes an important department of the local affairs out of the hands of all but the clergy (for as a rule the lay managers are dummies) and so there is a double loss. Not only does the administration of an enterprise largely by means of government grants lose the wholesome supervision of a miscellaneously-composed body of laymen. The laymen lose one of the very few fields of public co-operation open to them." J. Morley, *The Struggle for National Education* (1873), p. 43.

151 In 1891 there was a population of 149. *Kelly's Directory, North Yorkshire* (1893).

152 Carlton Husthwaite, School Board Minute Book, 1884–97. 6 December, 1890. 375 SB/BD (North Riding C.R.O.).

153 Rev. W. M. Blandford to Education Department, 24 July, 1888. Ed. 9/22. "Country parishes seldom contain the elements of a board that would be at once willing and able to enforce attendance of children at school. Even a powerful resident landlord might shrink from the novel and odious task of imposing penalties on his neighbours for not sending their children to school, and it is a duty which would certainly not be readily undertaken by one clergyman in a thousand." Report of H.M.I. Mr. J. Bowstead for 1871, BPP. 1872 XXII, pp. 45–6.

154 Rev. G. H. Aitken to the Bishop of Winchester, 23 May, 1902, Davidson MSS. (Lambeth Palace Library).

155 G. Christian (ed.), *James Hawker's Journal. A Victorian Poacher* (1961), p. 93.
Elected in 1893 under the occupation of "Shoe Hand", Hawker rose from 4th in the Poll to 2nd for his second term in office. Although a regular attender at Board meetings, he is recorded as having spoken once only— in support of a motion to pay pupil-teachers a 10s. grant earned by them at Annual Inspections. Oadby School Board, Minute Books 1887–99, 7 March, 1895. E/MB/A/241/1. (Leicestershire C.R.O.).

156 L. M. Springall, *Labouring Life in Norfolk Villages 1834–1914* (1936), p. 106.

157   Bratton Fleming School Board, Minute Book, 1884–1903, 5 May and 2 October, 1890. 849C. (Devon R.O.).

158   Elsing School Board, Log Book 1877–1900. 14 August and 18 December, 1894, 30 May, 1895 (Norfolk and Norwich R.O.).
An account of the effects of the changeover from a rural parochial school to school board management is given in M. K. Ashby, *The Country School. Its Practice and Problems* (1929), p. 50.

159   Miller to Kekewich, 7 April, 1891. Great Yarmouth. Ed. 16/224.

160   For background to the activities of the Board, see D. Gray, *Nottingham, from Settlement to City* (1953), pp. 83–4.

161   A. G. Chamberlain, District Auditor to School Board, 16 November, 1889. Nottingham Ed. 16/246.

162   W. Abel, Clerk to the School Board to Education Department, 18 November, 1889, *ibid.*

163   Hodgson to Kekewich, 25 March, 1890, *ibid.*

164   J. Hirst Hollowell to Education Department, 26 November, 1889, *ibid.*

165   Kekewich to Hodgson, 7 February, 1890. Nottingham Ed. 16/246.

166   White to Pringle, 17 November, 1892. West Ham Ed. 16/84. White added, "No doubt the West Ham Board writes in fear of the Publicans."

167   Miller to Kekewich, 10 June, 1897, *ibid.*

168   W. F. Fry, District Auditor to Dudley School Board, 3 July, 1888. Dudley Ed. 16/327.

169   Fry to Education Department, 17 January, 1889. Dudley Ed. 16/327.

170   Lindsell to A. T. Cory, 1 September, 1880. Huddersfield Ed. 16/365.

171   Sandford to Mundella, 4 September, 1880, *ibid.*

172   60 and 61 Vict. Ch. 32.

173   An Association of School Boards had been formed in October, 1893. One of the Association's first tasks had been to investigate "the difficulties which had been experienced relative to the payment by School Boards of subscriptions to the funds of the Association, and of the expense of the representatives who attended the meetings". *The School Board Gazette*, Vol. 1, No. 3, March 1899, p. 235.

174   School Board to Education Department, 8 January, 1901. Liverpool Ed. 16/170.

175   Sandford to Spencer, 21 February, 1881. Althorp MSS. In the larger cities, some did exist. The Gem Street School, under the management of the Birmingham School Board, was opened in 1888. It was designed for children who were too poor and dirty for ordinary board schools and no fees were charged. *Victoria County History—Warwickshire*, Vol. 7 (1964), p. 513.

176   Norwich School Board, Minute Book No. 2, 1874–6, 9 July, 1874 (Norfolk and Norwich R.O.).

177   E. W. R. Simpson, Clerk to the Board to Education Department, 18 February, 1875. Norwich Ed. 16/225.

178   Cumin to Norwich School Board, 30 March, 1875. Norwich School Board Minute Book, No. 2, *supra.*

179   *Ibid.*, 15 July, 1875.

180   Mr. Latham, an Assistant Commissioner for the Endowed Schools in reporting on the King Edward VI School Charities, Norwich, in June, 1877, mentioned "there is a party on the School Board led by Mr. Tillett, formerly M.P. for the borough, who if I am correctly informed are supporters of the Birmingham views in favour of free education with the help of Charities to relieve the rates". Report 12, June, 1877. King Edward VI School, Norwich, Ed. 27/3613.
An extra opportunity to air his views occurred when he became Editor of

the *Norfolk News*, a widely-read weekly Liberal journal. J. J. Colman of Norwich was one of the proprietors. Rev. Dr. A. Jessopp, Rector of Scarning, to Charity Commissioners, 14 January, 1880. Scarning Ed. 21/12996 (P.R.O.).

181 Norwich School Board Minute Book, No. 2, 24 March, 1875, *ibid.*

182 *Norfolk and Norwich Gazette*, 25 May and 31 July, 1875.

183 *Eastern Daily Press*, 16 August, 1877, and Norwich School Board Minute Book, No. 3, 1877-8, 30 October, 1877.

184 Hodgson to School Board, 7 September, 1877. Norwich Ed. 16/225.

185 Cumin to Sandon, 9 February, 1878. Norwich Ed. 16/226.

186 Sandon to Cumin, 29 March, 1878, *ibid.*

187 Forster to Ripon, 13 December, 1871. Wolverhampton Ed. 16/277. Ripon replied on the same day, "I entirely agree".

188 Drewery to Hull School Board, 29 January, 1876. Hull Ed. 16/333.

189 Forster informed Sandon during the final stages of the 1876 Act in Parliament that the Liberal Party greatly disliked Guardians as education authorities. "They can only be reconciled to the Guardians by the knowedge that if the new local authority works badly, the ratepayers can get rid of it by getting a School Board." Undated, but probably July, 1876. Harrowby MSS. Vol. LII, f. 378.

190 C. C. Case, Clerk to School Board to Education Department, 8 March, 1877. Maidstone Ed. 16/119.

191 Sandon to Sandford, 21 March, 1877, *ibid.*

192 20 December, 1877. Maidstone Ed. 16/119.

193 14 June, 1880. Althorp MSS.

194 Most of the arguments for retaining a fee were however based on the principle of parental responsibility for their offspring. Sir Charles Reed, Chairman of the School Board for London, proudly told a meeting in 1876 that "London has never had a free school, nor even a free place as such. Deficient as the people are in letters, they are not as a rule so lacking in moral responsibility as to wish their neighbours should bear their burdens for them". "Address on Elementary Education" in the *Transactions of the National Association for the Promotion of Social Science, Brighton Meeting, 1875* (1876), pp. 87-8.

195 F. D. Blyth to Mundella, 10 March, 1881. Low Leyton Ed. 16/80.

196 W. H. G. Armytage, *A. J. Mundella* (1951), p. 229.

197 Mundella to Sandford, 15 March, 1881. Low Leyton, *supra.*

198 Chamberlain to Mundella, 7 October, 1885. Mundella MSS., Box 2.

199 Mundella to Chamberlain, 11 October, 1885, Chamberlain MSS. JC5/55/8.

4

The Operation of Local Management Under the School Boards

ORGANIZATION OF LOCAL MANAGEMENT

With the passing of the 1870 Act and the establishment of school boards, the varying constructions subsequently put upon Section 15 of the Act made possible the extension of popular government in schools:

> "The School Board may, if they think fit, from time to time delegate any of their powers under this Act except the power of raising money, and in particular may delegate the control and management of any school provided by them, with or without any conditions or restrictions, to a body of managers appointed by them, consisting of not less than three persons."

School boards were given the discretion of removing "all or any such managers" from time to time: they were also to determine the number and stipulate the powers of any body of managers. The Act did not attempt to define the manager, merely stating in Section 3, that

> "The term 'manager' includes all persons who have the management of any elementary school, whether the legal interest in the schoolhouse is or is not vested in them."

It was therefore left open how far "control" and "management" were compatible under the school board, which was ultimately responsible for the financial soundness of administration.

A number of school boards in large towns did not use the powers of delegation allowed under this section and retained central management of their schools. At Salford, which was without board schools for many years, the board, it was stated in 1879, "have not thought fit to delegate the management of their schools to any body of managers but have appointed a Committee from their own number to carry on the work".[1] At Hull, a school management committee, consisting of five members of the board and chairman as *ex officio* member, were named managers.[2]

Similarly, Sheffield managed the schools through its education sub-committee of seven members. It selected teachers, and recommended them to the board and visited the schools "as often as possible".[3] Where a management sub-committee existed, as in this instance, other aspects of the board's work were dealt with by a number of sub-committees with titles such as general purpose, finance and buildings, often with different personnel.

One reason advanced by boards who were reluctant to delegate management was that in many instances they had inherited not only a large number of voluntary schools, transferred to the school boards, but also, as for example, in London,[4] and Manchester[5] a large proportion of the existing voluntary school managers; a number of these had had limited experience in management and many found difficulty in working under a more bureaucratic system.[6]

In some towns management was delegated to voluntary school managers. At Walthamstow, Essex, a member of the board was appointed correspondent and treasurer, but after two years the managers requested the board "to manage its own affairs"; the board complied with this expressed wish to give up local management of schools.[7]

Firm control over school management by boards through the operation of a school management committee had the advantage of lessening the possibility of disagreements between the board and local committees of managers. It could, however, often generate its own friction within the board. A member of the Shrewsbury School Board questioned the resolution adopted at the first meeting of the newly-elected board: "That the attendance, sites and buildings, school management and finance committees are each to consist of the whole Board, three to form a quorum". The board met as such on the second Thursday in each month and the various committees on the first and third Thursdays. At a meeting of the school management committee on 6 May, 1886, a letter from the Education Department was read. The clerk had prepared a reply to this, and by a majority of the committee it was ordered to be at once forwarded to the Department. A member of the board objected to this procedure on the grounds that the letter asking for certain information had been addressed to the board.

"The matter", he told the Department, "has *never been before* the Board at all, and the reply forwarded to the Department is *not* the reply of the Board. It is not the first time I have felt it my duty as a member of the Shrewsbury School Board to protest against this practice, which has already resulted in a late case in placing the Board and the School Management Committee in very unpleasant and conflicting situations."[8]

Even in the case of a large and well organized school board, such as at Bristol, there could be confusion regarding the delineation of functions between the school management committee and other committees. Here, the organization was based on the division of the city into four districts, each represented by "standing committees" with four members of the board operating in each district,[9] except for Ward Four, which had three only; the school managers appointed for each district were basically the district members and in addition five to eight local persons.[10] The committees, as well as supervising schools, superintended the work of attendance officers within each district, authorized summonses and heard statements of parents on whom notice had been served.[11] The members then met as a school management committee once a month to decide on policy matters such as the appointment of teachers and the provision of school accommodation.

A meeting of the school board was convened on 25 March, 1887, to receive a report on school management, presented by the vice-chairman of the board, the Rev. V. R. Thomas. The following dialogue ensued with another member of the board.

> *Mr. Gould:* "There are two or three matters in that Report which do not belong to the School Management Committee—provision for accommodation of children belongs to the School Attendance Committee and there are several matters referred to in the Minutes now read to us upon which I shall presently make a report as Chairman of the School Attendance Committee.
>
> *Thomas:* "I think the Chairman of the School Attendance Committee is out of order altogether. We do not touch the question of district (i.e. managers' work) but the question of accommodation in our schools. There is overcrowding and we are responsible for the Management.
>
> *Gould:* "We do not refer to the question of district. The duty of the Chairman is to refer the matter to the School Attendance Committee. It is not right that the Chairman of another Committee should take up the work of a Committee to which certain work has been delegated— this work has been delegated to the School Attendance Committee."[12]

Thomas attempted to pacify his colleague by pointing out that the recommendation of one committee in coming before the board would be helpful to the work of another committee. But there were further protests from another member, the chairman of the building committee, who insisted that the function of the school management committee was to receive reports and look after the equipment of the schools: if it had been content to report that the schools were overcrowded without recommending that extra accommodation should be provided, this would have been acceptable.[13]

The matter was settled by the chairman, Mr. Mark Whitwell, a businessman of vast experience in committee work,[14] who suggested the precedents of other corporate bodies in instructing their clerk to draw the attention of one committee to another committee's report, or better still, for the committees in question to hold a conference.

Closer liaison was made possible at Manchester where after a few years' experience, the school management committee was merged with the general purposes committee to form a sub-committee.[15] Where the board member was also chairman of local managers, as in London and Leicester, a ready channel of information existed; this was often the managers' only means of communicating their views to the board. Herbert Birley, the powerful and energetic chairman of the Manchester School Board, found time to be manager of some twenty schools in Manchester and Salford. In contrast, at a Leicester school, the local managers were unanimously moved to send a resolution to the Leicester School Board stating,

"In as much as the Reverend Father Hawkins, the board's representative manager of this School, has only been present at one meeting of the Managers the Managers would be greatly obliged if such arrangements could be made as would bring them into more direct touch with the Board."[16]

Two types of school board management have so far been explored: first, where the boards had retained full control and acted as managers and secondly, where a mixed system obtained of school board and local managers with a dominance of the former element. A third system was for large powers to be delegated to local managers. The Cross Commission particularly praised Liverpool, one of a number of such cases, for remitting the entire management of each school to a local board of managers, carefully selected in the first instance by the school board and afterwards co-opted by the local managers themselves. The Board, it stated,

"find that men of business, who have had the conduct of large enterprises, are found to be generally efficient members of local boards of managers, as their acquired knowledge of mankind guides them in the selection of teachers and in the exercise of effectual supervision, without encroaching upon the legitimate sphere of the teachers' duties and responsibilities."[17]

The ordinary duties of the board's managers were to take care of the fabric of the school, to maintain the staff at proper strength, and make necessary appointments of teachers; to take care that discipline and instruction of schools were good, and to make the preparations necessary for annual inspections by Her Majesty's Inspectors.

A handbook called *Suggestions to the Managers of Public Elementary Schools* was published by the School Board of Liverpool in 1880, a *vade-mecum* for the initiation of inexperienced local managers. The handbook suggested that one or two managers with the necessary leisure should acquaint themselves with its contents, and should concentrate during each visit on a few of the principles set out in the handbook. The headings were entirely practical: "What to Notice when Classes are at Work" included the observation that the teacher should as a counsel of perfection

"Always catechise in a lively and cheerful manner so as to prevent the children's attention from slumbering. Never allow a few quick clever children to answer more than their share of the questions, but take care that every child's mind is exercised."[18]

Teaching from a chair occasionally was recommended in

"that it accustoms a young teacher to remain stationary in a position from which the whole class can be commanded at once instead of roaming about in front of it, as most young teachers are apt to do."[19]

Under the London School Board, local managers were given similar functions: nomination of teachers, visitation of schools and examination of teachers' returns. Selected managers were also to attend "Notice B" committee meetings, held to enforce bye-laws for school attendance, visit cookery centres and act as managers of pupil-teachers' centres.

The School Managers' Manual, issued as a result of a meeting of the London School Board Committee of representative managers, also gives a résumé of local managers' duties and concludes,

"Managers under school boards are urged to cooperate in every way with all those engaged in the work of education, so that they may be part and parcel of a system and not in any way in antagonism to the Board. When any difficulties or points of difference arise between the Board and the Managers, the latter should request an interview with the Board, or ask that a deputation from the Board may confer with the Managers, for matters in dispute can be far better settled by personal interview than by correspondence."[20]

Not all boards shared this view; the West Bromwich School Board, returned for a second time without a contest and virtually with the same membership, considered at its meeting on 31 March, 1874, a request from the managers of two of its schools for periodical conferences of managers. After discussion this suggestion was "deemed inadvisable."[21]

An enlightened administrative system existed within the area of the Northampton Board. Here, a joint managers' committee, consisting of the managers of all the schools, met monthly to consider and report to the board on a great number of matters. They dealt with such affairs as the arrangements for the conduct of evening schools over which the managers had power to introduce or withdraw subjects, and to dispense with the services of any teacher. Sites and buildings, defective children and pupil-teachers' supervision also came within their jurisdiction.[22]

Most towns suffered from a shortage of local managers; besides the unrewarding nature of the work as compared with school board membership, the ever-growing number of board schools led to an increased demand for them.

Frequent resignations of local managers under the Leicester Board led to the suggestion by the chairman of managers of one school that the secretary put himself in communication with Mr. Hudson "with a view to obtaining names of any persons in the neighbourhood who would be likely to act as Managers".[23]

Finally, one more variation in the pattern of local management under school board administration may be noted. Some boards adopted the concept from the voluntary schools of "visitors" to schools. Often their functions were indistinguishable from those of the board members who worked in defined districts and who scrutinized the work of the schools; at Oldham, for instance, a school board member was appointed to each school as visitor and a record of visits was kept and read at the monthly meeting of the schools and general purposes committees.[24]

Bristol provided an example of a local visitors' sub-committee. This was formed in April, 1887, by the Bristol Board in an attempt to delineate the functions of the board's committees following the situation revealed by the school management committee's report the previous month. "Bristol differed from other large cities in having a larger proportion of well-to-do residents, and of families in which no children are to be found," wrote the authors of a book on Bristol about this time.[25] This made available a large number of people who, whilst not wishing to take on the responsibility of management, were willing to devote one year to being local visitors, with special responsibility for paying visits to the schools during one particular month in the year; the work was lightened by having three or more visitors attached to each school. The emphasis was on the word "local" as it was intended that the visitors would become attached by local loyalties to the school, attending and officiating at such events as prize distributions. The system was organized so that at the end of the month, the visitor would report in writing to the clerk regarding the condition and progress of the school for which he was responsible; every half year, in June and December, all the visitors of each school, with the member of the Bristol Board who was also visitor for the month acting as chairman, held a meeting. Finally, early in the year there was a general annual meeting of all members of the board and all the visitors.[26]

Inevitably, the local visitors began to assume or request managerial functions; a year after the establishment of the system, the local visitors were asking the school management committee for powers to grant leave of absence not exceeding one day to head teachers.[27] Although the scheme worked well, the need for continuous local management was not settled and the number of visitors to the schools formerly fixed at "three or more" was four years later down to "one to three".[28]

The existence of the different forms of management under school boards allowed under Section 15 of the 1870 Act ranged from full delegation to total retention of powers by the boards. This can be accounted for in terms of the circumstances surrounding the election of boards, the size of the board and complexity of organization, the proportion of voluntary to board schools, the availability of a sufficient supply of suitable local managers and the relationships between the boards and the schools generally. Certainly the Education Department, besides not being empowered by the Act to interfere with local arrangements, providing the work of the school board proceeded satisfactorily, did not feel competent to advise on matters requiring full knowledge of the history of the local situation. This was summed up by Cumin, the Secretary of the Department, in an early Minute relating to the Hull School Board:

> "It seems to me", he wrote, "almost impossible to control a School Board in a matter which must be so much better understood by persons on the spot than by any one in London."[29]

THE ACTIVITIES OF LOCAL MANAGERS

It has been seen that the extent of delegation of functions varied from board to board. Where small boards existed, there would often be little or no difference between the work carried out by the board members themselves and the local managers under large boards. For example, the school board at Cottingham in East Yorkshire practised the system of one member a month visiting the schools, checking the registers and signing the log book. At the election in 1886, William Stephenson secured a seat on the board; as he explained later to the Education Department,

> "The principal cause of my success was the desire as expressed (in election leaflets and speeches) to visit our various schools from time to time, to see how the children were progressing, occasionally hear them read, or examine their work etc. . . . Our members say they can and will prevent me."[30]

The matter was sent through the Hull M.P., William Sanders, to the Vice-President, who directed the Board not to interfere with Stephenson's activities and added that

"it is very desirable that members of school boards should show a personal interest in the schools under their management and to exercise beneficial interest on the children."[31]

Where school boards delegated only a little of their work to managers, the matters dealt with became trivial. The regulations for school managers issued by the Reading School Board left little scope for initiative. Although they were to have the control and management of the several schools for which they were appointed "subject to the general approval of the Board and by such orders and directions as shall from time to time be made and given by the Board", the managers were not given power to act in any matter involving the ownership or tenancy of school premises, to make any substantial addition to or in the buildings,

"nor to give orders for repairs thereto, nor alter or provide new fittings or furniture, beyond an expenditure on any one occasion for either of the above-mentioned purposes of the sum of £2; nor to dismiss or engage teachers, assistants and pupil teachers."[32]

In contrast to this, Burton-on-Trent managers were not only enabled to select teaching staff, but heads and assistant teachers applying were required to give a trial lesson before them.[33]

Most of the managers' dealings naturally would have been with the teachers. Despite suggestions contained in handbooks to managers "that any interference with the methods or authority of the teachers should be carefully avoided", unfortunate incidents occurred from time to time. One of the five managers of the Eastern District Girls' School, Southampton, the Rev. S. Scott, visited the school on 1 October, 1891. According to the headmistress's entry in the log book,

"The Rev. Scott entered the school at 10 minutes past Ten o'clock this a.m. and interrupted me in my duty, requesting that I should reserve my speech until he had gone; and in a very dictatorial manner demanded the Attendance Book and made his comments on the same in the presence and hearing of the whole staff and school assembled in the main room."

This matter was brought before the school managers' committee; the chairman, noting the seriousness of the charge made, asked the headmistress, Mrs. Darling, to be present and to make a fuller statement. The Rev. Scott mentioned at the meeting that "he would be very sorry to do anything that was derogatory to the nature of her position or in any way to be disrespectful to her. On the Chairman giving this assurance to Mrs. Darling, stating that she had the full confidence of the Managers, Mrs. Darling expressed herself satisfied with the Rev. Scott's apology and thanked the Committee for their expression of confidence."[34]

Local managers could also, on the other hand, iron out misunderstandings between the board and the Education Department. An unsatisfactory report on a teacher under the Norwich School Board by H.M. Inspector Mr. F. Synge, was referred to and investigated by the school managers; in clearing the teacher, the managers

"felt that something was due to the fact that the Inspector could not understand the pronunciation of the boys, just as the boys could not understand him."[35]

Few accounts seem to have survived of the day-to-day activities of local managers as distinct from the many biographies and auto-biographies of ex-school board members. Some flavour of the routine of their work, however, can be gathered from the entries of two such managers, Thomas Carver and Arthur Rendell, over the space of six years, in the managers' minute book for Christow Street Board Infants' School, Leicester. Carver must have devoted much of his time to the school, being chairman of the managers and making weekly visits. An early start to the school was essential[36] and deviations from this pattern were noted.

"I reached school this morning at 9.30 having overslept myself through a bad attack of neuralgia during the night. The maid neglected to call me and I did not wake until 9 a.m."[37]

An entry from the log book showed that Carver had in some instances to overrule his fellow managers.

"Mr. Carver has informed me", wrote the headmistress, Miss Jones, "that the wearing of a Dunce's Cap in school as proposed by the Managers is not allowed by the Board."[38]

Later, Carver refused admission to several babies "as the room is so full and as Miss Jones has no-one to help her I am afraid she may be overworked."[39]

One of the functions of managers often, as in London and Liverpool, was to supervise the work of the school caretaker. Arthur M. Rendell, a fellow manager of Carver's, was led into an embarrassing situation because of his zeal in pursuing the less than efficient caretaker of the school.

"*1896 Early November.* Visits daily because the place is unclean.
"*Nov. 12.* There was one small ball of clay prepared today for the modelling lesson in the first class, sufficient only for 23 children. A teacher had to go to the caretaker's home to ask him to prepare more.
"*Nov. 13.* I asked the caretaker not to come into school during school hours several times, but he still persists in doing so. He said he could come in just when he wished. . . . His manner was most unpleasant.
"*Nov. 26.* I sent for some soap this afternoon as there was not sufficient for the children's use in the lavatory. The caretaker did not send enough so I sent to him again. He then came into the lavatory in a great passion saying if I wanted soap I could fetch it myself. He made such a noise that several mothers congregated in the entrance to listen. This is the second time he has been disagreeable about the soap this week."[40]

Apart from the routine work connected with the functioning of the school, from the late 1880s onwards, the attention of school managers was drawn increasingly towards Article 146 of the Code which expressly laid down that they were to have regard to the mental, moral and physical welfare of the scholars. In 1887, the London School Board appointed a special committee, with a brief

"to report whether such changes could be made in the school curriculum as should secure that children leaving school should be more fitted to perform the duties and work of life before them."[41]

This could best be secured within the school by curriculum changes, extension of Froebelian methods into senior schools and the introduction of Slojd (Swedish educational handwork) and the extension of cookery to all girls of eleven and over.[42] Another recommendation dealt with the value of out-of-school activities, towards which the personal help of the local managers of the school boards was sought.

The committee of representative managers of the London School Board organized a series of six lectures for school managers in 1889 and 1890 to promote this movement.

One speaker, Miss Ada Heather-Bigg, suggested that "evenings of amusement" should be organized for schools by small committees.

"These committees should consist, if possible, of a certain number of managers, of the headmaster of the school and of such ladies and gentlemen residing in the locality as are willing to serve and perhaps past scholars of the schools."

This suggestion harmonized with the advice given in the *London School Board Managers' Manual* in 1885 that in order to promote goodwill between parents and teachers, managers should organize occasional entertainments in the school buildings, in which the children should take part, and which would give the opportunity of bringing parents into personal relation with the teachers.[43]

It was proposed, for example, that once a fortnight the school hall be thrown open, to children of the higher standards, for dancing —"quadrilles, lancers, polkas, Highland schottisches, and even waltzes";[44] This scheme was eagerly taken up by school managers and members of society.

Stewart Headlam, the colourful Church reformer and friend of stage actors, became chairman of the evening schools committee on the London School Board. Headlam arranged social evenings on Saturdays and on other nights; when the work was got through promptly, there would be quarter of an hour's dancing. His biographer tells a story typical of Gorst, the Vice President, in connection with this.

"I remember", wrote Headlam, "that a Minister—perhaps Gorst—coming upon such a scene, declared that he had found the boys and girls dancing away the 'Consolidated Fund'."[45]

Unlike board managers, local managers continued in office until such time as they resigned. This was not clear at first and the clerk to the Plymouth School Board wrote to the Department on 22 October, 1873, asking for information on the position of managers when the board went out of office, especially whether their appointments were cancelled or if they must be newly appointed by the succeeding board. No information existed in the Education Department on this important point. Sandford, the Secretary, was asked to give an opinion on this. In the absence of positive evidence to the contrary, Sandford presumed that managers and officers of the board continued in office under the new board.[46] W. G. Lumley, the Department's Counsel, amplified Sandford's statement:

"The Managers continue unless they are members of the Board, in which case they may individually cease to be Managers if they cease to be members of the Board, but this may be open to exception if they were appointed as Managers without reference to their being members."[47]

The influence of the permanent staff of the board in relation to the functions and the activities of the managers will next be examined.

SCHOOL BOARD CLERK

Lord Harrowby, a former Vice-President of the Committee of Council on Education, writing to Lord Salisbury on the effects of the growth of the school boards on the voluntary sector, remarked,

"People forget when talking of the Ratepayers' Check the great and growing power of that most able set of men—the Clerks of the large Town School Boards . . . as the members of the Board constantly change and *they* remain, mostly masters of the position."[48]

This view was widely shared; efficiency in all branches of administration and business had become more essential with the growing bureaucratization of organizations.[49] One advocate of this attitude wrote:

"The only security for the permanent efficiency of the schools is in remitting them to official management. If there be one thing more than another which has contributed to the greatness and prosperity of England it is the permanency of the official staff in every department, whatever change of Government may take place. Whether Mr. Disraeli or Mr. Gladstone preside in Downing Street, the machinery of Government is always under the control of the same experienced hands and a change of administration produces little more immediate effect than the setting of the sun today and its rising in the mornings. So it will be with the School Boards when the machinery of management has been properly organized. Whatever changes may come in the *personnel* of their members . . . the permanent staff will remain and the schools will not suffer from the absence of competent officials to control and direct them."[50]

The archetypal school board clerk was G. H. Croad, who help office from the formation of the School Board for London in 1871 to his death in September, 1902, a span of thirty-one years. An unusually shy, diffident and retiring man, he had started up the administrative work of the board with a staff of six. By 1902, it consisted of 500 clerks, 450 visiting staff, 500 school keepers and 14,000 teachers.[51] At the other end of the scale could be found many examples, such as the Deeping St. James School Board, Norfolk, which in 1876 appointed as a full-time school clerk Mr. G. H. Dean, a meticulous and autocratic man, to supervise its three schools.[52] Despite the difference in size of the respective boards, the backgrounds of the two clerks were similar to each other and to the majority of other clerks. They were both ex-headmasters, and in some instances, as at that of the Stoke-upon-Trent Board,[53] were from the schools of the city in which the board operated.

In country districts a number of them held such appointments with more than one board and therefore had experience in a wide variety of situations. Unlike his town colleagues, a clerk to a rural board was often a solicitor or a solicitor's clerk. Multiple appointments could, however, lead to the clerk having divided loyalties. A dispute arose between two school boards in East Yorkshire, Burstwick and Thorngumbald, which were adjacent urban districts, over

L

a boy who had removed himself from a school in Thorngumbald and was attending one in Burstwick. In this, he was supported by his parents. The Burstwick Board enquired into the benefit they might expect from the grant which the boy would earn from the other board; at the meeting of the Burstwick Board, the clerk, who acted for both boards, had to smooth over difficulties as best he could.[54]

The duties of the clerk varied according to the size of the board.[55] Besides accompanying managers and visitors and acting as secretary to their committees and to the managers' meetings, the clerk often performed full managerial functions. In some instances, indeed, this title was bestowed on him. At Birmingham, the report for the school board for 1876 mentions,

> "The Board has never appointed separate bodies of School Managers but has always preferred to manage schools by means of a Committee of the Board, *the Clerk being the official Manager and Correspondent for all the schools*."

In addition, up till midsummer, 1874, the regular superintendence and examination of the schools was conducted by the clerk to the board until it was realized that with the increase in the number of the schools this was no longer practicable.[56] Similarly, at Hull, the clerk visited schools, reported systematically on their condition and conducted intermediate examinations in each of them periodically.[57]

In January, 1900, Mr. Arthur Whitehead, the clerk to the Rawtenstall School Board, Lancashire, in a letter to the Education Department, claimed that, in the course of his official duties, he had the right to act as manager. This arose out of a communication with H.M. Inspector for the area, Mr. Holman, who informed the clerk that the latter had no right to check the registers of attendance at the schools and referred him to clause 6 of the Code, 1889–1890. This clause laid down that the accuracy of the registers had been entrusted to the managers, so it followed that a clerk could not act as a manager. Whitehead's indignation over the matter stemmed from the fact that he had been checking the registers of both day and evening schools for over seven years, had recorded that fact and signed in the log books on each occasion, and no objection had so far been made. Further, there was supporting evidence to justify his contention. He told Holman:

> "that in the clause of the Appendix of the Code, reference is made to *certificates to be signed by Managers* in Form 9 and that as these are directed in Form 9 itself to be signed by the Clerk to the Board where Managers are not appointed under Section 15 of the Elementary Education Act the Clerk does act as Manager in the very clause he relies on and it is natural to suppose he can act as Manager under the rest of the Section."

He therefore contended that:

"where Managers are not appointed under Section 15 and no such Managers have been appointed by the Board, the Clerk can check the Registers."[58]

There was some confusion within the Education Department as to the policy of the Department on this issue. It was intended that E. K. Chambers of the Department should reply that the verifying of school registers was the duty of members of the school board and "my Lords attach the greatest importance to the due fulfilment by members of this duty", and should quote, as had the H.M. Inspector, the current regulations that "The Managers are required to visit the school". John White, a Senior Examiner, queried this reply. Chambers, however, pointed out to him Circular 217 and the earlier Blue Book of 1886–7, Section 18, Appendix 3, which had read: "The Managers or *someone deputed by them* should visit the school." The italicized clause appeared again in the Blue Book of 1889–90, but disappeared in the following year's Regulations to Inspectors, and had never re-appeared; apparently, a member of the legal department, Mr. Lewin, had re-drafted these regulations in 1891 and the words were omitted. Chambers added "there are no papers to show why". (White thought that this clause was omitted "solely with a view to preventing Voluntary Managers from deputing Register verification.")

White concurred, and ordered Chambers's original reply to be sent, commenting,

"I confess to some sympathy with this Board Clerk, seeing that we accept his signature in lieu of Managers for all Returns on Form 9B, but I see you are quite right about the precedents and the recent ruling has Mr. Tucker's (the former Principal Assistant Secretary) authority."[59]

Although the effect of this ruling was to make a sharper distinction between paid officials and school managers, nevertheless the work of the clerk throughout the period overlapped in practice very much with that of school managers. The extent of a clerk's duties can be seen in the daily diary of the school board clerk of Exeter, John Austin, who held the post from 1880 to 1899. Besides attending meetings of the board and acting as secretary to committees, paying bills, and before the change of rules, examining school registers from time to time, Austin was responsible for preparing and delivering notices on parents for non-attendance, and with one attendance officer for the city, made personal enquiry after seven or eight children who had had notices. On Tuesday, 24 January, 1881 all the schools were visited and were found to be thinly attended. An analysis of H.M. Inspectors' Reports for the year was prepared and submitted in June, 1887 to the assembled teachers at St. Mary Arches Street Girls' School in the presence of five managers. Earlier in the year, on 10 February he had noted, with reference to the Cross Commission: "Wrote the answers to the questions on the Forms sent by the Royal Commission". The preparation and delivery of notices for all members of the finance committee and of the next board meeting were his sole responsibility. The scope of the work was so wide that it is not surprising to find that sometimes papers were mislaid. We read for 13 March, 1884,

> "Answered all the candidates for Assistant Mistress' Office, informing them of the appointment of Miss Lydia Williams,"

followed the next day by the anguished entry, "searched for Birth Certificates".[60] The managerial aspects of Austin's work, with his frequent visits to schools and his wide knowledge of school organization, placed him in a superior position to the ordinary school managers.

With the formation of the Association of School Boards in March, 1893, on the initiative of the clerk to the Manchester Board, C. H. Wyatt, who became the honorary secretary, the status of the clerk was enhanced. Each board could send one clerk and two members to the meetings and a forum for the exchange of views was thenceforth possible.

LOCAL INSPECTORS

The need for a more expert evaluation of the work and life of a school than could be provided by managers was appreciated by many boards. None put the case for it more bluntly than the Swansea School Board in its annual report for 1876:

> "To aid in the performance of its duties the law permits of the deputation of many of its powers to bodies of managers appointed under the Act of 1870. It has been found necessary in the case of each school taken by the Board to appoint such a body. . . . The managers however, have the disadvantage of not being trained to look at matters with the eye of one technically associated with education; and the same disadvantage applies also to the members of the Board themselves. For the purpose of advising the Board and managers in the performance of their task, the Board, in the autumn of last year, determined to appoint an Inspector of Schools."[61]

Discussing the merits of inspection of board schools by bodies of local managers, as at Liverpool and London, Joseph Chamberlain, as chairman, told the Birmingham School Board:

"We have thought such a system objectionable on two grounds; in the first place, because this voluntary inspection tends in a great number of cases to become perfunctory and inefficient, and because, in the second place, where it is efficient, it is likely to lead to clashing of authority between the committee outside the Board and the Board itself. We have therefore preferred to appoint an efficient inspector."[62]

As with school board clerks, most of the local inspectors were ex-school teachers.[63] The ideal qualifications required for the post envisaged by the Rev. John Rodgers, chairman of the school management committee of the first School Board for London, were successful elementary teaching together with a university degree: "experienced that he may understand the work in which he is to engage and a degree that he may command a good standing among his fellows."[64]

Other boards rapidly followed London's lead, including Nottingham, Newcastle, Norwich and Hull.[65] At Sheffield, a "superintendent", with twenty years' teaching experience, was appointed to inspect schools and test the efficiency of the instruction given between the times of Government inspection.[66] At Birmingham, the division of responsibilities was more clearly defined with the appointment of the inspector of board schools and a separate post of register clerk, whose duty it was to examine all registers and account books kept by the teachers. Here, the inspector reported to an examinations sub-committee of the board, not the school management committee as in London and other towns.[67] Some of the poorer boards, whilst seeing the necessity for them, could not afford to appoint inspectors; Salford, for instance, for three months a year used the services of Mr. John Sutton, an inspector of the Manchester Board schools.[68]

The interposition of the local inspector between H.M. Inspector and managers raised problems of division of responsibility for management. Local inspectors' reports were usually sent to the board, although in some instances the managers were the recipients, and were a link between the local inspectors and the teacher. The Leicester School Board found it necessary to issue a circular to its local managers in September, 1895, to enquire from managers

"whether any reports have been received from the Board's Inspectors or Inspectress and if so whether the contents have been made known to the assistant teacher. This the Board finds is not invariably done and it is very necessary that the assistant should be informed of any remarks made by the Inspector."[69]

Furthermore, it could be seen that the local inspector merely duplicated the work of H.M. Inspector in examining scholars. When the new London School Board was elected in 1885, a motion was passed:

"That in the opinion of this Board the present dual system of inspection is unnecessary."

The school management committee investigated the question and recommended for the forthcoming year

"that the work be arranged in the direction of inspection rather than examination."[70]

With the introduction of the Promotion List for teachers and the increasing power of local inspectors in appointing teachers, the complaints of the London local managers that their powers were being diminished over time were not without foundation. (At Leeds the inspector approved syllabuses submitted by head teachers.[71])

The teachers soon realized that it was to the local inspector rather than the managers that they should look for further advancement.[72] This was increasingly true after the late 1880s when H.M. Inspectors largely withdrew their superintendence from London schools. A sub-committee of the school management committee of the London School Board, set up in 1901 to enquire and report upon the alleged defect both in teaching and discipline in the schools of the board, obtained replies from twenty-four individual representative managers on these topics. These replies indicated a readiness to defer to the judgment of the local inspectors and in no instance advanced any dissentient views.[73]

The erosion of local managers' powers and functions under school boards was an inevitable consequence of the increasing complexity of working, which was paralleled by the trend in central government during this period; and the consequent greater demands for expertise in a number of fields which the local managers, by the nature of their appointments, were unable to meet. In addition, as within all organizations, the growth of bureaucracy created internal stresses.

A description and analysis of the work of local managers under the School Board for London may bear out some of these points.

THE SCHOOL BOARD FOR LONDON

The system of local management adopted by the School Board for London illustrated the difficulties of management when it was uneasily divided amongst a number of different interest groups.

The School Board for London consisted of members elected for the divisions corresponding to large vestries. A number of members represented the divisions for the purposes of management; these were called divisional members. The day-to-day management of the schools was carried on by local or representative managers who were elected in a variety of ways.

Initially, the board had not deliberately pursued any positive policy with regard to the appointment of managers. Between 1871, when the board was established, and 1873, when the first board schools were built, the transfer to the board of a number of voluntary schools raised the problem of continuity of their supervision. It was resolved, therefore, in 1872, that eight managers should be appointed for each transferred school, of whom four should be nominated by the outgoing body of managers. Of the remaining four, one was always to be a member of the board: the remainder were persons to be recommended by the divisional members. When the new board schools were built, the power of the divisional members was greatly increased; all eight managers from then onwards were to be recommended by the divisional members.[74]

Thus for the rest of the board's existence there were three parties involved in school management: the board itself, working through a school management committee, the divisional members and the local managers. The board framed a "Code of Rules" which changed from time to time, setting out the duties and powers of school managers; but as the board was unable to attend to their administration, the work devolved very largely upon the managers themselves. The balance of power was a constant source of friction; the board's problem was to decide how to give the local managers sufficient power to secure their continued interests in the schools without the board divesting itself of responsibilities which were properly theirs.

The chief functions of local managers were initially fourfold: to select the teaching staffs, including headmasters of the schools; to visit schools, check registers and pay regard to premises; to examine complaints against teachers; and to draw up annual reports of schools which would guide and assist the school management committee in deciding the needs of and future policy for the schools. Matters such as deciding upon school curricula and the amount of fees to be charged were outside their jurisdiction.

Schools were grouped into units of two or three, with the number of managers being a maximum of twelve and fifteen respectively. Where grouping took place, a chairman of local managers would be elected, who would be either a divisional or a local manager. Correspondents, selected from the managers, were chosen for each group, but with the growing burden of administrative work, paid correspondents for each division replaced them.

The procedure for electing local managers was not standardized, as has been noted above. There seems also to have been variations in methods of election as between one division and another. In some cases the divisional member promulgated his own nominations for local managers and sent them to the school management committee direct for approval; in others, the member and the local managers drew up separate lists, but disagreements frequently made this system unworkable.[75] The divisional member, in such a dispute, had the final word. However, persistence on the part of local managers often led to an acceptance of their candidates. One witness, Rev. C. H. Turner, chairman and manager of a group of schools, told a special committee,

> "We have had occasionally a difficulty in getting the Managers we nominated appointed. One of two persons have been refused by the Divisional Members though the persons so refused were better known to us than to them . . . but we kept on renominating and at last got them appointed."[76]

One divisional member constituted a quorum at a meeting, but where protests from local managers were likely, as in Marylebone, he would be reinforced by colleagues from the division. One witness before the Cross Commission mentioned that the great majority of the people who took an interest in education did not know the way and had no idea of the methods to be adopted to become a manager.

> "I have been asked by several gentlemen, how does so-and-so become a Manager? What has he to do? Whereupon I have said, I do not know what you can do but write to the Board member and say that you would you would very much like to serve."[77]

It was clear that divisional members would be able to make their point of view known at the school management committee, whilst managers would have to rely upon sending formal deputations to the board.

Alternative modes of electing local managers were put forward at various times. That a committee should be formed for this purpose raised the question of its composition, and one suggestion was that it should be composed of local managers. Another was that three different bodies should be responsible for their election: the Education Department, to safeguard its interest; the school board, to safeguard the interests of ratepayers, and representatives from the teaching profession.[78]

By 1882, the local managers, following a deputation to the board, were able to secure an inquiry into the appointment, duties and privileges of their body.[79]

The committee's report recommended that the existing system of appointing local managers by divisional members should continue, but that vacancies occurring be made

> "by the Board upon the nomination, either of a majority of the Divisional Members at their meeting, or of the local Managers, with the assent of a majority of the Divisional Members at their meeting."[80]

A similar committee five years later endorsed the findings of the earlier one on this point.[81]

One interesting outcome was that the local managers, on their own initiative, then formed a representative committee, consisting of representatives of schools which met once a month during the sessions of the London School Board to compare experiences in order to improve the quality of management.[82]

APPOINTMENT OF TEACHERS

Another matter over which the divisional member and local managers took issue was in the appointment and subsequent supervision of teachers, both assistants and heads. Initially, the local managers were responsible for these appointments as well as dealing with complaints by or against them. How far the board member as divisional member should take part in visiting schools, which was a function of the local managers, was difficult to decide. One manager stated, "I have often wanted to see a Divisional Member at a school, but I have never had an opportunity".[83] T. H. Huxley, however, during his service on the school board, opposed a suggestion that board members should be entitled to enter the schools, declaring that they "could not be allowed to come in and set the authority of the teacher at defiance".[84] Sir Charles Reed, chairman of the board from 1876 to 1881, on the other hand, preferred visiting schools which

"gave him also opportunities of intercourse with the local managers on whose willing co-operation he felt the success of the School Board system in no small degree depended."[85]

A number of local managers giving evidence before the 1887 committee voiced the opinion that teachers should be instructed to confer more with managers, and not so much with divisional members, so that managers were kept more in the picture.[86] With the increasingly political complexion of the School Board for London in the 1880s, any attempts by divisional members to bring pressure to bear on the schools for political ends only strengthened the local managers' dislike of the members' powers. In July, 1887, a special committee of the school board reported on an alleged breach of privilege by Mr. Stonelake, a divisional member. It found that

"a gross breach of privilege had been committed by a member of the Board in sending bills in connection with the election for Vestry men to the Headmaster of the Anglers' Gardens School, for distribution to scholars."

Stonelake had sent the circulars to schools, ordering the teachers to distribute them to their pupils. The headmaster, Mr. Ernest Brett, appearing before the committee, remarked: "It had some influence with me, Mr. Stonelake being a member of the Board." In announcing their findings, the committee recommended

> "that the teachers involved should be informed that the direction of a Divisional Member does not relieve them from the necessity of carrying out the rules of the Board, to [which they should strictly adhere."[87]

The local managers in exercising their function of appointing headmasters were equally not free from criticism. They had no formulated criteria to apply, and the lack of any systematic method of promotion made for difficulties. The 1887 special committee, dealing with the promotion of teachers, highlighted the danger that where a particular teacher was known to the managers who had an appointment to make, their minds might be unduly prejudiced in favour of such a teacher, who although possibly good in every respect, might not have deserved promotion to the same extent as may a teacher quite unknown to them.[88]

Few managers were averse to the suggestion that the modest Promotion List for selection of headmasters, then in the hands of the school management committee, should be made more comprehensive by inviting teachers to apply to be placed on it; managers could then make their selections from it. This was the first move towards centralization in selection of staff; two years later, in 1889, in spite of much protestation by local managers, the school management committee took over selection of headmasters, leaving only the appointment of assistants in managers' hands. In this way, the divisional members' powers were strengthened.[89]

LATER DEVELOPMENTS

At the same time as the Cross Commission was hearing witnesses from the London School Board, the latter's own special committee was seeking evidence on the functions and duties of managers. The committee of representative managers were invited to submit suggestions for an improved system. One suggestion adopted by the special committee but not rigorously enforced, was that a list of managers should be prepared at the end of every year, showing the attendances made at schools and managers' meetings; if no material contribution had been made by particular managers then they would be obliged to resign. The special committee stipulated that managers would fall under this category if they had "failed to attend one-third of the Managers' meetings and had not made at least three visits to schools during school hours".

It was not made clear who would make the recommendations or how the vacancies would be filled up. The representative managers requested that this should be left to local managers, who would recommend to divisional members the changes to be made, both in the way of deletions and substitutions. If the divisional members did not accept the recommendation of the managers, one or more of the divisional members was to confer with the managers on the subject before the list was sent up to the board.[90]

Another suggestion adopted was that in order to obtain good local managers, especially in areas where few persons of leisure were likely to live, it would be expedient if the school board kept at the iroffices a list of persons willing to act as managers, with their names and addresses and references, and that the board should let it be publicly known that they would be glad to receive names to place on the list.

Re-grouping of schools was also recommended; in order that managers could have experience of more than one school, no school should have a separate body of managers. To allow for more intensive visiting, managers were able to serve on the committees of only two groups of schools, rather than three as was formerly the case. Although the committee made suggestions regarding the powers and duties of managers, the witnesses who had given evidence were restricted to managers; in this way, an incomplete picture of the situation was given.

The last special committee on the appointment, duties and privileges of local managers in 1892 was far more comprehensive in scope than the previous ones. This was a powerful committee comprising, amongst others, Professor Gladstone, Rev. Stewart Headlam, Rev. Edward Schnadhorst, Mr. Sharp and the then Hon. Lyulph Stanley, with W. Roston Bourke as chairman.

It was decided to secure evidence from both managers and teachers. Chairmen of managers were to complete a circular under a number of headings within a fortnight of receiving it; the committee of representative managers were to draw up a statement of their views on various questions affecting local management; and every head teacher was sent a circular asking for the following information:

"The extent to which Managers have personally aided them in their school work, and co-operated in the various movements associated with the work of the Schools, e.g. Children's Country and Holiday Fund; Boot Clubs; Voluntary Agencies for the supply of Cheap or Free Breakfasts, Dinners, etc.; Cricket and Football Clubs; Visits to Public Institutions, etc.

"To what extent Managers by frequent visits to the Schools have become thoroughly acquainted with the staff and with the various wants and difficulties connected with the Schools."[91]

From the beginning, there were signs that the demands of local managers to have restored to them the privilege of appointing head-masters and caretakers would be difficult to achieve. The chairman of the special committee was W. Roston Bourke, the Principal of Hollo-way College, a private school; he was a Moderate member of the Board, moving towards the position he came to occupy during his last three years on the board as an independent educational repre-sentative.[92] He issued and distributed a memorandum to the com-mittee which he had originally drawn up when calling for its establishment.

The memorandum was an inflammatory one, which inevitably drew protests from the committee of representative managers on the grounds that the issues in question were pre-judged. Some examples drawn from the document illustrate this. Bourke wrote:

> "I WANT TO COMMIT MORE WORK TO THE LOCAL MANAGERS, but I fear to do it, because I want to place that work in more capable hands. . . . Local managers who are not interested in their work are WORSE THAN USELESS because they can be brought up from time to time at the solicita-tions of friends to vote and by such vote the men and women who know best the wants of the schools are overruled."

Then follows a list of examples of local managers' patronage.

> "THERE IS A WANT OF LOYALTY AND DISCIPLINE among the local managers. Surely some means can be found by which confidence can be restored and the work of our local managers rendered more effective for the purposes for which they exist, i.e. to foster the schools committed to their care."[93]

Following this, Bourke put forward three suggestions for future policy:

> Firstly, greater care should be exercised in choice and appointment of local managers. Secondly, they were no longer to recognize the principle of co-optation among local managers. "It would never do to allow a recalcitrant body of local managers to strengthen themselves against the legitimate action of the divisional members, or even against the policy of the Board. Thirdly, the Veto must be with the members first locally and finally here (i.e. the Board).[94]

William Bousfield, chairman of the representative committee, and Bourke, whilst differing widely in their views on local managers, independently of each other agreed that a new council or committee was required; this would interpose and lessen the causes of friction between the local managers and divisional members and act as arbiter where necessary. Bourke recommended a representative divisional council to be formed in each division. The members would be elected by the respective groups of local managers and the divisional members would be *ex officio* members of the council. Questions of policy could be remitted to them for their opinion; they could do all that the promotion sub-committee had recently taken over in selecting head teachers. Other functions which would be entrusted to the council would be to advise on the qualifications of persons proposed as local managers, the means of securing better attendance, consideration of the course to be adopted by superintendents of visitors in prosecuting parents for non-attendance, and the hearing of complaints of improper action on the part of any body of local managers.

> "By this means," wrote Bourke, "managers and members would find themselves working together in a common cause, the onus of unpopular local action would be upon members and managers conjointly, unity and harmony would be promoted and the real work of the Board could be better carried on."

In the final recommendation of the special committee, some concession was made to the wishes of local managers in that all future nominations by divisional members were to be examined and reported upon by the school management committee; hitherto the divisional members' nominations had hardly been questioned unless a protest had been made to the committee.

Some reduction in the number of local managers was also recommended. There had been a steady expansion from the original eight managers for each school to a maximum of twelve and up to twenty managers for two or more. Now the number was to be a maximum of six for a single school, nine for two grouped schools, and twelve managers for three or more schools.[95] Considering the nature of the work of the local manager in London, the report's comment that "the Committee found it somewhat difficult to differentiate duties from privileges" was a just one.

Towards the end of the century, the work of local managers was further diminished with the alteration in the method of selecting assistant teachers direct from college. This function was taken over by the Board's inspectors from July 1900. The cordial co-operation of the managers was invited by the Board:

> "This could best be accorded by the Managers selecting and nominating teachers from the list without requiring them to attend before them."[96]

The reaction of the managers of Tooting Graveney School on receipt of this letter was a typical one. They deplored the change in the new method of selecting teachers and stated that "any further curtailment of the Managers' responsibilities will, in the opinion of this Committee, tend to prevent ladies and gentlemen undertaking the duties of Local Managers."[97]

QUALIFICATIONS OF MANAGERS

All parties concerned in management under the School Board for London were generally agreed that the qualifications of many local managers were inadequate for the work. Of the seventy-eight chairmen of local managers who replied to the circular issued by the 1887 committee on the powers and duties of school managers, twenty-two referred to the unsuitability of managers for their duties.[98] It was calculated that between one-fifth and two-thirds of them came within this category.

The social class from which managers were drawn was one of the points often mentioned. Lady Stevenson, giving evidence before the Cross Commission, remarked on the composition of a committee of which she was chairman in the Chelsea area,

"I can mention one instance where a Divisional Member appointed without any recommendation from the Managers, a man who drove a cab; he was a cab proprietor, but he always drove his own cab. You cannot suppose that he was a man who could attend and do good service."[99]

The amount of time which could be devoted to regular school visiting favoured either retired ladies and gentlemen or those with a certain amount of leisure. One difficulty arose where, as in many instances, managers were customarily appointed largely from within the divisions where they resided.

"I believe", mentioned a lady manager, "there are several ladies and gentlemen in Marylebone who would be pleased to become Managers of schools in Divisions in which it is not possible to obtain qualified Managers."[100]

Leisure and knowledge of the schools did not always go together, but it seemed acceptable that the latter was of less importance. J. G. Fitch observed in 1887, that the number of people of education and leisure who had been successfully enlisted for local management was on the increase.[101]

The clergy, who would be expected to form an integral part of local committees, objected initially to serving on them, but later changed their minds.[102]

In 1892, the committee of representative managers protested that

"there is nothing in the existing rule which excludes suitable people of any condition of life from becoming Managers."[103]

Other individual managers claimed, however, that the shortage of suitable managers would continue unless an increase in their powers was made.[104]

In view of this conflicting evidence, it may be interesting briefly to examine the backgrounds of local managers in one year, 1884. This has been chosen for two reasons: first, it is half-way between two important special committees of the School Board for London which were concerned with management, and secondly the impact of politics on the selection of school managers had not yet made itself fully felt. The analysis (see Table A) is based on a return showing names, addresses and occupations of managers of board schools for the year ending 1884,[105] and excludes divisional members. No comparative return exists for this latter group.

The formulation of satisfactory social class categories for the late nineteenth century is a difficult one. Here the categories are based partly on those suggested by the recent studies of H. J. Dyos[106] and by G. W. Jones.[107] One of the difficulties arises out of the fact that the description of managers' occupations are based on their own statements and in some instances may be somewhat grandiose. A number of the descriptions were vague, e.g., merchant, educationalist and builder, which give a less than complete idea as to the size of the enterprise. Fortunately, only one member out of the 1,475 failed to name his occupation.

The heading of 'gentlemen' and 'ladies' indicated that no occupation was being followed. In all instances the 'military' managers who included representatives of both Army and Navy were retired. 'Law' is self-explanatory. 'Medicine' does not differentiate here between surgeons and doctors. The miscellaneous professions consist almost entirely of 'accountants', 'architects', 'surveyors' and 'writers'.[108] 'Church of England' clergy are differentiated from 'Nonconformists and others', the last mentioned category consisting of one Roman Catholic and one Church of Scotland priest. 'Merchant and managerial' includes owners or managers of businesses employing at least five people. 'Sub-managerial' comprises employers with some responsibilities such as supervisor or head clerk; 'Shopkeepers' include petty entrepreneurs employing fewer than five, and 'skilled workers' comprise such occupations as coopers, printers and gas-fitters. 'Teachers' are here entered as a separate category in order to extrapolate the education interest taken in management, and 'publicans' similarly, in order to test if the temperance issue was an important one in the elections.

A number of tentative conclusions can be drawn from the table: the leisured class constituted the largest element, being nearly one-third (31 per cent) of the total number of local managers, whilst the pro-

TABLE A

OCCUPATIONS OF LOCAL MANAGERS OF THE SCHOOL BOARD FOR LONDON, 1884

Division	Total	Gentlemen No. %	Ladies No. %	Military No. %	Law No. %	Medicine No. %	Miscellaneous No. %	Church of England No. %	Nonconformists No. %	Merchant & Managerial No. %	Sub-Managerial No. %	Publicans No. %	Shop-Keepers No. %	Skilled Workers No. %	Teachers No. %
City	152	19 13	43 28	3 2	6 4	6 4	4 3	23 15	9 6	16 10	8 5	– –	8 5	3 2	4 3
Finsbury	105	3 2½	22 21	– –	4 4	2 2	2 2	23 22	5 5	11 10	9 8	– –	17 16	3 2½	4 4
Lambeth East	311	45 14	36 11½	2 ½	12 4	11 3½	24 8	37 12	15 4½	21 7	61 20	– –	28 9	14 4½	5 1½
Greenwich	110	16 14½	19 17	4 4	6 6	1 1	– –	15 13½	8 7	13 12	16 14	– –	7 6	2 2	3 3
Hackney	141	23 16	26 18½	– –	2 1½	1 ½	4 3	27 19	12 8½	9 6½	14 10	– –	17 12	4 3	2 1½
Lambeth West	268	25 9½	43 16	2 ½	11 4	7 2½	11 4	35 13½	15 5½	22 8½	34 12½	5 ½	24 9	20 9	14 5
Marylebone	133	23 17½	63 47½	3 2	– –	2 1½	7 5	16 12½	2 1½	7 5	4 3	2 1½	1 1	– –	3 2
Southwark	108	5 4½	12 11	– –	– –	7 6½	3 3	16 15	6 5½	9 8½	14 13	– –	25 23	11 10	– –
Tower Hamlets	75	6 8	10 13½	– –	1 1	– –	1 1	24 32	4 6	6 8	4 5½	– –	8 10½	10 13½	1 1
Westminster	72	6 8½	16 22	9 12½	– –	– –	1 1	10 14	1 1	14 20	2 2½	– –	13 19	– –	– –
	1475	171 11½	290 19½	23 1½	42 3	37 2½	57 3½	226 15½	77 5½	128 8½	166 11½	7 ½	148 10	67 4½	36 2½

	%
Leisure Class	31
Professions	10½
Church	21
Merchant and Managerial	8½
Sub-Managerial	22
Skilled Workers	4½
Teachers	2½
	100

SOURCE: Return showing Names, Addresses of Managers of Board Schools, October, 1884. School Board for London (School Management Department) SBL. 1510 (Greater London Record Office (London Section)).

fessions accounted for only about a tenth $(10\frac{1}{2})$. Church influence was not very dominant at this time, amounting to one-fifth (21 per cent).

The paucity of working class representatives is borne out by the figures—some $4\frac{1}{2}$ per cent of the total.

Although it was claimed that there were too few ladies on the committees, these account for about one-fifth of the total membership $(19\frac{1}{2}$ per cent), but it is within the divisions themselves that the maldistribution is borne out. They composed 11 per cent of the total management in Southwark for instance, and $47\frac{1}{2}$ per cent in Marylebone: similarly, for gentlemen the figures are $4\frac{1}{2}$ and $17\frac{1}{2}$ per cent respectively. The relative distribution of this category of managers suggests that there was not a great deal of movement between divisions. There was high correlation between professional people and Church dominance in the divisions, except in Tower Hamlets where, with a small professional element, Church representation accounted for almost one-third of the total body (32 per cent). Surprisingly, in areas of high Nonconformist influence, such as Peckham, Lambeth, Brixton and Hackney, this was not reflected in representation, although this seems to have been the case in voting at general elections.[109] The merchant and managerial element was strongest in Westminster amounting to one-fifth, which was to be expected from a division which included Soho, Piccadilly and the Strand.

Lambeth East provides a good illustration of the predominantly white-collar population or sub-managerial category in Peckham; here, one-fifth of the representation came from this class.[110] Similarly, Southwark with a large shopkeeper contingent of nearly one-quarter (23 per cent) of the total managers accurately reflected the nature of the area. Less than one-twentieth $(4\frac{1}{2}$ per cent) of the managers were skilled workers. Of the sixty-seven members, most of them were, in terms of wages, in occupations which ranked them as "labour aristocrats", such as printing, ship-building and the building trade with a small scattering of medium wage earners such as boot-makers, and none in the lower ranks.[111] There is no evidence to suggest that the temperance issue had any effect on school management in London; only two divisions, Lambeth West with five and Marylebone with two returned publicans as such, amounting to $\frac{1}{2}$ per cent of the total. Teachers employed by the London School Board were not eligible for managerships. The 36 $(2\frac{1}{2}$ per cent) representatives were almost all headmasters and principals of colleges; for example, those of the two training colleges, Southlands and Whitelands, and the headmasters of Alleyn's and South London High School.

Despite considerable variations in the composition of management committees from division to division, the overall impression is that the professional and sub-managerial classes accounted for the bulk

M

of representation. How far the ladies and gentlemen were efficient managers, that is to say, knowledgeable in school matters, cannot be determined from statistics alone. Certainly only a small percentage of this category of managers would have had children of their own attending the board schools.

Efficiency, as has been seen, was also measured by conscientiousness in and regularity of visiting schools, and also attendance at managers' meetings. The only return on attendances was made in 1892.[112] (See Table B.)

On the whole, the claim often made in London that a minority of managers were responsible for shouldering the bulk of the work is not borne out by this table. The number of committee meetings varied enormously; West Lambeth easily claimed the record with 305 meetings in a year, that is, almost one every weekday throughout the year, yet one-third of the managers attended at least 75 per cent of these, as Column 3 shows. It is true though that, taking London as a whole, a large number rarely attended meetings. The figures for visits to schools are less impressive; in four of the ten divisions, over a half of the managers paid fewer than three visits to their schools during the course of the year. On the other hand, in Chelsea and Tower Hamlets, about half the total managers paid twelve visits or more. However, the table might possibly be misleading in this respect, as it is not clear if it should be interpreted as visits to *each* of the managers' schools, the departments of the schools or *all* of the managers' schools. Also managers' commitments varied from division to division according to the number of schools allocated and unless the total number of schools involved in each division is known, a truly accurate comparison cannot be made.

In the final analysis, the conflict of interests which existed between divisional members and local managers was an unreal one; for the supreme power rested with the board itself and major policy changes, such as that affecting the right to appoint headmasters, and the terms on which managers could appoint assistant teachers, were effected by it without much difficulty.

This was clearly shown in a memorandum on managers written for Balfour by Graham Wallas, once described as "the second most powerful man to Lyulph Stanley on the School Board", during the last crucial stages of the Education Bill in October, 1902. Balfour in his Manchester speech of 14 October (see Chapter 7) made it clear that the whole question as to the reality of representative government in the schools depended upon the relative meaning of "control" and "management" in the Bill. Wallas particularly fastened on to a paragraph in the speech relating to London, claiming in a memorandum to Balfour that he:

TABLE B

SCHOOL BOARD FOR LONDON
RETURN: LOCAL MANAGERS' ATTENDANCES AND VISITS
SUMMARY

DIVISION	No. of Mgrs	No. of Meetings held	Committee Meetings				Visits paid to Schools			
			75% & upwards	50% & upwards	25% & upwards	less than 25%	12 times & upwards	6 times & upwards	3 times & upwards	less than 3 times
City & Westminster	105	85	24	54	76	29	17	35	59	45
Chelsea	201	147	77	36	36	52	97	31	22	51
Finsbury	265	188	37	59	66	67	75	34	42	33
Greenwich	304	238	101	55	54	99	76	39	31	154
Hackney	251	199	49	51	57	94	52	36	49	114
East Lambeth	253	165	76	75	69	33	37	45	45	126
West Lambeth	403	305	95	114	109	89	140	89	61	125
Marylebone	172	89	24	43	43	62	67	31	31	44
Southwark	185	131	42	41	50	52	85	25	16	59
Tower Hamlets	270	207	51	75	62	82	142	36	25	67
Total	2,409									

source: Special Committee on the Appointment, Duties and Privileges of Local Managers, 6 July, 1892. School Board for London. SBL. 403 (Greater London Record Office [London Section]).

"was wrong in his statement as to the position of 'local Manager' under the London School Board. It must be remembered that the word 'Manager' has a technical meaning in educational administration. . . . They are members of local consultative committees whose advice is given, and generally though not always taken by the Boards, as to the nomination of assistant teachers under conditions settled by the Board; inquiry into friction, etc., the Board reserving the power (which it constantly uses) of refusing to accept their recommendations in any one of those particulars. In order to make this clear the London School Board have again and again informed the Board of Education that they are the 'Managers' of their own schools, and that all the communacitions from the Board of Education relating to any one of the schools and directed by the Code to be sent the 'Managers' must be sent to them."[113]

The 1903 Education (London) Act enabled the schools in each borough to be grouped and the number of managers to be determined as may be thought desirable, although both of these decisions were to be made by the individual metropolitan borough council. It was left to the London County Council to decide what powers, if any, beyond the actual visiting of schools it would give to managers. Two-thirds were appointed by metropolitan borough councils and one-third by the London County Council. Thus the trend which had been apparent throughout the board's existence of increasing centralization was continued. Sidney Webb, writing in 1904 on the subject of London's educational organization, believed it would be a calamity for the board schools to lose the devoted services being rendered by the majority of existing managers, but warned that there would be great differences between

"the somewhat haphazard recommendation at present made by the tiny group of managers, at scantily attended meetings, often dominated by a single personality, and those coming up from a well organized London Education Committee combining the experience of various groups of schools, advised in advance by the clerk and the inspector, duly checked in the central office, and definitely confined to the execution in detail of a declared policy of the central body."[114]

The days when the initiative of individuals and committees of managers could be taken had gone, and Webb remarked,

"In so far as the recommendation of the London Education Committee had received the concurrence of the inspector, were found to be within the scope of the work of the local body, and within the estimates for the year, and could be certified as in the line of the policy already decided on, they might safely be printed in the smallest type at the end of the School Management Committee's agenda, to be approved en bloc, unless particular objection was made."[115]

REFERENCES

1 Salford School Board, Report for the three years ending September, 1879, p. 4.

2 Report on the Proceedings of the Kingston-upon-Hull School Board during its three years of Office, February, 1871–January, 1874.

3 J. H. Bingham, *The Period of the Sheffield School Board, 1870–1903* (1949), p. 14.

4 The School Board for London presented so many exceptional features of management that this has been dealt with separately in the last section of this chapter.

5 S. D. Simon, *A Centenary of City Government, Manchester, 1838–1938* (1938), p. 242.

6 H. B. Binns, *op. cit.,* p. 316.

7 *History of the Walthamstow School Board, 1880–1903* (1903), p. 21.

8 E. Myers to Education Department, 10 May, 1885. Shrewsbury Ed. 16/254.

9 Interestingly, there was no ward representation of School Board members. To avoid costly and troublesome elections for casual vacancies, the general rule was to select as the new member one whose views resembled those of the previous representative. G. E. Stone, *Bristol, As It Was and As It Is* (1909), p. 167.

10 Review of the Proceedings of the Bristol School Board, January, 1871–November, 1873, p. 6.

11 Bristol School Board Minute Book No. 1, 1871–73, 27 October, 1871. MB/B1 (Bristol Archives Office).

12 Bristol School Board: Report of Meetings 1885–88, pp. 20–1, MSS. Minutes, MB/B6 (Bristol Archives Office).

13 *Ibid.,* p. 27.

14 Mark Whitwell (1826–1903) was Vice-Chairman of the Bristol School Board 1871–80 and Chairman 1880–89. *Contemporary Biographies, Bristol in 1898,* (1899), Vol. 1, p. 77.

15 Manchester School Board, Proceedings of the School Management and Organization Committee 1873–5, 20 September, 1875 (Manchester Central Library, Archives Dept.).

16 Leicester, Belper St. Junior Department, Managers' Minute Book 1894–7, 9 February, 1897. 19 D.59 VII 450 (Leicester Museum, Department of Archives).

17 *Cross,* Part III, Chapter 3. School Management, p. 68.

18 Liverpool School Board Suggestions to *the Managers of Public Elementary Schools* (1880), p. 14.

19 *Ibid.,* pp. 20–1.

20 F. C. Mills, *The School Managers' Manual* (1885), pp. 28–9.

21 West Bromwich School Board, 2nd Triennial Report, 1876, p. 3.

22 Northampton School Board, Joint Managers' Committee Minutes 1899–1903. Northampton Borough Education Records (Northamptonshire C.R.O.).

23 Leicester, Belper St. Junior Department, Managers' Minute Book, 1892–4, 19 October, 1892, *supra.*

24 Oldham School Board, Report for years 1886–8, p. 5.

25 J. F. Nicholls and J. Taylor, *Bristol Past and Present* (1882) Vol. 3, p. 264.

26 Bristol School Board, School Management Committee, Minute Book 1886–91, 21 April, 1887, MB/E1 (Bristol Archives Office).
27 *Ibid.* 21 June, 1888.
28 *Ibid.* Minute Book 1891–6, 7 February, 1895, MB/E2.
29 Cumin to Drewery, 29 January, 1870, Hull Ed. 16/333.
30 Cottingham School Board, Minute Book 1877–92, 12 February, 1886 (East Riding C.R.O.).
31 *Ibid.*, 25 February, 1888.
32 Reading School Board, Resolution of Board with respect to the powers to be delegated to Managers of Board Schools under Sec. 15 of the Elementary Education Act, 1870. Minute Book, Vol. 1, 1871–2, 7 February, 1872. RSB M/1. (Reading Corporation Archives.)
33 Burton-on-Trent School Board, Triennial Report, 1879–83, p. 8.
34 Southampton School Board, Eastern District Girls School, Managers' Committee Minute Book, 1886–93, 12 October, 1891. SC/E 75 (Southampton R.O.).
35 Norwich School Board, Surrey Rd., Horn's Lane and Prospect Row Schools, Managers' Minute Book, 1872–92, 24 January, 1882 (Norfolk and Norwich R.O.).
36 School managers' manuals emphasized the importance of this point. The Liverpool School Board's *Suggestions to Managers* (1880), p. 14 stated. "It is very desirable that managers should invariably make an effort to be present a quarter of an hour before the school opens in the morning. The opening of the school tests most completely its order and discipline." *The London School Managers' Manual* (1885) p.16 gives the reason for such visits: "to see that the Teacher is present in accordance with the regulations and that the children collect and fall in in a quiet and orderly manner."
37 Leicester, Christow St. Infant Board School, Managers' Minute Book, 1892–1914, 7 December, 1893. 19. D.59 VII 338 (Leicester Museum, Department of Archives).
38 *Ibid.*, 12 July, 1892. Managers' attitudes towards the punishment of pupils throw an interesting light on their philosophy of education generally.
    A Lancasterian school manager recorded in 1818 that "three boys confin'd in the strong Room broke out by knocking down part of the wall on the school side." Tottenham Lancasterian Day Book, 1813–22, 29 July, 1818. E.Mx.3 (G.L.R.O. [Middx]).
    A compromise solution was found at Taunton where the managers suggested to the teacher "that he do not strike the boys during school hours but when he finds it necessary, to punish them out of school hours." Taunton Central National School, Minute Book 1836–42. (Somerset R.O.). Managers' attitudes were perhaps best summed up by a discussion at a meeting in May, 1886 at Riseley, Bedfordshire, where the managers supported the master in administering corporal punishment. "They agreed also with the Chairman in thinking that if they had not been well licked themselves when boys, they would have been even worse men now than they are." Riseley National School, Managers' Minute Book, 1871–90, 11 May, 1886. S.D. 2812/1 (Bedfordshire C.R.O.).
39 Leicester, Christow St. Infant Board School, 12 July, 1892. Managers' Minute Book, 1892–1914. 19. D.59 VII 338 (Leicester Museum, Department of Archives).
40 Leicester, Christow St. Infant Board School, Managers' Minute Book 1892–1914. 19. D.59 VII 338 (Leicester Museum, Department of Archives). National studies are lacking but a recent study of the social composition

of the Leicestershire School Board suggests that it corresponds approximately with that of the local managers in London rather than with the Board itself. Of the fifty three members who served in the six Leicester Boards, there were three women and fifty men: of the men thirteen were clergy (eight Church, four Nonconformists, one Roman Catholic), ten manufacturers and merchants, seven professional men, three managers, five shopkeepers, nine artisans and three gentlemen of no occupation. A. Gill, "The Leicester School Board 1871–1903" in B. Simon (ed.) *Education in Leicestershire 1540–1940* (1968), pp. 156–77.

41 Sentiments expressed some seventy years later in, for example, official publications such as *Half Our Future* (1963), Ch. 16, "The Subjects and the Curriculum", pp. 124–7 and *The New Curriculum* (1967), pp. 18–19.

42 School Board for London. Report on the Subjects and Modes of Instruction in the Board's Schools. Recommendations, 29 February, 1888. SBL. 792 (G.L.R.O. [London]).

43 W. Bousfield, *Elementary Scholars. How to Increase Their Utility, being six lectures delivered to the Managers of the London School Board in 1898 and 1890* (1890), pp. 27–8.

44 W. Bousfield, *supra*, p. 129.

45 F. G. Bettany, *Stewart Headlam: A Biography* (1926), p. 149.

46 Sandford to Lumley, 24 October, 1873. Plymouth Ed. 16/51.

47 Lumley to Sandford, *ibid.*, 25 October, 1873.

48 Harrowby to Salisbury, 16 July, 1891. Salisbury MSS. A similar view had been expressed by H.M.I. Mr. Sewell in 1881. "I continue to repeat a suggestion I made ten years ago, that members of the School Boards should go out of office in detachments as the members of local boards do. A continuity of policy would thus be secured and officers of the board would be less likely to be at the mercy of the clerk, the only permanent depository of its tradition." BPP. 1882 XXIII, pp. 422–3.

49 For an exposition on the theory and development of bureaucracy, see P. M. Blau, *Bureaucracy in Modern Society* (1965), Chapter 2.

50 W. Hughes, "Notes on Elementary Education" in *Transactions of the Manchester Statistical Society op. cit.*, pp. 32–3. cf. W. O. Lester Smith, *Education* (1962), p. 142.

51 *School Board Gazette*, Vol. VIII, No. 3, September, 1902, pp. 192–3.

52 C. R. Burchnall, *The Story of Education and the Schools of Deeping St. James* (1957), p. 21.

53 E. J. D. Warrillow, *A Sociological History of the City of Stoke-upon-Trent* (1960), p. 293.

54 Letter from Chairman of School Board to Education Department, Burstwick School Board Letter Book 1892–1903, 4 March, 1902 (East Riding C.R.O.).

55 On the appointment of the Manchester Board in December, 1870 the chairman himself dealt with the correspondence. The first task of the newly appointed Clerk was to go round the schools with a foot rule, measuring the existing accommodation. N. Morris, "Manchester and the Supply of Schools" in *Manchester and Its Region: a survey prepared for the Meeting of the British Association* (1962), p. 217.

56 Report of the work accomplished by the Birmingham School Board during the six years ended 28 November, 1876 (1876), p. 73.

57 Hull School Board, 2nd Triennial Report, 1874–7, p. 12.

58 29 January, 1900. Rawtenstall, Ed. 16/146.

59 White to Chambers, 17 February, 1900, Rawtenstall, Ed. 16/146.

60 Exeter School Board, Daily Diary of John Austin, School Board Clerk, 1880–7 (Exeter City R.O.).

61 Triennial Report of the School Board of the United District of Swansea, November 1876, p. 16.

62 Birmingham School Board, *Six Years of Educational Work in Birmingham* (1876).

63 The interchangeability of the roles of school board inspector and clerk can be illustrated by the example of the appointment to the Birmingham School Board in 1882 of Mr. Barnes, who had been clerk to the Kings Norton Board for the previous three years. Report of the Birmingham School Board, November, 1882, p. 57.

64 G. A. Christian, *English Education from Within* (1922), pp. 165–6.

65 E. L. Edmonds, *The School Inspector* (1962), p. 100.

66 Bingham, *op. cit.*, p. 14.

67 Birmingham School Board, *Six Years of Educational Work in Birmingham* (1876).

68 Salford School Board, Report for year ending September, 1879, p. 4.

69 Leicester School Board. Circular No. 170, 11 September, 1895. 19. D.59 VII, 450 (Leicester Museum, Department of Archives).

70 *School Board Chronicle*, 20 March, 1886.

71 Leeds School Board. Report of Chief Inspector of the Board, September, 1899, p. 16.

72 "Gradually the criterion of real power passed from 'grants' which had been controlled by the Board of Education inspection to 'promotion of teachers', in which the active agents were the officials and chiefly the inspectors of the local authority." G. A. Christian, *op. cit.*, p. 152.

73 See Appendix C. Answers of Individual Representative Managers to Questions Set by Sub Committee. Vol. II, pp. 160–2. July, 1902.

74 T. A. Spalding, *The Work of the London School Board*, (1900), p. 110.

75 *Cross*. Evidence. Diggle Q. 30230.

76 School Board for London. Report of Special Committee on the mode of election and powers of managers, 1887. Evidence. 13 July, 1887, p. 20. SBL. 1509 (G.L.R.O. [London]).

77 *Cross*. Evidence. A. C. Rogers Q. 28449.

78 This was also brought out in the Annual Report to the Committee for Council on Education by H.M. Inspector, Mr. N. Stokes for 1879, BPP. 1880 XXII, p. 403.

79 School Board for London. Special Committee on Managers of Board Schools, their constitution and Powers, 1882. SBL. 404 (G.L.R.O. [London]).

80 School Board for London. Report of Special Committee on Managers, 2 August, 1882, para 2.

81 Special Committee on the Mode of Election and the Powers of Managers, December, 1887. SBL. 1509. (G.L.R.O. [London]). But the system continued unchanged.

82 Spalding *op. cit.*, p. 112.
    Sydney Buxton, later 1st Earl of Buxton, became the first Chairman of the Committee of Representative Managers in London. At their opening meeting in 1884, Mundella and Forster had addressed the managers. Buxton, in inviting another ex-Vice-President of the Council to attend the following year told Lord Harrowby, "The managers are *much* in need of encouragement." Buxton to Harrowby, 10 June, 1885, Harrowby MSS., Vol. LII, f. 70 (Sandon Hall, Staffs.).

83 School Board for London. Special Committee on the Mode of Election and Powers of Managers, 1887, *supra*, p. 26.

84 C. Bibby, *T. H. Huxley* (1959), p. 160.
85 C. E. B. Reed, *Memoir of Sir Charles Reed* (1883), p. 173.
86 Special Committee, 1887, *supra*, pp. 14 and 34.
87 School Board for London. Sub-Committee on Alleged Breach of Discipline of a Member of the Board, Mr. Stonelake, 18 July, 1887. SBL. 792 (G.L.R.O. [London]).
88 Special Committee on the Mode of Election, 1887, *supra*, p. 21.
89 But in 1892, the School Management Committee gave the local managers the function of selection of headmasters from short lists of three candidates drawn up by the Committee.
90 One witness before the 1887 Special Committee, Major Wade, a local manager, stated, "We have had Managers come into our Committee without the smallest introduction whatever. Nobody knew them. We received them courteously, paused to know their business and it has turned out that they were new Managers. It is awkward for them and for us." Evidence, 4 May, 1887, *supra*.
91 School Board for London. Special Committee on the Appointment, Duties and Privileges of Local Managers, March, 1892. SBL. 403.
92 T. Gautrey, *Lux Mihi Laus: School Board Memories* (1937), p. 61.
93 Special Committee, 1892. Memorandum, with suggestions by the Chairman of the Special Committee, 6 April, 1892. SBL. 403, pp. 1–2.
94 Memorandum, p. 3, Special Committee, 1892, *supra*.
95 Report of the Special Committee, 15 February, 1893, p. vii, SBL. 1511.
96 Appointment of College Teachers, G. H. Croad to Local Managers, July 1900. Sigdon Rd. Group, Dalston. Managers' Minute Book, 1898–1903. EO/PS/6/94 (G.L.R.O. [London]).
97 Tooting Graveney School, Managers' Minute Book, 1886–1893. 13 July, 1900. EO/PS/6/101 (G.L.R.O. [London]).
98 Special Committee on the Mode of Election and Powers of Managers, 1887. Appendix III, p. 188.
99 *Cross*, Evidence Q. 26424.
100 Mrs. Heberden, 2 November, 1887, Special Committee 1887, p. 36.
101 *Cross*, Evidence Q. 57752.
102 *Ibid*, Rev. T. W. Sharpe, H.M.I. Q. 4749–50.
103 Letter, W. Bousfield, Chairman of the Committee of Representative Managers to Special Committee on the appointment, duties and privileges of Local Managers, 26 May, 1892, SBL. 403.
104 *Cross*, Evidence, Sharpe, Q. 4994.
105 SBL. 1510 (G.L.R.O. [London]).
106 H. J. Dyos and A. B. M. Baker, "The Possibilities of Computerising Census Data", in H. J. Dyos (ed.) *The Study of Urban History* (1968), especially pp. 103–7.
107 G. W. Jones, *Borough Politics: A Study of Wolverhampton Town Council, 1885–1964* (1969), pp. 350–68.
108 13 architects, 11 accountants, 6 artists, 5 surveyors, 4 writers, 2 civil servants, 1 keeper at the British Museum and 1 actuary.
109 H. Pelling, *Social Geography of British Elections 1885–1910* (1967), p. 55–6.
110 See H. J. Dyos, *Victorian Suburb* (1961).
111 A ranking of trades in 19th and early 20th centuries can be found in E. J. Hobsbawm, "The Labour Aristocracy", E. J. Hobsbawm (ed.), *Studies in the History of Labour* (1964) pp. 280–6.
112 Special Committee on the Appointment and Privileges of Local Managers, 6 July, 1892. SBL. 403 (G.L.R.O. [London]).

113 Wallas to A. J. Balfour, Memorandum on Managers, undated but late October, 1902. Ed. 24/15 (P.R.O.).
114 S. Webb, *London Education* (1904), p. 44.
115 *Ibid.*

5

Issues Affecting the Appointment of School Managers

Apart from the issues relating to the functions of managers under different school boards and in voluntary school settings, at least three other variables in the situation may be discerned which affected the representative aspect of management. These were the limitations placed on parents, women, and "the working class" as managers. Although they will be dealt with separately, these categories overlap a good deal.

PARENTS AS MANAGERS

The representation of parents on managing bodies has recently become a prominent issue, following the evidence submitted to the Plowden Committee; the debate has ranged through official publications,[1] research studies,[2] educational magazines,[3] political pamphlets,[4] and the popular press.[5] It is interesting to observe that a similar movement was evident in the 1890s on much the same issues.

Following the evidence given before the Cross Commission on the subject, its Report gave a guarded welcome to the presence of parents as managers and concluded,

"So long however as the parents are not a preponderating element, we should be glad to see them represented on the committee of management. But, while voluntary schools do not receive aid from the rates, there seems to be no sufficient reason why the management clauses of their trust deeds should be set aside, in order to introduce representatives of the ratepayers."[6]

Frederick Temple, giving evidence before the Newcastle Commission in 1861, had favoured parental representation in the election of managers of voluntary schools.[7]

Certainly, a case could be made out for parents as representatives on account of their payment of fees to the school and therefore their help in supporting it. Some writers believed, on the contrary, that the parent was ill-equipped for this task. One such writer, J. C.

Tarver, in an article entitled "Education and Parental Control", poked fun at the parent as manager. For one thing

> "people who are very particular about the education of other people's children ignore their own convictions when they select a school for their own sons."[8]

Unlike a normal commercial transaction, the person who pays for education is not the person who receives the benefit, and it is therefore impossible to accept the judgment of the person being educated. Conflict, he implied, is necessary and even healthy: the parents want "good results" and the methods employed for this are of lesser importance:

> "It is surely obvious that even if good results could be quickly obtained, only a very small minority of parents are fitted by previous training to appreciate them, for which reason parental strictures upon a school curriculum are invariably limited to finding fault with the writing, the arithmetic, the geography, and the absence of colloquial teaching of modern languages."[9]

He concludes with a final thrust and a direct appeal:

> "Immediate parental control is certainly not to be recommended for any school. Madam, would you like to feel that the destinies of your beloved Tommy were in the hands of your neighbours, Mrs. Smith and Mrs. Jones and that horrid Mrs. Brown?"[10]

More fundamentally, as Professor Findlay pointed out almost fifty years ago, it never occurred to anyone that the parent could or should exercise a voice in management

> "for the very idea of elementary education sprang from pity for poor folk who could *not* organize, could *not* pay, could *not* realise what was good for their children. It is not surprising therefore that the organizers of schooling from the first compulsory Act of 1870 to the last of 1918 treated 'the parent' as a prospective enemy, to be coerced by threat of summons and penalty."[11]

There were at least two more immediate causes which prevented parents becoming managers. The first was the nature, in voluntary schools, of trust deeds which often stipulated that the management committee should consist of contributors to the school, and variation of a trust deed was a costly affair. Even where no restriction was placed on office holders, it was natural, given the financial situation of voluntary schools, that subscribers should have priority both as the electing body and also for candidature as managers. Unless parents were also subscribers, the need for parents *qua* parents as managers, was not easy to defend.

J. P. Norris, an ex-H.M.I., advanced the plea that such representation would go far beyond any pecuniary advantage and that the school would gain an "accession of morals".

"The parents," he argued, "would begin to regard it as an institution belonging to themselves in a great measure. Hitherto they have felt that it is the parson, or the squire, or the mill owner that is inviting them to one school rather than to another; they have a notion that they are in some way 'obliging' the managers of that school. Their attachment to a school in whose administration they have no concern is proportionately loose; and hence much of the evils complained of—apathy, want of co-operation with the teachers, irregular attendance, removal of their children for the most frivolous reasons."[12]

As an inspector some forty years previously, Norris himself had pleaded for such parental participation and had noted in his reports isolated instances where this had worked well.[13]

Politically, the issue became alive through a number of factors: the rise of representative bodies, such as county councils, political movements resulting in wider enfranchisement, the opportunities offered in school board elections which, although not specifically offering parental representation, gave an opportunity for a wider range of representation than offered by voluntary schools; and the findings of the Cross Commission, which stimulated public discussion on the role of parents in education. In 1890 and 1891 Bills were presented to Parliament to facilitate parental representation in the management of voluntary schools but they received no support. The preambles, identical in both cases, pointed to the necessity for such an Act. Often the schools were so situated that they were the only ones accessible to the parents of children attending them; therefore they should be represented. The Bills would have made subscribers, parents or any inhabitant householder of the neighbourhood eligible to elect representatives to participate in management "without regard to religious denomination, any trust deed, management clause, agreement or other document".[14]

The Free Education Act of 1891 had the potential to alter drastically the relationships between parents and managers. On the one hand, the "subscriber" argument was thereafter considerably weakened though it was not altogether discounted; on the other, it could be said that parents' most important and often only means of exercising influence in the running of the school—i.e. payment of fees—had been greatly diminished by direct Government subsidy. A. H. D. Acland, shortly to become the Liberal Vice-President, expressed this point of view in a debate on the Bill.

"We have not heard a word as to control going along with the payment of fees. What kind of influence or control do the Government propose to give to the parents? At present, at any rate, through the payment of fees a parent has some kind of reasonable relation towards the managers of the schools, but under the Government proposals it is possible that there will be managers who will not represent the wishes of the people at all."[15]

It was just this objection that Kekewich, the Secretary to the Department, had hoped to meet at an early stage of the Bill's proceedings. He proposed to the Cabinet that in any voluntary schools receiving the fee grant, the parents should be represented on the committee of management. An order was to be issued by the Education Department directing managers to call a meeting of parents attending the school at which a representative parent or parents should be elected, forming at least one third of the total number of persons comprising the committee. Each parent would have one vote (voting papers might be used) and the managers would be required to certify annually, before receiving the fee grant, that the required election had been held.[16]

The denominational difficulty was not to be solved by Kekewich's scheme. Parents participating in voting would be of the same denomination as the other managers, thus denying possible minority representation. Some special provision for Welsh schools was contemplated.[17]

This proposal for parental representation received only lukewarm political support. R. W. Dale, an opponent of free education on the Cross Commission, wrote to Chamberlain about this time:

"The proposal to give the parents as such power to elect representatives on the managing boards seems odd; if when they were paying fees they had received this power there would have been reason in it; but to give them special representation at the moment they cease to be special contributors seems hardly reasonable. And they are a fluctuating body which seems another objection to it."[18]

Chamberlain himself, the earlier champion of the representative elements in local government, showed little positive enthusiasm for the scheme. In an article on "The Problem of Free Education", *The Times*, whilst agreeing with the notion of parents of scholars being associated with the management of the school, mentioned the difficulties which might arise in carrying out such a proposal:

"It is put forward rather as a counsel of perfection to be pressed voluntarily upon school managers than as serious material for a new Education Act; for to quote Mr. Chamberlain's words, 'If they (the managers) would not do that, then he should still say, whether with representation or without it, he was in favour of making all schools free, and he should leave the issue of the denominational schools to be fought on other grounds altogether'."[19]

There was a divergence of opinion within the Church of England on this question. Canon Gregory, representing the National Society, suggested to Lord Cranbrook (Lord President at the time of the Free Education Bill),

"that there be placed upon the committee of management of every free school a minority and say one, two and at most three, of the parents of the children attending the school, to be elected by all the parents of such children."[20]

Unlike Kekewich's scheme, this would not have confined election solely to the parents of the same religious persuasion as that of the school. A more extreme view was taken, some time after the passing of the Free Education measure, by the Bishop of Coventry, who was to figure conspicuously later during the operation of the Voluntary Schools Act (see Chapter 6). At a meeting of the Church school managers and subscribers of the Archdeaconry of Birmingham, the Bishop remarked on the so-called "inalienable right of the parent in the management of the school". Where, he asked, did that right come in?

"His lordship cited the management of private schools, public schools such as Eton, Rugby and Harrow, and the Board Schools, where there was no parental control. He did not find on the School Boards any representative of parents. He found representatives of the Ratepayers, but not of parents as parents. The fact was that the management of schools went with the payment of schools, and that payment was divided between the State, which took the greatest part, and the management, and the State left either to the locality or the denomination which found the remainder of the money the rest of the management. He did not find in private, public, or Board Schools, any inalienable right of the parents to have a voice in the conduct of the schools."[21]

There was some evidence to back up this harsh statement. A special committee was set up by the London School Board in 1887 "to investigate the Mode of Election and the Powers of Managers". One of the questions put by the committee was as to the advisability of allowing the parents of children attending the school, or the ratepayers, to elect representatives to serve on the various committees of managers, but the almost unanimous feeling was against the suggestion.[22]

Despite the fact that the 1891 Free Education Act made no mention of the representation of new elements in the management of schools,[23] between the passing of the Act and the end of the century there was a gradual and increasing appearance of parents on managing bodies. Church school boards, which were the executive element of the Church Day Schools Association, occasionally included this element in their constitutions. The Manchester and Salford Church Schools Board, "formed so as to become the managers of such schools as may be handed over to it under Sections 6 and 7 of the Elementary Education Act, 1891", consisted of twenty-one members—the Lord Bishop, five members nominated by the Church Day Schools Association Committee, three to be appointed by the trustees and managers (voting together) of the Church schools in the district, and "six to be elected by the parents of the scholars in the schools managed by this Board, so soon as the number of schools in connection with this Board amounts to six, a proportional number being elected by parents previous to that time". The members were to hold office for three years.[24]

The Church schools in Middlesex seem to have adopted parent-managers more readily than others did. In common with the Manchester scheme, this system was more likely to be successful where a grouping of schools had taken place for financial purposes, electing a common committee. This had been made possible by Section 7 of the 1891 Act, but the clause was an entirely permissive one. At Friern Barnet, five schools had grouped together to form a general schools committee. The subscription component, however, was still a requirement. It was agreed at a meeting held ten days before the Act came into operation

> "that parents of all scholars at each school should be invited to subscribe 2s. 6d. a year to each school respectively and those subscribing that amount or upwards should be entitled to elect annually for each school respectively two Consultative Managers from among their own number."[25]

This plan was afterwards carried out but the interest in this scheme was not subsequently maintained. In the election of parents in November, 1900, only four were present out of which two were elected. The following year's meeting was cancelled as no one attended, and the previous year's managers agreed to continue in office.[26] In single schools such generous representation was unlikely.[27]

On the whole, the parent-representatives' role in most managers' meetings was indistinguishable from the others. Only rarely did the parent make any special contribution to the proceedings. One of the few examples recorded demonstrated the delicacy of his position: the possibility of appearing to criticize the school whilst attempting to give constructive advice. In this instance, the master, the other managers and the parent-manager were fortunately of one mind.

A Lancashire school, Lindale National at Grange-over-Sands, elected Mr. Stephen Shackley as parent representative in June, 1898. A practical and useful member of the committee, by September of that year he had voluntarily cleaned the gulleys and spouts of the school free of expense and had advised that the schoolmistress's house should be built in the spring rather than at that time of the year. Of greater importance was the fact that at the school committee meeting he moved a resolution:

> "That H.M.I. be respectfully asked to explain why he had reported the children to be slovenly in appearance. Both Parents and Master had been very careful as to this matter, and it was generally believed that the children did appear clean and tidy."

The master, Mr. Irving, agreed with Shackley that the Inspector should be asked to explain. H.M.I. Mr. Bernays, the author of the report, was sent a letter the following week by the secretary of the committee quoting Shackley's protest and requesting an explanation. Bernays assured the school in his reply that what he had observed on that occasion was "exceptional" and was not to be taken as a general criticism.[28]

The Voluntary Schools Act of 1897 establishing associations of voluntary schools on diocesan lines raised further problems of parent representation. The governing bodies of associations were to be elected by managers or "representatives" of the managers, and it was doubtful if a parent would be elected to the governing body unless this was proposed by school managers. During the course of the passage of this Bill through the Commons, an amendment was introduced which would have specified that parents would be a necessary element in the governing bodies. It was suggested during the debate that parish meetings should be called annually to elect representatives of parents, but the amendment was heavily defeated.[29]

The main opportunity for settling the parent-manager issue came with the 1902 Education Act. Chamberlain, in a letter to *The Times* of 24 April, 1902, outlined his plan for putting education under a single local authority "working through a representative committee". Similarly, he suggested that managers at voluntary schools should "receive on their Committees representatives of Ratepayers and parents of the Children". At that time, the Education Bill contained neither of these proposals and they subsequently became a matter for debate in Parliament.[30]

N

A new element had entered into the situation with the changed concept of the nature of the administrative authority to be responsible for education. Who, in fact, were the new local authorities intending to represent? As early as 1895, Gorst, when devising his abortive Education Bill, which assumed the establishment of larger authorities for education, wrote to Balfour:

> "As regards the representatives of the new authority placed upon the Boards of Management of associated schools, they are intended to represent not the people of the locality, but the new authority itself, acting as the Agents of Government in the distribution of an Imperial Grant. I do not recognize any right on the part of the ratepayers of a rural parish, or of an urban district not a county borough, to a voice in the distribution of money paid out of the National Exchequer."[31]

Seven years later, during the debate on the constitution of managers for the county councils in July, 1902, McKenna had denounced the Bill as withdrawing all management from the parents and giving it over to the clergymen of the parish.[32] Balfour, in reply, pointed out that the local education authority was to be the fundamental and supreme local authority

> "and managers, whether of voluntary schools or of schools provided by the local education authority, possessed, and could only possess, a very subordinate position indeed as regarded anything connected with the secular education of the schools."

Nevertheless, he proposed bearing in mind the important contribution that parents as parents could make to management, that in non-provided schools, one of the two representatives of popularly elected bodies "must be a parent".[33] The notorious Clause 7 of which this suggestion formed a part, was later dropped by the Government. The evening before the Bill left the Commons, a final attempt was made by the Opposition to reinstate Balfour's provision for parent-managers, but it was heavily defeated.[34]

Whilst these events were in train, the Vicar of Eccles, Manchester, had written to the Bishop of Winchester, supporting the idea of parental representation on managing committees, based on twenty-five years' personal experience of serving on school boards and as a school manager.

> "What we need to create and foster is real interest and sense of responsibility in parents. If they have a legal right to elect representative managers, it will make them 'rise to the occasion' as nothing else could. Our inviting them to do so now is regarded with the same languid interest as is an invitation to elect a 'Voluntary Church Council' by our parishioners, for they know we are not giving them any real legal power or status.

"There is humour about the suggestion too. All the parents who come to the clergyman to complain that their children are being unfairly treated would go to their Representative Managers under the proposed system, which would give the poor parson great relief!"[35]

The result of the Act was that, in the case of provided schools only, the county councils were compulsorily required to have a committee of managers: for the voluntary schools there were to be four foundation (i.e. denominational) and two representative managers. No conditions were attached to the nature of the representative managers' appointments, parents not being specifically mentioned. Parochial electors were to have a voice in the management as of right through their parish council and it was possible in this way for parents to be represented. The Lincoln Diocesan Board of Education actively encouraged an extension of the principle of parental control in management; a scheme suggested by the Department for electing a parent manager was that the electorate should be limited to parents of "regular children", namely those who had made 75 per cent of attendances and had been at the school for two years.[36]

It can be seen that, from the publication of the Report of the Cross Commission to the passing of the 1902 Act, a series of opportunities presented themselves to the Education Department and later the Board of Education, for establishing a parental element in school management. Despite the voluminous literature on the subject during the period, there seems to have been little genuine demand from parents themselves for representation. This is understandable for a number of reasons: lack of expertise in this field resulting from lack of opportunity, the reluctance of many people to take on the task of management which mainly consisted of fund-raising, the passing interest of the job and the uncertainty of the parent's role on the committee. The politically interested would have found their outlets in more influential fields.[37] It is only recently that the role of the parent-manager has been perceived as a potential link between the school and the wider community.

WOMEN AS MANAGERS

This section is concerned with the exercise by women of managerial or quasi-managerial functions rather than as owners of schools, which has been dealt with in Chapter 2.

Because of the nature of the task, which required a certain amount of leisure time, the work was carried on very largely by the wives and daughters of middle and upper class families. A characteristic of all types of female participation in this work was its short-lived and spasmodic nature. Family, entertaining, travelling commitments and marriage accounted for much of this. This seems to have been true of both voluntary and school board membership. To take one example, during the thirty-three years of existence of the London School Board, only half the lady members served for more than a term of three years.[38] Nevertheless, the presence of women on the larger school boards was consciously sought after: from 1873 onwards, for example, the Birmingham School Board was never without a woman member.[39]

In country districts especially, the philanthropic and religious leanings of families often found their outlet in the schools.[40] Dorothea Brooke in George Eliot's *Middlemarch* is perhaps a typical character of her time: living in a village with her uncle at Tipton Grange, "a young lady of some worth and fortune, who knelt suddenly down on a brick floor by the side of a sick labourer and prayed fervently as if she thought herself being in the time of the Apostles", and who took part in teaching at the village school.[41] Or a little later, there was Lady Kate Amberley, fourth daughter of Lord Stanley of Alderley, who recorded in her diary:

> "We examined the first classes together in sums, dictation, geography and the Bible and the three best got prizes and so on with other classes. It was a great encouragement for children and mistresses who had never had prizes or treats. We have announced it for another year so it will be a stimulus to Education and we shall examine in English, History and Physiology besides—I shall give them the books."[42]

The interest taken in the schools by the ladies was not always quite so selfless. The British and Foreign Schools Society entrusted the management of affairs of the girls' department to a committee of ladies as early as 1815. Their object in undertaking the duty was

> "to excite a general interest in the minds of the sex in behalf of the lower class of females. The benefits which may be expected to arise are invaluable. It is well known that of female servants, the majority cannot read, and it is very rare to meet one who is capable of writing a legible hand."[43]

Sewing was also a desirable accomplishment. It is not surprising therefore to read a typical log book entry such as that at Oxborough, Norfolk, "Lady Bedingfeld visited the school and examined the copybooks and the needlework most minutely".[44] Lord and Lady Vernon of Sudbury Hall, Derbyshire, in a similar manner

> "taught the children of the village school to take an interest in country affairs and appreciate the beauties of nature . . . they wanted to bring up children to be useful on the farms and the brightest they wanted for the better posts on their estates."[45]

Powers of full management were granted in voluntary schools to women in some instances: in others it remained a male prerogative. In the British Schools system, especially, women were often given the full management of the school including, in many instances, financial responsibility. At York, for example, the school committee of Bishophill Senior Girls' School consisted entirely of women. The personnel had remained stable over a great number of years. The report for 1875 regretted the departure of Marie Richardson, who had relinquished the office of treasurer, "a post she had so efficiently filled for eleven years".[46]

The Kingston Public School at Kingston, Surrey, provides an early example of a fully formed and entire ladies' committee. Opened in 1818 under the presidency of the Earl of Liverpool, it provided that "the management of the Girls' School should be under the exclusive direction of a Patroness, and not less than four Vice-Patrons and a superintending Committee of Ladies". The committee set to work with a will, performing a wide range of functions. One questionable activity was the method prescribed for dealing with misdemeanours and the future prevention of more serious offences among the children:

"A label expressive of such offences committed be conspicuously affixed to the offender for a stated time. Among such offences are Falsehood, Theft, Irreverence in the House of God, Bad Expressions, Disobedience to Parents, Disrespectful Conduct to the Mistress and Violent Behaviour to Schoolfellows."[47]

By 1858 the committee were reminding pupil teachers:

"that they are not in their present positions merely as show pieces. The ladies are very sorry to see the pupil teachers dress so unsuitably to their stations; they fear the time bestowed on their dress has prevented their giving their due attention to preparation for their duties."[48]

Drastic action such as was resorted to by the Winchester Central National School Ladies' Committee was seldom emulated. On 30 August, 1820, the committee went together to a parent of one of the children, Mrs. Beard, to remonstrate with her on her conduct in coming to the school and abusing the headmistress "using ill language before the whole school". As Mrs. Beard refused to apologize, the Mayor of Winchester was appealed to; the unfortunate woman was summoned to the Guildhall where the Mayor "found the offence such as would have authorized him to commit her to Bridewell unless the ladies would sooner accept her apology". The ladies chose the latter alternative, stipulating that she made either an apology in the newspapers or in the presence of the ladies and the whole school. Surprisingly, the latter course was preferred. The account concludes,

> "She appeared in the school accordingly on Monday, 2nd September, made her Public Apology and requested that her children might be continued in the school, which was granted."[49]

Occasionally, women managers were appointed in a predominantly male committee. There were often difficulties to be overcome. Miss Charlotte Cubbins, a woman manager at Stanwell, Middlesex, made strenuous efforts to drill the children in reading and arithmetic. Children were sometimes kept in after school. One father consequently took his child out of school without asking leave; the same afternoon he was obliged to apologize to the chairman of managers, Sir John Cubbins, Miss Cubbins's father, who remonstrated with the parent. Later, a pupil teacher was called before the committee and made to apologize for having "behaved impudently" towards Miss Cubbins.[50]

Direct representation on school boards by women was common, but the Exeter School Board furnishes a unique example of the retention of a ladies' committee in a board setting. The committee, which flourished throughout the board's existence (1871 to 1904), was naturally expected to supervise needlecraft and act as visitors to the schools; but in addition it reported directly to the board and was able in time to expand its activities. Mrs Beatrice Temple, wife of Frederick Temple, then Bishop of Exeter, was a member from its establishment in 1871 and later president of the committee; thus she remained until Temple's translation to London in 1885. Close cooperation between the board and the committee was assured because of the predominantly Anglican majority on the school board.

Much good welfare work was done by the committee. In 1881 Mrs. Temple requested the gentlemen of the Exeter School Board to grant a bedstead for the infants department of a school,

> "as it is generally considered that in order to ensure a healthy development of the mental and physical powers, much sleep is required in early years. . . . Some of the children attending the new Town School are under three years of age and become extremely drowsy in the afternoons, one having slipped off a bench when slumbering and hurt itself last summer."[51]

By the turn of the century, a number of interesting innovations had been introduced by the committee, including an exercise in home-school relationships. Many of the Exeter schools were in the poorer district of the city, and the committee spent much time in home visiting. It was considered desirable to interest the mothers of pupils in the work of the children and successful evening meetings for parents were held in schools.[52]

Apart from London and Liverpool, where a third of the local managers were women, representation of women on school boards was both minimal and sporadic.[53] At Southampton, where local management was delegated to school managers' committees, that of the Eastern District, consisting of four men, early in its existence resolved to invite three ladies to join them. One was the wife of the correspondent and the other two ladies were wives of school board members.[54] This policy does not seem to have operated in the other districts of the town.

Women members made their greatest impact in social aspects of education. At Leeds, Mrs. Catherine M. Buckton gave a course of lessons in "Physiology and the Laws of Health" to the pupil-teachers and the elder scholars.[55] Margaret McMillan, a member of the Bradford School Board from 1894 to 1902, laid stress on "Ventilation, School Baths and Medical Inspection".[56] During the previous decade another member of the same board, Miss Edith Lupton, had campaigned singlehanded against home lessons; and this terminated successfully with a High Court case in which her actions were vindicated.[57] On the Manchester Board, Miss Mary Dendy succeeded Mrs. C. P. Scott, wife of the editor of the *Manchester Guardian*, in 1896, and took a keen interest in advancing domestic economy in the schools.[58]

In country districts, with very much smaller boards, it was less likely that women would be represented. The exception to this is occasionally found where a local notable person expressed an interest in the work. At Stapleford, Cambridgeshire, for instance, which was a rural parish, Her Grace the Duchess of Leeds had been one of the four school board members from its beginning in 1876 until 1893 when she left the district; she was also responsible for providing the materials for the girls' fancy work and selling the articles when made.[59]

Participation of women in school management was not unexpectedly to be found on its largest scale in London. They could serve both as school board members or as local managers. During the London School Board's existence twenty-four out of the three hundred and twenty-six individuals who served as members were women. A number were motivated by their wish to ameliorate the home conditions of the children as, for example, Miss Susan Lawrence and Miss Honner Morten, the latter being one of the four Fabians returned in the 1897 London elections.[60] It also attracted feminists—Mrs. Emmeline Pankhurst and Miss Henrietta Miller—

and others with special causes such as Mrs. Annie Besant who had with Bradlaugh become a fervent propagandist of "anti-religious secularism". One woman member, Miss Bayliss, had the distinction of heading the poll for the London School Board.[61]

Far more numerous were the lady local managers.[62] In 1884 there were 290 in the metropolitan boroughs, almost one-fifth of the total number.[63] The work seems to have been undertaken both extensively and intensively. The London lady managers, like those in other parts of the country, were drawn almost exclusively from the middle class. Difficulty was experienced occasionally in restraining some of them from acting beyond their jurisdiction in the face of manifest injustice towards children. Jane M. E. Brownlow was a local manager in the Finsbury Division where Lord Beauchamp, the Progressive Party Divisional member,[64] was responsible for the local managers of the division. A personal friend of Lord Beauchamp, Miss Brownlow illustrates the growing interest of women in social issues and the desire for more education amongst middle class women in the 1890s. A society had been started exclusively for ladies with a similar outlook. On 7 December, 1898, Miss Brownlow wrote to Lord Beauchamp:

> "On February 23rd Mr. Fawcett is going to open our Debate declaring 'That the Government were right to relax the compulsory clauses of the Vaccination Act.' Could you, will you, come and oppose? We usually have 250 to 300 people—and Lady Elizabeth Best (who is my cousin) and I are doing our best to suppress fads and bring our members to view things from a quite common-sense point of view. There are a great many women in our Club who have never thought about anything but dress and society before they joined us. They are usually inclined to rush into extremes and to sentimentalise.
>
> "Your help will be just invaluable to us who are trying to make ourselves reasonable."[65]

The machinery for dealing with urgent matters under the School Board for London, immense as it was, was a complex and necessarily bureaucratic one. Miss Brownlow was unable to resist direct action in a bad case of truancy and contacted the superintendent of school attendance herself. She wrote:

> "Dear Lord Beauchamp,
> "I fear that as usual I have let my zeal overstep prudence. Going to Bowling Green Lane on Wednesday or Thursday I found Mr. Gibberd in real distress over the case of —— ——. I feel with the Master that every day's delay is dangerous in this case. The child may be past saving if allowed to go on much longer. So I sat down and wrote a letter, of which I enclose a draft. Of course I manifestly overstepped my duties. Still I do feel this is a thing I must do in special cases. Human souls can't

be tied up in red tape—and one can't wait for managers meetings and such formalities while boys are being ruined for life.

"Still if I get into trouble I deserve it for I am too hasty and too independent, and therefore I don't appeal to you for help, but merely report my indiscretion as you have taken an interest in the affair."

Beauchamp, a kindly soul, noted on the letter: "It (the case) will come up tomorrow night. Can you prevent Saunders from snubbing her?"[66]

Despite such examples, there was increasing recognition of the contribution of the work of women on school boards; but the prejudice shown against them was not always easily overcome. In 1895, the School Board for London nominated a woman to represent them on the Council of Charterhouse School; the Council protested that a male member was preferable, but the board stood its ground.[67]

A fundamental issue, that concerning the legal right of women to be eligible for school board or managerial service, was not cleared up until 1902. In a debate on the Bill in July of that year concerning an amendment which would have included the addition of the words "of both sexes" after the word "managers", Mr. Ernest Gray, one of the teachers' representatives, stated that for many years voters had held their tongues as to the position of women on school boards, but he was told that if the point were raised in the Law Courts it was very doubtful whether it would be found that women had a right to serve.[68] Despite the denials of the Attorney-General that there might be some disqualification at common law, the matter remained in some doubt. Another lawyer member disagreed with the Attorney-General, stating that in a legal sense, the married woman was not a personality; she was merged in the personality of her husband, and therefore both sex and *couverture* were disabilities for a seat on a board of school management.[69] Charles Dilke, a notable feminist advocate, demonstrated that the Courts had upheld views diametrically opposed to the intention of the House of Commons.

This confusion arose out of a conflict between statutory and judicial pronouncements. The Married Women's Property Act of 1882 had established proprietary rights for women. In 1889, the Interpretation Act, Section 1 (1) (*a*) further specifically provided that unless the contrary intention appeared words importing the masculine gender should include females; doubtless, it was this Act which the Attorney-General had in mind during the debate. The same year as the Act was passed a law case (*Beresford Hope* v. *Lady Sandhurst*)[70] found that where a statute dealt with the exercise of public functions, unless that statute expressly gave power to women to exercise them, the true construction was that the powers given were confined to men.

It was an anomalous position for women managers; women filled the majority of the teaching posts and the Board of Education and local authorities had women inspectors. Balfour clearly had not been aware of this difficulty and agreed to clear up the matter, so far as the Bill was concerned, by inserting words in the definition clause "which would make it the avowed and deliberate intention of the Government absolutely to encourage women's continuing participation in school management".[71]

In the Act, Section 17 (3) (c) provided "for the inclusion of women as well as men among the members of the Committee". Taking the wording broadly, it seemed as if each particular scheme, in order to comply with the wording, must provide for the inclusion of several women; this would be more in accordance with the letter of the Act than a scheme which provided for only one. In fact, it was thought possible to construe the word "women" generally and in accordance with this construction, a number of schemes were submitted by councils and approved by the Board of Education which did not provide for the inclusion of more than one woman.[72]

The provisions of this section were taken up by councils with varying degrees of enthusiasm. Many managers appreciated the need for the continuance, and indeed, expansion of the help given by their lady colleagues. J. H. Arkwright, a manager for over forty years of a small Herefordshire village school, may be taken as a typical example.

An influential figure, a county councillor as well as Lord-Lieutenant of the County,[73] Arkwright appealed for support at a meeting of his local parish council in March, 1903, for his proposal to appoint another woman (the existing one was his wife) as manager on the school committee.

> "I am trying", wrote Arkwright, "to persuade the County Council Education Committee to put women in every dominion of management. I think that one-third should be women, so should like to set the example by doing it here."

His reason for advocating the proportion of one-third women on every school committee was that "the girls are at least one half and they on many points are outside the province of male management".[74]

After twenty years of experience in management, the School Board for London endorsed the value of its women members; the final committee appointed to enquire into modes of management concluded that "there should be two, three or four women on a Committee of Local Managers, of which the maximum number of managers is six, nine or twelve respectively".[75] One of the merits of the School Board for London had been that women were members with the same responsibilities and powers as men. Under the proposed L.C.C. Education Bill women were not allowed to be members of the Council; however, thanks to the endeavours of J. Scott Lidgett, the Methodist leader of the Board, this situation was altered.[76]

Although limited in numbers, women had by 1902 gained the right to take part in school management, and this right was never subsequently challenged.

WORKING PEOPLE AS MANAGERS

A less easily definable interest group in the management of elementary schools was the body described in contemporary documents as "working people". The avoidance of the term "working class" merely skated over the difficulties of terminology;[77] nevertheless the fact remains that after the coming of the school boards, there seems to have been a genuine attempt in some of the larger towns to make it possible for working people to participate in the management of schools.

Professor Simon has shown how, in the early days of the school boards, an increasing number of working men stood for election, often with little success.[78] By the mid 1880s, trade councils or trade union branches made more organized challenges and later the Socialist Democratic Federation and Fabians carried this on up to the end of the century.[79] Working class interests were, in places such as London, being served by representatives normally belonging to a different social stratum. One of the few working-class members of the School Board for London, J. M. T. Dumphreys, a Southwark leatherworker, was a Conservative working man.[80]

During the formation of the early school boards, teachers occasionally expressed an interest in representation, possibly partly in the hope of raising their low status and partly to influence the proceedings of boards.[81] One of the earliest school board elections, at Tynemouth, Northumberland, produced a non-sectarian teachers' candidate in John Manor, for twenty-one years headmaster of one of the largest schools in the town. Manor was elected to the first board but because of the bitter sectarian rivalry on the board does not seem to have made much of a mark.[82]

Greatest interest in the possibility of electing working people as managers was found in the School Board for London. A number of special committees investigated the appointment and duties of local school managers and the evidence given before them by existing school managers provides a rich store of material for illustrating contemporary attitudes towards the subject.

Up till quite late in the history of the boards, the possibility of working people as representatives had not occurred to many managers. Typifying this attitude was the evidence of Major Wade, chairman and manager of a group of schools:

> "We have no working men; neither artisans nor mechanics on our Committee. I personally should not object to them; but I do not know what particular value they would be above anyone else. It has never occurred to me that it would give the parents more confidence if some of the managers were working men."[83]

The special committee concluded in 1887, that at that time there were no working men of the artisan class on the committees of management upon which the witnesses served, and opinion was divided as to whether it would be advisable to appoint them. The balance of opinion was, however, in favour of electing them, as in the case of other managers, "if they were qualified, or had any special knowledge which would be helpful".[84]

A later inquiry in 1892 into this subject showed that in the intervening five years there had been a shift towards more definite attitudes by both divisional and local managers on the possibility of securing a fair proportion of working people on the committees of managers.[85] Their replies ranged from a Tower Hamlets representative, himself a coppersmith, "There are five mechanics on the local Committee", to the Vicar of Greenwich's short comment "Utopian".[86]

Eight main obstacles lay in the way of wider representation:

1. *Organizational: time available.* The nature of a working man's duties would prevent regular visits to schools, an important function of the School Board for London managers. One manager noted that regular visiting would be especially difficult in "tidal districts". Those working people already elected as managers were able to attend evening meetings only and most managers' meetings were held during the day. Others, who had been specially accommodated to work with an evening class committee, soon fell off attending. A retired civil servant noted that "Independent gentlemen are wanted who could devote their whole time to the schools".

2. *Lowering of status.* Many of the replies hinted at this motive in wishing to exclude working people from management. The Rev. J. E. Kempe, rector of St. James's, Piccadilly,[87] made this point manifest:

> "I most emphatically deprecate the introduction of working people into the Committee. They have no claim to be represented. They would lower

the status of the Committees and prevent some of the most valuable persons from joining."

And a Lambeth manager, a clerk by occupation, was equally certain that "nearly all the present managers would, I believe, resign". In London, the question of status of local managers was of particular importance *vis-à-vis* the divisional members and any suspicion of dilution was regarded as a move to strengthen the hand of the divisional member.

3. *Political*. The concept of school management was essentially a middle-class one, involving the ideal of service rather than gain. Political movements of the Left showed an increasing interest in education at this time, for example, the Trades Union Congress, and infiltration of representative bodies for overtly political ends was regarded as dangerous and undesirable.[88] A military outfitter confirmed this, but without giving first-hand evidence. "Working men inclined to assist in the working of schools are either Ultra-Sectarians or Socialist Radicals." A more hopeful reply came from a Hackney minister: "This is quite possible if politics are excluded."

4. *Apathy*. "Generally working people do not care for the trouble," concludes one manager. The vicar of Marylebone demonstrated this fact: "In this neighbourhood," he said, "the testimony of Managers, Teachers, and even the Caretaker, is that no suitable working people are to be found." Others submitted that there was no desire by working people to serve; many who did soon resigned. This problem of apathy in London management was not, however, confined to working people.

5. *Expense*. The cost involved in travelling to and from schools, and attending the numerous committee meetings was usually prohibitive to wage-earners.[89] If standing for election to a school board, the situation was even more difficult. The Rev. Arthur Jephson, a London School Board member, on hearing that a fellow Progressive member had been nominated as a candidate, wrote:

"I am not much elated by the news that you have already selected an election agent. I fear lest you fall into the hands of sharks . . . a School Board election is quite unlike a Parliamentary one and it needs the greatest care not to run to expense. For though your Lordship might be glad to spend largely on the election, your would-be fellow members are not able to do so and the expenses, display, advertising, and the hundred and one matters of electioneering finesse need to be carefully watched lest they run up to an amount some of us would find difficulty in paying."[90]

6. *Working people's attitude*. Linked with the apathy already referred to and perhaps one of the main reasons for it, was the lack of support

given by a candidate's fellow workmen. It is doubtful, too, if his endeavours were particularly appreciated by them; possibly they might be interpreted as a desire to achieve some social distance from them. Rarely was this sentiment put into words. However, one such example did occur at the rural parish of Eversholt in Bedfordshire, following the successful election of a working-class representative, William Steward, to the local endowed school governing body in November, 1873. He had been elected at a public meeting of burgesses after both Liberal and Conservative parties had agreed to avoid a political fight by nominating the three best men each party could find. The manager at the meeting, in proposing Steward's nomination, described him as "one whose intelligence and up-rightness in all public matters would make him a good representative man of the working class on the new Governing Body."

Steward, in his acceptance speech, noted the lack of enthusiasm in the result from his fellow workers and his reply was suitably cynical.

"As a counsellor watches the case of a client, so shall I endeavour to watch the case for the people. I cannot expect the support of all among the working class; there are many crochety ones. John Bull, it is said, loves a lord: and some working class would rather be represented by broadcloth, even if it covers a noodle, than by fustian, even if it clothe a philosopher. Others are envious and jealous; they don't like to see a fellow workman noticed more than they are and if they cannot shine themselves, would rather not see anyone else shine."[91]

On the other hand, in rural school board contests, there was a slightly greater chance of election where the choice of candidate was limited. When a school board was ordered to be formed at Arnold, Nottinghamshire, in 1877, on the petition of fifteen ratepayers, an effort was made to avoid a contested election. "For that purpose, Mr. Julius Kohn, whose election was considered highly probable, withdrew in favour of Mr. James Shirtcliffe, the workingman's candidate", who was elected fourth out of the five in the poll.[92]

7. *Possible friction with teachers.* The occupation–social class–education link, although not expressed in so many words at the time, did not equip the working person to be a manager. Put bluntly by a wharfinger manager, "Lack of education of such people might cause want of respect from Teachers", and a vicar: "Teachers do not care to be supervised by ignorant persons". Certainly the working man would be at a disadvantage in carrying out his managerial duties, which would often include the appointment of teachers. Taken with the growing resentment of the teachers towards "interference" by managers as a body, the presence of working men would be highly

unacceptable to many of them. Embarrassing situations might arise like the following one at Dewsbury, Yorkshire. The headmaster of the local charity school wrote to the Education Department in May, 1871, protesting at the intrusion of a sub-committee of the school board into his school. As a result of this, an adverse report on the school was about to be laid before the Education Department by virtue of the casting vote of the chairman of the board, a small tailor who rented a house worth about £8 per annum. In his letter to the Education Department on this incident, the headmaster wrote:

"When the Sub-Committee of the Board came to the school, one member was called away almost as soon as he entered, then only two were left. One of the remaining two, I understand, never attended a day school; and on his desiring to see a boy work a sum in practice I wrote down the following: Can you tell me the cost of 3,468 tons of hay at 11¾d. per ton? I asked the member to work it himself but he refused to do so; and I feel sure the Lords of the Council would not sanction him as my assistant."[93]

8. *Working people as ratepayers.* It was conceivable that a plan put forward earlier by a Lewisham manager might have been a satisfactory basis for electing working-class managers. "I consider," he told a special committee of the School Board for London in 1887, "it would be a good thing if, in certain districts, managers were elected by the ratepayers—as for instance in such thickly populated districts as Deptford. I think that the managers would then be more representative, that there would be a fairer representation of the 'working class' than there is under the present mode of election."[94]

One difficulty in carrying out this plan was that a great majority of working people were not ratepayers.[95] It was calculated at Birmingham in 1873 in connection with a scheme which would have given burgesses responsibility for electing two-thirds of the governing body of the King Edward Schools, that of the 50,000 burgesses in Birmingham, 40,000 were compound householders, namely occupiers of houses with a net annual value of less than £10 per annum, and so exempt from paying rates. Thus it was claimed that control over the government of the school would pass into the hands of non-ratepayers.[96]

A similar argument could have been and was used in London with reference to working-class representative managers. Generally they were not direct ratepayers and as a result, as the rector of St. Paul's, Covent Garden warned, "working people's influence is not likely to promote economy". A chartered accountant cautioned "that much care must be taken in the selection of working men. Their presence should be courted rather sparingly. They receive all the benefit and contribute little or nothing".

It was also unlikely, in the voluntary schools, that the working people would qualify for managers as subscribers; at least there seems little evidence which points to this. The ratepayer argument was probably the strongest one of all, especially in London where the educational budget was of huge proportions.

In spite of these various factors which militated against working-class people as school managers, there were a number of them carrying on the work successfully. Outside London, this mode of representation was virtually unrecognized. In many ways, it was an unsatisfactory classification; those who worked under the system were labelled in an undesirable way. Perhaps the most fundamental weaknesses of this system were that there was no machinery, either suggested or in existence, for throwing up likely candidates; and in addition, the special contribution which a working person could make to a committee of managers was never defined. The Report of the 1892 London School Board Special Committee on Management concluded that although representative managers gave their general assent to the principle of working-class managers, they did not consider that any extensive change could usefully be made. "Still," the Report concluded, "the Representative Managers would always welcome the aid of intelligent working men and women, when such can be found, willing and able to bestow the necessary services."[97]

REFERENCES

1   Plowden Report, Vol. II. Primary School Management Preliminary Report. Appendix 13, (1967), pp. 602–16.
2   *Royal Commission on Local Government in England. Research Studies 6. School Management and Government* G. Baron and D. Howell, (1968).
3   "Active Role for Parents" in *Times Educational Supplement*. 20 June, 1969; "Decline of the governing class" by Anne Corbett in *New Society*, 1 May, 1969.
4   R. Watts *Parents in School* (1971) pp. 5–6 published by the Bow Group.
5   "What about Parent Power?" by David Rogers in *Sunday Times*, 5 October, 1969; *How to be a School Manager or Governor* issued by The Home and School Council, (1969) raises some of these issues, pp. 29–30.
6   *Cross*, Report, Part III, Chapter 3, p. 67. Sir Henry Holland, then Vice-President of the Committee of Council on Education in the 1886 Salisbury Ministry, wrote to Cross: "I think Voluntary School Managers should hesitate before they apply for help from rates. If they have such help, the ratepayers will insist upon being represented on the Managers list, and upon seeing to regulating the accounts and proceedings of the Schools." 8 September, 1886, Cross MSS., B.M. Add. MS. 51275, f. 216.

7 Newcastle Commission on Popular Education in England, Evidence Q. 331, BPP. 1861, XXI. Vol. VI.

8 J. C. Tarver, *Some Observations of a Foster Parent* (1897), p. 133.

9 J. C. Tarver, *ibid*, p. 135.

10 *Ibid.*, p. 137.

11 J. J. Findlay, *The Children of England* (1923), p. 130.

12 J. P. Norris, *The Education of the People. Our Weak Points and our Strength* (1869), p. 6.

13 Committee of Council on Education, Report, 1851–2, BPP. XXXIX, p. 724.

14 A Bill to facilitate the Representative Management of Voluntary Schools, BPP. 1890, IX 37 and BPP. 1891, X 635.

15 *Hansard*, Vol. CCLIII, 3rd Series, House of Commons, 8 June, 1891, Col. 1848.

16 Free or Assisted Education. 8 December, 1890. G. W. Kekewich. Cab. 37/28/61 (P.R.O.).

17 Later in the history of the Bill, Sandford, then very much concerned with Scottish education, forecast "that the Government will either propose no change in the Management of schools—or move the election of two Parent Managers. I fancy that, as in Scotland, they will start on that basis, and then if necessary accept two parents." Sandford to Harrowby, 3 May, 1891, Harrowby MSS., Vol. LIV, f. 100.

18 Dale to Chamberlain, 28 April, 1891, Chamberlain MSS., JC. 5/20/18. This same argument was advanced by a sample of Chief Education Officers in a recent study. *Royal Commission on Local Government in England, Research Studies, 6 op. cit.*, p. 77.

19 *The Times*, 19 May, 1891.

20 Minutes of Conference between Robert Gregory, W. H. Smith and Cranbrook, 11 February, 1891, Cranbrook MSS., HA 43. T501/190 (Ipswich and E. Suffolk R.O.).

21 *Birmingham Daily Gazette*, 26 May, 1897.

22 School Board for London. Report of the Committee on the Mode of Election and Powers of Managers, December, 1889, SBL. 1509, p. 192 (G.L.R.O. [London]).

23 W. H. Smith, Leader of the House of Commons during the later stages of the Bill's progress in the Commons, appealed to Chamberlain for his help in this matter. "I came down to the House hoping to find you but I hear you are at Birmingham. I am in some anxiety about Fowler's (H. H. Fowler, Liberal M.P. and friend of Chamberlain) instruction to provide for 'local representation' in the supervision of schools. It would frighten the majority of Parsons to death if it was carried, as anything may be included within the phrase *local* representation. I hope, therefore, if your friends wish the bill to pass, that they will resist the instruction unanimously. I think we should be obliged to drop it if it was carried." 26 June, 1891, Chamberlain MSS., JC5/65/19.
Three days later Chamberlain wrote: "I spoke against Fowler's amendment to the Free Education Bill which demanded the control of the voluntary schools." Chamberlain MSS., Diary: Memoranda of Events, 1880–1892. JC8/1/1.

24 Manchester and Salford Church School Board. Report of the Church Day School Association, 1892. Appendix, pp. 16–17. (Manchester Central Library Archives Department.)

25 Friern Barnet, Friern Lane Parochial Schools, Minutes of Committee, 1854–97, 21 August, 1891. DRO.12.I/G3/3 (G.L.R.O. [Middx]).

26 *Ibid.*, 19 November, 1900 and 11 November, 1901.

27   One or two parent-managers seemed to have been the usual number elected
     for any one school. Exceptionally, at Winchester, the Central National
     School parents met and elected three of their number as members of the
     committee for two years. Winchester Central National School Minute
     Book, 1866–1925, 3 December, 1894. 67/BX/DRI (Winchester City
     R.O.).

28   Lindale National Day and Sunday School, Managers' Minute Book,
     1890–1903, 25 October, 1898. PR2803/3/12. (Lancashire R.O.).

29   *Hansard*, Vol. XLVII, 4th Series, House of Commons, 15 March, 1897,
     Cols. 691–4.

30   Northbrook to Chamberlain, 24 April, 1902. Ed. 24/21.

31   Gorst to Balfour, 21 December, 1895. Balfour MSS. B.M. Add. MS. 49791,
     f. 10.

32   *The Manchester Guardian*, 17 July, 1902, had hinted that the new Prime
     Minister intended to make the board of local management in a school
     consist of representatives of trustees, representatives of the local authority
     and representatives of parents.

33   *Hansard*, Vol. CXI, 4th Series, House of Commons, 21 July, 1902, Col.
     838.

34   *Ibid.*, Vol. CXIV, 4th Series, 19 November, 1902, Cols. 1424–30.

35   Rev. F. D. Cremer to Bishop of Winchester, 17 August, 1902. Davidson
     MSS. (Lambeth Palace Library).

36   L. A. Selby-Bigge to R. L. Morant, 4 February, 1903, Ed. 24/245.

37   In 1888, the Cross Commission, in an attempt to discover the extent of
     parental participation in management, issued circulars to schools in ten
     sample counties. It was found that there were 1,721 such managers in all,
     Lancashire (750) and Lincolnshire (204) between them accounting for
     more than half the total number. BPP. 1888 XXXV, p. 406.

38   T. Gautrey, *op. cit.*, p. 27.

39   J. H. Muirhead, *Birmingham Institutions* (1911), p. 368.

40   The various societies which came into existence during the early part of the
     nineteenth century encouraged domestic missionaries. For instance, by
     1821, the British and Foreign Bible Society had no fewer than 10,000 lady
     visitors. M. J. Quinlan, *Victorian Prelude. A History of British Manners
     1700–1830* (1941), pp. 156–7.
     The habit of visiting the poor gave the ladies a remarkably complete
     picture of the home life of the children attending the local schools. An
     example of the detailed knowledge of the conditions and characteristics of
     each household can be seen in "Notes on Tiddington Village Oxon School
     and on village people, written for the information of the new Incumbent,
     Ernauld Lane, by his predecessor's wife, Lady Georgina Bertie, 1868."
     Albury MSS., D.D. Par. Albury b.3 (Bodleian Library, Oxford.)

41   G. Eliot, *Middlemarch* (1965 edn.), pp. 31–3.

42   B. & P. Russell (eds), *The Amberley Papers* Vol. 2, (1966 edn), p. 529.

43   *British and Foreign Society. Address of the Ladies Committee for Promoting
     the Education of Female Children belonging to the Labouring and Manu-
     facturing Classes of Society of Every Religious Persuasion.* (1815), p. 10.

44   Oxborough Roman Catholic School, Log Book 1879–1925, 2 June, 1886
     (Norfolk & Norwich R.O.).

45   Account of life on the Vernon Estate, Sudbury, Derbyshire, in the late
     19th century. Memoirs of F. T. Howard, Vicar of Hucclecote, (1868–1959)
     dictated, p. 8. D531/8 (Gloucestershire C.R.O.).

46   York, St. Mary Bishophill British Girls' School, Managers' Minute Book,
     1850–77. (York City Library, Archives Department). Acc. 118/257.

47 Kingston Public Schools, Ladies' Committee Minute Book, 1818–78, 4, December, 1818 (Surrey R.O.).

48 Kingston Public Schools, Ladies' Committee Minute Book, 1818–78, 7 February, 1858 (Surrey R. O.).

49 Winchester Central National School, Ladies' Committee Book, 1813–25 30 and 31 August, 1820. 67/BX/DRI (Winchester City R.O.).

50 Stanwell Girls' and Infants' School, Committee Minute Book, 1876–94, 2 December, 1880 MCC/E (Stanwell) (G.L.R.O. [Middx]).

51 Mrs. B. Temple to Exeter School Board, Ladies' Committee Minute Book Vol. 1, 1871–1901, 16 May, 1881 (Exeter City R.O.).

52 Ladies' Committee Minute Book 2, 1901–4, 31 October and 13 November, 1902, *supra*. It is interesting to note that Mrs. Cowie, the wife of the H.M.I. for the district, was a member from 1901.

53 It was calculated in June, 1876 that for the 1,249 board schools in England, excluding London, attended by girls, only 221 lady managers had been appointed under section 15 of the 1870 Act. Return by Counties of School Boards having and not having schools under their Management. BPP. 1876, LIX.

54 Southampton School Board, Eastern District Schools, School Managers' Minute Book, 1872–86, 20 February, 1873. SC/E 74 (Southampton Civic R.O.).

55 *Souvenir of the Leeds School Board* (1903).

56 A. Mansbridge. *Margaret McMillan* (1932), p. 32.

57 A. J. Evans, *A History of Education in Bradford During the Period of the Bradford School Board* M.A. Thesis, Leeds University, (1947), pp. 77–81. This is also well-documented in a long letter to the Education Department from the School Board Chairman, P. B. Myers, protesting at this. 26 December, 1878. Bradford, Ed. 16/357, Pt. II.

58 H. McLachlan, *Records of a Family 1800–1933. Pioneers in Education, Social Service and Liberal Religion* (1935), p. 47.

59 Stapleford School Board, Minute Book 1875–88, 14 September, 1882. R60/8/1/37 (Cambridgeshire C.R.O.).

60 A. M. McBriar, *Fabian Socialism and English Politics, 1884–1918* (1962), p. 202.

61 *Hansard*, Vol. CXI, 4th Series. House of Commons, 28 July, 1902. Col. 1431. Mr. H. Lewis.

62 In July 1873, the School Board decided that ladies should be appointed to every body of managers. School Board for London, Minutes of Board Meetings, Vol. 3, 1873, p. 680.

63 Return showing Names, Addresses and Occupations of Managers of Board Schools, 31 October, 1884. SBL. 1510 (G.L.R.O. [London]).

64 William, 7th Earl Beauchamp, K.C., P.C., K.C.M.G., 1872–1938. Mayor of Worcester 1895, Governor of New South Wales 1899–1902, Lord President of the Council 1910 and 1914–15. *Burke's Peerage Baronetage and Knightage*, (1963).

65 7 December, 1898. Correspondence of Lord Beauchamp, School Board Member, 1897–1900. SBL. 1884 (G.L.R.O. [London]).

66 Undated, but probably 1900. *ibid.*

67 W. W. Morrell, *Wesleyan Education: An Appeal to the Members of the. Conference of 1895* (1895), p. 6.

68 *Hansard*, Vol. CXI, 4th Series, House of Commons, 28 July, 1902, Col 1427.

69 *Ibid.*, Col. 1427. Dr. J. G. Shipman.

70 Law Reports. 23 Queen's Bench Division, 16 May, 1889, p. 91.

71 *Hansard*, Vol. CXI, 4th Series, 28 July, 1902. Col. 1430.

72 G. Edwardes Jones and J. C. G. Sykes, *The Law of Public Education* (1904), p. 132.

73 *Hereford Journal*, 27 May, 1905.

74 Arkwright to Mr. Powell, Chairman of Parish Council, 23 September, 1903. Arkwright MSS. A63/IV/HB/521 (Herefordshire C.R.O.).

75 Report of the Special Committee on the Appointment, Duties and Privileges of Local Managers, 15 February, 1893. SBL. 1511 (G.L.R.O. [London]).

76 R. E. Davies (ed.), *John Scott Lidgett, A Symposium* (1957), p. 137.

77 Asa Briggs has shown that the dividing lines between classes in the nineteenth century were extremely difficult to draw; and that the significant divisions inside what were conventionally regarded as class were often more significant than divisions *between* the classes. "The Language of 'Class' in Early Nineteenth Century England" in A. Briggs and B. Saville (eds) *Essays in Labour History* (1960), p. 70.
    For a sophisticated analysis of social class in terms of voting behaviour, see J. R. Vincent, *Pollbooks: How Victorians Voted* (1967), pp. 28–30.

78 In the north of England, and in Lancashire especially, there was a number of working-class members of school boards, representing Non-conformity rather than class interest. G. I. Hawkes, *The Development of Public Education in Nelson* (1966), p. 115.

79 B. Simon, *Education and the Labour Movement 1870–1920* (1965), pp. 147–154.

80 T. Gautrey, *op. cit.* p. 76.

81 A country parson wrote of an ex-teacher who was a member of the local school board: "Having got on to the Board he did what he could to make the position of the new Head as difficult as possible. He could not however do very much as he was in a minority of one. We passed a rule by which only the Chairman and two other members were deputed to visit the Schools This prevented him from personally interfering in the management." Rev. G. H. Aitken to Bishop of Winchester, 23 May, 1902. Davidson MSS. (Lambeth Palace Library).
    The Lambeth Association of the N.U.E.T. in 1872 appointed an "election committee made up of representatives of each ward and by which means they hoped to influence school board elections and secure the return of men who possessed a real knowledge of educational work and sympathy with the labours of the teachers". The intention was to spread this approach to other parts of London and the provinces. D. M. Thompson, *Professional Solidarity Among the Teachers of England* (1927), p. 65.

82 B. G. Everett, *The Early Years of the Tynemouth School Board* M.A. Thesis, Newcastle University, (1963), pp. 14 and 22.

83 Special Committee on the Mode of Election and the Powers of Managers. Evidence, 4 May, 1887, p. 7. School Board for London, SBL. 1509 (G.L.R.O. [London]).

84 Special Committee, 1887, *supra*. Report, 14 December, 1887, p. 192.

85 Special Committee on the Appointment, Duty, and Privileges of Local Managers, 1892. Summary of Replies to Circular of the Special Committee Addressed to the Chairman of Local Managers, 6 April, 1892. SBL. 1511 (G.L.R.O. [London]).

86 *Ibid.*

87 The occupations of the Chairman of Local Managers were not given in the Summary. These are taken from Annual Returns of Managers of Board

Schools, 1892–94. School Board for London. General Purposes Dept. SBL. 1514. (G.L.R.O. [London]).

88 This was less true at national level. Pakington and Sandon had been involved in a plan to support working men in politics in 1871. The plan was stillborn because of premature publication in *The Times*. Pakington to Sandon, 17 October, 1871. Harrowby MSS. Vol. LIII, f. 278.
It was inevitable by the nature of events after the successive Reform Acts that working-men would be returned eventually to Parliament. In a letter to Akers-Douglas, the Government Chief Whip, Stafford Northcote observed: "I should be very glad to see two or three Conservative Working men in Parliament; and perhaps it might be well to run a candidate or two in connection with the London Workmen's Association . . . the selected candidate would go to the Association, prove himself to be a *bona fide* working man and show that he has a reasonable expectation of support." 5 April, 1885. Chilston MSS. U564 C 306/5 (Kent Archives Office).

89 An exceptional instance of working class initiative was recorded by H. D. Oakeley when H.M.I. in the Durham district in the early 1870s. One pit village with nearly 300 children possessed no schools at this time. "Practically the whole population of the village were pitmen, and they applied to the owners of the colliery to help them to build a school, but without any success. The men took the matter into their own hands, every one of them contributed, and a school was built, and they had the good sense to obtain two excellent teachers, husband and wife, by offering a liberal salary. My visits to this school gave me great pleasure. The colliers appointed four or five of their body to act as managers, who took the greatest interest in the school." H. D. Oakeley, *My Adventures in Education* (1939), pp. 39–40.

90 A. W. Jephson to Lord Beauchamp, 29 July, 1897. Beauchamp MSS. SBL. 1884 (G.L.R.O. [London]).

91 *Bedfordshire Mercury*, 15 November, 1873.
Lord Hobhouse, who had been both a vestryman and a member of the School Board for London, wrote in 1888: "The fact is that the artisan classes of London are perfectly supine about their local affairs. They will make a great fuss and agitation over a Parliamentary election, when they may succeed in sending to the House of Commons a man who will be one in 670, and who may once or twice a year have to speak or vote on some subject directly bearing on their lives. But when it is a question of a Vestry or a School Board, which does not seem so grand a thing, they will not stir a finger to return a man whom they trust, though he may every day be engaged in matters which directly concern the education of their children." L. T. Hobhouse and J. L. Hammond, *Lord Hobhouse – A Memoir*, (1905), pp. 159–60.

92 Anon., *A History of Arnold, Nottinghamshire*, (1913), p. 147.

93 C. Rogers to Education Department, 1 May, 1871, Dewsbury, Ed. 16/360.

94 Special Committee on the Mode of Election and the Powers of Managers, Evidence, 15 June, 1887, F. Morson, SBL. 1509 (G.L.R.O. [London]).

95 This difficulty could be overcome sometimes by a verbal sleight of hand. At Duntisbourne Abbots, Gloucestershire, a general meeting of householders was convened in May, 1893 to elect a committee for the school. The meeting, which was well attended, engaged in a heated discussion "as to whether or not other than ratepayers could be elected; the Chairman holding that all householders for whom rates are paid are *ipso facto*

ratepayers." Duntisbourne Abbots National School, Minute Book, 1893–1902, 25 May, 1893. P122. SC1/1. (Gloucestershire C.R.O.).

96 Select Committee on the Endowed Schools Act (1869), 1873. Evidence, W. Mathews, Chairman of the Board of Governors, King Edward's School, Birmingham. Q. 3082. BPP. 1873 VIII.

97 Report, 26 October, 1892, p. 5, School Board for London, SBL. 403 (G.L.R.O. [London]).

6

Innovation in Administration:
The Voluntary Schools Associations

The main object of the 1891 Elementary Education Act had been to give financial assistance in the form of a fee grant to all managers willing to offer free education; but of great interest to voluntary managers especially was that Section 7 officially acknowledged for the first time the possibility and advantages of the grouping of voluntary schools, whilst not generally interfering in the management of individual schools. Such Associations had existed for a number of years.[1] They had arisen partly as a result of the increasing competition from the school boards, and in an attempt to break down the isolation felt by individual voluntary school managers. By 1897 the National Society had listed Church Day Schools Associations in twenty-two towns. Most simply aimed at saving schools from extinction, but at Sheffield, a school handed over to the school board was actually reclaimed and rebuilt in 1896.[2]

Early examples of Associations are those at Chester and Manchester. At Chester in 1876, one-fifth of the city's schools were under the supervision of the British School Association, consisting of twenty-five to thirty ministers; other gentlemen of various denominations, Church as well as Nonconformist, had four schools under their care.[3] The Manchester and Salford Day Schools Association, founded in 1875, was possibly the first and most highly organized Association. A Church of England organization, it was affiliated to the Manchester Diocesan Board of Education, virtually taking over its functions, its area of operations being conterminous with that of the school board districts of Manchester and Salford. The Association, in the best nineteenth century Mancunian tradition, collected much statistical information in the area regarding surpluses and deficiencies of school accommodation but, more important, gave a pecuniary grant to schools if they appeared to be in need of help. A condition of this was that a member of the committee had a seat on the board of management of the school.[4] Another condition of the grant was that the managers should admit its organizing inspector into the school. Following the Free Education Act, a more ambitious programme was undertaken. A Church School Board was established in 1892 which took over the secular management of the schools "that were either so weak or so self-distrustful that they would be likely to be handed over to the School Boards".[5] Managers and trustees were represented on it as well as parents of pupils in affiliated schools. Schools could be "affiliated" to the Board even though they were under school board management.

A typical system of representation was formulated by the Federation of Church Schools in Southampton in its scheme of 1896. Each committee of managers of these schools elected two representatives as members of the council, of whom one was to be a clergyman and one a layman. The representatives were to be elected by the subscribers of all the schools, each person having between one and five votes according to his subscriptions. Nominations were made by annual subscribers at a meeting held not less than three weeks before the election was to take place. The votes were counted under the superintendence of the chairman of the council, assisted by assessors appointed by the meeting.[6]

Occasionally where no school board existed in a town, the membership of such an Association could be widened. At Dover in 1883, the Dover Public Elementary School Managers Association included members of the school attendance committee and the town clerk.[7]

It was not unnatural that many voluntary school managers should be reluctant to "associate" and belong to a group of schools rather than continue as an individual entity.[8] But the need to federate became more urgent in the 90s: the voluntary schools had been hard hit, especially in the north, by the freeing of the board schools. Acland's Circular 321 issued in 1893, which struck at the poor administration in voluntary schools and emphasized the benefits of centralization, was beginning to be recognized. Manuals for voluntary school managers of the 1890s put forward the need for federation,[9] to safeguard school trusts, to establish and administrate a central fund to help weak schools and to prevent, if possible, the transfer of voluntary schools to school boards. Bishops issued circulars to the clergy of their dioceses recommending

"as soon as possible after the passing of the Education Bill (1891) Church Day School Associations shall be formed in all our large towns and educational districts to watch the progress of educational change, to give help and advice to school managers within the areas committed to them, and when it is so resolved to become the council of confederated schools."[10]

Central banking was one of the advantages of federation. Schools of an Association were able to amalgamate their accounts; as the school years of individual schools ended at different times, a common bank account made it possible for schools to be tided over the point at which funds were very low by an advance lent from a school whose grant had recently been paid. This system worked very successfully, for example at Norwich, Leeds, Manchester and Rochester.[11]

To be effective, the Association had to be something more than a paper union, but on the other hand it was necessary that it should not savour of interference by an outside body. One solution to this was found at Alnwick in Northumberland. The plan of the Duke's Commissioner, E. G. Wheeler, was to establish an office in Alnwick under the supervision of the School Management Sub-Committee of the Newcastle Diocesan Society, to act as a "sieve" for all communications between school managers and the Education Department. Copies of correspondence between the school managers and the Education Department were filed centrally, as was information on schools. After a year's working, it was found that by this system unpaid claims upon the Education Department owing to schools, in all amounting to £900, had been recovered; that in other counties, arrears had been recovered to a very considerably larger amount; that building alterations had been carried out at twenty-six schools, for which economical plans had been supplied free of cost; and that in twenty-one cases the building requirements of the Government were either modified or withdrawn, at a saving of £4,000.[12]

After the dramatic collapse of the Liberal Government in 1895, the time was ripe to redress the balance in favour of the voluntary schools. This had been pledged in election addresses, and the Salisbury Ministry and the Church supporters were mindful that the existing state of the schools had come about largely as the result of Conservative legislation implemented by a Liberal administration.

Proposals to meet the situation were initiated by Sir John Gorst, then the new Vice-President of the Committee of Council on Education.

Gorst sent the first rough sketches of the new Education Bill to Balfour, Leader of the Commons, on 6 December, 1895. His main proposals, contained in a second draft a few days later, were: to give grant aid to poorer voluntary schools, abolish the 17s. 6d. limit and exempt schools from rates. Much more controversial was Point 6 of his plan: "I regret the maintenance of the Cowper-Temple clause as a relic of religious intolerance and an unnecessary interference with liberty."[13]

One of the main features of Gorst's plan was the proposed creation of a new educational authority based on the county council, which would co-ordinate and direct elementary and higher education. This new authority would act as a strong counterweight to the

THE BEARS AND THE BUN.

9.   This cartoon appeared in *Punch* during the passage of the Voluntary Schools Bill in 1897. The figure in the foreground is A. J. Balfour

powerful school boards and would fill the gaps in counties and county boroughs which had no school board. Gorst was conscious of the difficulties attendant upon his idea of giving power to the new authority to assist rate-aided schools in rural parishes, and admitted that "its unfavourable reception by everybody has not surprised me. But some alternative to the establishment of a School Board in rural parishes is urgently demanded."[14]

The new authority would take over many of the functions of the boards, would administer the grant and be responsible for regular inspection instead of the Education Department. Representatives of the authority would, in return, be placed on boards of management of assisted schools, a startling departure from any previous conception of the role and function of the school manager. But Gorst regarded this representation as a necessary safeguard against indiscriminate distribution of a grant to schools which were not necessitous. The difficulty, however, still persisted. "If you give to all alike, you waste public money on schools that do not need it. If you make a distinction, you run the risk of managers making away with their resources, to qualify themselves for the special grant."[15]

Chamberlain called Gorst's proposals "the maddest I have ever seen in the course of my life".[16] Whilst now prepared to help voluntary schools, Chamberlain, the chief spokesman for the Unionist wing of the party, considered that such provisions as the repeal of the Cowper-Temple clause, the limitation of school boards and the power to raise a local rate in aid of denominational schools "would provoke something little short of a rebellion against the Liberals and all Nonconformists of whatever denomination".[17]

The functions of the board of local school managers propounded by Gorst were also questionable. It was proposed to empower the local education board to erect schools which would afterward be managed by the new local board of school managers. The latter would not have the power to raise money, even for the expenses of management, and it seemed probable that there would be conflict between the spending body and the taxing body. It was also left vague how deficiencies in school accommodation and the relationships with the Education Department would be dealt with.

The omens for a sound Bill were not promising. Balfour complained to Salisbury on the same day as Gorst's suggestions were received: "The Committee of the Cabinet on Education have met twice and on each occasion have laid down the basis for a Bill. No Bill has been prepared or is in process of preparation and Sir John Gorst does not appear to agree with the principle provisionally accepted by his colleagues and not at the same time objected to by himself." Balfour suggested that Salisbury should write to Gorst, requesting him to have both his own and some suggestions by Kekewich embodied in draft Bills.[18]

As was anticipated, the Education Bill in its final form, still containing a number of Gorst's contentious features, particularly the Cowper-Temple clause repeal (Clause 27), was defeated when it was presented in May, 1896,[19] and the proposed new education authority never materialized. A member of the Conservative Office had collated reports from "trustworthy agents" in all parts of England and Wales as to the feeling with which the Bill was regarded by Liberal Unionists. In every case, he informed Balfour, the withdrawal of the Bill had been greeted with distinct relief:

> "No one seemed to have a good word for the 27th Clause. It was condemned by Churchmen and Nonconformists alike. Much of the country was hostile to the creation of a new Education Authority, partly because it constituted an attack on School Boards but, surprisingly, more because of delegation of some of its powers by the Education Department. Nothing in the whole controversy is more noteworthy than the widespread objection to any diminution of departmental authority."[20]

For some who were less politically committed, the discussion which Gorst had raised on the proposed new authority had been valuable. The patchwork system of education authorities was not satisfactory and Gorst's attempt, although misguided and politically motivated, contained the germ of the ultimate solution. G. B. Lloyd, a Birmingham banker who had been narrowly beaten for a place on the Birmingham School Board in 1870 as a Society of Friends' candidate,[21] saw some merit in the Bill. He regarded it as a wise one, especially in its main feature—that of subordinating all public elementary schools whether board, or voluntary, to the local governing body of each county or county borough.

> "The plan, borrowed from America, of electing specialists by popular vote to manage special work, is *always* a bad one, whether in railways or hospitals or schools or any other department of work. The talkers and extremists are sure to be elected in that way. The specialists should be chosen by a superior authority representing Common Sense and they should report to and obtain sanction from that central authority."[22]

The withdrawal of the Bill had produced a calming effect on most Unionist supporters but this was largely due to the belief that when it was reintroduced the following year, it would be less far-reaching in character.

The lesson was not lost on the Government. The Lord President, the Duke of Devonshire, broke the news to Gorst that after the disaster of the 1896 Bill, the Government could not tolerate the possibility of a repetition. "I think," wrote Devonshire to Balfour in November, 1896, "I had better take the opportunity of telling him (Gorst) that you will take charge of the Bill and that he will not be held responsible for its deficiencies."[22a]

Balfour, Salisbury's nephew, had taken over the Leadership in the Commons on the death of W. H. Smith. Walter H. Long, M.P. (later Lord Long) wrote to the Government Chief Whip supporting Balfour's nomination, but added "his only fault, if fault it can be called, is a sort of indolence and a strong contempt for popularity—but his sense of duty is strong enough to overcome all this".[23]

Balfour's task was a difficult one. His association with the previous Bill had made him very much aware of the pitfalls which awaited any further attempt after only a short lapse of time. The approach to the question in Cabinet discussions would prove of vital importance.

Devonshire broadly laid down the lines which he would favour. It was important that everything should be done to give the Bill the appearance of a temporary measure, rather than an attempt at a final settlement. Devonshire appreciated that there was an irreconcilable difference of opinion between supporters of voluntary schools themselves, as well as between supporters of board schools and voluntary schools, as to the ultimate solution of the problem.[24] The Cabinet had now wisely decided to bring forward their new educational policy not in one but in several Bills, and this Voluntary Schools Bill was to be the first of them. Both Balfour and Devonshire agreed that the main features of the Bill should be the ending of both the 17s. 6d. limit and the payment of rates by voluntary schools; and that a special aid grant from the Treasury should be paid to voluntary schools on a varying scale. Of special interest and of far-reaching importance to voluntary school managers for the next five years, was the suggested mode of distributing the grant. Devonshire's only mention was "that such grant should be paid to Associations".[25] Balfour, on the other hand, in a Cabinet paper, whilst agreeing separately that the grant should be paid "as far as may be, not to individual schools but to Associations of schools", went on to discuss some of the problems which might arise out of the formation of Associations. The area and organization of the Associations, he believed, could be left to Associations themselves to decide; the outstanding point to be settled was whether the subvention was to be roughly graduated according to the needs of different kinds of locality, or whether the whole responsibility for distribution was to be left to the Associations. A difference in the award between town and country schools, Balfour was convinced, would be calamitous. His solution therefore was to leave the whole responsibility of distribution to the Associations.[26]

Balfour's suggestion was felt by some of the Cabinet to be "too ecclesiastical" in flavour and excited vehement opposition on the grounds that large sums of public money would appear to be State subventions to particular denominations. He appreciated the possibility of creating invidious distinctions between the denominations and the difficulty of defining the criteria for assessing the needs of individual schools.

> "The reasons . . . are not of a kind which can be unanswerably enumerated in black and white. They would, in this plan, be the result of the Inspectors' impressions modified, it might be, by the representations of the school managers, and if, say, in the case of Liverpool, it were found that 8s. per child were given to the Roman Catholics and only 6s. per child to the Church, I think the feeling aroused would be of a most serious character."[27]

His solution was a compromise: that the Department should only be responsible for distributing the grant within the limits of each Association belonging to the same denomination.

> "It will probably be difficult in any case to induce the voluntary schools even in their own interests to submit to the advice of their own religious community. They would undoubtedly refuse to submit themselves to the advice of any other."[28]

Balfour realized that when the Education Department had settled the areas in which federation was to take place, there were already in existence many schools associations which provided the nucleus of the new Associations. Finally, he believed that an Association

> "could not only give valuable advice to the Department in distributing the grant among the members of the Federation (thus acting as a buffer between the Department and public criticism) but may also do valuable educational work in co-ordinating the independent units of what we are pleased to call our 'voluntary schools system' as at present composed."[29]

Between Balfour's submission of his first plan relating to the structure and functions of the new Associations, there had been no shortage of suggestions for alternative administrative units. Sir John Hibbert and Hart-Dyke favoured a body which could deal with necessitous schools, both board and voluntary. They suggested that instead of an Association, a commission of three persons, consisting of voluntary school and board representatives and a neutral chairman, would report to the Treasury.[30] Cranbrook reverted to the earliest times of grant distribution, suggesting the National Society and the British and Foreign Society as the agents.[31] A week later, Hart-Dyke had abandoned his original proposal and just before the Cabinet meeting on 19 November, 1896, suggested the county council as the most appropriate authority, although he recollected that "the storm raised lately by the Bill in the House and the general excitement outside, no doubt terrified the county authorities and made them anxious to repudiate the responsibility of dealing with such a mass of inflammatory material."[32]

All these suggestions were received by Salisbury with alarm. Not only were the Cabinet deeply divided in their views on Associations, but the whole purpose of the proposed Bill, it seemed to Salisbury, was slipping away. He therefore put forward three main objections to Balfour's suggestions, which were summarized as follows:

Distribution of money. The effect of this arrangement will be described as an attempt to withdraw the details of the legislation from the cognizance of Parliament.

Relief of necessitous schools. The Bill aims at stimulating the efficiency of voluntary schools. "I object to this proposed enactment, because it does not put the relief of poverty in the foreground, as the object to which the special grant is to be devoted."

Formation of Associations. England is to be divided into a number of Divisional Committees consisting of such number of the Inspectors of the district as the Department may select; and of an equal number of other persons nominated by the Association. This would be the main function of the Association. Inspectors would have to furnish Associations with information concerning the finance and state of a great number of schools in an Association. "The control which they (Associations) are to exercise can only be applied by managers who, as they are not independent, will not be volunteers. Both these sets of officers must be paid, and they must be appointed and be at work *before* the governing body is recognized. . . . I have a very strong impression that at least 50 per cent of these governing bodies will never come into existence." [33]

This completely different representation of the functions of new Associations was of Salisbury's own devising.[34] Balfour, the dutiful nephew of the elderly Prime Minister, could only register a protest at the scheme in a letter to Salisbury which clearly shows his opposition to the proposals:

"I am quite indifferent *what* proportion the Inspectors are to form of the whole local advisory body. In the draft scheme I have made them a half; but a third or a quarter will suit my individual views quite as well. In my original plan (as you may remember) I gave them *no place at all*; but left the *whole* distribution to the organized Association.

"I devised the new plan
(1) to meet your objections to the appearance of a purely ecclesiastical control;
(2) to meet your views on the incompetence of the Church to organise itself for educational purposes. But—curiously enough—there is a struggle between the Department and such representation of the

voluntary schools as I have seen, each party pulling in the direction precisely opposite to that which might have been expected.

"The Department are anxious to relieve themselves and their Inspectors as far as possible of all responsibility. Mr. Brownrigge, Secretary of the National Society, and Archdeacon Wilson both declare that the voluntary schools would have much greater confidence in the Inspectors than in any other body which could possibly be devised!"[35]

An opportunity occurred unexpectedly shortly after this for Balfour to re-state his views to the Cabinet. Kekewich had noticed that Balfour's Minute accompanying the draft Bill, which was to be laid before the Cabinet on the 21 November, had no provision in it that an Association should necessarily possess a governing body, which was an essential buffer between the Education Department and the school.[36] It also transpired that Balfour's Minute distributed to the Cabinet did not appear to be entirely understood by its members.[37] Accordingly, at the Cabinet's request, Balfour summarized the arguments of, on the one hand, Salisbury's and Chamberlain's draft clauses for inclusion in the Bill and, on the other, his own. The paper is a skilful piece of writing, displaying Balfour's cool, logical mind and his capacity for clarity of exposition. Briefly, the main difference between the two parties was that Chamberlain and Salisbury simply required the Education Department to distribute as best it could the grant among the voluntary schools in proportion to their property; whilst Balfour favoured denominational Associations which should advise the Department on the distribution of the grant among their constituent schools, and that the amount of the grant should be determined by the number of children in average attendance in the schools of the Association and not by "poverty".

Balfour, in discussing Salisbury and Chamberlain's proposals, mentioned that the definition of "poverty" was taken from Lord Salisbury's paper of 30 November, i.e. "if, in the judgment of the Department, the Managers, from causes beyond their own control, are unable without exceeding the income of the school, to make adequate provision for the maintenance and conduct of the school." Disarmingly, Balfour continued, "This I have introduced in accordance with the express direction of the Cabinet, and it was accepted with such unanimity and enthusiasm that it is with some diffidence that I express my doubts as to its merits", and then proceeded to demolish the arguments propounded in favour of the clause. Most of the memorandum is devoted to a vigorous defence of his views and a demonstration of the impossible burden which would fall on the Department in attempting to determine the distribution among 16,000 voluntary schools each year, and the unenviable task of the Education Minister in Parliament who, year after year, would

11. SPENCER CAVENDISH, 8TH DUKE OF DEVONSHIRE (1833–1908)

12. JOSEPH CHAMBERLAIN (1836–1914)

have to defend the allocation of the money. Unlike Salisbury, Balfour believed that 90 per cent of the voluntary schools would associate. He ended the memorandum with a plea to entrust the managers with this task: "With regard to all the schools that associate, the Department will practically be supported by the knowledge and advice of those who, after all, have the very best opportunity of knowing what are the needs of their voluntary schools, and have the strongest interest in seeing that these needs are supplied."[38]

Balfour's memorandum clearly swayed the Cabinet towards his suggested solution.[39] When the new draft of the Bill was circulated to the Cabinet on 12 January, 1897, it was virtually in its final form. The only point outstanding which had previously been discussed in Cabinet was that relating to the relief of school buildings from rating. On balance, Balfour was against rate relief by direct enactment. "If the Exchequer is responsible for rates, the County will at once screw up the assessment of the schools to the highest possible point."[40] The existing system was extraordinarily arbitrary and inequitable, but curiously enough, there were few concrete facts about the rating of schools in the possession of either the Local Government Board or the Education Department.

Balfour suggested that the simplest solution, following a recent analogy of an Act exempting scientific institutions from rates, was to exempt managers from any local rate except to the extent of any profit which they might derive from the letting of the premises. What was certain, Balfour informed his colleagues, was that "If nothing is done in relief of rating, we shall certainly have some of the East End Managers plaŷing the part of martyrs, and compelling the rating authority to distrain their goods."[41] The Cabinet readily agreed with Balfour, and added an appropriate clause; the Bill was now almost ready for presentation to Parliament.

The debates on the Bill in the Commons, which lasted for seven nights (4–11 March, 1897), were concerned almost entirely with Clause 1 relating to aid grant to voluntary schools. It became obvious during the proceedings that Balfour was unclear as to the precise relationship envisaged between managers and the governing bodies of Associations: that is, whether the bodies were to be representative or elective bodies, a point of some importance in the actual operation of the Act, as will be seen later.

In reply to a proposed amendment on this point, Balfour's uncertainty is seen.

"He must oppose the introduction of the word 'elective' upon this among other grounds—that it would tie them down to some method of creating a representative advisory body consisting of certain individuals, who would vote under certain conditions at certain times and places,

P

R E S O L U T I O N

adopted at a meeting of the Management Committee of the

CULCHETH BRITISH SCHOOL,

held on Tuesday, July 7th, 1903.

That this Management Committee of the Culcheth British School
at its final meeting rendered necessary through its duties having been
transferred to the Education Authority established by the recent Act
of Parliament, expresses its high appreciation of the invaluable services
services rendered by the Chairman, Councillor William Trevor J.P.; the
Treasurer, Mr. James N. Walker, and the correspondent to the Education
Department, Mr. William H. Egerton, not only to the Committee but to the
surrounding neighbourhood as the officers of an educational institution
which has during its whole history ranked high in efficiency.

Mr. Trevor's connection with the School began in the year 1869
when it was first established. He had previously been a member of a
small Sub-Committee appointed in 1866 to gather "information respecting
Government Day Schools." He acted as correspondent to the Education
Department and only ceased to so act on his appointment as Chairman of
the Committee on January 14th, 1890. During the whole of this
period of 35 years he has been indefatigable in his attention to the
affairs of the school and, after the head master, the success of the
school was mostly due to the wise policy he always pursued, based as it
was on an enlightened conception of the moral and material value of a
good education.

Mr. J. N. Walker became a manager in 1899 and from 1897 he has
acted as Treasurer. Mr. Walker's skill as a financier specially fitted
him to discharge his onerous duties with great advantage to the school,
and no one brought to bear upon its administration a fuller knowledge of
the powers vested in the managers or a greater sympathy with every effort
which was made to make the School more useful.

Mr. Egerton was Auditor from 1883 to 1890 and in 1889 he was
elected a manager. In 1890 he succeeded Mr. Trevor as Correspondent
to the Education Department, a position he still holds. Mr. Egerton
has many excellent qualities but he excels in nothing so much as in
executive work. His continuous application to the duties of his office
has been of the highest value to the School.

The high estimation in which the School is deservedly held is
largely consequent on the wisdom which these officers, and others who
have passed away, have always shewn in their administration of its affairs.
The cardinal principle of their policy has been to secure and to retain
when secured, the best teachers they could afford and the managers
cannot in recognising the services of their officers omit to testify to
their good fortune which the School has experienced in being served by
a head master who for 35 years has given tone and character to the whole
institution. Mr. Lakin has ever been an earnest, industrious, admirable,
teacher; a strict disciplinarian who disliked idleness and carelessness
and who sought to develop habits of sincere and earnest application in
his scholars.

13. AFTER THE 1902 ACT
This resolution describes the activities of the managers in unusual
detail, 1903

according to some of the methods with which the system of local government had made them familiar. Representative bodies they must be; elective bodies he thought they ought not to be, or at least, need not be. It was possible, for example, that the schools represented would be of such a number that no election was necessary. A number of managers of each school might meet together and form an association; on the other hand, it might happen, without a formal election, that the managers of the various schools should signify to the Education Department that they were entirely satisfied with the representative body which should be created by some less formal methods."[42]

The threatened mutiny of the Liberal Unionists against the Bill never eventuated, thanks to Chamberlain's stout defence in the debate following the introduction of the Bill on 5 February, 1897. As a witness of the scene commented:

"For the ex-President of the Birmingham School Board when it was on the warpath, the ex-President of the National Education League which fought Mr. Forster when he showed tendency to further lapse into compromise—for him to appear as the champion of a Bill which, according to his old colleague, Mr. George Dixon, 'imported into the education question the most unprecedented and extraordinary injustice to Board Schools', was a sight to see."[43]

To ensure that no obstruction would hold up the Bill, Balfour took the unusual course of refusing to accept any amendments at all in Committee; the Committee had twelve sittings between 1 and 18 March, 1897, and because of this procedure the Report Stage was avoided. Balfour had learnt his lesson from the previous year. Griffith-Boscawen, an M.P. from 1892 to 1906, who described himself as "a Churchman, a Conservative and a Tariff Reformer", later reflected that "it was, no doubt, rather ignominious to be obliged to resort to such tactics, which destroyed the deliberative character of the House altogether for the time: but they were justified by their success".[44]

By the beginning of April, the Act was on the Statute Book.[45] It was a brief Act consisting of five sections, two of which were concerned with definition only. The main features were the repeal of the 17s. 6d. limit, its replacement by an aid grant payable to voluntary schools up to 5s. per scholar, and exemption from rates. Although Balfour's advice on the conditions for making the grants to schools had been largely taken by his Cabinet colleagues, the functions allotted to the Associations were the result of a compromise solution. The aid grant was to be distributed by the Education Department "in such manner and amounts as the Department think necessary" (Section 1(2)), but the Association could submit a scheme for distribution to the Department (Section 1(4)). If Associations of schools were constituted in such areas and with such governing bodies representative of the managers as approved by the Education Department, the Association would be given a share of aid grant counted according to the number of scholars in its schools at 5s. per scholar, and a corresponding share of any sum available after distribution made to unassociated schools (Section 1(3)). Finally, a school could be excluded from receiving a share of the aid grant if it unreasonably refused or failed to join an Association (Section 1(5)).

It had not been decided at the time the Act came into operation if there were to be different rates for town and country schools which would result in variations of the rate. Devonshire and Balfour accepted Kekewich's proposal for a differential—5s. 9d. for town scholars and 3s. 3d. for country, provisionally for two years.[46] No account was taken of population;[47] a Minute of 16 June stated that a voluntary school which on 1 April, 1897, was situated within the district of the London County Council, a county or municipal borough or urban district was for purpose of allotment of aid grant, a town school.[48]

The Act, though a temporary measure, was an acceptable one. Board schools received similar relief from rating in the same year and the abolition of the 17s. 6d. limit temporarily appeased the opponents of the favoured treatment of voluntary schools.

More than any other sector of education, the voluntary school managers were to be affected by the operation of the new Act. The nature of these changes will now be examined.

GOVERNING BODIES AND THE WORK OF THE VOLUNTARY SCHOOLS ASSOCIATIONS

One of the Senior Examiners in the Department, C. L. Kingsford, reviewing the work of the Associations in 1902 remarked

> "It was never intended that the benefit of Voluntary Schools Associations should be purely financial. The establishment of Associations was devised to promote the better organization of the schools as a whole. In this they have been entirely successful."[49]

For the school manager in 1897, however, the future pattern was not clear. For one thing, as a contemporary wrote, "each body of managers was inclined to think that their own school was a very special case, and their own difficulties quite exceptional".[50] How far the large Association, geographically remote from their own schools, would understand their problems was an open question. Interference in the management of schools was, to a certain extent, expected. Against this would be the advantages which would accrue from

working with other managers, often for the first time, on committees
dealing with a whole range of schools, which offered a chance to
discuss common problems.[51] The executive functions of the Associations were entrusted to governing bodies; much depended, however,
on their individual constitutions, which were to consist, it will be
remembered, of "representatives of managers". The Education
Department had not prescribed any rules for the constitution of
Associations, but left such organization to local initiative; it took
responsibility for approving each Association's constitution, the area
of operation and composition of the governing body, but intended
to interfere as little as was necessary thereafter.[52]

Four days after the Act had become law, the Education Department issued Circular 394 to all managers of voluntary schools,
suggesting that if they had not yet taken any step toward association
they should, as soon as possible, "communicate with the managers
of those voluntary schools in your neighbourhood with which the
association of your school would seem most natural and desirable,
or with any bodies or persons who may appear to you authorised to
confer and arrange with you on behalf of such schools". In order to
expedite the first allocation of aid grant to such Associations, the
details of the proposed Association were to be sent to the Department
within three months of the Circular.[53]

AREA

The area of the Association was taken to be the diocese or archdeaconry in the case of Church of England, the diocese only for
Roman Catholic schools. The Wesleyan and British schools divided
their areas into geographical regions of England, and the Jewish
schools had a national Association. By 1898, there were 75 Associations—46 Church of England, 11 Roman Catholic, 11 British and
other schools, 6 Wesleyan and 1 Jewish.[54] (See Appendix A.)

The minute issued with the Circular on 9 April, mentioned that
"an Association would not be recognized by the Department unless
it extends over a sufficiently wide area and includes a large number of
schools". Three days later the Department was called upon to define
the area intended, following a letter on the subject from the proposed
Diocese of York Association of Schools. This huge diocese was
composed of four archdeaconries, each of which was divided into
32 rural deaneries of varying size. Some 522 voluntary schools were
to be found in the area. The Bishop of Beverley wrote to the Department suggesting five possible alternative groupings;

    (*a*) An Association for each rural deanery
    (*b*) A grouping of rural deaneries

(c) Four Associations, conterminous with the four archdeaconries
(d) Four Associations, but with a separate Association for the three county boroughs
(e) One diocesan Association[55]

The Education Department, whilst favouring one Association, agreed that the diocese might be an unmanageable size, "but," wrote John White, "whether we should approve the division of this into as many as four parts is a question of policy which I can only refer".[56] Kekewich thought that larger areas than these were contemplated by the Government.

> "What I think nobody outside the Department understands is that these Associations will have to work by a Committee, and that there is really not much greater difficulty in working an Association for a large area than for a small one; and that, probably, the larger the area the more stable and well governed will be the Association."[57]

Gorst sent the papers on to Devonshire for a final decision as to the minimum number of schools below which an Association was not to be recognized (28 April, 1897). Devonshire considered that a decision at this stage, with no experience of the working of the Act, was premature. Whilst agreeing that the larger the area of an Association the better, he shared some apprehension with the diocese that, for the distribution of the aid grant, the very large area with a correspondingly large governing body might be found to be unworkable; a small committee for the distribution would need to be appointed.[58] Eventually, the one governing body for the diocese was approved.

All the Associations were denominational. An attempt to form an Association of colliery schools was rejected by the Department,[59] but managers of an individual school were free to join an Association of a different denomination. The managers of Mattersey Church of England School, Nottinghamshire, for example, having received no aid grant from the Nottingham Association, left it to join the Midland Counties of British Schools Association.[60]

A typical Church Association governing body was that of the Salisbury Diocese. It consisted mainly of delegates of local committees who had been elected by the managers of the schools, assembled on the basis of two representatives from each school plus one extra member for every additional department. These representatives met in the rural deanery, electing a chairman, and one delegate for every nine departments of associated schools in the deanery to serve on the governing body for three years. At least half the members of the governing body were to be selected by laymen. (The rural deanery of an Association was often entitled the Sub-Association of the diocese.) The delegates were to meet and could co-opt not more than sixteen additional members, so that the governing body was then complete. For administrative purposes the governing body delegated all possible duties to two or more advisory committees on archidiaconal or county lines (the diocese including parts of Wiltshire and Dorset); one of these duties was to be superintending the division of schools among local committees and advising them as to their duties as well as on the distribution of the grant.[61]

For the larger Associations, such as that of the Staffordshire Diocese which had eighty-nine members on the governing body, the representation on the district committees was limited to one elected member for every two thousand children, except in the rural parts of the diocese.[62]

Where the Association represented an archdeaconry of a diocese only, as in the Surrey (Diocese of Winchester) Association, the governing body was very small, comprising only twelve. Here, the elaborate system of committees was unnecessary. Managers elected one representative to serve on the governing body for every 200 children in attendance during the previous year. The governing body was called the "Central Council" and the archdeaconry was divided into "divisions" rather than deaneries. A novel feature of this scheme was that the divisions were each to elect a "Consultative Committee" which sent detailed reports on the state and efficiency of every school in its division.[63]

POWERS AND DUTIES

The Act had not specified the extent of the governing bodies' functions and the pragmatic approach was often the only one available to associations. A number of common characteristics, however, do emerge. Governing bodies were allowed to transact their business in their own way: they could decide whether an Association was open to all voluntary schools or confined to those of a particular denomination. They could ascertain whether aid grant paid to a school had been properly expended before recommending another grant, but could refuse to give to managers details of its distribution. It was possible to approve a change of purpose of expenditure recommended by a previous governing body.[64]

Interference with the management of individual schools was discouraged, and taking over the management of a school was regarded as inexpedient.[65] Governing bodies were not able to impose conditions as to the manner in which the grant they recommended was to be spent nor guarantee grants for future years. Nor should they pronounce what should be, for example, the minimal salary or minimal staff. They could not authorize the transfer of subscriptions from one school to another.

One of the questions most frequently asked of the Department was the position regarding the expenses of the Association. The Education Department refused to allow any part of the grant aid or income of the school to be applied to such purposes. A note on a policy file of the Department stated,

> "considering the very large sum assigned to voluntary schools under the Voluntary Schools Act, it would not appear to be a large demand to make upon the supporters of those schools that they should themselves contribute to the expense of the Association by means of voluntary contributions for the purpose."[66]

This included postage, stationery and travelling expenses incurred during the course of their work.

Records of Association meetings have only rarely survived, but perhaps a typical example of how expenses were met is provided in the proceedings of the Diocese of Chichester, Pevensey Sub-Association. At its first meeting on 2 September, 1897, the chairman, Sir Evan C. Nepean, C.B., stated that

> "there were certain expenses attending the meeting of the Sub-Association and suggested that each member should subscribe 2s. 6d. All those in the room paid this and the amount subscribed was 20s. The Rural Dean wrote to say that he had hired a room at Lewes for the early meeting of the Sub-Association at cost of ten shillings. It was resolved that this amount be repaid to him."[67]

The organization and constitution of governing bodies raised the most fundamental problems for managers of individual schools. Procedurally, there was no rule laid down as to the number of persons required to constitute a governing body;[68] this ranged from three members (Isles of Scilly Church of England Association) to 203 (London and District British Schools Association). Members of governing bodies who were school managers could be present while a grant for the schools which they represented was under consideration.[69] The proportion of laymen to clergy was usually, at Kekewich's insistence, about a half, although an exception was made for Roman Catholic schemes. When that of the Roman Catholic Westminster Diocese was submitted by Cardinal Vaughan, he requested one-third membership of laymen. John White of the Department remarked on the file,

> "There would be a real difficulty in securing more than one-third laymen (who would not be mere 'lay figures' as well as laymen) on many Roman Catholic governing bodies."[70]

The draft constitution submitted by the Truro Diocesan Schools Association in 1897 included a requirement that the choice of representative of the managers must be a member of the Church of England, a qualification which the Education Department would not allow.[71]

In this connection, one of the anomalies in the wording of the Act was that, whilst it mentioned in Section 1(3) that the governing body must be "representative of the managers", no closer definition was attempted. No further clarification is found in the Voluntary Schools Association Precedents Book of the Education Department, which at one point merely states in a case of 1897, "that an Association must be generally accepted by managers within it before approval".[72] This implied that, provided the proportion of lay to secular was secured, the presence of managers on the governing body was of lesser importance.

Early in the life of the new Act, this point was put to the test in Birmingham. The Worcester Diocesan Association's constitution was submitted on 24 May, 1897. The governing body of the Association was to be elected by three archidiaconal "councils" or "boards" for Worcester, Coventry and Birmingham. The councils or boards were not only to elect governing bodies but to draft schemes of distribution for their respective archdeaconries; the schemes for Worcester and Coventry were passed, but the Department challenged that for Birmingham. This was mainly on two grounds: firstly, that it was intended to continue an already existing Birmingham Church School Board as the new governing body of the Association, and secondly, that this body was not elected by managers either directly or indirectly and therefore violated Section 1(3) of the Act.

The Birmingham Church School Board came into existence in 1895[73] to oppose the programme of the New Education League which had become active in the Midlands.[74] A strong centralized body had aided schools in the archdeaconry with grants amounting to £5,000 in the course of two years. Out of this, a Voluntary Schools Defence Association was formed (later to be called "the Church Schools Association"), and a number of gentlemen formed a provisional committee with the aim of examining means of strengthening the finances of the Birmingham voluntary schools.[75]

On the passing of the 1897 Act, the Board called a meeting of managers which accepted the offer of the Church Schools Association to become their Association under the Act.[76] The Department made it known that this form of Association was unlikely to be acceptable, as the governing body was non-elective. One of the leading persons in the Association was the Bishop of Coventry, "an excellent educationalist and friend to the Association"[77] who, unlike his senior colleague, the Bishop of Worcester, favoured separate archdeaconries rather than one diocese.

The Bishop of Worcester, wishing to settle the difficult problem of the Birmingham Archdeaconry and its proposed independence, suggested at a Birmingham Church Schools Association meeting that their name should be changed to "The Church Schools Board of Education for the Archdeaconry of Birmingham", and that the Council out of its number would send a certain proportion of representatives to the Diocesan Association. The preparation of all schemes for the Department, and management, would rest with the Board: he hoped that, strengthened by the admission of all associated school managers, it would take part in the election of the Council.[78]

Although this proposal was accepted, the Bishop of Coventry called a further meeting on 28 June of "all subscribers to the Birmingham Board and of all Managers of Church Schools in the Archdeaconry who had joined the Association". Admission was by ticket, and it appears, according to the Bishop, "from the tickets before me that the meeting was attended by 97 Managers, by three teachers, by one lady who may or may not have been a Manager, and by myself. In short, the meeting was to all intents and purposes strictly a Managers' meeting."[79]

It was proposed to continue collecting funds for the schools as well as to carry on with the work in connection with distributing aid grants. The Bishop, however, stated that he intended to defy the agreement arrived at at the May meeting on the grounds that there would be confusion in the schools if they had two different societies to deal with. He felt that

"the work of the Archdeaconry would be more thoroughly done, and more effectively done, if the managers could be persuaded to join forces with the subscribers to the Board and form one society."[80]

This motion was unanimously approved by the meeting and the Bishop of Coventry submitted that as the Church school managers of the diocese had been fully consulted, the constitution for the Board should be approved. He further claimed that the Department had not the power to reject it on the ground that other than school managers assisted in the election of the governing body, and that it was the wish of the managers to appoint the Board in its present form.

In a letter to the Department, Coventry showed why the presence of subscribers on the governing body was, in many ways, more desirable than that of school managers. After pointing out that "defects in education will never be remedied unless subscribers with a wider outlook than the ordinary school managers are brought into close touch with the whole body of school managers", the Bishop continued:

> "Further, it is quite certain that the ordinary School Managers are not likely to assist the Department much in the way of maintaining subscriptions. It will be their interest to form the lowest possible estimate of the subscribing power of the parish. . . . It is our conviction that by interesting wealthy Churchmen in education as distinct from the cause of the local school of a particular parish, we shall be able by degrees greatly to raise the whole tone of Churchmen in this district on educational questions. But if large subscriptions are invited, subscribers must be secured in some voice in the distribution of their subscriptions. . . . It is not enough to trust to co-optation to secure this end."[81]

Kingsford and Lindsell of the Department saw the Bishop on these matters. It was a difficult case.

> "The question practically is", wrote Kingsford afterwards, "can a body not elected by Managers either directly or indirectly be recognised as the Governing Body of an Association if the Managers have agreed so to accept it? Here the Board is not actually the Governing Body, but it will elect the representatives of the Birmingham Archdeaconry on the Governing Body of the Diocesan Association, and will in effect discharge many of the powers of a Governing Body."[82]

The solution seemed to be either to establish similar Sub-Associations in the other two archdeaconries, which neither desired, or to make the governing body of the Birmingham Board more representative.

One more attempt to make the constitution acceptable to the Education Department was made by the Bishop by accepting the second alternative. It was a blatant misinterpretation of the term "representative"; on 31 August the Bishop announced the election of "nine representatives of Managers" to serve on the governing body of the Diocesan Association; it included himself, the treasurer of the Board, and seven other influential clergy and lay people. Ingeniously, it was suggested that

> "to simplify matters, the nine representatives on the governing body of the Diocesan Association should also be the Executive Committee or Council of the Sub-Association for the Archdeaconry, and that such Council should have power to co-opt additional members and to appoint the officers of the Sub-Association."[83]

The Department once again were obliged to reject the scheme on the grounds that it "confuses with the Sub-Association under the Voluntary Schools Act for your Archdeaconry, a 'Board' and a 'Council' constituted in a manner which, in the Department's opinion, is not contemplated by that Act, and for certain 'objects', detailed in the scheme, of which the greater number seem quite beyond the scope of the Act".[84]

Coventry, in his Report of the Archidiaconal Council of Education for 1898, complained bitterly of the possible curtailment of the Birmingham Board's activities which since 1895 had included maintaining pupil-teachers' classes, and assisting schools in obtaining cookery and manual instruction.

"The Education Department rigorously confined the Associations formed under the Voluntary Schools Act, 1897, to the one duty of distributing the Aid Grant and has, in the judgment of your Council, so far defeated the intentions of the Government as expressed in the speeches of leading Members."[85]

The Department remained obdurate on this point, insisting that all Associations and Sub-Associations under the Voluntary Schools Act should confine themselves strictly to the distribution of the aid grant. The charge made by the treasurer of the Association that this principle "was adopted as a concession to certain political suscepti-bilities and to the fears of those who dreaded the power and influence which the new Associations under the Act might have over the voluntary schools system"[86] was not an accurate one. For one thing most Associations were geographically widely distributed, as com-pared with school boards, and this was an obstacle to large-scale concerted action.

It has been seen that the expenses for supporting Associations had to be found by the Associations themselves, and this often restricted their activities. In spite of the latent intention of the Act to secure better co-operation between managers of schools, the strong indivi-dualism of the managers of voluntary schools would have made very close co-operation, except in dire financial circumstances, unlikely. Sub-Associations, in fact, such as at Birmingham or Manchester, which were almost conterminous in area with the local school board, were able to act with more cohesion; but the Department regarded the Associations as at best a temporary expedient and for this reason did not relish the possibility of conflict with school boards.

TEACHERS AS REPRESENTATIVES

One further point was that the smooth working of the governing bodies assumed an identity of interest among the participating members which was not invariably the case. Besides the lay/clergy, subscriber/manager divisions, the vexing problem of the "representa-tion of the managers" still remained. One other possible element had received little mention during the debates on the 1897 Act—the obvious one of teacher representation on governing bodies.

Balfour sent a draft copy of the Voluntary Schools Association Bill to the Bishop of Rochester in January, 1897. At the same time he asked for an account of the constitution of the Rochester Diocesan Board of Education with special reference to the appointment of the Committee, and how far it was representative of the schools or the managers. Mr. Brownrigge of the National Society had suggested earlier to Balfour "that there might be some safeguard (in the Bill) against the Education Department forcing on the Governing Bodies representation of the Teachers or Ratepayers. The managers of the schools of an Association ought to elect the Governing Body, the Education Department having the power to see that this was done, but not having the power to create a hostile constituency."[87]

Professor Tropp has shown that by the end of the nineteenth century the educational ideals of the National Union of Teachers had united both board and voluntary school teachers. Whilst being just as concerned with the conditions of rural schools as with the inadequate salaries offered to voluntary school teachers, the Union demanded again and again that "education ought to be in the hands of bodies, intelligent, active, educated, acting over sufficiently wide areas to prevent local jealousies from creeping in and injustice to teachers being done".[88] Until such authorities were established, it was argued, teacher representation on governing bodies would be a valuable step forward.[89]

Three months after the Act had been in operation, teacher representation on governing bodies was very slender. Of thirteen Church of England Associations approved, only Rochester with four and Ripon, with two, had included teachers in their number; of the ten British and Undenominational Federations only London had co-opted teachers, eight in all. The six Wesleyan Federations, on the other hand, had thirty-six teachers.[90]

Ernest Gray, an ex-elementary school teacher, along with J. H. Yoxall, had been elected to Parliament in 1895 as the first teacher representative; in conversation in the House with Gorst in July, 1897 on this topic, he informed Gorst that Article 85(e) of the Code, which forbade a teacher "to undertake duties not connected with the school", was an obstacle to teachers being elected as representatives of managers on governing bodies of Associations. Since that conversation, Gray had been informed by one of the teachers in the Eastbourne district that in the Chichester Diocesan Association, the Archdeacon had ruled that teachers could not be among the managers' laymen representatives on the electoral body, let alone the governing body. Gray asked Gorst

"Now may I take it from you that Article 85(*e*) will not be allowed to interfere with the freedom given to Managers by the Voluntary Schools Act, but that teachers will be permitted to serve upon the Federations if sent there by the Managers of individual schools, or by groups of Managers, or if co-opted by the Governing Body in accordance with the terms of their scheme?"[91]

The Chichester scheme, which had been approved, required by Clause 6 that the electoral body "shall consist only of managers", but no such limitation applied to the governing body which was to consist of "representatives" (Clause 8). Gorst believed that a rule, not aimed especially at teachers but requiring that all who took part in the election of the governing body should be managers, was not unreasonable providing election of other than managers to the governing body was not thereby obviated.[92] Kekewich, with characteristic shrewdness, asked John White,

"Do you think that a governing body would be 'representative of the managers' if the managers were not given free choice of their representatives? If the choice is allowed to be limited by the exclusion of a particular class, it might be limited by the exclusion of all classes, except e.g. the clergy."[93]

Gorst agreed, but added that the governing body might not specifically forbid teachers as such, but they might forbid anybody not a manager taking part in the election.[94]

Strictly interpreted, the governing body could be said to be more absolutely representative of the managers by being elected by managers only, but this was not the point at issue. The Department's field of action was limited to supervising the operation of this vaguely-worded Section 1(3) of the Act; presumably, they would be called upon to act only if a manager of the Association objected to the provision, on the grounds that it hampered his choice of an elected delegate. As to the interpretation of Article 85(*e*) of the Code, the Department had already given a ruling in two cases that "service on the governing body of an Association to which a school belonged, would not, in their Lordships' opinion, be the discharge of a duty connected with the school within the meaning of Article 85(*e*)",[95] thus making it clear that a teacher must not so serve. This accorded with precedents formed prior to the Voluntary Schools Act, that duties connected with a number of schools could not be considered duties connected with the school: even when the school formed one of the number. By analogy, the fact that Article 71 of the Code refused recognition to a teacher who was a member or officer of any school board or school attendance committee would also include the joining of a governing body. John White submitted to Gorst that:

"any interpretation of the Article 85(*e*) which would permit a teacher to undertake, during his school hours, duties connected with several schools provided his own school was one of them would be an implied change of policy and relaxation of the old rule, enabling us to guard against neglect by teachers of what is surely their *primary* duty—the teaching of their own school."[96]

Kekewich subscribed to this view, pointing out that membership of a governing body might involve, for instance, attendance at the meetings of the Diocesan Society. How far it could be held that it was the "duty" of the master to serve on the governing body, even if designated in the same sense that teaching was, was a moot point.[97]

Gorst realized the dilemma in which he had been placed. It would have been difficult for him to accept the interpretation of the staff of the Department, though it was legally correct. As recently as 10 May, 1897, he had replied to a question in the House that "The Committee of Council would not refuse to sanction the appointment of teachers of schools attached to Associations to be members of the governing bodies of such Associations."[98] Gorst remarked to Kekewich that "after what has been said in the House of Commons by Mr. Balfour and myself on the subject, we cannot make use of Article 85(*e*) as a prohibition to their serving as such, without laying ourselves open to a charge of breach of faith".[99]

The question was left unanswered, and the Department felt their way cautiously, treating each case individually. Gray, however, had become something of a teachers' champion and brought to Gorst's notice other contraventions of the Act. In February, 1900, the governing body of the Chester Diocesan Association proposed a change in the constitution whereby "managers can only elect managers to represent them on the governing body".

> *"By an accident"*, wrote White to Gorst, "the revised constitution was approved by us (the Department) without our having before us the required assurance that it was generally acceptable to the associated managers."

(Gorst noted in the margin, "I assured the House of Commons a few days ago that accidents never happened in the Education Department.")[100] In fact, the governing body included one teacher who had been co-opted, and the power to co-opt as members of the governing body persons who were not managers of schools still remained.

Gray protested that, though Roman Catholic and Nonconformist Associations had freely admitted teachers to governing bodies, some by election, others by co-option, in the great majority of Church of England Associations "every attempt has been made to exclude them, and the information which reaches me shows that this systematic and intentional exclusion is doing more to destroy the attachment of teachers to Church of England schools than all the financial strain which rested upon them before the passing of the Act".[101] Still walking the narrow tight-rope, the Department maintained that where, as in the Chester Diocese, the Association prescribed that only managers shall elect managers as representatives, the Department would not withhold assent; but that it also approved schemes under which managers might elect any representatives.[102]

In a further letter to the Department, Gray, who had devoted considerable time to an examination of the subject in anticipation of asking a question in the House on 12 March, said it was clear to him that the authors of the Act had intended that managers should be at liberty to send a teacher to represent them on the governing body.

"I can honestly say that a large number of managers are deeply regretting, and protesting against, decisions which are depriving them of that liberty. Contests are being waged in a number of Diocesan Associations on the subject, and those who have wished to secure this representation have again and again found themselves excluded by the introduction to the scheme of the words 'from their own body' making it imperative that the managers should select none but managers to represent them.

"An old friend of mine, Mr. Ellison, the Vicar of Windsor, tried by formal resolution to secure the inclusion of teachers in the Oxford Governing Body, and was defeated."[103]

In his reply in the House, Gorst denied that any pledge had been given by the Government that the Department would refuse to approve the rules of an Association which did not admit of the representation of managers by teachers.

"Under the circumstances the Committee of Council are not prepared to decide at present whether this governing body have gone beyond the provision of the Act."[104]

Gray drew the Department's attention to perhaps the most extreme example of the exclusion of teachers. The Newcastle Diocesan Association's amended constitution, which had been approved by the Education Department, provided (Rule 4) that managers only could elect one of their body as the representative for the school on the ruridiaconal committee in every rural deanery, and that the governing body should be elected by the committee. Under Rule 3, even co-opted members had to be managers.[105] The managers of one school, St. Thomas's National School, Newcastle, on 12 January, 1900, defied this ruling and appointed a master, Mr. John Nicholson, to represent them on the Newcastle Deanery of the Association.

10. A. J. BALFOUR (1848–1930)

6.　SIR JOHN SOMERSET PAKINGTON, later 1st Lord Hampton (1799–1880)

"On his presenting himself at their first meeting to which he was called, he was told that he could not be allowed to sit with them on account of his being a teacher."

The chairman of the rural deanery subsequently wrote to the school managers, stating their objection to him. The managers, supporting Mr. Nicholson, pointed out to Gorst that "if the Master is disqualified, the Managers will not be represented on the Board."[106]

Morant had now entered the Education Department; he took over the case and ordered the Newcastle Diocesan Association's rules to be looked into.[107] It transpired that the Association's amendment had been agreed to by the managers in eleven of the twelve rural deaneries. The Solicitor-General was asked for an opinion; he decided that the constitution of the governing body was a matter for the schools which formed the Association to agree upon. This settled the matter, although Morant assured Gray that the "Board of Education have always urged on Governing Bodies the desirability of framing their rules so as to admit of teachers being appointed representatives but that they had no powers to insist upon it".[108]

The precedents established relating to a teacher's participation on governing bodies were not encouraging: he or she could be excluded from election to the Sub-Association or the governing body, and from any co-option to the latter body. Nor had it been established, even if these obstacles had been overcome, that the teacher would not be prevented from attending by the operation of Article 85(*e*) of the Code. The Education Department's interpretation of this Article had shown that attendance at such meetings was not to be regarded as part of a teacher's duties. The hard-won and valuable experience of the teacher was, as a result, in the majority of cases, not made use of by the Associations. An opportunity for an interesting experiment with a form of combined school management was thus lost.

ORGANIZING MASTER

Perhaps the main agent involved in the functioning of the Voluntary Schools Act was the organizing master or organizing teacher. His relationship with the Associations, managers and teachers provides some insight into the administrative complexities of operating the Act.

Organizing masters pre-dated the Act,[109] and the Cross Commission especially praised the work of those employed in Rochester, Huddersfield and Bradford. The circumstances under which the organizing master was appointed by the Church Association at Huddersfield have been mentioned earlier in Chapter 2.

No organizing teachers were employed except by the Church of

England, and these were usually the servants of diocesan boards, although the National Society engaged a number whose services could be lent to diocesan boards where necessary. Invariably, they were certificated teachers of good experience and were often regarded with much jealousy by ordinary teachers. Their functions were more varied than those of H.M. Inspectors or of board school inspectors, and could include inspecting, examining and organizing schools, advising managers with respect to school buildings, finance, staff, accommodation and appliances, and organizing pupil-teacher instruction; also they could assist in the preparation of aid grant schemes for approval by the Education Department, enquire into trust deeds, and assist managers in their official correspondence with the Department.

A difficulty was the method of payment of the organizing master. The Minority Report of the Cross Commission recommended that one half of his salary should be paid by Government grant, but this was not taken up. Although no aid grant was to be applied to meeting the expenses of the Associations, in certain cases the Education Department allowed it towards the organizing teacher's salary under Article 5 of the Code. Frequently the remainder of the salary was contributed out of private subscriptions for his other work in connection with the Associations; in some instances, as at Lincoln, the principal organizing teacher[110] was also the assistant secretary of the Association and in others he was actually the secretary.[111]

Some Associations appointed sub-committees to supervise the work and, often, the appointment of the organizing master and his terms of service. In the Salisbury Association, the organizing master's salary for the Archdeaconry of Sarum was to consist of a £1 grant from each school visited by him, a fee of 5s. per half day plus travelling expenses; and a sum of up to £5 for postage, with an additional £10 from the grant given by the Diocesan Board of Education. The master was also at liberty to inspect, examine or advise on buildings, etc. in the case of schools not in the archdeaconry, "as to which he shall make his own terms, provided he gives his first care to schools in this Archdeaconry".[112] Morant believed that a "fairly typical case" of an organizing master before the passing of the Voluntary Schools Act would be an officer who received £200 per annum, and that since then he would have received an additional £150 per annum for visiting schools and conducting correspondence under that Act.[113]

In spite of the widening range of functions following the Voluntary Schools Act, the organizing master usually remained a servant of the diocesan board. Between Associations there was little formal contact, but as an Education Department official remarked in 1902, "There is an Association of Organizing Teachers, who like other officials, love to hold conferences."[114]

A number of Associations determined that, as a condition for recommending the school for aid grant, it accept an annual visit from the organizing master.

Kekewich thought that it would be possible for an Association to draft a constitution which made acceptance of the organizing master's visits to its schools a condition for admission to the Association; but unless this was stated, the visit could not be enenforced.[115] White, on the other hand, did not consider it reasonable for managers to refuse a visit from "any proper person, sent at a proper time, to obtain proper information about the school for the governing body".[116] Kekewich agreed that the governing body had a perfect right to insist on the managers of an assisted school admitting a person sent to ascertain particulars as regards the needs of the school:

> "But that is not the usual function of an organizing master. And I do not think that Associations at all intend that his visits should be paid solely for that purpose. To force a school to admit (and doubtless pay for) an organizing master as such, would be to my mind interfering with the management of the school, which we have said over and over again is not the purpose of Associations."[117]

After three years' experience of the working of the Associations, White wrote that a governing body had the right, if necessary, to expect a school to receive a visit from an "expert" to report to them on the condition of the school and that, if he were refused admission, the aid grant could be curtailed.

> "But such expert would enter the school as a mere enquirer and observer, not claiming to 'organize' or to exercise any power or authority whatever."[118]

In practice, however, many Voluntary Schools Associations sanctioned the organizing masters' visits to schools to inspect and examine scholars. In the Wakefield Association, he visited all schools twice a year, in June and October. A sample examination of the work was made at the first visit and this was completed at the second visit.[119]

Many schools resented the organizing master for a number of reasons: the managers often regarded his visit as an interference with the management of the school and as an attack by a friend. Also, his status was questionable: as an ex-schoolteacher, he lacked the authority of H.M. Inspector or the many impressive school-board inspectors. An unfavourable report could result in the loss of aid grant. The teachers disliked the visits even more: they were already

subject to the supervision of the managers and surprise visits from
H.M. Inspectors. The organizing master represented yet another
intrusion; the advice offered was superfluous, but most of all, with the
ending of formal individual inspection by H.M. Inspectors in 1895,
the organizing master's reintroduction of this system seemed
insupportable.

Occasionally, managers misconstrued the functions of the organizing master with unfortunate results. On the afternoon of 28 June,
1897, Mr. Boyling, the organizing visitor for the Northamptonshire
Diocesan Education Society, paid a visit to Stowe-Nine-Churches, a
small Northamptonshire hamlet. "The mistress," records the log
book, "felt cheered and encouraged by his visit." The following day,
Mrs. Ladkin, the teacher in question, received notice from the
rector that the school committee were to meet in the schoolroom the
same evening and required her presence. That evening, Mr. Roberts,
one of the managers, called for her at the school house and took her
in to the meeting.

> "I went in. The Rector said the managers had come to the conclusion to
> ask for the written undertaking in preference to giving the usual three
> months notice, and to accept one month."

The schoolmistress was taken aback and refused to do this, asking
for time to consider the matter. The rector then handed over the
organizing visitor's report.

> "I said I thought it was unjustified and monstrous, read from my copy
> his remarks upon my methods of teaching—that I did not see that they
> were necessary, viz.
> "(1) *Oral lessons* should always be illustrated. They always have been
>   illustrated. I do not think Mr. Boyling saw the museum or cases in
>   the room I was two or three years procuring at great expense, time
>   and trouble.
> "(2) *Arithmetic* should always be taught by blackboard demonstration.
>   It has always been—I know no other way, and so on.
>   "Mr. Boyling did not hear or see me teach any subject except to give a
> few lines of dictation."

The matter was adjourned for a fortnight. Before the next meeting
the rector and chairman of managers, the Rev. Starmer, must have
sensed that the committee had acted hastily, but that they could not
readily retract without losing face. Accordingly, when the mistress
was present at the August meeting he assured her that "as far as he
was concerned, and he believed that his colleagues would agree
with him, he was perfectly satisfied: we were driven to the present
attitude by the Department". Mrs. Ladkin, a woman obviously of
some spirit, replied that in her opinion "the organizing visitor was

not the Department and his conduct would not be sanctioned", and handed in her resignation to take effect from December. The assistant teacher also resigned.

There was an unexpected sequel to this some two months later, recorded by Mrs. Ladkin in the log book.

"On October 22nd, St. Lukes Day, the school attended a service at church at 9 a.m. Returned at 9.40. At 10.45 the class marched out for recreation. In a minute or so the mistress received a message that an 'Inspector' had arrived. On returning to the schoolroom the mistress found Mr. Boyling, the organizing visitor, there. I told him that I had not expected another visit from him as I was about to leave. He expressed great concern to hear this and asked how his report could have brought about such a result. I told him my committee had read all his suggestions to mean that I was ignorant of those methods or that I did not use them. I told him I always had taught arithmetic from the blackboard. 'As to oral lessons,' I asked, 'had he noticed the museum or pictures on his previous visit?' He answered 'Yes, or I should have ordered one.' (If organizing visitors can order museums with effect, how is it they are so rare?) He said had he then anticipated such a reading and rendering of his report he would have taken care to word it differently. He had not dreamt that I should be leaving."

In spite of attempts by the managers to persuade Mrs. Ladkin to withdraw her resignation, she remained adamant. The year ended with a final flourish from her:

"21st Dec. 1897. Mrs. Ladkin closed her career as Mistress in this school, *and* as a School Mistress, and made her last entry this day."[120]

By the time of the issue of the Board of Education's Circular on Schemes under the Voluntary Schools Act relating to the distribution of grant aid, in 1901, only lukewarm support was offered for Associations to encourage the use of organizing visitors.

"The Board", it stated, "do not desire to debar the governing body of an Association from the exercise of a wide discretion, but it is hoped that grants of this class will, as a rule, be confined to cases where the services of the 'Organizing Visitor' are admittedly desired and necessary. The Board of Education will in no case allow the acceptance of the services of an Organizing Visitor to be made a condition of grant."[121]

This was a blow to the Associations. The issue of the Circular coincided with a report of the National Union of Teachers which displayed much animosity towards the organizing visitor and his "needless services". A manager member of an Association was moved to write to the Duke of Devonshire, the Lord President, as a result:

"If the organizing visitor is shut out of a school, the governing body is shut out, and the scheme is prepared very much in the dark. It is bad enough to have governing bodies that can be turned out by apathetic managers if they make themselves unpleasant, but it is infinitely worse to have the door of the school shut against the governing body by the Board of Education. It is very disheartening and the more so as it seems clear that it is under the influence of the teachers that this retrograde step is taken."[122]

With the passing of the 1902 Education Act, the work of the organizing master came to an end. Morant considered that it would be undesirable to provide compensation for their services, as the conditions under which individuals of different Associations had been employed varied; the possible claimants for compensation would be numerous and would include persons of very varied degrees of merit.[123] Whilst it was undesirable in the view of the Education Department to require local authorities to take over the services of organizing masters in every case, it was hoped that some of the best would in fact obtain employment under the new authorities. J. Blount Green, the energetic organizing master of the Wakefield Diocesan Association and acting president of the Organizing Inspectors Association, protested in vain to the Education Department on their non-inclusion in the Bill:

"that after long years (twenty and more in some cases) of endeavour, their means of livelihood would be taken away. And why? Simply because they have remained faithful to the cause of denominational education, which the Bill now before Parliament seeks to uphold."[124]

SUBSCRIPTIONS AND THE VOLUNTARY SCHOOLS ACT

One of the most striking results of the Act was the great improvement in the premises and equipment of voluntary schools. In the years 1899 and 1900, the expenditure of voluntary schools on books, furniture and apparatus per head, was actually greater than that of the board schools. Similarly, there was a very substantial increase in the sums spent in minor improvements to school buildings. But the aid grant, which in 1902 was running at about £600,000 annually, was not sufficient to secure financial stability, in spite of increased annual grants under the Code resulting from increased efficiency. By 1900, the financial strain was once again being felt and two years later the indebtedness of the Church schools was equivalent to the amount of aid grant given.[125]

The Department intended to combat the growing indebtedness by requiring school managers to make greater efforts to increase the amount of voluntary subscriptions. In 1899, Circular 416 to voluntary schools stressed this point:

"My Lords have noticed with regret that in some districts the voluntary contributions have shown a marked tendency to decline. . . . They believe that the diminution of income from this source arises chiefly from the apathy or neglect of individual bodies of Managers, and is for the most part confined to certain classes of schools. . . ."

After praising governing bodies of Associations for their efforts in this cause, and in reporting to the Department cases where voluntary contributions were in their opinion inadequate, the Circular continued in a way that raised a furore amongst governing bodies:

"In some instances, however, My Lords doubt whether the Governing Bodies have not taken too narrow a view of the duty that rests with them in this respect under the Voluntary Schools Act. In the case of those schools where after due warning voluntary contributions are not forthcoming, or are less than might be reasonably expected, it will be the duty of the Governing Body to reduce the amount of Aid Grant, or even to withhold it altogether. I am to add that My Lords may be unable next year to give Their sanction to recommendations to Aid Grant to schools whose Managers have not made reasonable efforts to secure for them a proper measure of local support."[126]

The lack of a reliable index of the subscribing potentialities of an Association proved a difficulty. The Surrey Association protested to the Education Department that "the seeming wealth of a district as shown by its rateable value is misleading. A seemingly wealthy district may, for the purposes of the Act, be quite the reverse." The Association quoted Englefield Green as an example. The rateable value was drawn principally from three public institutions and three wealthy residents who were members of the Jewish faith. Two of the institutions together subscribed fifteen guineas per annum (a school board rate would have been about £200) while the other, a Government institution, refused to subscribe anything although the Association educated fifty of its children.[127]

A serious difficulty threatened to arise in some dioceses, from the action of the Education Department in accepting the opinion of their Inspectors against that of the Associations on the ability of parishes to increase or maintain their contributions. The Department had in some cases, it was alleged, superseded the decisions of the governing body; in other cases it had issued warnings to schools without consulting or even giving information to the governing body, thus usurping the Association's responsibility.[128]

In Cumberland, a manager of a Roman Catholic school at Millom explained to the Department why his subscriptions had been falling steadily over the years. There were no well-to-do people in the parish. "Only two out of six blast furnaces here are working owing to the high cost of coke. The men erecting a sea wall here are only earning 25s. per week in fine weather and about 10s. per week in wet weather." The owners of works and gentry "obstinately refuse as they say they have to pay far too much to meet the great expenditure of the ten Board Schools in the district", and to the fact that "we are already collecting subscriptions among my poor people for the erection of a new Infant School ordered by the Government Inspector".[129]

The Catholic Associations, the poorest bodies in the country, were hardest hit by the Circular.[130] In 1899, the Department instituted enquiries in respect of the decrease in voluntary subscriptions within the most influential one, the Salford Diocesan School Association. As a result the managers of twenty-four individual schools submitted explanations. The Department examined these, and then warned the Association that voluntary contributions included, in addition to the donations of individuals or societies, all net sums derived from offertories, concerts, entertainments, bazaars and voluntary rates. The secretary of the Association bitterly commented:

> "If, then, a Rector on some occasion finds himself able to help the School Managers by handing over to them the proceeds of a Sermon, Concert or Bazaar, the managers are to be thenceforth, year after year, called to account and worried for explanation in case the Rector is unable to make his occasional gift into an obligatory and annual Subscription!"[131]

The need for greater stringency in supervision of allocation of aid grant, ensuring that the managers of individual schools were endeavouring to obtain subscriptions and exercising economy in school expenditure, and the scrutiny of their claims for aid grant, lent great importance to the smaller units of the Association.[132] The Wiltshire (Sub-Association) Archidiaconal Committee had pioneered a thoroughgoing scheme for elucidating the financial state of the schools in its area and for recommending grants to the governing body. On receiving the returns from the schools, via ruridecanal committees, they were classified under four heads, namely, non-necessitous, fairly necessitous, necessitous and specially necessitous. In the first year of operation, the governing body declined to consider appeals from schools save "only under very special circumstances". As a result of experience gained, a revising sub-committee, consisting of the chairman, vice-chairman and secretary of the Sub-Association and one representative of every rural deanery, had been established, complete with bye-laws which governed the distribution of the grant. The managers of every school received notification of the grant and were able to appeal to a full area committee; a representative of the school was allowed to appear before it.[133]

Usually, about half of the aid grants were earmarked for staff and salaries, equipment and apparatus being a much smaller proportion. The governing body of the North Salop Voluntary Schools Association allocated its aid grant to necessitous schools according to average attendance, in conformity with the classification of town and country schools as set out in the schedule issued by the Education Department. It reserved, however, 10 per cent of the total grant to be applied to meet particular cases which appeared to call for exceptional treatment by the governing body.[134]

Exceptionally, a town within a diocese might make its own arrangements to form a sub-area. In the Lincolnshire Diocesan Association, for example, Lincoln itself presented a tightly knit area which made a fairly logical unit. It began its existence in October, 1897 as an Association of voluntary schools with a lay chairman, but as the Wesleyans and the Free Church Council refused to participate it became a Church organization the following year.[135] By March, 1898, the governing body of the sub-area discovered that "the average of voluntary contributions per school appears to be 2s. 1¼d. as against 6s. 10d. per scholar in the whole of England and Wales".[136] This, of course, rendered the sub-area liable to be refused grant aid. The best explanation that it could offer was, in the words of the chairman:

> "That four out of the thirteen schools are new schools completed within the past three years; and that not even the most sanguine could hopefully set to work to raise voluntary subscriptions in Lincoln on a due scale, until the results of the Education Act of 1897 had been ascertained."[137]

In December, immediate action to save the situation was called for. The Dean of Lincoln at the newly formed Council presented a scheme for raising and distributing a sustentation fund for 'necessitous schools' in the city. All managers were required to submit approximate balance sheets to the Council (illegal under the Act) and by June, 1899, loans were granted to schools to meet overdrawn balances at 3½ per cent "on such security as the Finance Committee may deem sufficient". As this proved difficult, the Council passed a resolution in July stating that "so long as the Council are paying the interest (on the debt) . . . the buildings shall be under the management of a committee consisting of representatives of the three parishes of the Council"; this proved to be even more difficult to arrange and on 23 February, 1900, a sub-committee was set up "to see how the above resolution can be carried out".[138]

By 1901, the financial difficulties experienced by managers had drawn other denominations into the Council and a new constitution was drawn up. The managers of each school were to elect two representatives with co-option; all members of the Council had to be subscribers. The Council's main functions were to provide new places where necessary, to undertake, in spite of past experience, where desired, the management of any of the new or existing schools, and to advise managers how to deal with the Board of Education.[139]

The final report of the Council in fact showed much more modest achievements: school holidays in the town had been standardized (one teacher and one manager from each school had attended the Council to consider common action); the migration of teachers from one school to another without consultation of both sets of managers had been stopped; and the facilities of the City Public Library were now available to children.[140]

In spite of ingenious efforts by Associations to centralize financial control, the fund-raising efforts were not enough. A Parliamentary Return of "Public Elementary Schools which have been closed since the commencement of the Voluntary Schools Act 1897" lists a great number of reasons for the failures of individual schools.[141] There is no doubt that the decrease in attendance at voluntary schools was due largely to the superior conditions of the board schools by the end of the century; and that the demands made by the Inspectors and the Education Department on the voluntary school managers to bring their schools up to an efficient standard could not in most cases be met.[142]

Where, however, managers refused to join an Association, H.M. Inspectors, although having no authority in this matter,[143] would make their own views quite clear to them. A letter marked "Very Private" from H.M. Inspector, Mr. E. M. Kenney Herbert, to a chairman of managers in Buckinghamshire bears this out:

> "£ s. d. is a trouble everywhere, but you ought not to put it first as a difficulty, because your managers have deliberately refused to call the school necessitous and to seek for any share of the aid grant. If you really have not got the funds for the payment of a full efficient staff, you ought to pocket your pride and obtain an aid grant to provide salaries."[144]

Under Section 26 of the 1902 Education Act, the Voluntary Schools Act was repealed as from 26 March, 1903, but Associations could continue to exist in a perpetually diminishing degree until 25 September, 1904, which was the appointed day when their schools were to come under a local education authority.

The formation of Voluntary Schools Associations had introduced a new concept of management into the voluntary schools system, that of operating under a centralized authority on a representative basis.

Although, except in individual cases, governing bodies received no official or social recognition among educational authorities,[145] the value of their contribution towards the organizational efficiency of the voluntary schools within their Associations from 1897 onwards has not received the recognition it deserves.

The Voluntary Schools Act had, for the first and last time in the century, secured some unity of action amongst voluntary schools managers. Financially, the lack of rate aid made more than partial success of the Act impossible; but the operation of governing bodies representing the interests of managers over large areas was a success. Canon Norris, writing shortly after the passing of the 1902 Act, summed up the general results of the Voluntary Schools Act:

"There is more cohesion and confidence among managers; there is greater efficiency in the schools; there is more accurate and particular knowledge of the details of the various schools at headquarters; there is a much larger income from voluntary contributions; in short, schools are stronger and management more careful and better. These are no insignificant advantages, and supporters of voluntary schools have every reason to be thankful for the much abused Act of 1897."[146]

REFERENCES

1   In February, 1884 the then Bishop Vaughan set up a Voluntary Schools Association, a militant body with a definite programme—that of obtaining a 25 per cent increase in grants for Church schools. The Association was originally conceived as a mouthpiece for all denominations, but under Cardinal Manning, it became the official Catholic organ for disseminating information on the education question. A. McCormack, *Cardinal Vaughan*, (1966), pp. 171–2.

2   *School Guardian*, 20 March, 1897.

3   J. K. Montgomery to Education Department, 10 May, 1876. Chester Ed. 16/25.

4   Report of the Manchester and Salford Church Day Schools Association 1886, p. 8. 372/942/M6. (Manchester Central Library, Archives Department.)

5   Report of the Manchester and Salford Church Day Schools Association, 1892, p. 9. 372/942/M6. (Manchester Central Library, Archives Dept.) The Board was successful in its activities, earning 1s. 1¼d. per head more than the average in Church schools in the country and a little more than the Board schools. p. 10, *ibid.*

6   Scheme for the Federation of Church Schools within the Borough of Southampton, 20 February, 1896. PR21/19/2. (Southampton R.O.).

7   Letter to Education Department, 21 January, 1884, Dover Ed. 16/114. The Association continued to flourish until well into the present century. See J. B. Jones, *Annals of Dover* (1691), p. 427.

8   But sometimes the demands of Associations eliminated some schools from membership. At Huddersfield, all affiliated schools were required to have

three bona fide managers. Fifteen schools were unable to fulfil this condition. *Cross* Evidence, Rev. R. Bruce, Q. 44369.

9   See, for example, T. More, *The Education Brief on Behalf of Voluntary Schools* (1890), pp. 81–2.

10 Bishop of Manchester, Circular letter 31/7/1891. M45/5/1/32. (Manchester Central Library, Archives Department.)

11 W. F. Norris, *op. cit.*, (1904), p. 109.

12 *The Times*, 7 January, 1895. "The Federation of Voluntary Schools."

13 Balfour MSS., B.M. Add. MS. 49791, f. 10.

14 Balfour MSS., B.M. Add. MS. 49791, f. 10.

15 Gorst to Balfour, 21 December, 1895. Balfour MSS. B.M. Add. MS. 49791, f. 9–10.

16 Chamberlain to Duke of Devonshire, 15 December, 1895. Chamberlain MSS. JC5/22/157.

17 Memorandum on Draft Scheme for an Education Bill, 16 December, 1895. Balfour MSS. B.M. Add. MS. 49773, f. 86.

18 6 December, 1895. Balfour MSS. B.M. Add. MS. 49690, f. 122–5.

19 This Clause was attacked with great effect by Asquith during the Second Reading of the Bill on 5 May, 1896. See *The Education Bill. Speech delivered by the Rt. Hon. H. H. Asquith, M.P., in the House of Commons* (1896), pp. 18–19.

20 Arthur Pye-Smith to Balfour, Balfour MSS. B.M. Add. MS. 49769, f. 85.

21 *Birmingham Gazette,* 19 November, 1870.

22 G. B. Lloyd to G. H. Kenrick, a member of the Birmingham and Midland Education League, April, 1896. Letters etc. relating to the Birmingham School Board 1867–1902 collected by J. H. Lloyd. 529347 (City of Birmingham, Public Reference Library).

22a 7 November, 1896. Balfour MSS. B.M. Add. MS. 49769, f. 12.
    Devonshire had written to Salisbury a little time earlier (13 September): "I do not know whether Balfour spoke to you before leaving London, but I am pretty sure that he does not think that Gorst's conduct of another Education Bill would lend to its success. . . . Is there any chance of changes which would place the Education Department in other hands?" Salisbury MSS.

23 W. H. Long to Akers-Douglas, 14 October, 1891. Chilston MSS. U564 C346/4. (Kent Archives Office).

24 Proposals for a Bill. Printed for the use of the Cabinet, 10 November, 1896, written 7 November, 1896, Devonshire. Cab. 37/43/43. (P.R.O.).

25 *Ibid.*, p. 3.

26 Paper printed for the use of the Cabinet, 10 November, 1896, written 8 November, 1896, Balfour. Balfour MSS. B.M. Add. MS. 49698, f. 14.

27 Paper printed for the use of the Cabinet, 19 November, 1896, written 16 November, 1896, Balfour. Balfour MSS., B.M. Add. MS. 49698, f. 18.

28 Paper printed for the use of the Cabinet, 19 November, 1896, written 16 November, 1896, Balfour. Balfour MSS., B.M. Add. MS. 49698, f. 19.

29 *Ibid.*

30 Hibbert to Gorst, 13 November, 1896. Balfour MSS. B.M. Add. MS. 49769, f. 117. Devonshire had independently written to Balfour agreeing with many of Hibbert's suggestions, 18 November, 1896, *ibid.*, f. 119.

31 Cranbrook to Gorst, 16 November, 1896, *op. cit.*, f. 131.

32 The authority for Distribution of Special Aid Grant to poor Schools, 20 November, 1896. Hart-Dyke, *ibid.*, f. 139–41.

33 Memorandum on the Education Bill. Printed for the use of the Cabinet,

1 December, 1896, written 30 November, 1896, Salisbury. Balfour MSS., B.M. Add MS. 49698, f. 20–23.

34 Salisbury wrote privately to Balfour enlarging on the official document. "There are three forces contending for the mastery of the educational field. 1. The Economists, 2. The Religionists, 3. The Educationists. If your Bill passes, the result will have been confiscated by the Educationists. The Education Department of course consists only of educationists. We know from Acland's brief reign that their demands are practically unlimited. Where the 3 Rs were enough 20 years ago, now you must have French, pianoforte playing and trigonometry; and no doubt German and astronomy will come next. The educationist is one of the daughters of the horse leech; and if you let him suck according to his will, he will soon have swallowed the slender increase of sustenance you are now tendering to the voluntary schools. You are pouring water into the tub of the Danaides. You had much better give no grant at all, and let the money go to build an ironclad." 20 November, 1896, Balfour MSS., B.M. Add. MS. 49690, f. 181–2.

35 Balfour to Salisbury, 22 October, 1896, Salisbury MSS.

36 Kekewich to Balfour, 20 November, 1896, Balfour MSS. B.M. Add. MS. 49769, f. 133.

37 Note accompanying Memorandum explanatory of the Action that will be taken when the Education Bill becomes law. 30 November, 1896. Devonshire, *ibid.*, f. 143.
This was not surprising as at this time no record of Cabinet proceedings were kept. Balfour agreeing with Salisbury a few years later that this situation should be changed, stated: "A brief record of Cabinet decisions would be a convenience. My own memory in such matters is very untrustworthy and I sometimes find it difficult, after our confused discussions, to recollect even the instructions which I have received on matters which I have myself brought before it." 22 April, 1900. Balfour MSS. B.M. Add. MS. 49691, f. 100.

38 Memorandum for the use of the Cabinet, 8 December, 1896, written 7 December, 1896, Balfour. Balfour MSS., M.B. Add. MS. 49698, ff. 24–6.

39 Balfour's achievement was a notable one in view of the fact that the Cabinet had earlier voted 10 to 8 in favour of a rough draft of the Bill being prepared, based on Chamberlain's and Devonshire's proposals rather than Balfour's. Chamberlain Memo. 2 December, 1896, Chamberlain MSS., JC5/5/26.

40 Balfour to Salisbury, 6 January, 1897. Salisbury MSS.

41 Printed for the use of the Cabinet, 13 January, 1897, written 13 January, 1897, p. 2, Balfour. Cab. 37/44/4. (P.R.O.)

42 *Hansard*, Vol. XLVII 4th Series, House of Commons, 11 March, 1897, Col. 520.

43 H. W. Lucy, *A Diary of the Unionist Parliament 1895–1900* (1901), p. 126.

44 A. S. T. Griffith-Boscawen, *Fourteen Years in Parliament* (1907), p. 116.

45 Voluntary Schools Act, 1897. 60 Vic. Ch. 5.

46 Devonshire to Balfour, 6 May, 1897. Balfour MSS., B.M. Add. MS. 49769, f. 153.

47 John White of the Education Department noted one of the difficulties which could arise if a definition of a town or country school based on the population of the area alone were adopted. Taking Urban Districts, which were to be classified as "town schools", there were at that time 68 in England and Wales with populations ranging from 979 (Hedon, E. Yorks.) to 4,822 (Wells, Somerset). 29 April, 1897. Ed. 24/23.

48   G. E. Jones and J. C. G. Sykes, *The Law of Public Education* (1904), p. 720.
49   Minute, 21 March, 1902. Ed. 24/20.
50   W. F. Norris, *op. cit.*, p. 112.
51   Records of discussions at managers' meetings on the advisability of joining an Association show that many members had doubts on the matter. At a Somerset school, among the objections put forward were "the choice of Diocese as the area of the Association, the confining of the Association to Church Schools and the fact that the clergy and laity had not been consulted as to the best area to be chosen". Kingston St. Mary Parish School, Managers' Minute Book, 1888–1903, 24 May, 1897. 18/7/2. (Somerset R.O.).
52   A request was sent from the governing body of an Association to the Education Department for the names of headmasters of the schools in their area and the salaries paid to them. The Department refused to give this information on two grounds: "(1) for our own sakes, (2) for the sake of the Governing Body, who should be looked on as friends of the Schools in the Association, not as spies in league with the Education Department." W. Loring to J. White, 4 June, 1897. West Riding, British Schools Association. Ed. 48/9.
53   Circular to Managers of Voluntary Schools. Voluntary Schools Act 1897. 9 April, 1897. Kekewich. BPP. 1897 LXVIII.
54   Return of the several Associations formed under the Voluntary Schools Act 1897 with their Areas and the Number of Persons forming the Governing Body of each Association. BPP. 1898. LXX 541.
55   12 April, 1897. York Diocesan Association. Ed. 48/12.
56   White to H. W. Simpkinson, 26 April, 1897, *ibid.*
57   Kekewich to Gorst, 27 April, 1897. York Diocesan Association, Ed. 48/12. This optimistic view was not widely shared. One assessment of the situation forecast that "the work of the Education Department will be increased and rendered more difficult by the necessity of consulting associations . . . representing such large areas as to be less capable than the Department's own officers of ascertaining the real wants of the several neighbourhoods". Committee Meeting of the British & Foreign Schools Society, 26 February, 1897. 92nd Annual Report for 1897, p. 16.
58   Devonshire to Gorst, 1 May, 1897. York Diocesan Association, Ed. 48/12.
59   Bebside Colliery School, 1897. Precedent Book. V.S.A. 1897, p. 97. Ed. 127/2.
60   Mattersey Church of England School, Managers' Minute Book, 1895–1960, 31 January and 7 March, 1899. SBX 50/2 (Nottinghamshire C.R.O.).
61   Salisbury Diocesan Voluntary Schools Association, 1st Year Book, 1898. Report p. 5. 594/62 (Wiltshire R.O.).
62   Bishop of Lichfield's Letter to Rural Deans on the Scheme for the Staffordshire Diocesan Voluntary Schools Association, 26 April, 1897. Sutherland MSS., Lilleshall Agency Records. D593 N/3/11/6 (Staffordshire C.R.O.).
63   Surrey (Diocese of Winchester) Voluntary Schools Association. Scheme 12 September, 1897. Ed. 48/2.
64   Derby Diocesan Voluntary Schools Association, 1900. Precedent Book, V.S.A., p. 19. Ed. 127/2.
65   Precedent Book, V.S.A., p. 20. Ed. 127/3.
66   Chichester Diocesan Association, 1898. Precedent Book, V.S.A., p. 3. Ed. 127/2.
67   Meeting of Pevensey II Sub-Association of Voluntary Schools, Diocese of Chichester. Minute Book, 1897–1912. 232/25/13 (E. Sussex R.O.).
68   Where the Association elected very large governing bodies, as in the case

of the Salford Diocesan Roman Catholic Association which had 171 members, the Department suggested that a Clause should be added to the scheme to the following effect: "The Governing Body shall further have power to appoint local sub-committees as it may from time to time think fit." White to Bishop of Salford, 10 August, 1897. Minutes of the Meetings of the Governing Body of the Salford Diocesan School Association, 1897–1908. RCDT. 4 (Lancashire R.O.).

69 Clifton and Newport Roman Catholic Diocesan Association, 1899. Precedent Book V.S.A., p. 4. Ed. 127/2.

70 White to Simpkinson, 14 July, 1897. Westminster Roman Catholic Diocesan Voluntary Schools Association. Ed. 48/7.

71 White to Secretary of the Association, 31 July, 1897. Truro Diocesan Voluntary Schools Association. Ed. 48/4.

72 Lydiard Tregoze National School, Wilts, 1897. Precedent Book V.S.A., p. 97. Ed. 127/2.

73 Before this, there had been an Association of Voluntary School Managers in the city which instituted a system of inspection of schools and had discussed all measures directed to their common welfare. *Handbook of Birmingham. Prepared for the Members of the British Association, 1886* (1886), p. 60.

74 In a circular which was issued on 25 October, 1895, the Birmingham and Midland Education League stated as its aims "(1) to resist the demands now being made for increased aid from parish funds to schools under private denominational management, (2) to provide a universal system of education under the local control of the elected representatives of the ratepayers." Scrapbook of G. H. Osborne 1867–1907. 243371. (Birmingham City Reference Library).

75 *Birmingham Daily Post*, 13 November, 1895.

76 *Ibid.*, 24 May, 1897.

77 Simpkinson to Kekewich, 15 July, 1897, Worcester Diocesan Voluntary Schools Association, Ed. 48/10.

78 *Birmingham Daily Post*, 1 June, 1897. The Archdeaconry of Worcester had already appointed a Council consisting of sixty representatives of managers. *ibid.*, 27 May, 1897.

79 Bishop of Coventry to Education Department, 9 July, 1897, Worcester Diocesan Voluntary Schools Association, Ed. 48/10.

80 *Birmingham Daily Gazette*, 29 June, 1897.

81 9 July, 1897, Worcester Diocesan Voluntary Schools Association, Ed. 48/10.

82 H. M. Lindsell to White, 12 July, 1897, *ibid*. The Department had previously been obliged to recognize the Exeter and Durham Diocesan Boards as governing bodies of Associations, which somewhat weakened the Department's case.

83 Circular to Managers of the Birmingham Archdeaconry, 31 August, 1897.

84 Simpkinson to Kekewich, 15 July, 1897. Worcester Diocesan Voluntary Schools Association, Ed. 48/10.

85 3rd Annual Report of the Birmingham Archidiaconal Council of Education, 1898, p. 8. (Birmingham City Reference Library.) This was no doubt based on Balfour's own statement in the Commons on 6 February, 1897 that "the Associations will be able not merely to give pecuniary assistance, but assistance in many other ways to their constituent units".

86 *Birmingham Daily Gazette*, 14 December, 1897.

87 Bernard Mallett to Talbot, 20 January, 1897, Balfour MSS., B.M. Add. MS. 49789, f. 86–7.

88   A. Tropp, *The School Teachers: The Growth of the Teaching Profession in England and Wales from 1800 to the Present Day* (1957), p. 172.

89   Occasionally, teachers were actively involved in the formation of an Association. The West Riding Association of Undenominational Schools, which included amongst its aims the improvement of staffing and an increase of salaries, was one such example. Initially, it was suggested that the teachers in Leeds, Bradford, Wakefield and Sheffield "should secure a room for the meeting, either free of cost or at a small charge", to press for such an Association, and that their managers should be invited to the meeting. Circular, 18 May, 1897, West Riding Association of Undenominational Schools, Ed. 48/9.

T. H. S. Escott suggested the establishment of local councils for educational purposes, consisting of Crown nominees, university representatives and teachers. The latter might be chosen by headmasters in conference and by assistant masters. For the latter category it was deemed "advisable to select the teachers' members by the direct vote of the class immediately concerned". *Social Transformations of the Victorian Age. A Survey of Court and Country* (1897), pp. 164–5.

90   *The Schoolmaster*, 10 July, 1897.

91   Gray to Gorst, 7 July, 1897, Ed. 24/82B.

92   Gorst to White, 14 July, 1897, *ibid.*

93   Kekewich to White, 16 July, 1897, *ibid.*

94   Gorst to Kekewich, 19 July, 1897, Ed. 24/82B.

95   Gorst to Chichester Diocesan Voluntary Schools Association, 26 July, 1897, *ibid.*

96   White to Gorst, 22 July, 1897. Ed. 24/82B. This rule did not apply to the post of Secretary of an Association. The South Devon and Cornwall Branch of the South Western Association of British and other Voluntary Schools, which included schools in Cornwall, Devon, Dorset, Somerset, Wiltshire and Hampshire, was given in 1897, to the headmaster of the Plymouth Public School without any apparent reaction from the Education Department. Report of the Plymouth Public School for the year ending 30 September, 1897, p. 5 (Plymouth Public Library, Archives Department).

97   Kekewich to Gorst, 26 July, 1897, Ed. 24/82B.

98   *Hansard*, Vol. XLIX, 4th Series, House of Commons, 10 May, 1897, Col. 92.

99   Gorst to Kekewich, 26 July, 1897, Ed. 24/2B.

Balfour had remarked during the debate on the Bill, "I have never suggested that the Education Department should prevent teachers being on the governing bodies." *Hansard*, Vol. XLVII, 4th Series, House of Commons, 15 March, 1897, Col. 701.

100   Gorst to White, 3 March, 1900. Ed. 24/82B.

101   Gray to Gorst, 5 March, 1900. Ed. 24/82B.

102   White to Kekewich, 5 March, 1900, Ed. 24/82B.

103   Gray to Gorst, 7 December, 1900, *ibid.*

104   *Hansard*, Vol. LXXX, 4th Series, House of Commons, 12 March, 1900, Col. 589.

105   Gray to Gorst, 2 August, 1900. Ed. 24/82B.

106   S. S. Walton, Secretary to St. Thomas' School Managers' Committee to Gorst, 6 April, 1900, Ed. 24/82B.

In rare instances, school managers were prepared to support the nomination of a teacher in the face of opposition from the governing body of the Association. At the initial meeting of the Lancashire and District Association of British Schools in May, 1897, the Committee of Culcheth British

School, Lancs. sent two representatives—a manager and Mr. R. Lakin, the headmaster of the school since 1868. Lakin was nominated for a seat on the provisional committee but this was ruled out of order on the ground that he was not a manager. At a managers' meeting on 20 May "Mr. Lakin went fully into this matter and stated that the Education Department recommends and permits Teachers to be represented on the Committee of the Association".

The following month, the provisional committee invited the school to send two *managers* to its next meeting to consider the report and approve or amend the draft constitution. The school managers "expressed disapproval of the action in ruling the nomination of Mr. Lakin out of order, and appointed Messrs. W. Trevor and R. Lakin as representatives to attend the meeting". Lakin's nomination was finally accepted by the committee. Culcheth British School, Newton Heath, Manchester. Managers' Minute Book, 1891–1903, 20 May and 1 June, 1897. M36/13/1/2 (Manchester Central Library, Archives Department.)

107 R. L. Morant to White, 4 August, 1900. Ed. 24/82B.
108 14 January, 1901. Ed. 24/82B.
109 The first one to have been appointed by an Association was probably by the Manchester and Salford Church Day Schools Association in 1875 on the recommendation of Archbishop Tait. But as early as 1839, an organizing master seconded from the National Society had inspected and advised on method and arranged evening refresher courses for teachers at Southwell, Notts. on behalf of the Lincolnshire Diocesan Board. Report for 1839 (Lincoln Public Library.)
110 Some Associations employed several organizing teachers.
111 An objection to the Staffordshire Diocesan Voluntary Schools Association employing the organizing teacher as auditor was made by the Department in 1898. Precedent Book, V.S.A., p. 60. Ed. 127/2.
112 Salisbury Diocesan Voluntary Schools Association. 1st Year Book 1898. Report, pp. 8–9. 594/62 (Wiltshire R.O.).
113 Memorandum: Organizing Inspectors of Voluntary Schools, November 1902, p. 3. Ed. 24/26.
114 C. L. Kingsford to Morant, November, 1902. Ed. 24/26.
115 Kekewich to White, 16 July, 1897. Ed. 24/82B.
116 White to Kekewich, 17 July, 1897, *ibid.*
117 Kekewich to White, 20 July, 1897, *ibid.*
118 White to Morant, 14 May, 1901, Ed. 24/82B.
119 Report of the District Committee for the Deaneries of Huddersfield, Halifax and Silkstone for 1898, pp. 5–6. Wakefield Diocesan Voluntary Schools Association. Ed. 48/6.
120 Stowe-Nine-Churches Church of England School, 1897–1918, Log Book. 28 June to 21 December, 1897 (Northamptonshire C.R.O.).
121 p. 3, March 1901.
122 14 May, 1901. Ed. 24/82B.
123 Minute R.L.M., November, 1902. Ed. 24/26.
124 J. Blount Green to Morant, 26 November, 1902. Ed. 24/23.
125 Minute C. L. Kingsford, 21 March, 1902. Ed. 24/20.
126 Circular to Voluntary Schools Associations. Scheme for Distribution of Aid Grant, 29 March, 1899. Kekewich.
127 R. Nares, Hon. Secretary of the Association to Education Department, 26 February, 1898. Surrey (Diocese of Winchester) Voluntary Schools Association. Ed. 48/2.
128 Report of the Governing Body of the Manchester Diocesan Association of

R

Church Schools, 26 October, 1900. Bishop of Manchester. 45/5/1/80
(Manchester Central Library, Archives Department).

129   Rev. W. Perrin to Gorst, 6 December, 1890. Ed. 24/82B.

130   In spite of this handicap, not a single Catholic school was abandoned to the
Boards between 1870 and 1902, although 1,500 other voluntary schools were
given up to these authorities. H. O. Evennett, *The Catholic Schools of
England and Wales* (1944), p. 21. Much of this achievement was due to the
activities of T. W. Allies, Secretary of the Catholic Poor School Committee
from 1853 to 1883. See M. H. Allies, *T. W. Allies* (1907).

131   Salford Diocesan School Association. Report to be submitted to the
Governing Body at Meeting of 31 August, 1898. RCBT4 (Lancashire
R.O.).

132   This had happened automatically in some instances. In the York Diocesan
Association where the governing body was weak and took little interest in
the work, the Archdeaconries practically carried on the organization.
J. R. Dasent remarked on this situation to a fellow Assistant Secretary,
W. I. Ritchie, on 23 October, 1902: "If it were not for the Bill, I should stop
a good many cases, doing the work the G.B. ought to do for us." York Diocesan Association of Schools. Ed. 48/12.

133   Salisbury Diocesan Voluntary Schools Association. 1st Year Book, 1898
Report. p. 9. 594/62 (Wiltshire R.O.).

134   North Salop Voluntary Schools Association: Suggested Scheme for Distribution of Aid Grant 1897–8. Sutherland MSS. D593. N3/11/6 (Staffordshire C.R.O.).

135   There were ten Church of England and three Wesleyan schools at this time
in Lincoln. F. J. W. Ruddock, *Directory of the City of Lincoln*, (1897),
p. xxi.

136   Lincoln Diocesan Association of Voluntary Schools, Sub-Area, City of
Lincoln. Diocesan Board of Education Minute Book 1897–1902, 6/1/1
(Lincolnshire Archives Office).

137   Memorandum for Governing Body by R. A. McBriar, 8 March, 1898, *ibid.*

138   Lincoln Central Council for Voluntary Schools, Minute Book 1898–1902,
13 December, 1898. 6/1/2 (Lincolnshire Archives Office).

139   Lincoln Central Council for Voluntary Schools. Fourth Year Book ending
31 December, 1902, *ibid.*

140   Lincoln Central Council for Voluntary Schools. Report for 1902, p. 7
(Lincolnshire Archives Office).

141   Return of Public Elementary Schools not provided by School Boards,
Closed or Transferred to School Boards since the commencement of the
Voluntary Schools Act, 1897, giving in each case Reason assigned by
Managers for Closure or Transfer. BRP. 1899. LXXV.

142   The vicar of St. Oswald's, Sowerby in North Yorkshire wrote a letter to
the Department on 19 August, 1899 which summed up the feelings of many
other voluntary school managers: "In our case, we have received £45 per
year from the Aid Grant. But we have been obliged to increase our staff at
an expense of £85 per annum; and have spent £119 on structural alterations.
We were better off without the Aid Grant, if it is only to be a ground on
which more demands are to be made." Rev. E. de V. Bryans to Education
Dept. York Diocesan Association of Schools, Ed. 48/12.

143   H.M.I. could not attend the meeting to discuss the formation of an
Association, nor could he serve on the Governing Body. He could, however,
if invited, attend as advisory assessor. Precedent Book, V.S.A. 1897,
p. 125. Ed. 127/2.

144   Swanbourne National School. E. M. Kenney Herbert to Rev. F. Pinkhorn,

10 February, 1901. Fremantle MSS. Box 34, Bundle 4 (Buckinghamshire R.O.).

145 Perhaps the most notable instance of such recognition was the conferring on eight Midland Church of England Associations and the Midland Associations of Catholic, Wesleyan and British Schools, the right to nominate one governor each to the Mason University College, Birmingham from 1897. S. Royle Shore, Hon. Sec., Worcester Diocesan Association to Education Department, 13 March, 1899. Worcester Diocesan Voluntary Schools Association, Ed. 48/10.

146 W. F. Norris, *op. cit.*, p. 114.

7

The 1902 Act and the
Recasting of Management

By the turn of the present century, it was agreed amongst Churchmen that no final solution to the plight of the voluntary schools would be arrived at without a share in the rate aid, as with board schools. But a number of events had occurred since the 1897 Act which inevitably tied up the fates of both religious and secular systems of elementary education.

In 1899 a more unified central agency for education, the Board of Education, capable of dealing with both elementary and secondary schools came into existence; the Act establishing the Board provided for the continuance in office of the Lord President and Vice-President for the time being. One important addition was Gorst's new private secretary, Robert Morant, whose work at the Office of Special Inquiries and Reports had attracted Gorst's attention and who was henceforth to be intimately concerned with educational legislation. Morant's enquiries had led to the Cockerton judgment in 1900 which made illegal school board expenditure on higher education; this paved the way for the Government to pass a measure the following May which made counties and county boroughs the local education authorities for secondary education. What now remained to be settled was the future relationship between secondary, technical and elementary education and the maintained and voluntary schools. The focus of this chapter, therefore, will be the impact of the proposed and actual legislation during this period and its subsequent effects on school management.

What seems surprising, in view of his past record and known dislike of school boards, was that initially Gorst[1] should have been put in charge of the Bill to deal with education in the crucial session of 1901–2.[2] As early as 25 July, 1901, Balfour had warned Devonshire of the delicacy of the negotiations before them—"to deal with a certain number of School Boards who are sulky, a certain number of Borough Councils who are ambitious, and a certain number of County Councils who are somewhat slow". In all this Gorst, alleged Balfour, was moved to spend some of that time "in directing the administration and re-casting official letters in a manner which suits *his* views but does not suit ours".[3] An abortive attempt had been made two years earlier by Almeric Fitzroy, Devonshire's Secretary, to induce Balfour to give Gorst the vacant Chief Charity Commissionership in view of the latter's strained relations with Kekewich and his "attitude of slumbering rebellion" towards the Lord President.[4]

According to his biographer, Morant, at that time a Senior Examiner in the Department, drew up a masterly memorandum for the consideration of the appropriate Cabinet Committee, which stressed the importance of the religious question:

> "The only way to 'get up steam' for passing any Education Bill at all in the teeth of School Board opposition will be to include it in some scheme for aiding denominational schools."[5]

Morant's own close connections with the leading Church figures proved valuable in future negotiations. When it had been decided that Balfour would be the obvious person to steer such a Bill through the Commons, it was arranged that Morant should win Balfour over to his point of view at an intimate luncheon arranged at the Bishop of Rochester's Palace at Kennington.[6]

However, Balfour, in his first memorandum to Morant, was not optimistic on the prospects for voluntary school managers who, with the Church's blessing, desired to have all their current expenses connected with secular education paid out of the rates. In exchange, they were to hand over their existing buildings but would engage to maintain them in the future. Balfour argued that the bargain would be a one-sided affair.

> "If the buildings to be handed over are equal in cost and quality to the Board Schools of the District, the Managers of Voluntary Schools will no doubt be making a very handsome present to the community for which they might well demand a *quid pro quo*. But I take it that in a very large number of cases the buildings are inferior to the Board Schools, and that if the Voluntary School Managers were required to bring them up to that standard their financial position would hardly be improved by the change."[7]

Of the many proposals put forward at this time by the Church party for tackling this question, the most influential and far-reaching one was contained in a memorandum written by Lord Hugh Cecil, a High Churchman, and a relative of both Salisbury and Balfour. The scheme had a number of bizarre features, such as the one relating to the future appointment of teachers by voluntary school managers. Cecil proposed that managers should nominate the teacher to the proposed education authority, who might reject and refuse to give their reasons in writing. The managers could submit the name a second and third time; if after three nominations the managers and the authority were unable to agree, the appointment would be decided, in the case of an unassociated school, by the Education Department. Where a school belonged to an Association, it would be decided by a body called the "Visitatorial Committee", of which a majority would be appointed by a governing body of the Association and the remainder would be decided by the education authority. In either case the right of appointment would be absolute.[8] But the main proposals were impractical—that every voluntary school was to receive the whole cost of maintenance from public funds: and to provide and repair buildings out of subscriptions, which, under Cecil's scheme, would continue; that the new education authority would have full control of secular education and existing managers would have full control of religious education; and that teacher dismissal was in the control of the managers in respect of religious instruction and education authorities in respect of secular instruction.

What emerged from Cecil's plan was that rate aid would be available to denominational schools but the management of individual schools would remain. Cecil was aware of suggestions that the "control difficulty" might be met by having public representatives on the boards of managers, but rejected this on two grounds:

"First, from the Church point of view there is much more danger of Managers being overcrowded or ill-treated than of a great Association who could make a loud fuss, and secondly a small parochial body is the worst place for bitter and unnecessary quarrelling."[9]

Morant, in receipt of the memorandum, quickly saw Cecil, who modified his position somewhat when Morant pointed out some of the difficulties—such as what was to happen to the special aid grant and the method of applying rate aid to voluntary schools. This meeting had another purpose: to try out a suggestion for a draft Bill which Balfour and Morant had worked out together at Balfour's Scottish house at Wittingehame. Morant was delighted to note that many of Cecil's demands would be met by theirs,[10] which included permission for new authorities to maintain or aid public elementary schools and provision for transfer of duties from school boards to county, county borough and urban districts.

Much to Morant's chagrin, Devonshire consulted three school board supporters, Kekewich, Ilbert, the Parliamentary draftsman, and even Acland, the former Liberal Vice-President—"as usual, a happy collaboration going on, of which the poor old Duke is blissfully unconscious but unhappily the victim".[11] When, therefore, at the beginning of November, 1901 the three different draft Bills were ready to present to the Cabinet, Morant disclaimed any authorship of the Bills and said they were unworkable.[12] He also urged Balfour not to let any definite decision which left elementary voluntary education out of the Bill be taken at the coming Cabinet meeting.[13] The nature of the discussion at the meeting which, Morant claimed, "so frightened the Duke and (I believe) J. C(hamberlain)", was influenced by the receipt of a letter a few days beforehand by Devonshire from J. Powell Williams of the Conservative Office, who had been travelling the country and sounding opinion. He expressed the view that the political signs were that if a policy of supporting denominational schools from rates were adopted, it might have a damaging effect on the Liberal Unionist Party, especially on the Radical Unionist wing.[14] Balfour viewed the situation pessimistically. He remarked to Morant at this time:

> "You will see by this that I am in the lowest possible spirits about the whole question, and I am beginning to think it far more insoluble even than the South African problem."[15]

The three draft Bills which Devonshire circulated at the Cabinet meeting on 5 November consisted of two which dealt with secondary and elementary schools and one with secondary alone. Briefly there were two alternative strategies outlined in the accompanying Minute; a permissive Bill by which county councils, boroughs and urban district councils would take over the work of school boards, while non-county boroughs and urban districts would enjoy complete autonomy as to elementary education either through school boards or through their own councils. This was not a very satisfactory plan. The alternative was much more drastic—abolishing the school boards at once and making the county the authority for elementary as well as secondary education. County councils could levy rates for this purpose.

Both drafts undertook to give aid to voluntary schools, but under different provisions as to conditions and securities for efficient management. What emerges from Devonshire's memorandum is the fact that even at this stage the Cabinet had scarcely discussed "the principle of giving rate aid in any form to Voluntary Schools".[16]

It was clear that a division of opinion in the Cabinet would follow from the nature of its Conservative/Liberal Union composition. Devonshire reminded Archbishop Frederick Temple at about this time that support for rate aid for voluntary schools was "almost exclusively from Church Associations and not from political organizations . . . it would involve the disruption of the Unionist Party as at present constituted".[17] As a result of Cabinet discussions, Balfour suggested a number of alterations in the draft Bill, which Devonshire did not consider improvements,[18] including optional local rate aid for the voluntary schools. Many members of the

Cabinet rallied behind Chamberlain, the leader of the Liberal Unionists, who expressed his personal belief that rate aid to managers was both wrong and politically inexpedient.[19]

A few years earlier, Chamberlain had written to Hicks Beach[20] on this subject in the hope that they could agree to working on the same lines.

> "Personally", wrote Chamberlain, "I do not want the Voluntary Schools to yield to the Board Schools with a great increase in the Rates in consequence. But I believe it will be impossible to give them aid from the Rates without Ratepayers' consent."[21]

Devonshire, his old friend, was won round to Balfour's view[22] that a logical scheme must take cognizance of all schools in a particular county or county borough, and held that "we meet with hopeless difficulties at every step if these authorities are compelled to ignore the schools which are educating more than half the children of England".[23] Devonshire followed this up by meeting Chamberlain three days later on 6 December, 1901; it seemed possible that Chamberlain would accept a Cabinet decision which gave local authorities permissive powers to grant rate aid, though he considered this to be unwise. Devonshire gloomily remarked,

> "It is quite possible that we should be met by an amendment on our own side, making it compulsory on the local authority to finance all Voluntary Schools. If this were carried we should have either to drop the Bill or break up the Government."[24]

Surprisingly, for once, Gorst and Devonshire found themselves in agreement. A further meeting of the Cabinet Education Bill Committee on 9 December ended in deadlock only three days before the next full Cabinet meeting.[25]

Before any further progress could be made, it was necessary to win over Chamberlain. He was then at the height of his powers, taking a prominent part as Colonial Secretary in the conduct of the Boer War which was then raging.

> "By 1900," it has recently been claimed, "he was probably far better known in the country than either Salisbury or Balfour . . . regarded with implacable hatred by the Liberals, adored by the Imperialists, Joseph Chamberlain stood forth as the most controversial and the most famous statesman of his time."[26]

Morant, at a famous interview with Chamberlain on 11 December to test out Chamberlain's reaction to rate option for voluntary school managers, recorded the conversation in hastily jotted down notes. Chamberlain obviously saw the managers' function in a very circumscribed light after the transfer to a local authority had been effected. The recorded conversation also displayed Chamberlain's ignorance of Church managers' functions at the time.

Chamberlain	*Morant*
"(14) The Managers would *only* arrange the Religious Instruction. Nothing to do with the secular teaching, nor the appointment of teachers.	(14) But then there is not a single School that would consent to transfer if Managers have no rights at all and cannot appoint teachers.
"(15) Oh, no. The Managers care *only* for the Religious Instruction hour: and *that* we should give them.	(15) That is quite out of date. It was so in 1870, but nowadays it is felt that they must have a religious man to do all the secular teaching. Things have changed since 1870 on this point.
"(16) I did not know this. Is it not only true of Romans?	(16) Oh, no. It *was* only true of Romans: now Anglicans have learnt it, and will fight for it, even to rate war, it is said."[27]

Chamberlain was not convinced by Morant's persuasive arguments. He had been warned by Devonshire on the day before the Cabinet meeting that Balfour and he had found it impossible to leave out rate aid for voluntary schools.

At the meeting, both Devonshire and Balfour stressed the impossibility of the Committee carrying out the original brief given to it by the Cabinet. The instructions had been to prepare a draft Bill dealing with elementary as well as secondary education and to provide for the universal, not permissive extinction of school boards; that it should repeal the Cowper-Temple Clause; and not give powers to the new authority to aid voluntary schools from local rates.[28] Rate aid, whether optional or compulsory, should be given permanently and to every school in the area of a local authority. Devonshire added that if matters could not be settled, it would be better to confine the Bill to secondary education only.[29]

It is not clear why, after this meeting, Chamberlain's views on rate aid changed; either the Morant interview had persuaded him, or political calculations[30] in the light of a coming election had been responsible for this conversion. Whilst he sympathized with Devonshire and the Education Committee on their "almost hopeless task", Chamberlain grudgingly conceded that a Bill dealing with primary education, rather than secondary education only, was essential next session. His suggestions were:

"Abolish School Boards.
"Set up a Municipal Authority for Education on lines of your draft.
"Give powers to this authority (or rather to the authority which elects

it) to make such grants and such schools for such times and under such conditions as may be agreed upon between the new authority and the managers of any Voluntary Schools in its district.

"If it is necessary to carry out this scheme to abolish the Cowper-Temple clause, let it go—although I would rather not raise this thorny subject if it could be avoided.

"Provide that in future—and in view of local responsibility—the Board of Education should be charged only with the duty of controlling *results*; the Board would make its own terms whether by the efficiency of the scholars separately or by the School as a whole, and the grant would be made according to a scale arranged by them, but they would no longer be responsible for the means by which these results were obtained. They would deal with educational efficiency but not with architecture, construction and sanitation and teaching staff."[31]

This concession seemed to clinch matters for the future progress of the Bill, but this did not take into account Salisbury's own very individual approach to all matters connected with education. Three days after Chamberlain's conciliatory letter to Devonshire, Balfour's Minute of 11 December, mentioning the necessity of permanent rate aid ran contrary to Salisbury's own thinking. Salisbury commented in a Cabinet memorandum:

"The moment that any School has a right to receive aid by asking for it, from that moment the subscription to that School will absolutely cease. The only motive that keeps the stream of school subscriptions running is the belief that if they are not paid the school will perish. The motive for paying them is gone if the school can rely upon the rates. The rates must be levied, and levied only on those parishes where the schools fall short of the expenditure required by the school. . . . I imagine that generally the new financial arrangement will present itself to the average tradesman of a country town or village as one by which he will have to pay a rate of a shilling in the pound which he never paid before, while the squire and the rector who have hitherto mostly borne the cost of education that falls upon the parish will henceforth pocket the difference."[32]

Balfour had at the meeting on 13 December circularized to Cabinet colleagues a draft clause for rate maintenance of voluntary schools. The effect of the clause would have been to prescribe the conditions under which the new "Council" would maintain schools in its area. Sub-clause 7 was particularly clumsy. Voluntary school managers were to pay the aid grant to local councils in return for maintenance and they were to contribute to the expenses of maintaining the school in proportion to the relative amount of time devoted to the catechism or formulary.[33]

The clause was amended at a meeting a week later, largely as a result of a paper circulated by Lord Balfour of Burleigh, Secretary of State for Scotland and a Unionist.[34] His main objection to the draft clause was that there was to be no check upon the expenses from voluntary school managers which the Council might be called upon to find. His suggestion was that whilst agreeing to the principle of rate aid, the deficiency between the Parliamentary grant and the cost of the scheme should be divided, a half being paid by the voluntary school managers and half by the new school authority out of the rates, and so save the whole cost being thrown on the rates. Subscriptions would continue to be raised. The power of audit of voluntary school accounts by the Council should be given.[35] Burleigh was hurt when Randall Davidson, Bishop of Winchester, attacked him for his views on the matter and assured him that "I am profoundly attached to the principle of a really religious education and I detest the Cowper-Temple Clause".[36]

In spite of the buffetings the draft Bill had endured during the discussions within the Cabinet, by 20 December, Morant had received Balfour's instructions as to the lines on which the Education Bill was to be drawn up. They included:

> "Work the matter as one Bill, but bear in mind that it *may* have to be separated into a Bill for Secondary and a Bill for Elementary.
> "Repeal Cowper-Temple. Insert the principle of Clause 27 of 1896.
> "Make Rate Aid possible on any terms, to any school and to any amount—free option.
> "No area to be rated in which the Voluntary School (if it has no Board School) gets no rate aid at all.
> "Over the rest of the area maintenance must be pooled as far as possible."[37]

There were many elements in this memorandum which augured well for the Bill. The possibility of working secondary and elementary education together, coupled with universal, if optional, rate aid, made the mooted "single authority" for education purposes more feasible.[38]

The acceptance of rate aid for all had consequences for management, especially in the voluntary schools. Morant, in a lengthy letter to Balfour on 3 January, 1902,[39] observed

> "that I have throughout assumed that, just as if rates go at all to a Voluntary School they must go for the whole nett cost of maintaining it and not require any subscription . . . any 'in and out' arrangement would not only be quite impossible for Voluntary School Managers as you showed in your Memorandum and as Gladstone showed in 1870, but would also make impossible any sound scheme of County finance."[40]

However, Balfour of Burleigh's proposals, drawn from Scottish experience, where subscriptions were matched with rates, were irrelevant in the English context: in Scotland, voluntary schools represented only a small minority of the total elementary schools.

What was later to be a fiercely contested point of the Bill was the repeal of the Cowper-Temple Clause and its consequences for the appointment of teachers by managers. Morant, however, urged

> "that no elected authorities can possibly gauge the religious character and colour of teacher candidates. This can *only* be attempted by persons professing themselves to be of the religious character and colour in question. Herein is the *raison d'etre* of what are called (wrongly) 'Voluntary Managers'. If, then, the Government intend to give favourable consideration to this strong feeling and are in favour of a system by which it may be possible that Elementary Schools shall be staffed by teachers of known religious character and colour, and that it shall not at any rate in some schools be wholly a matter of chance whether the men and women in charge of the children all day long for eight years of their life have any or no beliefs at all,—then we have at once a solid basis for continuing the present system by which the managers (not being an elected body) of denominational schools *can* exercise this discrimination, and teachers *can* be chosen for their work with some reference to their religious character and colour. If this be accorded it follows that the choice of teachers in these schools *must* be left with the managers, and that if there be any representation of the Local Authority still, these managers *must* be in a *majority* on the managing body of the school—otherwise the whole *raison d'etre* of the school is destroyed."[41]

Ratepayer control would be achieved by setting up the county council as the local authority over all elementary schools and would lay down requirements to be fulfilled by them, thus putting managers in the position of carrying out the authority's regulations.

What emerged immediately from these discussions was the need for more efficient management of all elementary schools which rate aid could effect. Devonshire, in a Cabinet memorandum, demonstrated the advantages of a more comprehensive administrative unit.

> "The substitution of larger areas for the present school districts also renders necessary some change in the management as distinct from the provision of their schools. It is proposed that the powers of the new authorities in these larger areas should in all cases be powers of supervision, direction and control, as distinct from management.
>
> "Thus every school will be subject to the control, in respect of its secular education, of the local authority, every school will be maintained by the local authority, and every school will be managed by a body of managers. The only difference which will be recognized between one school and another will be that the managers of schools which have been provided out of public funds, or have been absolutely transferred to the local authority, will be wholly appointed by the local authority, and that

the religious instruction given in them will be undenominational, while in the case of schools which have been provided from private resources, a majority of the managers will be appointed under the existing provisions and the religious instruction will be such as they may determine."[42]

Hicks Beach, who, with Salisbury, disliked the idea of rate aid to voluntary school managers, challenged Devonshire during the Cabinet discussion on the memorandum. Devonshire followed this up afterwards in a private letter to Hicks Beach in which he drew upon his own experience as a subscriber:

"I maintain entirely or almost entirely, around Chatsworth, four schools in four parishes and the average deficiency for the last three years which I have had to find is £203. If I withdrew my subscriptions the four parishes would be probably united in a School District, and to maintain the Schools at the same expenditure would require a rate over the four parishes of 10½d., of which I should pay £107, and the other ratepayers would pay £96. If my plan was adopted and all Schools in the County were maintained by a County Rate, and if the expenditure per child in the Voluntary Schools was raised to that which prevails in the Board Schools, a County Rate of 7d. or 8d. in the pound would be required. I should then have to pay (at 7d.) £74 and the other ratepayers £67. I could then, if I chose, pay all my own and my tenants' rates and save £62. Is there anything very terrible in this?

"Why should you or I who have maintained our Schools be put under any compulsion to continue our subscriptions when the Duke of Bedford who has never contributed any more than his share of the rates is not compelled to contribute anything, but perhaps will gain by the equalisation of his School Board rates over the whole County."[43]

This scheme was, however, largely acceptable to the Cabinet, Balfour's only doubt being the wisdom of dropping Burleigh's and his own plan for a continuation of subscription for "relieving the squire and parson at the cost of the farmer and the small tradesman". He preferred that teachers' salaries should be a charge on the county fund but managers would remain responsible for the upkeep of schools and hand over to the local authority the average amount which it had paid for teachers' salaries in the last three years. Gorst's marginal note on a surviving copy of the memorandum pointed out that "the more efficiently the income has been kept up the more the managers will have to pay; and the less efficiently, the less, and that for all time. This can, of course, be done, but it would not be regarded as just."[44]

Balfour favoured the appointment of one-third of the managers by the local authority and two-thirds by those who provided the schools: "Let the appointment of all teachers, whether in Board or in Voluntary Schools, be by the Managers, with a veto and a power of dismissal, on educational grounds, exercisable by the local authority."[45]

Morant worked out the financial implications of Balfour's proposals. Taking twelve voluntary schools at random in three different cities and county boroughs, he found that managers would in future have to raise, from voluntary contributions, one-fifth to a quarter of the total expenditure, and that would mean that the managers would have to find more money than they found at present in sixty-four out of the seventy-two schools.[46]

A compromise was reached and rate aid was left optional when the Bill was introduced into the House on 24 March. This was largely Morant's work. Writing to Randall Davidson[47] shortly after the decision to include the adoptive element in the Bill, Morant admitted

"it was the *only* way to get the Bill past J.C. in the Cabinet and that a free option Bill was the *only* thing they would look at until I tried *this*. Is it not an advantage at all events to get the Government themselves committed, in a Bill, to the principle of recognizing that the Schools *ought* to be part and parcel of supply, even though they fear to enforce it everywhere? None the less I lament the drawback."[48]

Morant's anxiety about the Bill's progress was not without cause. He told Beatrice Webb shortly after this of the state of affairs among those chiefly responsible for the fate of the Bill. Kekewich and Gorst were completely ignored, Devonshire incapable of grasping the complicated details and the Cabinet absorbed in other affairs, impatient and tired with the whole question of education. She noted in her diary:

"Impossible to find out after a Cabinet meeting, Morant tells us, what has actually been the decision. Salisbury does not seem to know or care and the various Ministers, who do care, give me contradictory versions. So I gather that Cabinet meetings have become more than informal— they are chaotic—breaking up into little groups, talking to each other without any one to formulate or register the collective opinion. Chamberlain would run the whole thing if he were not so overworked with his own department."[49]

The storm of opposition to the Bill, mainly from Nonconformists such as Dr. Clifford and Hurst Hollowell, crystallized itself very largely into an attack on Clause 7 of the Bill which dealt with the management of individual schools. The clause had mentioned only that all public elementary schools should be managed by managers appointed under Section 15 of the Elementary Education Act 1870, and in the cases of schools not so provided, by the persons who were managers for the purposes of the Elementary Education Acts 1870 to 1900 in proportion of two-thirds to one-third. Much of the subsequent discussion turned on the relative proportions of denominational to lay representation.[50] Gorst, shortly before he was deprived of his Vice-Presidency, saw the risk of the Bill being wrecked by two factions of the Liberal and Conservative Unionist Party—those who wished to extend popular control and thus increase the one-third proportion, and those who believed that two-thirds was the smallest proportion that would secure the denominational character of schools. Gorst wrote to Balfour,

"I have never myself thought the two-thirds majority of Managers a satisfactory security for the distinctive religious character of the schools; the two-thirds may be composed of absentee squires and church officials. The one-third of the ever present local Dissenters. . . . The Managers should be appointed partly by the Trustees and partly by the Local Authority. The proportion is to me a matter of indifference—whatever will best go through Parliament."[51]

At about the same time, Morant had confided to Bishop Davidson that Balfour was about to seek the Bishop's advice on a new line of suggested compromise "which he does not himself much like and which he thinks you would not like: very briefly, it is to give a majority representation on the management to the local authority, but to reserve to the existing managers the choice of all teachers and the religious instruction".[52]

The day that Balfour received Gorst's letter he took Salisbury's place as Prime Minister. The details of managers' powers under the new pattern of administration were still outstanding. One of his major tasks was to secure the settlement of this point during the next few months. Balfour's realistic appraisal of the role of managers under the new system during debates in the House did not take into account stronger emotions. That managers could possess "only a very subordinate position indeed as regarded anything connected with the secular education of the schools" as compared with the supreme local education authority, left out of account the hostility to religious representation on managing committees.[53]

Chamberlain advised Balfour that

"if the Bill is forced through the House in its present shape it will undoubtedly in my opinion kill the denominational schools. The minority of the Management Committees who will represent the principle of popular control will have a permanent grievance which will cause them to act on each Committee as a section apart, constantly putting sand into the wheels and opposing everything that is done by the other managers. There will therefore be permanent irritation and the system will break down under the strain. On the other hand, if the so-called popular representatives were in a majority, they would, I believe, in most instances take a commonsense view of the matter and try to make the system work smoothly and economically. A proportion of them would be from the first friendly to the denominational system, and those who were opposed to it would not have behind them any strong popular support if they were to act unjustly or discourteously to the clerical representatives."[54]

He followed the compromise suggested by Bishop Percival of Hereford, which was fully set out in a paper read to Church Congress[55] and a summary of which appeared as a letter in *The Times*.[56] The compromise referred to the 8,000 parishes where Church of England schools were the only ones available.

"The managers appointed by the Church shall have the Statutable right, whenever the office of head teacher is vacant, to require that all candidates must be members of the Church of England, other posts, such as that of assistant and pupil teacher being open to all denominations.

"The clergy of the parish shall have free access to the School at suitable times for the purpose of instructing their children in the doctrine of the Church of England.

"The managers appointed by the Church shall be one-third of the whole.

"The local educational authority shall nominate one-third, as proposed in the Bill.

"The remaining one-third shall be elected either by the parish council or by parish meeting."[57]

Chamberlain's own preference for a council majority of managers leaving religious instruction to be dealt with by a denominational minority, fitted in well with Percival's suggestions. Balfour's problem in accepting either plan was, however, as he told Chamberlain, "rather practical than theoretical". He pointed out the difficulty of a system under which the teacher was elected by a denominational minority and at the same time the servant of the elected majority of the managers.

"Moreover I have always had a great desire not merely to abolish the clerical preponderance in the management of secular education but the clerical preponderance also in the management of religious education. This, it seems to me, would be successfully accomplished by *my* plan without destroying the denominational character of the schools. It would not be accomplished by yours."[58]

He did, however, fear the reception of his plan by many Anglicans and all Roman Catholics in making laymen supreme in matters ecclesiastical, and with good reason.[59]

According to the Bishop of Rochester, Edward Stuart Talbot,[60] Chamberlain told Charles Gore, the Bishop of Worcester,[61] his good friend who was staying with him at this time, that "he never liked the Bill: that he would be glad even now to be out of office, but that the game has to be played, and that it is not the game to be defeated. The upshot is that he presses A. J. B. to have a conference between Nonconformist leaders presided over by himself!—no other of any use. . . . To rouse the whole Nonconformist folk to ire is bad; to cement an alliance between them and labour against the domineering priest is worse; and to let a new Liberal Party come in founded on this alliance worst of all. I see no way which does not destroy the Church School as we know it."[62]

Gore himself later told Winchester that Chamberlain, during this period, believed that the Government "is steering the ships on the rocks—the Unionists will not follow. He seemed ignorant of the state of mind of the Nonconformists."[63] In Chamberlain's version of his meeting with Gore, the Bishop had favoured a majority of popular representatives on managing bodies.

"Now if the other Bishops were ready to accept this", he told Balfour, "at such a Conference as I suggested to you, the Nonconformists, or at least the reasonable majority, would be satisfied. You would be protected from your own side by the Bishops and you would split the opposition into fragments."[64]

Morant wrote to Balfour's Secretary expressing his perturbation at Balfour's plan.

"This question of giving all six Managers the control of religious instruction and altering all the Trust Deeds so as to take it away from the parson who now has it is most horribly dangerous. Also I fear we shall get into awful quagmires if we begin to set up lay tribunals."

On the future handling of the measure a new factor had now to be taken into consideration. Devonshire, the Lord President, was replaced by Lord Londonderry as President of the new Board of Education upon its establishment in August, 1902. At the same time Gorst, as Vice-President, was succeeded by Sir William Anson as Parliamentary Secretary. Londonderry, with his Ulster connections, appreciated that the fate of the Bill could be profoundly affected by "Belfast influences upon the religious instruction question" and Londonderry's nervousness on this point was transmitted to Balfour by Morant.[65]

The general assumption was that the county authority and the Church representation on managing bodies of schools in the future represented different interests. In fact, in rural counties especially, there was a close identity of Church and county council interests. Thirty-eight out of the forty Church members of the Norfolk County Council from the total of seventy-five aldermen and councillors, sent a copy of a memorial addressed to the Archbishop of Canterbury

s

and to *The Times* stating their views. They wished for a majority of managers to be elected representatives of the county and parish but failing this, the antagonism could be mitigated by removing two grievances: whilst reserving head teachers' posts in Church schools, other posts should be open to all denominations regardless of trust deeds: and that it should be incumbent upon managers to provide, in addition to Church teaching, an alternative class conducted by one of the teachers on the staff, in accordance with the Cowper-Temple Clause.[66] The signatory of this letter, A. Lee Warner, was an old friend of Morant's; accordingly Morant wrote a private letter to him asking various questions. Warner's reply was a pre-eminently fair one, basing his arguments on educational and administrative rather than on doctrinal principles. He wrote to Morant,

> "You ask me 'Don't you think that the greater part of the Nonconformist opposition is based on complete mis-understanding of the Bill, arising generally out of deliberate misrepresentations and lies?' Emphatically No, in Norfolk. You are proposing to make a new departure, and the Nonconformists apprehend that it will stereotype the authority of the Parson, and hamper his elasticity by giving a fresh lease of life to the National Society. Are they wrong?"[67]

The attitude of the Church authorities towards Nonconformist minorities in education was, as typified by Percival, a sympathetic one. It stemmed partly from the anxiety to settle the education issue and partly from the anxiety shared by all denominationalists for the fate of the "single school areas" in rural parishes which were predominantly Church of England in character, i.e. where the school represented one denomination. Temple suggested a compromise plan to Balfour for schools in the hands of the Church. The Church would consent to confine instruction in her own formularies to two days a week. The Nonconformist could withdraw his children from religious instruction on Thursday and Friday, but not on Monday, Tuesday and Wednesday, and would thus be in the same position as if he were attending a board school. He added,

> "Many of the Clergy would not like it. But I am thinking of what is just; not of what is agreeable. And I would sacrifice much to conciliate our opponents, many of whom are very religious men."[68]

This plan was a variation on Clause 27 of the abortive 1896 Bill, which would have allowed accredited teachers of various denominations access to the schools. Balfour in replying to Temple enclosed a copy of a memorandum he had written for the Cabinet a fortnight before on single school areas, "from which you will perceive that my thoughts and your thoughts on the subject are running in the same channel".[69]

Balfour wrote a masterly document for the Cabinet entitled "Voluntary School Management under the Education Bill", in an attempt to get a decision on Clause 7. It started in a rather caustic fashion:

> "The main storm of educational controversy rages round the question of 'Management' in Voluntary Schools. Considering how little under the Bill these Managers have to manage, this seems rather absurd."

Broadly, two schemes, A and B, were put forward for consideration: Scheme A gave a majority among managers to the denomination to which the school belonged. B provided that a majority of the managers should be representative with special powers for the denominational element in certain "reserved subjects", namely, the right to select teachers and the right to settle the religious instruction curriculum. A number of variations of both schemes were put forward. The final choice, if a decision had to be made, in Balfour's views, lay between Scheme A Variation 1, and Scheme B Variation 3; in the first instance the body of managers would have complete control of all matters connected with the school, except those within the province of the education authority, notwithstanding anything in the trust deeds. Thus the managers would have full powers to deal with reserved subjects. In Scheme B Variation 3, reserved subjects were to be dealt with exclusively by existing denominational managers. All other subjects were to be dealt with by managers appointed in the same way as those for rate aided schools. Balfour's own predilection was for Scheme A.[70]

Morant submitted his comments on Balfour's proposals and referred to Scheme B in the following terms:

> "The existing slack system as to the appointment of Managers works at present as there is no particular reason to challenge the appointment of Managers in any case. In future, however, there would be, if Scheme B were adopted, a division of responsibility between two sets of Managers. These two bodies would have to deal with one another and in that case it seems almost impossible to avoid having validly appointed Church Managers."[71]

At this time, Morant wrote despairingly of Balfour to the Bishop of Winchester:

> "Now I know how blissfully he ignores newspapers and so forth and how incapable he sometimes is of realising that many popular misconceptions are in no way destroyed by even the best of arguments: so I fear he may be over sanguine in some directions, while I fear still more that he may be overbold in others."

As to how far religious instruction should be under the control of the Church managers,

"A.J.B. has always *counted* on their being in full control of it. It has been one of his pet points.

"If we raise this issue in the House, and if we propose to put it in the hands of any six persons, however chosen, of whom only one is a parson, the decision, practically, of what is the proper religious instruction for a Church of England School and what is not—we should be let in for the whole huge wrangle of a new Reformation Settlement, of Congregationalism in the Church of England, of a continuous unseemly wrangle in managing bodies."[72]

In urging Balfour to stand firm on the question of denominational managers, Morant was not alone. Devonshire, who still retained a special responsibility for the Bill in the Lords, told Chamberlain that there was little advantage to be gained by going back on the denominational majority of managers.[73] The alternatives put forward by Nonconformists were unrealistic in terms of day-to-day management of voluntary schools. A Gloucestershire M.P. and a moderate Churchman, Sir John E. Dorrington ("surely a good and typical man" noted Morant), writing to Morant, declared,

"I don't see any possibilities of compromise on the question of the proportion of representatives on the managing committees. To give a majority would be to give up Denominational Schools. Imagine a Roman Catholic with a majority of Nonconformists on the Committee and appointing a Baptist Head Teacher!"[74]

In all the discussions on the principles of the Bill, there had been little attempt to define the new role of manager, or indeed to look very closely at the existing role. Gorst, now free from official responsibilities,[75] wrote in *The Nineteenth Century* an article on the Bill in October, 1902 and speculated on the effects of local authority control on management:

"The name 'managers' is perhaps not an altogether happy one. It has certainly led to much misapprehension. These are no longer to be 'managers' in the sense in which those now responsible for Voluntary Schools are 'managers'. The 'managers' of the Bill are, as has been frequently stated, the 'creatures and servants' of the local authority. They have no powers except those specifically given them by Statute—or delegated by the authority. It does not follow that the authority may not entrust a great deal of discretion to particular bodies of managers and follow to a great extent their advice. . . . But all such discretionary powers would be dependent on the will of the authority who would have the right to withdraw them at any time from bodies of 'managers' with whose composition or conduct they were dissatisfied."[76]

So far as voluntary schools were concerned, the difficulties of definition were even greater. Balfour admitted in his Manchester speech on 14 October:

"I think some of the difficulty has arisen owing to a misunderstanding of one of the terms used in the Government Bill, the term 'managers'. I think it is very natural that anybody who saw the term 'manager' in the Bill would say, 'These are the people who have got control of the schools.' It is a mistake, but it is a natural mistake. I don't think it is a mistake for which either the Government draughtsman or the Government are responsible, because we have borrowed the term 'manager' from the preceding Act of 1870: 'management' and 'manager' are terms which do not carry with them the idea of control."[77]

In the debate on Clause 7 which followed a week later in the Commons, Harcourt, in asking Balfour for further clarification of this part of his speech, stated:

"The Act of 1870 gave no particular powers to the managers, who were usually the proprietors of the schools, and they were only in the position of private persons who earned grants by the fulfilment of the conditions proposed. The situation was now altogether altered. The managers admittedly were not managers in the sense that was understood under the Act of 1870, and it was to be regretted that the word 'managers' should have been applied in this case. These persons were a totally different class of persons, with different attributes and different duties altogether."[78]

The election of the four foundation managers, namely the denominational managers of voluntary schools, raised the question of the methods of selection with special reference to trust deeds. Balfour hoped that "the four denominational representatives shall be a reflection of the kind of body contemplated by the original trust deed, and as that original trust deed does not contemplate a clerically dominated body . . . (it) will not be any more than its prototype clerically controlled with a clerical majority".[79]

The facts of the case were often very different. Balfour himself had received numerous letters from managers pointing out the restrictions which would be placed upon suitable appointments if trust deeds were to be construed to include only persons strictly and legally appointed in pursuance of some power in a trust deed. An M.P. and manager of a number of schools, H. W. Worsley Taylor, gave an example of the difficulty:

"In two other schools with which I am connected the Managers were persons designated by the Trust Deed. But some years ago we, of our own motion, elected additional Managers—in the one case the Wardens and Sidesmen: and, in the other, certain persons chosen by parents of scholars—with a view to giving more popular representation—to the great advantage of the Schools as it turned out.

"In these cases again it may be held that there is no legal power to appoint such outside Managers—which would be a distinct loss.

"I submit for consideration whether, in view of the foregoing, it would be well to *enlarge* the definition of 'Managers' as contained in Section 2 of the Act of 1870."[80]

Archbishop Temple, in a letter to Balfour which was never sent, protested that

"if you are going to interfere with the Trust Deeds at all, are you not rather avoiding the respect due to the Trust Deeds if you make the accidental varieties of their forms impose for all times upon the school, to cover rural parishes with so great a variety of systems? As a matter of fact we have in ordinary usage worked out schools on a practically uniform system whatever was to be the wording of the different Trust Deeds."[81]

Before making his Manchester speech, Balfour had enquired from the Legal Branch of the Board of Education for guidance on the inviolability of trust deeds. The answer was that variation could be made. Moreover, it was discovered that as far back as 1886, the National Society had stated that they did not object to removal by scheme from trust deeds on National Schools of the Church qualification of the managers, and that this had been done in many cases.[82]

In the Bill, Balfour was urged to make provision regarding the election and terms of office of voluntary school managers. A Welsh rector, who was manager of joint schools with the vicar of an adjacent parish, had been dismissed because of the action of the other vicar, who was also secretary with everything in his hands, "and myself the Rector of this Parish unfortunately not being even Ex-Officio Manager without his nomination", had no redress. "If," he wrote to the Attorney General, "this happens to me, a *Rector*, we being now as a Parish *utterly without* representation and the schools shamefully *mismanaged in spite* of us—what about *other* Managers?"[83] His plan for election was that the clerical or trustee nominator would provide a list of those he approved; ratepayers would be allowed to choose at least half of them. The term of office would be three years. In fact, the mode of election of voluntary school managers was never written into the Act.

THE BILLESDON NATIONAL SCHOOL AFFAIR

During the closing stages of the Bill an important amendment introduced by a Government supporter, Colonel Kenyon-Slaney,[84] dramatically shifted the balance of power within denominational managing bodies away from the clerical element. Balfour had already stated in the House that "Religious education would be under the control not of one man and that man the parson of the parish, but of a Board of Six", [85] and again, at Manchester on 14 October: "I say that the typical case will be that, whereas the clergyman of the parish is at present sole manager of the education of his parish now, under the Bill, he will be one of six managers." [86]

The Kenyon-Slaney Clause vested the control of religious instruction in the hands of the body of managers as a whole. It is a fact that the amendment was accepted in order to appease Nonconformist opposition, but it is tempting to speculate that Balfour and Morant had been influenced in their attitude towards the question by such an issue being raised by the school managers of a Leicestershire school. Two significant pointers to support this theory are that firstly, no decision seems to have been arrived at before this specific case arose, and secondly, some of the school correspondence relating to the case was deposited in the Board's official papers in the months August to October, 1902, during which period the initial decisions relating to the Clause must have been taken.

On 15 May, 1902, the parents of seventeen children and the master, Frederick W. Clowes, of Billesdon Church of England School in Leicestershire, wrote to the Board of Education protesting at the action of the vicar, Rev. C. R. Fowke, the chairman and correspondent of managers, in regard to religious instruction. The parents had, on the previous two days, given notice in writing to the vicar that they were withdrawing their children (under the Conscience Clause) from religious instruction, which was given by clergy, and expressed a desire to have their children taught by the school master and school mistress, who held first and second class Archbishops' Certificates respectively. (Owing to the vicar's action, the congregation had dwindled from some 350 to about 20.) The vicar, an extreme Ritualist, refused to allow the master to teach children in religious subjects and the master in protest declined to teach secular work, as he knew the wishes of the parents. The Rev. Fowke then sent the children home.

In his letter to the Board of 28 May, 1902, Fowke maintained that as religious instruction given in the school was under his control, as vicar of the parish he had the right to take the whole teaching or any part of it himself at any time.

"To allow withdrawal from individuals," he wrote, "would cause endless confusion and be disastrous to the education of the children and the discipline of the school. It has been objected that the wording of the article in the Code is 'must not be compelled to remain', but unless children are told they can go home, they *are* compelled to remain. I submit that I have acted in accordance with the letter and the spirit of the 'Conscience Clause' and other directions of the Code regarding religious instruction."

The letter ended defiantly, "I feel it is a matter which concerns me only under the Bishop of the Diocese, so long as the 'Conscience Clause' is observed".[87]

Morant now took a personal interest in the case and directed that he should be kept informed of all further developments. This interest persisted throughout the conflict, which spanned the time from shortly after the introduction of the Education Bill in Parliament to the crucial days of October, 1902. Morant had obtained "by private information" the fact that the rector's letter had been written "in the teeth of wishes of three of the managers", who were unaware that it was ever sent.[88]

Shortly after this, the master was summarily dismissed by the managers at a meeting not duly constituted. The matter was now taken up by J. H. Yoxall, General Secretary of the N.U.T., with Lord Churchill, a manager of the school who had originally presented the living to Rev. Fowke. Yoxall's intention was to get the teacher reinstated without any public trouble if possible. Morant contrived to get the N.U.T., with Lord Churchill's approval, to write to the Board of Education as to the terms of the trust deed, which Morant had now seen. The deed, dated 1874, provided that the management should be vested in a committee, consisting of the vicar of the parish, churchwardens of the Chapel of Rolleston and two other persons being subscribers to the school, as well as annually elected ratepayers. Yoxall, in writing to the Board, stated that no such election by the ratepayers had taken place in the previous four years and that therefore the terms of the trust deed had not been complied with. Morant, noting that "the case is full of private difficulties"[89] ordered Cowie, the Assistant Secretary, to "kindly see that the matter received prompt attention and careful treatment, and is not just answered in a negative manner".[90]

The procedure was to refer the trust deed to the South Kensington Branch, who stated that they were limited in their jurisdiction as to holding an Inquiry, and that in fact the matter should go to the Charity Commission.[91]

Events moved swiftly. Subsequent to the matter being referred to the Commission, and the resulting correspondence, a managers' meeting was held. Two subscriber managers were duly elected and the master was reinstated. This last move came about only after threats of libel proceedings against the vicar had been made by the National Society, but the deadlock continued.

On 1 October, 1902, the Board of Education succeeded the Charity Commissioners in bearing responsibilities for schemes relating to voluntary schools. The following day, Lord Churchill sought a meeting with the Board. An account of what transpired was noted by Bruce. He suggested that

> "although the Scheme could be established upon receipt of sufficient application of two inhabitants, etc., such a course would seem of little advantage in present case, in which the crux of the whole matter was the Religious Instruction apparently, inasmuch as, apart from any power of the Board to alter trusts in this respect (and such power was very doubtful), it was unlikely that any such Scheme would go through, since National Society would certainly strenuously oppose a diminution of Vicar's rights under the Trust Deed, and would jealously guard against any alteration in provisions of Deed which might prejudice and affect their Society. Best course therefore would seem to be to find if possible some other building and for subscribers to be induced to withdraw their subscriptions from present School to the new building, which Whitehall Branch would possibly recognise and assist with Grant and withdraw Grant from existing School which would then of necessity have to be closed.

> "Lord Churchill was afraid no suitable other building existed but promised to ascertain this. He said he should be sorry if circumstances made the creation of a Board School necessary, but that almost anything would be better than the present state of affairs, and he was afraid that the lay Managers would attempt to take the law into their own hands by giving the Master their own instructions as to religious teaching or otherwise.

> "*Possibly* Vicar might resign before long. Mr. Bruce explained probable effect of Education Bill now before Parliament as regards the *management*, but explained that its provisions would not assist as regards the present difficulty, viz., the alteration of the existing trusts as to the Religious Instruction. Warned Lord Churchill to advise Managers to do nothing *ultra vires*, inasmuch as appeal would probably then be made to this Board and to National Society, when any illegal action upon part of Managers would have to be deprecated and effectually stopped. Stated that it appeared that the only way out of difficulty was either a new Vicar or provision of some other school building accommodation."[92]

The Board of Education was now in a dilemma. At an interview Lord Churchill had had in September with John White at the Board, Churchill had asked "whether if the other managers ousted Mr. Fowkes from it (i.e. Committee of Managers) *we* should interfere on his behalf. I guaranteed", wrote White, "that we should do nothing of the kind."[93] At a subsequent interview, White told Lord Churchill that

> "he need not fear interference by us of Whitehall on side of Vicar in any quarrel between Vicar and Managers as to what Deed required in regard to Religious Instruction. I said we constantly refused to interpret Deeds and that in this case we should be particularly careful to avoid all appearance of backing Vicar against rest of Parish."[94]

Taking the two statements together, it becomes clear that a revolt against the rector as manager or his enforcement of religious instruction in the schools left the Board helpless to interfere.

In this situation the next move was not surprising. The reinstated master of the school informed the Board on 8 November that the "bitter religious controversy" had broken out again. Over half the scholars of the school had now been withdrawn from religious instruction which the vicar still insisted, under the terms of the trust deed, in having sole right to give. A petition signed by Churchmen and Nonconformists begging the managers to arrange for the teachers to give religious instruction, was presented at a managers' meeting on Wednesday, 5 November; as a result the master received instructions from the managers to take the children to another building to be set apart for religious instruction, and there to teach Church of England doctrine. Clowes, the schoolmaster, mentioning that there was no provision for this on the time-table, asked, "I naturally wish to obey orders given by School Managers, but am I justified in being away from school from 11 a.m. to 12 noon each day?"[95] The Board's advice was unhelpful: Pooley, an Assistant Secretary, remarked to White, "I do not think that we can or should decide the question as between the Master and the Managers." Bruce suggested that the master might give religious instruction out of hours in a building other than a school building. This did not solve the basic difficulty of the master, who had been instructed by the managers to give religious instruction during school hours in school buildings. Another suggestion was that one of Her Majesty's Inspectors should hold a local inquiry.[96]

Until the Act was on the Statute Book it seemed that Article *85e* precluded the possibility of the teacher absenting himself from school premises during school hours. Morant's final words in the case to White therefore were: "I think with you that, all things considered it would be best that no answer at all should be sent."[97]

On 27 November the House of Commons passed by a huge majority the Kenyon-Slaney amendment, giving responsibility to managers as a body instead of to the vicar for giving religious instruction. Morant, whose minutes continued throughout the proceedings, noted with satisfaction three days after this event, "The case is exciting much attention and is one of the gravest local difficulty. But the Kenyon-Slaney Clause will stop *all* the trouble."[98]

Certainly Balfour was not driven to insert this amendment by House of Commons pressure. Almeric Fitzroy noted in his diary on the day the amendment passed in the House:

"It is curious that a Bill in the conduct of which the Government have exposed themselves to bitter attacks for their alleged surrender to ecclesiastical pressure should have been the occasion of a most remark-able demonstration of the little hold clerical influence has on the temper of the House."[99]

Balfour recorded his own account of the history of the amendment in a little known Cabinet Minute dated 6 December, 1902. It is, for Balfour, a passionately worded document and opens on an indignant note:

> "There seems to be a widespread impression that the policy embodied in the Kenyon-Slaney Clause has been 'sprung' upon the public, and that the Government have been driven to accept it at a late stage of the proceedings on the Bill by forces hostile to the Church. As I entirely differ from this view, and think that if there has been any change of opinion it has not been on the part of the Government, it may be worth while to recall the real facts of the case."[100]

Balfour stated that Clause 7 and Clause 8(1) (*e*) he understood to mean

> "that the management *for every purpose* of Denominational Schools was in the hands of a body of which two-thirds necessarily belonged to the denomination and one-third might or might not belong to it, but in any case were appointed by outside authorities. I was in error. It appears that the words taken in connection with the Act of 1870 have, in the case of schools governed by particular trust deeds, a different and less obvious signification" (obviously a reference to the reserved right of the vicar to religious instruction). "But how many are there among those who now object to the Kenyon-Slaney amendment who did not share my mistake?"[101]

To substantiate his claims that the substance of the amendment had been his intention well before the November crisis, Balfour quoted from various speeches he had made both in the House and on public occasions.[102] None date before May, 1902 when the Billesdon School conflict first arose.

LATER STAGES OF THE BILL

Shortly before the Bill passed through its final stages in the Lords, Temple asked Mr. Danckwerts, K.C., for his opinion on two points: first "the effect of the Kenyon-Slaney amendment on schools whose Trust Deeds provided that the superintendence of religious instruction shall vest in the Parish Clergyman". The opinion given was that "the effect of the Section must be that the Trust Deed must yield in favour of the governing intention and that is to leave the control with the managers and preserve only the characteristics of the religious instruction and that is to say, instruction in accordance with the tenets and doctrines of the Church of England". Temple's second question was: "How does the Education Bill affect the power of School Managers to withdraw their schools from use as Public Elementary Schools?" The answer gave no rise to optimism. The Bill would create practical difficulties in the way of producing non-compliance of a resumption of the school with its premises and trust fund, having regard to Section 7(1)(*a*), Section 14(1) and Schedule II para.14.[103]

The acceptance of the Kenyon-Slaney amendment produced great bitterness among Church leaders. Talbot of Rochester,[104] Davidson of Winchester and Gore of Worcester attempted a last ditch stand.[105] "The Kenyon-Slaney business seems to get worse every day," wrote Morant to Davidson. "We are rather fearing a difficulty at the Albert Hall" where Talbot and Gore and Hugh Cecil addressed a meeting;[106] the *Church Times* reported on it however as being "dull, decorous and important".[107] On the penultimate evening of the discussions on the Bill in the House of Lords, the three bishops attacked the clause and Archbishop Temple, by now ailing and partially blind, spoke, vainly, against it.[108]

The Education Act passed through the Lords on 18 December, 1902. During its passage, the school boards had been destroyed; in their place were established the local education authorities in the county councils and county boroughs, with the duty of maintaining and keeping efficient all public elementary schools, whether provided by themselves or by voluntary agencies. Politically, the Act had strained the Conservative Union alliance and roused the opposition of the Liberals.[109] Chamberlain wrote to Devonshire at this time:

"I told you your Education Bill would destroy our Party. It has done so. Our best friends are leaving us in scores and hundreds and they will not come back.[110] . . . The worst of the business is that after the Bill has passed the agitation will continue in its most serious form. What are you going to do with Town Councils that refuse to act and ratepayers who refuse to pay? D-mn the Bill!"[111]

Balfour, some six months after the Act was in operation, summed up the situation:

"It is, of course, true that our greatest offence, that of having been too long in office—is one that time cannot diminish. But the Education Bill fever will be allayed in twelve months and Ritchie[112] will, I hope, next year get another penny off his Income Tax."[113]

But some of the difficulties of implementing the system had yet to be put to the test. The "dual" system now operated, with religious instruction being undenominational in "provided" schools, and in the hands of the managers in "non-provided" ones. Appointment of teachers in "provided" schools was made by the local authority and in a "non-provided" school by the denomination to which the school belonged. Both systems were to be maintained by public funds.

FOUNDATION MANAGERS

Section 11(1) of the Act provided for the appointment of foundation managers to represent the denominational interests contemplated by the provisions of the trust deed of the school.

> "... but if it is shown to the satisfaction of the Board of Education that the provisions of the trust deed as to the appointment of managers are in any respect inconsistent with the provisions of the Act, or are insufficient for the purpose in that there is no trust deed available, the Board of Education shall make an order under this section for the purpose of meeting the case."

Although, as already stated, four was the normal number of foundation managers contemplated in the trust deed, where the local education authority was a borough or urban district it was suggested that the numbers might be six foundation and three local authority managers; in the case of a county council it should be eight and four respectively or other multiples of four and two, although it was admitted that in most cases twelve would be an inconveniently large number of managers.[114] An overwhelming proportion of voluntary schools in England and Wales—10,907 out of 13,796—had within the statutory three months applied to the Board for alteration of trust deeds as to the appointment of managers, many on the grounds that the former deeds were defective, in that some number other than four was stipulated therein.[115]

Neither the Act nor the subsequent explanatory Memorandum gave any clear lead on the methods of appointing the first foundation managers. In order to get the Act smoothly into operation, however, interim orders were issued to local education authorities, as well as to owners, trustees and managers, in order to enable these various bodies to have time to prepare their plans. Not all boards of managers were eager to hurry matters. For example, on 17 December, 1902, the day before the Act was passed, the managers of St. Silas' National School, Hunslet, Leeds, met in order to comply with the trust deed requirements and appoint another manager. "The Vicar reported that the day by day changes in the Education Bill had caused him to take no steps for the finding of another Manager and the meeting justified his masterly inactivity."[116]

Selby-Bigge, an Assistant Secretary, suggested to Morant that the best way of appointing the first foundation managers in all cases would be by co-optation by the existing managers for a limited period of one year:

"It would secure some continuity of management and would make a bridge between the old system and the new. In most parishes it is probable that the old Managers will, under *any* system, provide the first Foundation Managers but in some parishes the adoption of the new method might result in all the old Managers being displaced. In these circumstances the continuance of the school as a 'voluntary school' might be imperilled. I think that in ordinary parishes a body of Foundation Managers representing the existing Managers would be more likely to try to carry on the school on the voluntary system than a brand new body, who might possibly be elected with the express object of securing the transfer to the local education authority."

(Morant noted—"will be widely and hotly discussed".) Selby-Bigge's plan was largely followed.[117]

When a Final Order came into force, foundation managers would usually consist of an *ex officio* manager and three representative managers. The *ex officio* manager was the principal officiating minister of the ecclesiastical district or parish in which the school was situated. Representative managers were to be "qualified persons elected by qualified subscribers to the funds of the school at a meeting to be held triennially for that purpose". Their term of office was three years but they would in practice remain in office until their successors were elected. They were also eligible for re-election.[118]

The decision to grant subscribers the right of selecting foundation managers was not taken by the Board of Education without considerable debate. A number of alternatives were put forward including nomination by quasi-representative bodies such as Voluntary Schools Associations or Diocesan Boards. Sir William Anson, the new Secretary, suggested that co-optation would be open to the risk of placing the management of schools in the hands of a few rich persons; "foundation managers would find their field of subscribers narrowed by the blighting influence of the Education rate and will have to look out for colleagues who can help to keep the school going".[119]

The co-optative solution which was proposed was regarded as a temporary expedient rather than a long-term one. From his own experience of the administration of charities in rural districts, Selby-Bigge disliked co-optation. "Such bodies are often found to have been restricted for generations, to members of certain families or classes or political parties and they have cultivated immobility to a high degree. . . . In rural districts where the only possible members of a co-optative body are small farmers and tradesmen the risks of stupid prejudiced management are really considerable."[120] On the other hand, the traditional policy of the National Society giving subscribers the chief voice in the management of the school had many advantages. It presented some sort of electorate (a calculation showed that in only 10 per cent of Church of England schools had the number of subscribers fallen below eight); and, as has been seen earlier, the rights of subscribers under the trusts were not negligible.

One problem of an electorate consisting of subscribers was that to reduce the amount of qualifying subscription to, say, 2s. 6d., exposed the school to the risk of a "faggot" electorate. It was therefore suggested that the requirement should be for the electors to have been subscribers for two or three years previously.

"It seems to me", wrote Selby-Bigge to Morant, "that this practically removes the risk of the purchase of votes, e.g. by Dissenters merely to cause trouble. A man who will subscribe so persistently to a school to gratify spite or contentiousness would probably find a way onto any body of managers however constituted, and would almost certainly get himself appointed as a Local Authority's representative. The spiteful man has now no need to subscribe."[121]

THE WORKING OF THE ACT

The prickly relationship between managers of non-provided schools and the new local authorities in the early period of the operation of the Act was not unexpected. Local education authorities sometimes misconstrued the extent of their jurisdiction over the Church schools. Under Section 7(1) of the Act they were empowered to "maintain and keep efficient all public elementary schools within their areas"; in the case of "non-provided" schools, this was on condition that the managers of such schools carried out directions of local education authorities as to secular instruction, the number and quality of teachers to be employed and made the school available for inspection.

At Southampton, some of the managers at St. Mark's National School, "in response to a brief and ambiguous invitation", had attended a meeting of the school management sub-committee of the local authority on 18 September, 1903 on the question of school fees, "where according to the Managers they were treated with a lack of courtesy". This was followed by a peremptory letter from the secretary of the committee stating that as the local education authority had decided to abolish school fees in "non-provided" schools, all fees received since 1 June were to be paid to the borough treasurer, their division to be arranged later. Matters worsened when the chairman of the local authority had requested to be supplied with copies of all meetings of the managers, in itself a difficult request to comply with because of the nature of transacting business. The managers decided to consider this request "in connection with the wider subject of the relation of the Managers to the Authority". The chairman of managers, the Rev. E. N. Franklin, after a long discussion of the committee was understood to be of the opinion that Section 7(1)(*a*) "The Managers of the School shall carry out any directions of the Local Education Authority" did not give the authority to pass over the managers and to deal with the teachers and caretaker direct. It was resolved to convene a further meeting of the Southampton voluntary schools in order to consider a scheme embodying the duties of managers under the Education Acts, which was to form the basis of an understanding between the Southampton managers and the Southampton Education Committee.[122]

Where liaison with a local education authority was attempted by a diocesan authority, the active hostility of voluntary school managers became apparent. At a conference of clergy and church-wardens of the Durham Archdeaconry held on 6 November, 1903, a letter was read from the Chairman of Durham County Council in which he expressed his desire "to seek some happy middle path which, while wounding the consciences of none, will secure the education progress all desire".[123] The Bishop urged that "we should attempt to come to some arrangement with the County Council, as the Education Authority for the County Area" and to elect at the Conference a committee to confer with the County Council.

Briefly stated, the proposals for a concordat with the County Council were as follows:

> Church Schools should be leased for 3 to 5 years to the Authority at nominal rent with power on each side to revert to existing arrangements at the end of period.
>
> The Church Schools, being, during the term, rate-provided schools, the County Council would appoint four, and the minor local authorities, two Managers; but because of special owners of school buildings, two of County Council Managers should be appointed by owners or trustees of buildings and a third member should be a paid official of County Council, so that half of Managers would be directly interested in giving effect to the arrangement in spirit and in letter.
>
> That the County Council should appoint the teachers on the recommendation of Managers.
>
> That a syllabus of Religious Instruction should be agreed upon and used as part of the curriculum in all rate-provided schools on five days of the week and leased schools four days.
>
> That on one day per week, in rate-provided schools, clergy and ministers of all denominations should be free to instruct their own children in distinct tenets. A similar rule should apply to leased schools on two days a week, with an honorarium for teachers willing to teach religious instruction to be provided by Managers.

That on Sunday, the leased buildings should be at the command of the Church for religious purposes.

That the Education Authority should keep leased buildings in an up-to-date condition; provided that, if structural extensions and additions are needed, these shall be settled in consultation with the Trustees, who, if the lease be terminated, shall repay in a manner to be agreed upon, the then ascertained value.[124]

Although such arrangements were possible under Section 5 of the Act, a number of problematical points arose where agreements had been arrived at. The attitude of the National Society was clearly discernible in a circular distributed to managers on this topic, headed *"Latet Anguis in Herba"* (Snake in the grass), in August, 1903. The earlier Chester Concordat had proved unsatisfactory and another recent one with the Montgomeryshire County Council, which was very similar to the proposed Durham scheme, was "dangerous" on a number of grounds. For example, no provision was made for the filling up of vacancies for teaching staff "who are something more than merely nominal Churchmen and Churchwomen". So-called "Church teaching" by the teacher could be of a different flavour from what was intended, and furthermore it was no longer an integral part of the duty of a teacher if payment were separately offered.

On the use of "provided schools" on one day a week for denominational teaching: "Do our friends realise that the Cowper-Temple Clause does not allow any religious catechism or religious formulary of any particular denomination being taught?" As to the bait of local authority being responsible for repairs during the period of the experiment, with alterations and enlargements of building being subject to conditions of reimbursement, the circular questioned:

"Will it be possible three years hence to get the money to take our buildings out of pawn? If not, the schools will remain in the possession of the local education authority without any agreement."[125]

Further, a legal representative of the Board of Education distinctly pointed out to the Conference that "while a lease would be binding on Church Managers no agreement of this kind on the part of the present County Council could bind their successors."[126]

The complexity of the problem arose principally from the wording of the Act: in some instances, the intended effect of one section was cancelled out in another. A last minute plea before the meeting by a Church supporter of the Concordat demonstrated the difficulty. He argued that by Section 18(2) of the Act, all grants were made payable to the county council and power was reserved whereby the Education Department could refuse to pay any portion of the grants. Thus the

T

Department had lost control over the county councils unless Section 16 was invoked, whereby a writ of *mandamus* could have been issued:

> "a cumbersome costly and futile procedure, which they cannot, without great difficulty enforce without a popularly elected body, and certainly will not enforce for the sake of protecting the aggrieved Managers of a Church School."[127]

A recent event had confirmed the supremacy of the county council. At Todmorden, Yorkshire, the Council appointed a headmaster of a Church school, a man recommended by two Nonconformists; the Education Department refused to remonstrate with the County Council over this. The moral seemed, therefore, that managers in Durham should make the best bargain possible with the Council.

A more immediate threat was the absence in the Act of any provision which enabled managers to let or sell school buildings. If a hostile local education authority invoked Section 7(1)(*d*), whereby the local education authority could demand "such alterations and improvements in the buildings as may be reasonably required", many of the Church schools, which were in old buildings, would be in jeopardy.

> "If Trustees or Managers find themselves unable to do the repairs and refuse to do them, then the local education authority can do them and the school becomes a provided school and ceases to be a Church school. Even if the necessary repairs are carried out in the first instance and that danger is avoided there is the probability that in many cases, when Managers realise by practical experience that they are reduced to mere ciphers, possessing no control over the teachers and unable to order a single article for the school, they will not undertake the labour of raising funds for ordinary repairs and extensions, and will allow their schools to become provided schools."[128]

It followed that if managers could reach an agreement with the council before this stage, every effort should be made to do so.

The Nonconformist agitation which Chamberlain and others had feared continued, in the years following the Act, to remind the voluntary school manager of his tenuous position. It was no surprise when the 1906 Liberal Government was returned, that an Education Bill was introduced into the Commons by Augustine Birrell, which would have provided, if it had been translated into law, that from 1 January, 1908, no schools would be recognized as public elementary schools except those provided by the local education authority; this would have been effected either by compulsory transfer in certain circumstances or by agreement with the managers. Teachers were to be appointed only by local education authorities; and undenominational teaching could be given in all schools by existing staff, with some concessions to denominational teaching if this was a condition of transfer.[129] The effects of such an Act would have been to withdraw all powers from the voluntary school managers' hands. Devonshire proved to be a rallying point for moderate Churchmen in the Conservative Party. Shortly after the Bill was introduced into the House, Goschen remarked to Devonshire: "My first impression is that it is an intolerable Bill. . . . Like you I think the procedure as to Trust Deeds most arbitrary and tyrannical."[130] Hicks Beach, now Lord St. Aldwyn, wrote sourly: "I didn't like the Act of 1902 as I was afraid it would bring this Bill upon us."[131] Many Churchmen believed the situation called for a salvage operation rather than a large scale offensive: the Bishop of Ripon commented that it was better "frankly to accept popular control as a natural sequence of State and rate support".[132] Even the indomitable Hugh Cecil considered the situation hopeless.[133] Devonshire had formed a small and powerful committee to suggest amendments to the Lords, which ultimately proved successful in defeating the Bill in December, 1906 although it had passed through the Commons.[134] Further efforts two years later made no more progress.

The voluntary managers now had to work more closely with local education authorities and were more inexorably drawn into the national network than at any time previously. The main change lay in the nature of the representation on managing committees with their links between local government and Church authorities. But much had been saved from the previous regime: the voluntary managers still controlled religious teaching, subject to the Conscience Clause, as well as retaining responsibility for the appointment of teachers.[135] They were also left with the power, subject to the repayment of building grants and subject also to the Charitable Trust laws, to close their schools at any time, and could thus cause a serious deficiency of school accommodation.[136]

For many of the elected personnel who had given service under the school board system, there were mixed feelings. This can be most clearly seen in the case of London. A contemporary wrote: "In common with the rest of the municipal bodies of the country, the London County Council found itself (after 1902) called upon to undertake a new and formidable task which it had neither desired nor asked for." The new Council was responsible for all types of education and its methods of administration were in some respects radically different from the old, resulting in some diminution in the powers of individual school board members.

"The Divisional Members were *de facto* the chief administrative officers within their area; the Council appointed an Education Officer as their chief administrative official and in practice, though the principle was never laid down by Standing Order, the Education Sub-Committees did not proceed to discuss an important subject without the Chief Officer's report."[137]

An added irritation was that unlike school board meetings, the Council's Education Committee met at first in private, as with its other committees; as has been mentioned earlier, women were not eligible for election. A long-drawn-out battle had been fought between the Moderate majority on the Board from 1895 with the Government, to allow London to have its own water supply. Sir William Collins, one of the members, wryly remarked after the 1902 Act had been passed, "We asked for water and they gave us education."[138]

Despite such difficulties, administrative continuity in the transition from school boards to local education authorities was secured to a larger extent than might have been anticipated.[139] J. G. Legge has stated that by 1902 many of the most vigorous and experienced members of school boards were already members of town and county councils constituting the new local education authorities and were in readiness to form the basis of a new administration.[140]

The Act itself bore the hallmarks of compromise and expediency in many ways; furthermore it did not finalize the relationships between the Board of Education, the local authority and voluntary managers. The main achievement of the 1902 Act was, however, the establishment of a viable system of management for elementary education which remained virtually unchanged for almost half a century.

REFERENCES

1   Sir John Eldon Gorst (1835–1916). Entered Parliament in 1866; as party manager he laid the foundations for the Conservative victory of 1874. Became a member of the notorious Fourth Party in 1880. Solicitor-General 1885, Under-Secretary at the India Office 1890. Vice-President of the Committee of Council on Education 1895–1902. Gorst's undoubted ability in the political field was discounted because he had an unfortunate manner in his dealings with both colleages and opponents alike: his flippancy, outspokenness and sarcasm made him many enemies. "What a mountebank Gorst is", commented A. H. D. Acland to Asquith during the early stages of the 1902 Bill, "I wish you would chastise him." 15 July, 1901, Asquith MSS., f. 10. Salisbury himself had written a brutally frank letter to Gorst on the defects in his character some two years previously: "Speaking generally I should say that the cause of much of the hostility you have evoked, is that when you are defending the policy of the Government you give both friends and foes the impression that you are attacking it. Your manner of fencing seems to invoke a, not infrequent, back-hander aimed at those who are standing by your side, or behind you. You are

evidently unconscious of this peculiarity in your manner—but the impression that it exists prevails largely." 27 September, 1899, Salisbury MSS.

2 E. Eaglesham, "Planning the Education Bill of 1902", in *British Journal of Educational Studies*, Vol. IX, No. 1, November 1960, pp. 4–5.
The first draft of the Bill was dated 18 August, 1901 and Gorst remained in control of the Bill's planning until about the end of October.

3 Balfour to Devonshire, 25 August, 1901, Balfour MSS., B.M. Add. MS. 49769, f. 191. Chamberlain shared this view. He wrote to Salisbury at this time: "I wish the Duke could be persuaded to do more and Gorst did less." 23 August, 1901, Balfour MSS., B.M. Add MS. 49691, f. 146. Salisbury passed Chamberlain's letter on to Balfour without comment.

4 Sir A. Fitzroy, *Memoirs* (1925), p. 28.

5 B. M. Allen, *Sir Robert Morant, A Great Public Servant* (1934), p. 153. Sir Robert Laurie Morant (1863–1920). Assistant Director Special Enquiries and Reports, 1895. Private Secretary to Gorst, November 1899–June 1900. Senior Examiner, August 1900–November 1902. Acting Secretary, November 1902–March 1903. Secretary, April 1903–December 1911.

6 *Ibid.*, p. 155.

7 Balfour to Morant, September 1901. Ed. 24/14.

8 Memorandum on the Preservation of Voluntary Schools, September 1901, *ibid.* Cecil was described by a contemporary as "an intellectual and fanatical Churchman". H. W. Lucy, *Memories of Eight Parliaments* (1908), pp. 231–3.

9 Memorandum on the Preservation of Voluntary Schools, 1901. Ed. 24/14.

10 Morant to Balfour, 30 October, 1901, Balfour MSS., B.M. Add. MS. 49787, f. 29.

11 *Ibid*, 14 September, 1901, f. 20.

12 "Ilbert still drafts the things in a highly hostile spirit", Morant complained to Balfour on 1 November, 1901. "He admitted this morning that they (the Bills) could not possibly work as drafted", *ibid.*, f. 33.

13 *Ibid.*, 2 November, 1901, f. 35.

14 J. Powell Williams to Devonshire, 1 November, 1901, Ed. 24/16.

15 Memorandum to R. L. M. from A. J. B., November, 1901. Ed. 24/14.

16 Printed for the use of the Cabinet, 2 November, 1901. Devonshire. Cab. 37/59/111 (P.R.O.).

17 Devonshire to Temple, 19 November, 1901. Temple MSS. Official letters, Vol. 49, f. 415 (Lambeth Palace Library).

18 Devonshire to Salisbury, 2 December, 1901, Salisbury MSS.

19 Morant in a letter to Balfour on 7 December had pointed out that the majority of the Cabinet, who favoured State-aid rather than rate-aid, were confused in their thinking. The arguments used by Morant were largely accepted by Balfour. Blanche E. Dugdale, *Arthur James Balfour* (1936), p. 322.

20 Sir Michael Hicks Beach, 9th Bt., 1st Earl of St. Aldwyn (1837–1916). Chief Secretary for Ireland 1874–8 with a seat in the Cabinet from 1876; 1878–80 Colonial Secretary; 1885–6 Chancellor of the Exchequer; 1886–7 Chief Irish Secretary; 1888–92 President of the Board of Trade; 1895–1902 Chancellor of the Exchequer. Resigned in July, 1902. Created Earl in 1906.

21 20 July, 1895, Hicks Beach MSS., D 2455. PCC/86 (Gloucestershire C.R.O.).
In fact, Chamberlain and Hicks Beach were enemies of long standing. As Chancellor of the Exchequer in the last Salisbury Administration, Beach's interference in South African affairs had further exacerbated their differences. This was reflected in Cabinet opinion during the period of the

discussion on the Education Bill. It has been stated by Beach's biographer that in 1901 "many a tussle took place in the Cabinet between forces of unequal numbers. The majority of Ministers were ready enough to follow Mr. Chamberlain's lead in urging developments and experiments whether in domestic or imperial affairs. In the long run, only Lord Salisbury stood by his Chancellor of the Exchequer." Lady Victoria Hicks Beach, *Life of Sir Michael Hicks Beach* (1932), p. 159.

22 Although Michael Hurst has shown that from 1895 onwards Devonshire had become progressively more estranged from Chamberlain and more "tired of and disgusted with politics." M. Hurst, "The Liberal Unionist Alliance: Chamberlain, Hartington, and the Conservatives, 1886–1904", in *English Historical Review*, Vol. LXXVII, No. 302, 1962, p. 68.

23 Devonshire to Chamberlain, 3 December, 1901. Chamberlain MSS. JC 11/11/5.

24 Devonshire to Balfour, 6 December, 1901. Balfour MSS., B.M. Add. MS. 49769, f. 203.

25 Devonshire to Salisbury, 9 December, 1901. Salisbury MSS.
Salisbury's own pessimism at this point is caught in a letter to Edward Talbot, Bishop of Rochester, written on 7 December. "I am very much obliged to you for the kind tone of your letter. I wish I could reciprocate with assurances that would satisfy you, but I am not sanguine.
"When people talk of 'the strongest Government of modern times' they forget that we are a *Coalition Government*: that at least four, possibly more, of our most important members are still Liberals on all internal questions. . . . When we come to deal with questions which were burning issues 20 or 30 years ago, we never can have any security that the congenital internal divisions of the Cabinet will not declare themselves." G. Stephenson, *Edward Stuart Talbot* (1936), p. 143.

26 R. Blake, *The Unknown Prime Minister. The Life and Times of Andrew Bonar Law 1858–1923* (1955), pp. 41–2.

27 Notes on Conversation between Mr. Chamberlain and Mr. Morant on the Education Bill, 12 December, 1901. R.L.M. Ed. 24/17.

28 Instructions for the preparation of a Draft Bill on Education. Printed for the use of the Cabinet, 12 December, 1901, signed 12 December, 1901. Devonshire. Cab. 37/59/131.

29 Memorandum by the Cabinet Committee on the Education Bill, 12 December, 1901, written 11 December, 1901. Balfour. Cab. 37/59/130.

30 Chamberlain, during the Christmas recess, went so far as to join hands with Balfour in repelling an attack by Hicks Beach on the principle of local option. See the exchanges of letters between Chamberlain and Balfour, 1 and 3 January, 1902. J. Amery, *Joseph Chamberlain and the Tariff Reform Campaign. The Life of Joseph Chamberlain* Vol. 5 (1969), p. 91.

31 Chamberlain to Devonshire, 14 December, 1901. Devonshire MSS., 2nd Series 340. 2878.

32 Memorandum: The Education Bill, 17 December, 1901, pp. 1–3. Salisbury. Cab. 37/59/135.

33 Draft Clause for Rate Maintenance of Voluntary Schools, n.d. but probably 13 December, 1901. Balfour, Cab., 37/59/136.

34 Alexander Hugh Bruce, 6th Baron Balfour of Burleigh (1849–1921); from 1876, representative peer for Scotland in the House of Lords. A very able administrator. It was a source of irritation to him that he was often confused with A. J. Balfour, who was not related to him. Lady Frances Balfour, *A Memoir of Lord Balfour of Burleigh K.T.* (1925), p. 64, provides

an amusing example of this confusion. Lord Balfour was very tall and heavily built, in contrast to A. J. Balfour; this fact was depicted in a current cartoon of the two men and was headed: "The Slim Balfour and the Burleigh Balfour."

35 Memorandum: Education Bill: The Voluntary Schools, 20 December, 1901. Balfour of Burleigh, Cab. 37/59/138.

36 Balfour of Burleigh to Davidson, 27 November, 1901. Davidson MSS. (Lambeth Palace Library.).

37 The Memorandum is headed, "Mr. Balfour's instructions to me, December 20, 1901 as to lines of Education Bill. R.L.M." Balfour MSS., B.M. Add. MS. 49787, f. 51.

38 Herbert Asquith mentioned to T. D. Acland his own growing apprehension about the single authority. "It has become the shibboleth of three distinct educational parties who have nothing really in common, viz. (1) the Board School extremists (Channing & Co.), (2) the Teachers Trade Unions (Macnamara & Co.), (3) the more astute Denominationalists (Jebb & Co.). I feel pretty sure, as you do, that Devonshire will not be strong enough to confine his Bill to Secondary Education. And I am much afraid that there will be infinite confusion and division among us if, as is possible, he seeks to set up for both primary and secondary education the much demanded 'single authority'." 30 October, 1901. Letters to T. D. Acland MS. Eng. Letters d. 81. (Bodleian Library, Oxford.)

39 "I wrote a horribly long letter to Mr. Balfour yesterday before I received yours of yesterday", stated Morant to Sandars, Balfour's Secretary. "I wanted him to get it before he goes to the Duke at Chatsworth. . . . I have reason to believe that the Duke is so immersed in the Education problem that he won't be able to resist talking to A.J.B. about it." 4 January, 1902, Balfour MSS., B.M. Add. MS. 49787, f. 52.
Morant had calculated correctly in this. Balfour wrote to Salisbury after receiving Morant's letter: "I go to Chatsworth on Monday and Devonshire is sure to talk to me at length upon his educational schemes." 5 January, 1902, Balfour MSS., B.M. Add. MS. 49691, f. 120.

40 3 January, 1902. Ed. 24/18.

41 Morant to Balfour, 3 January, 1902. Ed. 24/18.

42 Memorandum: Rate Aid to Voluntary Schools, 5 February, 1902, Devonshire; written 4 February, 1902, pp. 2–3. Cab. 37/60/31.

43 Devonshire to Hicks Beach, 5 February, 1902, Ed. 24/19.

44 Memorandum. Education Bill: Voluntary Schools, 11 February, 1902. Balfour, pp. 1–2. Cab. 37/60/37.

45 Memorandum. Education Bill: Voluntary Schools, 11 February, 1902. Balfour, p. 2. Cab. 37/60/37.

46 Memorandum on Mr. Balfour's Proposals, February, 1902. Morant. Ed. 24/14.
In another Memorandum written during this month, Morant analysed the financial conditions of voluntary schools in fourteen typical counties, eleven typical county boroughs and London. He found that 56 per cent of the schools in the counties were "under water" in 1900, 63 per cent in county boroughs and 55 per cent in London. Balfour's proposals, therefore, as a long-term solution, were unworkable. Memorandum: Financial Conditions of Voluntary Schools. R. L. Morant, February, 1902. Ed. 24/13A.

47 Thomas Randall Davidson, Baron Davidson of Lambeth (1848–1930). Bishop of Winchester 1895–1903; Archbishop of Canterbury 1903–28. Created Baron 1928.

48 Morant to Davidson, 20 February, 1902. Davidson MSS. Davidson

was to play an important part in the discussions on the Bill, both Morant and Balfour often turning to him for advice. Balfour asked Davidson on occasion to write to him officially on the Church's view of education, to counteract the more unreasonable utterances of other Churchmen. "Of course," wrote Balfour's Secretary to Davidson, "you won't mention that *I* have begged you to write. Your personal acquaintance with Mr. B. is quite enough reason." F. S. Parry to Davidson, 6 December, 1901, Davidson MSS.

Davidson was described by one Nonconformist paper as having "a pleasant manner as well as a sharp tongue: he is terse and pithy and speaks out well: and although not an ornate orator he is a smart debater." *British Weekly*, 11 December, 1902.

49   B. Webb (ed. B. Drake and M. Cole), *Our Partnership* (1948), p. 240.

50   Campbell-Bannerman writing from Baden-Baden on 24 September, 1902 to a political friend remarked on the Bill: "They want the predominance of a sect in schools paid for by the rates. The thing is impracticable: denominational authority and public control won't row in the same boat. No halves or thirds or fiftieths on the managing board will do." J. A. Spender, *Henry Campbell-Bannerman* (1923), p. 76.

The earliest mention of this topic is contained in a lengthy letter from Balfour to Talbot, Bishop of Rochester, on 25 June, 1902. "I find a very widespread impression, that in spite of everything, the real control of schools will rest with the managers. In these circumstances we have also to consider whether any modification is possible or desirable in the scheme of local management laid down by the Bill." The alternatives suggested were "(*a*) stick to the Bill as then drafted; (*b*) provide that of the third of outside managers there should never be less than two; (*c*) as for (*b*) except that they should be two-fifths of the whole management; (*d*) give absolute equality or even the majority to outside elements. Balfour favoured (*b*) or (*c*) solutions. Balfour to Talbot, Balfour MSS. B.M. Add. MS. 49789, f. 165–6.

51   Gorst to Balfour, 11 July, 1902. Balfour MSS., B.M. Add. MS. 49791, f. 32.

52   Morant to Davidson, 1 or 2 July, 1902, Davidson MSS.

53   *Hansard*, Vol. CXI, 4th Series, House of Commons, 21 July, 1902, Col. 838.

54   Chamberlain to Balfour, 4 August, 1902, Balfour MSS., B.M. Add. MS. 49774, f. 7.

55   For full text of this see W. Temple, *Life of Bishop Percival* (1921), pp. 181–4.

56   29 July, 1902. In a further letter to *The Times* on 7 August, 1902, Percival criticized J. G. Talbot, M.P. and a High Churchman, for objecting to the election of parishioners. "In plain English, the complainant means that Mr. Talbot, like Mr. Kruger, desires to treat the parishioners at large as Outlanders—they are to contribute the money for the support of the school, but they are to have no real voice in the administration."

Talbot had also urged Bishop Davidson the previous month not to agree to a concession on the number of managers to be appointed by the "new authorities". "I should not have troubled you, but I heard that the recent Fulham Conference had led some of your Bench to look with favour on a proposal to give the majority to the outsiders on conditions; but no conditions could be satisfied if the outsiders (who in some places are sure to be hostile) had it in their power to manage the school." J. G. Talbot to Davidson, 7 July, 1902, Davidson MSS.

57   Morant noted on his copy of the letter: "In a school of 800 there would be 7 Non-conformists to 1 Church Teacher." Ed. 24/25.

58   Balfour to Chamberlain, 3 September, 1902, Balfour MSS. B.M. Add. MS. 49774, f. 19.

59 Cardinal Vaughan had already informed the Department of the Roman Catholic attitude towards the control of elementary and secondary education during the earlier stages of the Bill. No doubt Balfour now had Vaughan's memorandum: "Resolutions on Education"— in mind. For the text of this, see Ed. 24/14.

60 (1844-1934). Bishop of Rochester, 1895–1905; Southwark, 1905–11; Winchester, 1911–23.

61 (1853–1932). Canon of Westminster, 1894–1902; Bishop of Worcester, 1902–5.
Gore's nomination on 8 November, 1901 by Salisbury to the vacant see of Worcester came as a surprise. He had recently written to *The Times* attacking the British concentration camps in South Africa, and was associated in the public mind with Chamberlain, who had been partly responsible for the war. The opposition to his enthronement by the Church Association and allied societies led to a celebrated lawsuit in the King's Bench in February, 1902, in which Gore was successful. G. L. Prestige, *The Life of Charles Gore, a Great Englishman* (1935), pp. 228–31.

62 Talbot to Davidson, 4 September, 1902, Davidson MSS.

63 Gore to Davidson, 27 September, 1902, Davidson MSS.

64 Chamberlain to Balfour, 31 August, 1902, Chamberlain MSS. JC. 11/5/8.

65 Morant to Sandars, 28 August, 1902, Balfour MSS., B.M. Add. MS. 49787, f. 70.
The 6th Marquess of Londonderry made no great mark at the Board, but his amiable disposition won him many friends. J. W. Mackail, a Senior Examiner at the Department on the occasion of his retirement, wrote to him: "I may say that of the seven Lord Presidents under whom I have served, there was none whom I felt it a greater personal pleasure to serve than yourself." Mackail to Londonderry, 23 December, 1903, Londonderry MSS. (Durham C.R.O.).

66 *The Times*, 6 September, 1902.

67 H. Lee Warner to Morant, 8 September, 1902. Ed. 24/25.

68 Temple to Balfour, n.d. but September, 1902. Temple MSS. Official letters, Vol. 53, ff. 334–5.

69 Balfour to Temple, 1 October, 1902, *ibid.*, f. 336.

70 Voluntary Schools Management under the Education Bill, 24 September, 1902, written 6 September, 1902. Balfour, pp. 1–9. Cab 37/62/130.
For an interesting account of some of the pressure groups operating to secure an amendment to Clause 7, see D. R. Pugh, "The 1902 Act: The Search for a Compromise" in *British Journal of Educational Studies*, Vol. XVI, No. 2, June, 1968, pp. 164–78.

71 Morant to Balfour, 19 September, 1902. Balfour MSS., B.M. Add. MS. 49787, f. 81.

72 Morant to Davidson, 10 September, 1902. Davidson MSS.

73 Devonshire to Chamberlain, 2 October, 1902. Chamberlain MSS. JC 11/11/11.

74 Dorrington to Morant, 4 October, 1902. Balfour MSS., B.M. Add. MS. 49787, f. 87.
Morant realized that Variation 1 of Scheme A would not be acceptable to the Roman Catholics. During his stay with Balfour at Whittingehame shortly afterwards, Morant was able to tell Davidson on 28 September, 1902: "Forgive this scrawl. I gave all my energies to get him to give up the (1) of A, with success. The next one I will tackle him on tonight." Davidson MSS.

75 But he had promised Balfour in an interview on 7 August, 1902 "that

though he saw something to criticize in the Education Bill, he should never think of voting for an amendment which the Government regarded as. fatal", a promise which he kept. Notes on Interview. Balfour MSS., B.M. Add. MS. 49791, f. 36.

76   J. E. Gorst, "The Education Bill" in *The Nineteenth Century*, Vol. CCCVIII, October, 1902, pp. 586–7.

77   *The Times*, 15 October, 1902.

78   *Hansard*, Vol. CXIII, 4th Series, House of Commons, 22 October, 1902, Col. 499.

79   *Hansard*, Vol. CXIV, 4th Series, House of Commons, 19 November, 1902, Cols. 1395–6.

80   H. W. Worsley Taylor to Balfour, 3 May, 1902, Ed. 24/22.

81   Temple to Balfour, late September, 1902. Davidson MSS.

82   H. J. Simmonds to L. A. Selby-Bigge, 12 October, 1902. Ed. 24/242.

83   Rev. E. N. Townshend to Sir R. Finlay, 27 October, 1902, Ed. 24/25.

84   William Slaney Kenyon-Slaney (1847–1908), Colonel of Regiment 1887. Decorated at Tel-el-Kebir and retired from the Army in 1892. M.P. for Newport, Salop, 1886–1908.

85   *Hansard*, Vol. CXI, 4th Series, House of Commons, 21 July, 1902, Col. 841.

86   *The Times*, 15 October, 1902.

87   Billesdon Church of England School, Leicestershire, Ed. 21/10199.

88   Morant to R. J. G. Mayor, 2 June, 1902, *ibid.*,

89   Morant to C. M. Cowie, 3 August, 1902, Ed. 21/10199.

90   *Ibid.*, 8 August, 1902.

91   J. L. Carson to W. N. Bruce, 17 July, 1902, *ibid.*

92   Memorandum: Interview, Lord Churchill and W. N. Bruce, 2 October, 1902. Ed. 24/25.

93   White, 11 October, 1902. Ed. 21/10199.

94   White to E. K. Chambers, 30 October, 1902, *ibid.*

95   F. W. Clowes to Board of Education, 8 November, 1902, Ed. 21/10199.

96   H. F. Pooley to White, 20 November, 1902, *ibid.*

97   Morant to White, 2 December, 1902, Ed. 21/10199.

98   Morant to White, 1 December, 1902, *ibid.*

99   A. Fitzroy, *op. cit.*, pp. 112–13.

100   Memorandum: Education Bill, Kenyon-Slaney Clause relating to denominational education, 6 December, 1902, Balfour, p. 1. Cab. 37/63/163.

101   *Ibid.*

102   *Ibid*, pp. 1–2.

103   Education Bill, 1902, Kenyon-Slaney Clause and etc. Copy of Opinion of Mr. Danckwerts, K.C. 5 December, 1902. Temple MSS., Vol. 53, ff. 370–1.

104   Talbot wrote a long and bitter letter to Balfour at this time expressing his regret that the safeguard of a right of appeal to the Bishop in matters relating to religious instruction had not been enshrined in the final Bill. Balfour MSS., B.M. Add. MS. 49789, ff. 177–81.

105   See, for example, Gore's vehement letter to *The Times*, 5 November, 1902.

106   10 November, 1902. Davidson MSS.

107   21 November, 1902.

108   A Churchman wrote pessimistically to the President of the Board's wife at this time: "I noticed Lord Londonderry's peroration in his speech on the Education Bill, 'the Non-Conformist Lion lying down with the Anglican Lamb'. I hope however the Lion won't eat up the Lamb." G. A. Hutton to Lady Londonderry. 11 December, 1902, Londonderry MSS.

109   Asquith, for the Liberals, protested that "the Act lets loose large sums of money to be scrambled for by clerical managers, without any regulating

principle, and without any effective security, either for local or Parliamentary control." J. P. Alderson, *Mr. Asquith* (1905), p. 228. He did, however, during the final stages of the Bill, tell Davidson that "in my view 'popular control' is in no way inconsistent with the continuance of the non-provided schools of denominational teaching." Asquith to Davidson, 5 December, 1902, Davidson MSS.

110 Chamberlain to Devonshire, 22 September, 1902, Chamberlain MSS. JC 11/11/10.

111 *Ibid.*, 3 October, 1902. JC 11/11/12.

112 Charles Thomson Ritchie, 1st Baron Ritchie of Dundee (1838–1906). Chancellor of the Exchequer August, 1902 in Balfour's Administration: he resigned over the Tariff dispute in September, 1903.

113 Balfour to Devonshire, 4 June, 1903, Balfour MSS., B.M. Add. MS. 49770, f. 17.

114 Board of Education, Memorandum, Foundation Managers, 20 December, 1902, Sec. 17 (a).

115 Board of Education, Annual Report, 1902–3, Cd. 1763, p. 8.

116 St. Silas' National School, Hunslet (Leeds), Managers' Minute Book, 1890–1948, 17 December, 1902. Parish Records, No. 65. (Leeds City Library, Archives Department.)

117 Minute on the Appointment of Final Foundation Managers. Orders under Sec. 11. L. A. S. Selby-Bigge to Morant, 20 January, 1903. Ed. 24/245. File B.

118 Education Act, 1902, Appendix C. Typical Final Order for Church of England Foundation Managers.

119 Selby-Bigge to Morant, 4 February, 1903, Memorandum: "Election by Subscribers as to the Mode of Appointing Foundation Managers." Ed. 24/242.

120 Selby-Bigge to Morant, 4 February, 1903, Memorandum: "Election by Subscribers as to the Mode of Appointing Foundation Managers." Ed. 24/242.

121 *Ibid.*

122 Southampton, St. Mark's National School, Managers' Minute Book, 1894–1947, 22 October, 1902 to 4 December, 1903. PR 21/19/2. (Southampton Civic R.O.).

123 Letter. Bishop of Durham to Clergy and Churchwardens of the Durham Archdeaconry, 16 November, 1903. Correspondence: Diocesan Board. EP/Wi 91 (Durham C.R.O.).

124 Printed Proposals for a Concordat with Durham County Council, 1903. EP/Wi 92 (Durham C.R.O.).

125 *School Guardian*, No. 59, August, 1903.

126 Circular, *The Education Conference*, November, 1903, EP/Wi 91. (Durham C.R.O.).

127 Pamphlet To the Clergy, Wardens, and Managers of Church Schools in the Administrative County of Durham, W. Moore Ede, p. 2. November, 1903, EP/Wi 91 (Durham C.R.O.).

128 Pamphlet To the Clergy, Wardens, and Managers of Church Schools in the Administrative County of Durham. W. Moore Ede, p. 3, November, 1903. EP/Wi 91 (Durham C.R.O.).

129 Full details of the history of the 1906 Education Bill can be found in G. K. A. Bell, *Randall Davidson, Archbishop of Canterbury* Vol. I (1935), Ch. 29, pp. 510–40.

130 Goschen to Devonshire, 20 April, 1906. Devonshire MSS. 2nd Series 340.3214.

131 Lord St. Aldwyn to Devonshire, 6 June, 1906, *ibid.*, 340.3215.
132 Bishop of Ripon to Devonshire, 8 June, 1906, *ibid.*, 340.3220.
133 Lord Hugh Cecil to Devonshire, 8 June, 1906, *ibid.*, 340.3222.
134 Lansdowne to Devonshire, 16 November, 1906, *ibid.*, 340.3245.
135 Few voluntary managers felt as strongly about the change as Sir William Vavasour in the West Riding of Yorkshire, whose family had supported the village school during the previous forty years. The last entry in the school log book reads: "4 July, 1904, 12.30 p.m. Sir Wm. Vavasour is taking formal possession of the school, locking the door and keeping the key on account of not being able to make satisfactory arrangements with the West Riding County Council. We are stranded!" Hazelwood, St. Leonard's R.C. School Log Book, 1863–1904. Vavasour MSS., 1280. (Leeds City Library, Archives Dept.).
136 L. A. Selby-Bigge, *The Board of Education* (1934), p. 227.
137 F. G. Bettany, *op. cit.*, p. 163.
138 Quoted in A. G. Gardiner, *John Benn and the Progressive Movement* (1925), pp. 299–300.
139 In the new London County Council at this time, no fewer than twenty-one of its members had served on the School Board for London. G. A. Christian, *op. cit.*, p. 72.
140 J. G. Legge, *The Rising Tide* (1929), p. 5. This generalization has been borne out in a recent study. E. Midwinter, "The Administration of Public Education in Late Victorian Lancashire", in *Northern History*, Vol. IV, (1969), p. 194.

8

Conclusion

During the century with which this study has been concerned, it is possible to trace the emergence of the school manager from the largely undifferentiated and undefined body of men formerly responsible for the establishment of schools. The allocation of specific tasks, as a result of a growing volume of legislation and instructions from Government agencies, called for a body of individuals to put these into effect.

From simple beginnings, the work became increasingly sophisticated and time-consuming, especially after the introduction of the school board system. A hierarchy of managerial rank resulted from the various sizes of the administrative unit with which managers were concerned. Taking London as an instance, this ranged from the chairmanship of the School Board for London to the school board members, who would also be members for their division, local managers under the Board, and the voluntary school managers. In the intermediate range were those exercising quasi-managerial functions; and the activities of such influential bodies as the local visitors' sub-committee under the Bristol School Board and the ladies' committee at Exeter, as well as annual and assistant managers have been noted earlier. Much ingenuity was shown in devising new categories to fulfil specific tasks, which differed from area to area.

This study has examined examples of the relationships which existed between institutions such as school boards, town councils and ratepayers; and individuals such as the clergyman, landowner and subscriber. Although these have occasionally illustrated the effect of local influences, such as the rise of the plaiting industry in and around Bedfordshire, nevertheless it would be difficult to draw more than tentative conclusions in accounting for the variations in the pattern of management over the country.

Constraints on the activities of managers and their reactions to them, particularly by Government Departments or their agents, produced some interesting developments. For example, administrative decisions taken by the Education Department often drew a response from managing bodies, which led to discussions on matters of principle by administrators on the interpretation of managers' functions. Similarly, the constant redefinition of Her Majesty's Inspector's role in relation to the managers, which ranged from close co-operation under the Revised Code to an almost complete separation after the introduction of "surprise visits" in the 1890s, resulted in a corresponding adjustment in the managers' activities.

Again, the school board clerk's functions overlapped considerably with those of the managers under the board to the extent that, as has been seen, the Department were obliged to establish a precedent excluding the clerk from acting officially as a manager.

Perhaps one of the main difficulties facing managers in the nineteenth century was the lack of definition of their functions. With the voluntary school manager, tenure of office varied according to the custom of the place, and election could be by subscribers, ratepayers or trustees: more often than not, those who were willing to undertake the work were gladly accepted. As the school board was an *ad hoc* authority, the members often had only tenuous links with the town council. The position was not made easier where, for example, it was necessary to serve a precept on the council for the education rate. The nature of the work of the manager under a board depended on the particular organization for management of the schools which the individual board adopted. A manager could be a board member, local manager, or an elected manager for a school or group of schools.

Matters were not helped by the lack of any strong lead by the Education Department, which for the most part retained a neutral position in interpreting the manager's role. Professor Eaglesham, in discussing the administrative position of the Education Department in 1886 has stated:

"We see an Education Department holding tenaciously on to the system of standards as the heart of elementary education; worried by the conflict between the interests of School Boards and Voluntary schools; conscious that School Boards were in some cases unjust in using their powers of the grant regulations but reluctant to accept any additional responsibility for the Department."[1]

Some of the Inspectors of the Department pointed out this lack of support in their annual reports. H.M. Inspector H. R. Rice-Wiggin, wrote in 1876:

"Assuming a body of 'managers' to have been accepted by the Education Department, it is quite possible to ensure their having a knowledge of their duties, *by informing them what those duties are*. This is a point on which incredible ignorance prevails; and I believe that an immense step would be gained by the publication, either as part of the Code, or in some other form, of a plain detailed statement of the duties which managers are *expected* to perform. This would not only enlighten them, but would strengthen their hands in the discharge of their office. At present many 'managers' *dare* not face their teachers' dislike of 'interference'."²

Even where the duties were fairly clearly defined, however, a further difficulty in carrying them out often arose from those managers working under a school board. Clashes of political and religious philosophies in the proceedings of boards, as has been seen, were common. One member of the School Board for London from 1885, the Rev. Arthur W. Jephson, raised the question of motives for becoming a manager:

"Is it right to get elected a member of a public body, and when elected to work in the interests of some other outside interest? No one surely has any right to accept a position on a public body unless prepared to work for what he considers the object of that body. There are reasonable differences as to means and methods, but no one should join a Board with an intention of opposing or wrecking its main object."³

One interesting feature of the system of elementary school management was that although it relied very heavily upon middle-class support for its continuation, only a minority of managers had any personal experience of attendance at such schools or sent their own children to them. The consequences of a lack of knowledge and experience of the schools were pointed out in a manual for managers published in 1878:

"There is no training school or training for Managers. Many indeed, have by great pains and application overcome this difficulty, . . . but some do not see their deficiency, or trust to the light of Nature to make up for it, without any special effort on their own part; and much mischief is the result."⁴

For many middle-class people, the State-supported schools represented a threat to the security of the as yet largely unreformed grammar and endowed schools, to which they looked for the education of their own family. In addition, the rate levied for board schools was unpopular, the curriculum taught being often regarded as unnecessarily enlightened and expensive to provide. Both these views were widely expressed in pamphlets and books of the period. One, entitled *John Bull and His Schools. A Book for Parents, Ratepayers and Men of Business*, asked whether the benefits of free education had made board school pupils better workmen and better citizens than they might have been otherwise. W. R. Lawson, the author, had no doubts as to the answer.

"The Board School boy," he wrote, "has seldom much real vitality about him. As soon as he comes into contact with the working world he

QUO FAS DUCIT PROSPICE.

AN

ASSOCIATION

OF THE

MANAGERS AND GOVERNORS

OF

SCHOOLS

FOR THE

WORKING CLASSES

IN THE

UNITED KINGDOM.

EYRE & SPOTTISWOODE,
GOVERNMENT, LEGAL, AND GENERAL PUBLISHERS.
LONDON : EAST HARDING STREET, E.C.

Price, Half-a-Crown.
N.B.—*Half price to Managers and Governors of Schools.*

Urgent.

Ightham Knoll,
Sevenoaks, Kent,
19th January 1899.

SIR,

1. A FEW months ago a letter was circulated in the County of Kent, suggesting a combination of the Managers and Governors of Schools engaged in the education of that class of the community which is usually entitled the working class, and although it was only natural that proposals very wide in their nature should be received with a very necessary amount of caution, it has been gratifying to find that so many School Managers of weight and influence (both laymen and ministers of religion) in that county are in concurrence on the general principles which underlaid the measures which had been advocated; and that, subject to such amendments as might be ultimately deemed advisable, they were desirous of accelerating the formation of such an Association at the earliest possible date. *Origin of Association.*

2. This encouragement to persevere in an undertaking, not free from difficulty or anxiety, proceeds from the Managers or Governors of every description of school in that county, viz. :— *Every variety of Manager.*

> National,
> Church of England,
> British,
> Roman Catholic,
> Wesleyan,
> Endowed,
> Board, and
> Grammar.

3. From these I am at liberty to say that several of the National and Church of England Schools are represented by Rural Deans; the British Schools include that represented by the Secretary of the British and Foreign Aid Society; the Board Schools comprise, amongst others, that of the considerable town of Dartford (represented in Parliament of one by the most eminent authorities on education in this country); the Wesleyan Schools comprise that at the important town of Tonbridge, and the Roman Catholic Schools that at St. Mary Cray, under that highly respected priest, Father Edward Carroll. *Representatives.*

4. The Chairman of the adjoining county of Surrey, Mr. E. J. Halsey, has also written a letter warmly supporting the movement (*see* Appendix 1, page 19). *County of Surrey.*

A 2

14. An early attempt to form a National Association of Managers and Governors in January, 1899

Durham County Record Office

U

looks tired and limp. . . . What it has evidently done is to give him a strong dislike for manual labour. He keeps away from that if he can, and when in default of more congenial occupation he has to take it, he puts much less heart into it than their uneducated fathers did. What can the Board schools have done to him thus to reverse, as it were, his hereditary instincts?. . . Nine tenths of the boys who passed through Board Schools were necessarily destined for it in one form or another. But it was apparently not a congenial thought for Managers and teachers. They kept their thumb on it. Manual labour was tabooed in text books and among teaching subjects. It would not have been a welcome topic at Board meetings."[5]

Only drastic measures would restore the position of the middle-classes. Another writer stated the solution in a blunt manner:

"No scheme of education will be accepted as satisfactory by the middle class which does not provide for the entire separation of their children from those of a lower grade, a separation as complete as that which exists between them and the children of the upper classes. . . . One of two things only can relieve the pressure felt by the middle class: either the curriculum of the secondary schools must be raised, or that the Board and Voluntary Schools be reduced to a more elementary standard."[6]

In such a climate of opinion, the "manager" did not have the status of a person carrying out similar work but connected with a superior institution, such as an old grammar school, where the term "governor" had long been employed. The Oxford English Dictionary's definitions of the two terms bring out this difference. A "manager" is "a person responsible for the *general working* of a public institution (chiefly of an Elementary school, especially since the 1870 Act)": a "governor" is "one who *bears rule* in an educational institution" and the term dates back to at least 1607.[7] This distinction was consciously felt at the time. In 1899, a document written by school managers set out the reasons why managers ought to be styled "governors". Among them are the following:

"Those who manage education should have a superior title to those persons who manage railways, works and ordinary business operations. The title 'Manager' though used in the Minutes of the Education Department, cannot be considered a compulsory or everlasting title and a notification from a school that it had changed the title of the members of the Governing Body from Manager to Governor would no doubt be accepted. . . . No Manager of an elementary school would be likely to decline the acceptance of a higher title."[8]

Despite the difficulties noted above, it is a remarkable fact that throughout the century there was always available a body of people willing to take on this onerous and often unrewarding work. Motives included the philanthropic, religious and political; more often than not it stemmed simply from a sense of public duty. William Allen, a friend of Lancaster, who had been made a Fellow of the Royal Society in 1807 for a paper on carbonic acid, took up the Secretaryship of the British and Foreign Society School Committee and spent much time and labour in preparing a set of books and all the accounts. He wrote to Joseph Forster, a fellow Committee member:

> "I have been labouring as hard as ever I did in my own concerns in unravelling matters, and I have the satisfaction to inform thee that our waste book, journal and ledger are all posted up, as far as the materials permitted. I have raised between fifty and sixty heads in the ledger, which I believe will include all our present subjects."

For many years he recorded all the minutes of the Committee with his own hand and he told a friend: "This engagement has taken great hold of me for I have distinctly seen the importance of its bearings."[9]

Lyulph Stanley, later Lord Sheffield, a member and later Vice-Chairman of the School Board for London from 1876 to 1904, with only one short break, was a typical example of this selflessness. It was said of him by Graham Wallas,

> "Here was a great aristocrat, with many other calls on his time who had been a Fellow of Balliol, who yet toiled daily like a young commercial traveller with his reputation to make. He would come to the office at ten in the morning after having read masses of official papers and visited a couple of outlying schools, would sit continually on Committee after Committee, driving the business all the time, would go without his lunch and hastily swallow a cup of tea, and would still, even though he were in poor health, be toiling at seven or eight in the evening. Someone of less enduring nerves once asked him whether he never felt the work stale and monotonous. He answered that he sometimes did so and that then he used to go down to a school, walk through the classrooms and watch the possibilities of good and evil in the faces of the children until the passion for work came back to him."[10]

For two years until his health gave way in 1872, T. H. Huxley was also a member of the School Board for London. Besides undertaking his scientific work, Huxley was involved in membership of two Royal Commissions, became President of the Geological Society, the Ethnological Society and the British Association, was Governor of Owens College in Manchester, and filled the onerous post of Secretary to the Royal Society. On joining the School Board, he soon became involved with the selection of books and apparatus for schools and was a member of the works and general purposes committee, of the statistics committee, the school management committee and the divisional committee for Marylebone.[11] Arthur Hobhouse,[12] his close friend and a successful Chancery lawyer, wrote later of Huxley's "proud independence of spirit", that he was "intolerant of patronage, careless of titular honours, and indifferent to the accumulation of worldly wealth".[13]

Hobhouse had been concerned by Huxley's unpaid labours on behalf of the Board. He wrote to Huxley on 25 July, 1871,

> "A late conversation with you tended to confirm a notion which has crossed my mind repeatedly ever since you first agreed to work on the schoolboard: viz. that you must be incurring much personal sacrifice for the public good. An idea has occurred to me without its correlative question: whether it would be possible for me to bear a share.
>
> "If your only appreciable loss consists in the inroads made on your scientific pursuits there is no more to be said: I cannot help in that. But you have children and must earn money; and I can imagine that for that object you may have to do exhausting work not much tending to the advancement of science."[14]

Hobhouse concluded his letter by generously offering him £400 per annum, for the four-year term of office which it was possible to serve. Typically, Huxley refused to accept any financial help.

These examples of devotion to the furtherance of a more efficient system of management are extreme ones. For the most part, committees had to rely on men and women whose interest in the work waxed and waned; as a result the membership of many managing bodies was often transient with a nucleus of enthusiasts who ensured their day-to-day working. In spite of this, it can be clearly seen that boards and committees of managers were able to respond to the changing situations which confronted them, especially during the second half of the century, by devising new forms of organization.

From the time of the Management Clauses of 1847, which required that lay subscribers should have a share in the management of schools as a condition of the schools receiving building grants, committees absorbed the new element without any apparent strain. The twenty years between 1850 and 1870 saw a growing demand for local elected committees to supervise schools with the help of a rate. After 1870 the complex pattern allowed by the Act to school boards in their organization of management led to a wide variety of forms being adopted, many of great ingenuity. Perhaps it is in the voluntary field, though, that the flexibility of organization can be most readily seen. With the advent of the school boards, competition was experienced for the first time by Church managers. Co-operation with board managers was half-hearted; attempts at grouping schools and managers, as at, for instance, Manchester and York, led to wider experiments after the 1891 Elementary Education Act had officially recognized the grouping of schools, and many Church Day School Associations were formed. Little radical restructuring of the existing pattern was necessary with the Voluntary Schools Associations from 1897, but fundamental questions were raised here of the composition of governing bodies of the Associations. Unlike any of the then prevailing patterns of management, the 1897 Act afforded a unique opportunity for teachers and managers to work together on the governing bodies, a practice which even today is not universally recognized and which the 1902 Act did not further.

Managers became dissatisfied with their diminishing powers, as centralization of education policy increased. Also the lack of consensus among themselves arose because of the division between board and other managers. This resulted in the promotion of at least one scheme at the end of the century to unify managers and governors of all elementary schools and so form a powerful pressure group. In 1899, an *Association of the Managers and Governors of Schools for the Working Classes in the United Kingdom* was mooted by a Kent County Councillor, C. E. Luard. The manifesto issued stated,

> "Those individuals who are appointed either by popular election or selection to voluntarily manage the schools in this country have no cohesion one with another, except in those cases where for specific purposes associations exist . . . the National Society, the Diocesan Education Society, the School Board Association, etc. But Managers and Governors of schools do not at present possess an association which would enable them as a body to exercise the influence which seems to be imperatively necessary for the interests of this country."[15]

The plan was to elect district committees based on the administrative counties and county boroughs, with one representative from each, to form an executive committee of the Council of 206 members. It was envisaged that managers would be paid for their services.

> "This Committee", it was hoped, "would consequently be composed of the most hardworking and most capable school managers or governors in the United Kingdom, thoroughly representative in matters relating to the education of the working classes. These are the men who would be brought to the front and a certain proportion of them would run a fair and even chance of obtaining for the noble work on which they have for years been engaged, some substantial recognition of their labours."[16]

Finally, the Association expressed the desire

> "that it should simply form a very influential channel of communication between Managers or Governors and the Education Department or Board of Education and it may possibly come to pass that its Executive Committee might be deemed a very appropriate body for any Govern-

ment to consult, feeling that no surer pulse could be felt in any matter connected with the education of the working classes."[17]

There is no evidence that the Association captured the imagination of managers and governors; but it must be realized that this manifestation of interest in the re-shaping of the machinery of management was only one in a long series of experiments which had started half a century earlier. The ideal balance of interests in representation on managing bodies; the qualifications for membership: the tasks which should be entrusted to them: the optimum administrative grouping of these bodies: the means by which the local community could be actively involved and interested in such work at a time when central direction of local affairs was growing: these were questions constantly raised, and many have still to be satisfactorily answered.[18]

Writing shortly after the passing of the Balfour Education Act of 1902, J. E. G. de Montmorency, the educational historian and himself school manager, made out a strong case for the continuing need for the school manager as an integral part of the machinery of educational administration:

"It is true that the Managers of Elementary schools have little direct power but, in fact, the power by way of influence is very great. This vast class of unknown men and women who give freely of their time to local administration would become purely mechanical and bureaucratic, and the human, as opposed to the official, element would have hardly any place in our educational administrative system. The Managers very often know not only the teachers and the children, but also the parents, and convey to the minds of all directly concerned in the working of the educational machine, the knowledge that somebody is really interested in them and in the results produced. If School Managers can carry into the actual school buildings both sympathy and high educational ideas and ideals, there is a work done for education that no legislation could accomplish."[19]

REFERENCES

1　E. Eaglesham, *From School Board to Local Authority* (1956), p. 27.
2　Report for 1876, BPP. 1887, XXIX, p. 544.
3　A. W. Jephson, *My Work in London* (1910), p. 124.
4　J. G. Wenham, *The School Manager. His Office and Duties in Regard to Elementary Denominational Schools* (1878), pp. 7–8.
5　W. R. Lawson, *John Bull and His Schools. A Book for Parents, Ratepayers, and Men of Business* (1908), pp. 19–20. The remarks of a diocesan inspector of schools on the same subject supplement this view: "The bigger an educational system is, the more antagonistic is it liable to become to individuality. . . . The prospects of the results of heredity after many generations, say of the average board school child, would, probably eventuate in the production of an individual of the most ordinary type—prim, smug and

uninteresting." Rev. B. Reynolds, *National Education—Essay Towards a Constructive Policy* (1901), p. 46.

6 R. F. Hinder, *The Schoolmaster in the Gutter* (1883), pp. 26–7. Queen Victoria wrote to Gladstone in 1880: "The Queen wishes to observe that she had *long* been of the opinion that the elementary Education was of too high a standard—and useless in consequence, and thus a modification was desirable." P. Guedalla, *The Queen and Mr. Gladstone* Vol. 2 (1933), p. 105.

7 1923 edition.

8 *An Association of the Managers and Governors of Schools for the Working Classes in the United Kingdom* (1899), Appendix 3. Reasons for Adoption of the Title of "Association of School Governors", p. 21. EP/Wi 91 (Durham C.R.O.).

9 W. Allen, *Life of William Allen with Selections from his Correspondence* Vol. 1 (1846), p. 97. See also J. Sherman, *Memoir of William Allen F.R.S.* (1851), p. 109.

10 G. Wallas, "Lord Sheffield on the London School Board", in *Men and Ideas*, (1940), p. 83.

11 C. Bibby, *op. cit.*, p. 161.

12 Arthur Hobhouse, 1st Baron Hobhouse of Hadspen (1819–1904), 1845 called to the Bar; 1862 Q.C.; 1866 Charity Commissioner; 1869–72 Endowed School Commissioner; 1877–99 vestryman of St. George's, Hanover Square; 1882–4 Member of School Board for London.

13 L. Huxley, *The Life and Letters of T. H. Huxley* Vol. 2 (1900), p. 407.

14 Hobhouse to Huxley, 25 July, 1871. Huxley MSS. Vol. 18, f. 188–9. (Imperial College of Science and Technology, London University.)

15 *Op. cit.* Para. 7, p. 4. A parallel to this can be found in the recently-formed National Association of Governors and Managers (N.A.G.A.M.) which hopes to gain freedom for governors and managers "so that they can run their schools like private enterprises without having to pay so much lip-service to politicians". *Times Educational Supplement*, 6 March, 1970. An account of the inaugural meeting stated that "it was shown by the questions asked that there are undoubtedly plenty of muddy battlefields ahead. But it is hoped that the association will at least help those who theoretically run our schools to work out what on earth they are up to and who they are supposed to be." *The Observer*, 26 April, 1970.

16 *Op. cit.* Para. 22, p. 7.

17 *Ibid.* Para. 41, p. 11.

18 Some of these problems have been discussed in W. O. Lester Smith, *Government of Education* (1965), pp. 21–3 and D. M. Hill, *Participation in Local Affairs* (1970), pp. 145–51.

19 J. E. G. de Montmorency, *National Education and National Life* (1906), pp. 3–4.

Appendix

RETURN of the several ASSOCIATIONS formed under the VOLUN-
TARY SCHOOLS ACT, 1897, with their Areas, and the Number of
Persons forming the Governing Body of each ASSOCIATION. BPP.
1898 LXX

ASSOCIATIONS (46) MAINLY COMPOSED OF CHURCH OF ENGLAND SCHOOLS

Name	Area	Number of Persons on Governing Body
1. Bangor Diocesan	Diocese	25
2. Bath and Wells Diocesan	Diocese	43
3. Bedford	Archdeaconry	15
4. Berks	County	21
5. Bristol Diocesan	Diocese	26
6. Canterbury Diocesan	Diocese	60
7. Carlisle	Diocese	36
8. Chester Diocesan	Diocese	59
9. Chichester Diocesan	Diocese	99
10. Derby	Archdeaconry	68
11. Dorset	County	42
12. Durham Diocesan	Diocese	46
13. Ely	Archdeaconry and Isle	30
14. Essex (St. Albans)	Archdeaconry	52
15. Exeter Diocesan	Diocese	77
16. Gloucester Diocesan	Diocese	39
17. Hampshire	Archdeaconry of Winchester	28
18. Hereford	Archdeaconry	37
19. Herts (St. Albans)	Archdeaconry	28
20. Huntingdon	Archdeaconry	24
21. Isle of Wight	Archdeaconry	24
22. Lincoln Diocesan	Diocese	84
23. Liverpool Diocesan	Diocese	40
24. Llandaff Diocesan	Diocese	
25. London Diocesan	Diocese	89
26. Ludlow	Archdeaconry	44
27. Manchester Diocesan	Diocese	74
28. Newcastle Diocesan	Diocese	30
29. North Salop	Archdeaconry	29

Name	Area	Number of Persons on Governing Body
30. Norwich Diocesan	Diocese	90
31. Nottingham	Archdeaconry	60
32. Oxford Diocesan	Diocese	24
33. Peterboro' Diocesan	Diocese	126
34. Ripon Diocesan	Diocese	72
35. Rochester Diocesan	Diocese	75
36. St. Asaph Diocesan	Diocese	39
37. St. David's Diocesan	Diocese	58
38. Salisbury Diocesan	Diocese	63
39. Staffordshire	Archdeaconries of Stafford and Stoke-on-Trent	89
40. Sudbury	Archdeaconry	26
41. Surrey (Winchester)	Archdeaconry	12
42. Truro Diocesan	Diocese	37
43. Wakefield Diocesan	Diocese	71
44. Worcester Diocesan	Diocese	40
45. York Diocesan	Diocese	93
46. Isles of Scillys	Isles of Scilly	3

ASSOCIATIONS (6) OF WESLEYAN SCHOOLS

Name	Area	Number of Persons on Governing Body
47. London and South-East	Bedford, Berks, Bucks, Dorset, Essex, Hants, Hunts, Kent, London, Middlesex, Norfolk, Northants, Oxford, Suffolk, Surrey, Sussex (East)	84
48. Midland	Leicester, Staffs, Warwick, Worcester, and parts of Cheshire, Derby, Lincs (Kesteven), Notts, Salop and Yorks (W.R.)	45
49. North-East	Durham, Lincs (Lindsey), Northumberland, Yorks (E.R.), Yorks (N.R.), and parts of Lincs (Kesteven), Notts, and Yorks (W.R.)	34
50. North Central	Parts of Cheshire, Derby, Lancs, and Yorks (W.R.)	42
51. North-West	Cumberland, and parts of Cheshire, Lancashire, Salop, and Yorks (W.R.)	61
52. South-West	Cornwall, Devon, Gloucester, Somerset, Pembroke, Monmouth	22

ASSOCIATIONS (11) OF ROMAN CATHOLIC SCHOOLS

Name	Area	Number of Persons on Governing Body
53. Birmingham Diocesan	Diocese	23
54. Clifton & Newport Diocesan	Diocese	15
55. Hexham & Newcastle Diocesan	Diocese	23
56. Leeds & Middlesbrough Diocesan	Dioceses	38
57. Liverpool Diocesan	Diocese	43
58. Nottingham & Northampton Diocesan	Dioceses	24
59. Salford Diocesan	Diocese	171
60. Shrewsbury & Vicariate of Wales	Diocese and Vicariate	24
61. Southwark Diocesan	Diocese	31
62. South-Western	Dioceses of Plymouth & Portsmouth	10
63. Westminster Diocesan	Diocese	37

ASSOCIATIONS (11) OF BRITISH AND OTHER SCHOOLS

Name	Area	Number of Persons on Governing Body
64. Bristol & District	Gloucester, Hereford and parts of Somerset, Wiltshire, Worcester and Radnor	108
65. Cheshire & District	Cheshire and part of Staffordshire	92
66. Eastern Counties	Bedford, Cambridge, Lincs (Holland, Kesteven and Lindsey), Norfolk, Northants, Suffolk (East), Suffolk (West)	53
67. Lancashire & District	Lancashire and part of Cumberland	38
68. London & District	Berks, Bucks, Essex, Herts, Isle of Wight, Kent, London, Middlesex, Oxford, Surrey, Sussex (East), Sussex (West) and part of Hants.	203
69. Midland Counties	Derby, Leicester, Notts, Salop, Warwick and parts of Staffordshire and Worcester	84
70. Northern Counties	Durham, Northumberland, Westmorland, Yorks (E.R.), Yorks (N.R.), and part of Cumberland	123

Name	Area	Number Persons on Governing Body
71. North Wales	Anglesey, Carnarvon, Denbigh, Flint, Merioneth and Montgomery	45
72. South Wales and Monmouth	Brecon, Cardigan, Carmarthen, Glamorgan, Monmouth, Pembroke, and part of Radnor	47
73. South-Western	Devon, Dorset, and parts of Hants, Somerset, and Wilts.	131
74. West Riding of Yorks	Yorks (W.R.)	25

ASSOCIATION OF JEWISH SCHOOLS

75. Jewish	England and Wales	41

Bibliography

A. UNPUBLISHED SOURCES

Manuscript materials relating to the management of elementary schools, e.g. Managers' and Trustees' Minute Books, School Log Books, Account Books, correspondence between managers and the Education Department; School Board Minute Books, Annual Reports and political correspondence, have been drawn upon from the following record repositories:

(a) *County Record Offices*

Bedfordshire
Berkshire
Buckinghamshire
Cambridgeshire and Isle of Ely
Cheshire
Derbyshire
Devon
Dorset
Durham
Essex
Gloucestershire
Hampshire
Herefordshire
Hertfordshire
Huntingdonshire
Kent Archives Offices
Lancashire
Leicestershire
Lincolnshire Archives Office
Greater London—
London and Middlesex Sections
Northamptonshire
Northumberland
Nottinghamshire
Salop
Somerset
Staffordshire
Surrey
W. Sussex
E. Sussex
Wiltshire
Worcestershire
Yorkshire, E. Riding
Yorkshire, N. Riding

(b) *Joint Repositories*

Norfolk and Norwich
Ipswich and East Suffolk

(c) *Borough Record Offices*

Bristol Archives Office
Leicester Museum, Department of Archives
Liverpool Record Office
Reading Corporation Archives Department
Southampton Civic Record Office
Winchester City Record Office

(d) *Borough Libraries*

Birmingham City Library
Exeter City Library
Gloucester City Library
Leeds Public Library
Lincoln Public Library
Manchester Central Library
Plymouth City Library
Sheffield Public Library
York City Library

(*e*) *Universities*
Birmingham University
Bodleian Library, Oxford
Christ Church, Oxford
Imperial College of Science and Technology, London
London School of Economics and Political Science
University College, London
Sheffield University
Borthwick Institute of Historical Research, York

(*f*) *National Collections*
British Museum
Public Record Office

(*g*) *Private Collections*
Hughenden Manor, Bucks
Chatsworth, Derbyshire
Lambeth Palace, London
W. H. Smith & Son, London
Althorp, Northants
Sandon Hall, Staffs

(*h*) *Government Departments*
Department of Education and Science

Principal Manuscript Collections
Acland (Devon R.O. and Exeter City Library)
Akers-Douglas (Kent Archives Office)
Ancaster (Lincolnshire Archives Office)
Arkwright (Herefordshire C.R.O.)
Asquith (Bodleian, Oxford)
Balfour (British Museum)
Beaconsfield (Hughendon Manor, Bucks)
Beauchamp (Greater London R.O.)
Brougham (University College, London)
Burdett-Coutts (Lambeth Palace, London)
Cartwright of Aynhoe (Northamptonshire C.R.O.)
Chamberlain (Birmingham University)
Cobden (British Museum)
Cookson of Goosnargh (Lancashire R.O.)
Cowdray (West Sussex R.O.)
Cranbrook (Ipswich & E. Suffolk R.O.)
Cross (British Museum)
Davidson (Lambeth Palace, London)
Devonshire (Chatsworth, Derbyshire)
Fremantle (Buckinghamshire R.O.)
Gladstone (British Museum)
Hambleden (W. H. Smith & Son, London)
Hatherley (Staffordshire C.R.O.)
Harrowby (Sandon Hall, Staffs)

Hicks Beach (Gloucestershire C.R.O.)
Huxley (Imperial College, London)
Iddesleigh (British Museum)
Lancashire Public Schools Association (Manchester Central Library)
Londonderry (Durham C.R.O.)
Lyttelton (Worcestershire C.R.O.)
Manchester (Huntingdon C.R.O.)
Manvers (Nottinghamshire C.R.O.)
Monson (Lincolnshire Archives Office)
Mundella (Sheffield University)
Osborne (British Museum)
Pakington (Worcestershire C.R.O.)
Peel (British Museum)
Redesdale (Gloucestershire C.R.O.)
Ripon (British Museum)
Russell (Public Record Office)
Salisbury (Christ Church, Oxford)
Salvin (Durham C.R.O.)
Serrell (Dorset R.O.)
Spencer (Althorp, Northants.)
Sutherland (Staffordshire C.R.O.)
Temple (Lambeth Palace, London)
Whitbread (Bedfordshire C.R.O.)

Classes of Education Department Documents Consulted at the Public Record Office

Ed. 9 Secretary's Minute Books 1848–71
      1889–99
    Curiosities of School Board Elections
  10 Memorials to the Education Department
  11 Elementary Education: General Files
  16 Elementary Education: Supply Files
    School Boards
  21 Elementary Education: School Files
  24 Private Office Papers
  27 Secondary Education: Endowment Files
  48 Voluntary Schools Associations Files
  49 Elementary Education: Endowment Files
 127 Voluntary Schools Associations and Precedent Books
Cab. 37 Cabinet Memoranda relating to Elementary Education
    1882–1902.

All the following were published in London unless otherwise stated.

B. OFFICIAL PUBLICATIONS
(a) Royal Commissions
    (i) Popular Education in England (Newcastle) 1861 XXI.
    (ii) Civil Service Inquiry Commission (Playfair) 1875 XXIII,

(iii) Elementary Education Acts (Cross) 1886 XXV, 1887 XXIX and XXX, 1888 XXV, XXVI and XXXVII.

(iv) Civil Service Establishments (Ridley) 1888 XXVII.

(*b*) *Select Committees*

(i) The Education of the Poorer Classes 1837–8 VII.

(ii) Manchester and Salford Education 1852 XI.

(iii) The Constitution of the Committee of Council on Education 1865 VI and 1866 VII.

(iv) The Endowed Schools Act (1869) 1873 VIII.

(v) The Education, Science and Art (Administration) 1883 XIII and 1884 XIII.

(*c*) *Reports*

(i) Annual Minutes and Reports of the Committee of Council on Education 1840–1902.

(ii) First Report of the Endowed Schools Commission to the Committee of Council on Education 1872 XXIV.

(iii) Report of Dr. Crighton Browne upon alleged Overpressure of Work in Public Elementary Schools 1884 LXI.

(iv) Memorandum by J. G. Fitch Esq., Chief Inspector of Training Colleges on the Working of the Free School System in America, France and Belgium 1890–1 LXI.

(*d*) *Returns*

(i) Return showing by Counties the Number of School Boards which have and which have not Schools under their Management; also showing the Number which have Appointed Visitors for such Schools, and in the Girls Schools, Lady Managers 1876 LIX.

(ii) Return of the several Associations formed under the Voluntary Schools Act 1897, with their Associations and Number of Persons forming the Governing Body of each Association 1898 LXX.

(iii) Return of Public Elementary Schools not provided by School Boards which had been transferred to School Boards since the commencement of the Voluntary Schools Act 1897. 1899 LXXV.

(*e*) *General*

(i) Hansard.

(ii) Instructions to Inspectors.

(iii) Circulars to School Managers.

(iv) Copies of all correspondence which has taken place between the Committee of Council on Education and the Committee of the National Society upon the subject of the Management Clauses 1894 XLII.

(v) A Bill to Facilitate the Representative Management of Voluntary Schools 1890 IX and 1890–1 X.

(*f*) *Present Day Publications*

(i) Report of the Central Advisory Council for Education: Half Our Future, 1963. (Newsom Report).

(ii) Report of the Central Advisory Council for Education: Children and Their Primary Schools. Vol. 2—Research and Surveys, 1967. (Plowden Report).
(iii) Schools Council—The New Curriculum, 1967.
(iv) Royal Commission on Local Government in England: Research Studies No. 6—School Management and Government by G. Baron and D. Howell, 1968.

C. BIBLIOGRAPHIES AND REFERENCE BOOKS

Burke's Peerage, Baronetage and Knightage, 1963.
A. Christophers, *An Index to 19th Century British Educational Biography.* Education Libraries Bulletin Supplement No. 10. University of London Institute of Education, 1965.
The Dictionary of National Biography.
H. A. Doubleday and Lord Howard de Walden, *The Complete Peerage.* St. Catherine's Press, 1932.
B. L. Gabiné, *A Finding List of British Royal Commissions Reports 1860–1935.* Harvard University Press, 1935.
P. H. J. H. Gosden, *Educational Administration in England and Wales: A Bibliographical Guide.* University of Leeds Institute of Education, 1967.
The Imperial Calendar.
W. Matthews, *British Diaries: An Annotated Bibliography of British Diaries written between 1442 and 1942.* University of California Press and C.U.P., 1950.
W. Matthews, *British Autobiographies: An Annotated Bibliography of British Autobiography.* Published or Written before 1951. University of California Press, 1958.
J. E. Roscoe, *Dictionary of Educationists.* 3rd Edition. Rea, Walker & Inchbould, 1913–14.
A. Tropp, *Some Sources for the History of Educational Periodicals in England*, Vol. VI, No. 2, May, 1958. British Journal of Educational Studies.
P. J. Wallis, *Histories of Old Schools: A Revised List for England and Wales.* Department of Education, University of Newcastle-upon-Tyne, 1966.

D. NEWSPAPERS AND PERIODICALS

(a) *Newspapers*

Bedfordshire Mercury
Birmingham Daily Gazette
Birmingham Daily Post
Birmingham Morning Post
Bolton Chronicle
Bolton Weekly Guardian
Bradford Observer
Buckinghamshire Express
Derbyshire Advertiser & Journal
Devizes & Wiltshire Gazette
Eastern Daily Press
Essex Times
Glossop Chronicle
Halifax Guardian
Hereford Journal
Huddersfield Daily Chronicle
Leyton Express & Independent
Lincoln Chronicle

x

Macclesfield Courier & Herald
Manchester Guardian
Middlesex Chronicle
Norfolk Mail & Norwich,
  Yarmouth & Lowestoft
  Conservative Reporter
Norfolk News
Norfolk & Norwich Gazette
Observer
Oxford Times
Rotherham & Masboro'
  Advertiser
Scarborough Mercury
The Scotsman
Sheffield & Rotherham Independent
Sheffield Telegraph
Shropshire Guardian
Sunday Times
The Times
Tottenham & Edmonton Weekly
  Herald
Wallasey News
Wallasey & Wirral Chronicle
Walthamstow Express
Winslow Standard
Yorkshire Post & Leeds Intelligencer

(*b*) *Periodicals*
Bedfordshire Magazine
Blackwood's Magazine
British Journal of Educational Studies
British Journal of Sociology
British Weekly
Contemporary Review
Durham Research Review
Economic History Review
Educational Magazine
Educational Times
English Historical Review
Journal of Economic History
Journal of Educational Administration, Australia
Journal of Educational Administration and History, England
Law Times
Lincolnshire Historian
New Society
Nineteenth Century
Nonconformist & Independent
Northamptonshire Past & Present
Northern History
Papers for the Schoolmaster
Punch
Researches & Studies
The School and the Teacher
School Board Chronicle
School Board Gazette
School Guardian
The Schoolmaster
Times Educational Supplement
Transactions of the Manchester Statistical Society
Transactions of the National Association for the Promotion of Social
  Science
Victorian Studies

E. PAMPHLETS

H. Althans, *A Compendious Report of the Order of Proceedings and Actual Operations in the Central School of the British and Foreign School Borough Road*, 1831.

J. Beldam, *A letter to Rt. Hon. Lord John Russell on National Education*. James Ridgway, 1850.

Rev. H. W. Bellairs, *Work, the Law of God, the Lot of Man*. Groombridge, 1855.

Rev. T. A. Birks, *The Revised Code: What Would it Do? And What Should be Done with It? in a letter to Earl Granville, K.G.* Seeley, Jackson & Halliday, 1862.

British & Foreign School Society. *Address of The Ladies' Committee for Promoting the Education of Female Children belonging to the Labouring and Manufacturing Classes of Society of Every Religious Persuasion*. London, 1815.

Rev. W. F. Brown, *Our School Boards. A Contrast between the Expenditure of Board Schools and Voluntary Schools on Sites, Buildings, Administration and Maintenance*. Catholic Truth Society, 1895.

Six Years of Educational Work in Birmingham: An Address delivered to the Birmingham Joint Board by the Chairman, Joseph Chamberlain, Esq., M.P. Journal Printing Offices, Birmingham, 1876.

Rev. D. Coleridge, *The Education of the People. A letter to the Rt. Hon. Sir John Coleridge*. Rivingtons, 1861.

J. Fletcher, *Education National, Voluntary and Free*. James Ridgway, 1851.

J. Grote, B.D., *A Few Words on the New Educational Code and the Report of the Educational Commissioners*. Deighton Bell, Cambridge, 1862.

J. H. Hinton, *The Case of the Manchester Educationists. A Review of the Evidence taken before a Committee of the House of Commons in relation to the State of Education in Manchester and Salford*. John Snow, 1852.

J. Hirst Hollowell, *Education and Popular Control—A Genuine School Board System Wanted. A Reply to Addresses delivered by the Archdeacon of Manchester in May, 1898*. John Heywood, 1898.

T. J. Macnamara, *The School Board System in the Villages*. The Schoolmaster, 1895.

W. W. Morrell, *Wesleyan Education: An Appeal to the Members of the Conference of 1895*. Yorkshire Herald Newspaper, York, 1895.

Rev. H. Moule, *National School Expenses: How to a Large Extent These May Be Met. A letter to the Rt. Hon. W. E. Forster, M.P.* Wm. Macintosh, 1870.

National Education Union—Authorised Report of a Conference on Behalf of Voluntary Schools held at the Westminster Palace Hotel, London, 12th June, 1879. 1879.

Rev. W. D. Parish, *An Account of a Plan of School Management adopted for Five Years at Selmeston, Sussex*. Farncombe, Lewes, 1873.

Progressive School Board Election Council, *The Case Against Diggleism: Plain Facts concerning the Reactionary Policy of the Present Majority on the London School Board, 1891*. Alexander & Shepheard, 1892.

Rev. C. Richson, *Education: The Government Measure shown to be Susceptible of Improvement on its own Principles*. Longman, Brown, Green & Longman, Manchester, 1853.

J. H. Tillett, *The Church in Fetters*. Tracts of British Anti-State-Church Association No. 25. Published for British Anti-State-Church Association, 1850.

Souvenir of the Leeds School Board 1870–1903, Durhams, Leeds, 1903.

A School Manager, *National Elementary Education and the New Code, 1861*.

The Education Crisis. A Defence of Popular Management in Public Education. The National Education Emergency Committee, 1896.

Report of the Church, Schools, etc. in connection with the Messrs. John Bagnall & Sons, Ironworks, Golden Hill, W. Bromwich. F.P.B.N. Hutton, M.A., 1864, for private circulation.

A Schoolmaster in the North, *A letter on the administration of Parliamentary Grant for the promotion of education in Great Britain, addressed to a member of the House of Commons, 1864*.

National Education: not necessarily Governmental, Sectarian or Irreligious shown in a series of Papers read at the Meetings of the Lancashire Public Schools Association. C. Gilpin, 1850.

F.　MANUALS ON SCHOOL MANAGEMENT

Rev. H. Walford Bellairs, *The Church and the School: or Hints on Clerical Life*. James Parker, 1868.

J. R. Blakiston, *The Teacher: Hints on School Management*. Macmillan, 1879.

W. Bousfield, *Elementary Scholars—How to Increase Their Utility*, being six lectures delivered to the Managers of the London School Board in 1889 and 1890. Percival, 1890.

D. R. Fearon, *School Inspection*. Macmillan, 1876.

J. Gill, *Systems of Education: A History and Criticism of the Principles, Method, Organisation and Moral Discipline advocated by Eminent Educationalists*. Longmans, Green, Reader & Dyer, 1876.

J. Gill, *Introductory Text Book to School Education, Method and School Management*. Longmans, Green, Reader & Dyer, 1876.

P. W. Joyce, *A Handbook of School Management*. McGlashen & Gill, Dublin, 1867.

Liverpool School Board, *Suggestions to the Managers of Public Elementary Schools*, 2nd edition. Wm. Isbister, 1880.

F. C. Mills, *The School Managers' Manual*. Cassel, 1885.

W. F. Norris, *Elementary Schools*. Longmans, Green & Co., 1904.

T. Preston, *The School Board Guide and Teacher's Manual*. Wm. Amer., London, 1871.

J. G. Wenham, *The School Manager: His Office and His Duties in Regard to Elementary Denominational Schools*. Burns & Oates, Simpkin Marshall, 1878.

H. R. Rice-Wiggin and A. P. Graves, *The School Manager*, 2nd edition. Wm. Isbister, 1880.

G. WRITINGS ON AND BY HER MAJESTY'S AND LOCAL INSPECTORS

M. Arnold, *Reports on Elementary Schools 1852–1882* (ed. F. Sandford). Macmillan, 1889.

N. Ball, *Her Majesty's Inspectorate 1839–1849*. University of Birmingham Educational Monographs, Oliver & Boyd, 1963.

P. B. Ballard, *Things I Cannot Forget*. U.L.P., 1937.

Mrs. Brookfield, *Sermons by the Late Rev. W. H. Brookfield with a Biographical Notice by Lord Lyttelton*. Smith, Elder, 1875.

G. A. Christian, *English Education from Within*. Wallace Gandy, London, 1922.

E. L. Edmonds, *The School Inspector*, Routledge & Kegan Paul, 1962.

T. Gautrey, *Lux Mihi Laus: School Board Memories*. Link House Publications, 1937.

E. Holmes, *What Is and What Might Be: A Study of Education in General and Elementary Education in Particular*. Constable, 1911.

A. P. Graves, *To Return to All That: An Autobiography*. Cape, 1930.

J. Leese, *Personalities and Power in English Education*. Arnold, 1950.

F. Mayrick, *Memories of Life at Oxford, and Experiences in Italy, Greece, Turkey, Germany, Spain and Elsewhere*. J. Murray, 1905.

A. W. Newton, *The English Elementary School. Some Elementary Facts about it*. Longmans, Green, 1919.

J. P. Norris, *The Education of the People. Our Weak Points and our Strength. Occasional Essays*. Simpkin, Marshall, 1969.

H. D. Oakeley, *My Adventures in Education*. Williams & Norgate, 1939.

B. M. Sneyd-Kynnersley, *H.M.I.—Some Passages in the Life of one of H.M. Inspectors of Schools*. Macmillian, 1908.

F. H. Spencer, *An Inspector's Testament*. E.U.P., 1938.

A. J. Swinburne, *Memories of a School Inspector. Thirty-five Years in Lancashire and Suffolk* (Published by author). Snape Priory, Saxmundham, 1912.

R. G. Tatton (ed.), *Selected Writings of Thos. Godolphin Rooper, M.A., Balliol College, Oxford, late H.M.I.* Blackie, 1907.

R. M. Theobald, *Memorials of John Daniel Morrell, M.A., LL.D., Her Majesty's Inspector of Schools*. W. Stewart, 1891.

H. THESES

E. Benson, A History of Education in York 1780–1902, Ph.D., London University, 1932.

R. Charlesworth, The History of Education in Warrington. M.Ed., Manchester University, 1936.

A. J. Evans, A History of Education in Bradford During the Period of the Bradford School Board. M.A., Leeds University, 1947.

B. G. Everett, The Early Years of the Tynemouth School Board. M.A., Newcastle University, 1963.

C. E. Greenwell, The History of Education in South Shields. M.Ed., Newcastle-upon-Tyne University, 1935.

J. L. Hanson, A History of Education in Halifax During the 19th Century. M.Ed., Leeds University, 1940.

R. Harrison, A History of Education in Rotherham and District up to 1902. M.Ed., Bristol University, 1950.

H. J. Larcombe, The Progress of Education in Bristol. M.A., Bristol University, 1924.

A. W. Swann, Quakers and Education: A Study of Education in York in the 19th and 20th Centuries. Dip.Ed., University of Durham, 1967.

E. Stones, The Development of Education in Accrington 1790–1903. M.A., Sheffield University, 1957.

I. LOCAL HISTORIES

Handbook of Birmingham. Prepared for the Members of the British Association 1886. Hall & English, Birmingham, 1886.

History of the Walthamstow School Board 1880–1903. Printed for Board by Gilbert J. Marks, Walthamstow, 1903.

The Schools of Tottenham Through 400 Years: Exhibition of Records 1956: Catalogue. Tottenham Archives Committee 1956.

Anon: *A History of Arnold, Nottinghamshire*. Harvey B. Saxton, Nottingham, 1913.

T. S. Ashton, *Economic and Social Investigations in Manchester, 1833–1933*. P. S. King, 1934.

W. King Baker, *Acton, Middlesex*. Acton & Chiswick Gazette, Acton, 1913.

T. W. Bamford, *The Evolution of Rural Education: Studies of the East Riding of Yorkshire: Research Monographs No. 1, May 1965*. Institute of Education, University of Hull.

T. C. Barker and J. R. Harris, *A Merseyside Town in the Industrial Revolution, St. Helens, 1750–1900*. Frank Cass, 1959.

H. Bateson, *A Centenary History of Oldham*. Oldham County Borough Council, 1949.

J. Beswick, *History of the Village School, Royton*. Bolton, 1922.

J. H. Bingham, *The Period of the Sheffield School Board 1870–1903*. J. W. Northend, Sheffield, 1949.

C. W. Bracken, *A History of the Plymouth Public School*. Underhill Ltd., Plymouth, 1927.

A. Briggs, *Victorian Cities*. Odhams, 1963.

C. R. Burchnall, *The Story of Education and the Schools of Deeping St. James*. Peterborough, 1957.

O. Chadwick, *Victorian Miniature*. Hodder & Stoughton, London, 1960.

W. H. Chaloner, *The Social and Economic Development of Crewe 1780–1923*. Manchester U.P., 1950.

E. D. W. Chaplin, *The Book of Harrow*. Staples Press, 1948.

H. W. Clemesha, *A History of Preston in Amounderness*. University of

Manchester Publications No. LXVII Manchester University Press 1912.

R. Cookson, *Goosnargh, Past and Present*. Preston: H. Oakey, Printer, Fishergate, 1888.

C. S. Davies (ed.), *A History of Macclesfield*. Manchester U.P., 1961.

Rev. J. Silvester Davies, *A History of Southampton*. Gilbert, Southampton, 1883.

J. G. Dony, *A History of the Straw Hat Industry*. Gibbs, Bamforth, Luton, 1942.

T. B. Dudley, *A Complete History of Royal Leamington Spa*. Royal Leamington Spa: P. & W. E. Linaker, 1901.

J. Dyer, F. Stygall and J. Dony, *The Story of Luton*. White Crescent Press, Luton, 1964.

H. J. Dyos (ed.), *The Study of Urban History*. Arnold, 1968.

T. Dyson, *The History of Huddersfield and District from the earliest times down to 1932*. The Advertiser Press, Huddersfield, 1932.

J. F. Ede, *History of Wednesbury*. Wednesbury Corporation, 1962.

Rev. B. E. Evans, *The Story of Milton Malzor*. Wells, Gardner, Danton, 1925.

R. Fasnacht, *A History of the City of Oxford*. Basil Blackwell, Oxford, 1956.

A. Fried and R. M. Elman (eds.), *Charles Booth's London*. Hutchinson, 1969.

Rev. J. Denny Gedge, *The History of a Village Community In the Eastern Counties*. A. H. Goose, Norwich, 1893.

J. Glynde Jnr., *Suffolk in the Nineteenth Century: Physical, Social, Moral Religious and Industrial*. Simpkin & Marshall, London, 1856.

J. Godber, *History of Bedfordshire 1066–1888*. Bedfordshire County Council, 1969.

J. Goodwin, *Burwash and the Sussex Weald*. The Courier Printing & Publishing Co., Tunbridge Wells, n.d.

D. Gray, *Nottingham from Settlement to City*. Nottingham Co-op Society, 1953.

L. V. Grinsell (ed.), *Studies in the History of Swindon*. Swindon Borough Council, 1950.

A. G. Gummer, J.P., *Reminiscences of Rotherham. A Retrospect of Over Sixty Years*. H. Garnett, Rotherham, 1927.

F. Hardcastle, *Records of Burley*. Raleigh Press, Exmouth, Devon, 1951.

G. I. Hawkes, *The Development of Public Education in Nelson*. Nelson Corporation, Lancashire, 1966.

G. M. Hine, *The Lancastrian School for Girls, Chichester, 1812–1962. The Chichester Papers No. 26*. Chichester City Corporation, 1962.

M. Hinton, *A History of the Town of Reading*. Harrap, 1954.

J. Hole, *The Working Classes of Leeds: An Essay on the Present State of Education in Leeds and the Best Means of Improving it*. Simpkin, Marshall, 1863.

P. Holland, *Recollections of "Old" Swinton* W. Pearson, Swinton, Lancs, 1914.

J. Hirst Hollowell, *Heroism in a Yorkshire Village: The Fight for Naunton*

School. Northern Counties Educational League Series No. 17. Jas. Clark, 1898.

F. A. Howe, *A Chronicle of Edburton and Fulking in the County of Sussex.* Hubners, Crawley, Sussex, 1958.

J. Hutchins, *The History and Antiquities of the County of Dorset,* 3rd Edition, Vol. 1. John Bowyer, Nichols & Sons, 1861.

F. A. Hyett, *Glimpse of the History of Painswick.* John Bellows, Gloucester, 1928.

F. R. Johnston, *Eccles: The Growth of a Lancashire Town.* Eccles & District History Society, Eccles, 1967.

G. W. Jones, *Borough Politics: A Study of the Wolverhampton Town Council, 1885–1964.* Macmillan, 1969.

J. B. Jones, *Annals of Dover.* Dover Express, 1916.

H. C. M. Lambert, C.B., *History of Banstead in Surrey,* O.U.P., 1912.

J. Lawson, *Primary Education in East Yorkshire 1860–1902.* E. Yorkshire Local History Society, 1959.

J. M. Lee, *Social Leaders and Public Persons. A Study of County Government in Cheshire since 1888.* O.U.P., 1963.

J. Leyland, *Memorials of Abram (for private circulation only.)* Printed J. Heywood, Manchester, 1882.

E. S. Lindley, *Wotton-Under-Edge. Men and Affairs of a Cotswold Wool Town.* Museum Press, 1962.

P. Lucas, *Heathfield Memorials.* Arthur L. Humphreys, 1910.

W. Lyon, *Chronicles of Finchampstead.* Longmans Green, 1895.

S. E. Maltby, *Manchester and the Movement for National Elementary Education 1800–1870.* Manchester U.P. 1918.

J. D. Marshall, *Furness and the Industrial Revolution.* Barrow-in-Furness Library & Museum Committee, 1958.

F. S. Merryweather, *Half a Century of Kingston History 1837–1887.* G. Philipson, Kingston-upon-Thames, 1887.

W. E. Morden, *The History of Tooting Graveney, Surrey.* Edmund Seale, 1897.

N. Morris, "Manchester and the Supply of Schools" in *Manchester and its Region. A Survey prepared for the meeting of the British Association 1962.* Manchester U.P. 1962.

Rev. T. Mozley, *Reminiscences, chiefly of Towns, Villages and Schools,* 2 Vols. Longmans, Green, 1885.

J. H. Muirhead, *Birmingham Institutions.* Cornish Bros. Birmingham, 1911.

R. Newton, *Victorian Exeter.* Leicester University Press, 1968.

J. F. Nicholls and J. Taylor, *Bristol Past and Present,* Vol. 3. *Civil and Modern History.* J. W. Arrowsmith, Bristol, 1882.

A. Temple Patterson, *Radical Leicester. A History of Leicester 1780–1850.* University College, Leicester, 1954.

H. Pelling, *Social Geography of British Elections 1885–1910.* Macmillan, 1967.

N. Pevsner, *The Buildings of England:*
   Cambridgeshire (1954).
   Northamptonshire (1961).

Nottinghamshire (1951).

Yorkshire: West Riding (1959).

Penguin Books.

H. B. Philpott, *London At School. The Story of a School Board 1870–1904.* T. Fisher Unwin, 1904.

W. Potts, *A History of Banbury: The Story of the Development of a Country Town.* Banbury Guardian, Banbury, 1958.

W. F. Proudfoot, *Fawkham.* Arthur Barker, 1951.

E. Puddy, *Litcham, The Story of a Mid-Norfolk Village.* G. Arthur Coleby Dereham, 1957.

C. G. Ramshaw, *Concerning Todmorden Parish.* Todmorden Advertiser Office, 1911.

S. Rayner (ed. W. Smith), *The History and Antiquities of Pudsey.* Longmans, Green, 1887.

D. Read, *The English Provinces 1760–1960. A Study in Influence.* Arnold, 1964.

R. C. Russell, *A History of Elementary Schools and Adult Education in Nettleton and Caistor,* Part 1: 1800–1875. Nettleton W.E.A., 1960.

J. H. Scott-Tucker, *Parish of Stoke Fleming, Devon.* 1955.

R. R. Sellman, *Devon Village Schools in the 19th Century.* David & Charles. Newton Abbot, 1967.

H. Shortt (ed.), *City of Salisbury.* Phoenix House, 1957.

B. Simon (ed.), *Education in Leicestershire 1540–1940. A Regional Study.* Leicester U.P., 1968.

S. D. Simon, *A Century of City Government, Manchester 1838–1938.* G. Allen & Unwin, 1938.

T. A. Spalding, *The Work of the London School Board.* P. S. King, 1900.

L. M. Springall, *Labouring Life in Norfolk Villages 1834–1914.* G. Allen & Unwin, 1936.

A. Stokes, *East Ham: From Village to County Borough.* Wilson & Whitworth, E. Ham, 1933.

G. E. Stone, *Bristol As It Was and As It Is.* Walter Reid, Bristol, 1909.

M. Sturge-Henderson, *Three Centuries in North Oxfordshire.* Basil Blackwell, Oxford, 1902.

Rev. J. M. Swift, *The Story of Garston and Its Church.* A. M. Proffit, Garston, 1937.

P. F. E. Sykes, *The History of Huddersfield and Its Vicinity.* The Advertiser Press, Huddersfield, 1898.

R. and E. Taylor, *Rochdale Retrospect.* Corporation of Rochdale, 1956.

J. T. Ward, *E. Yorkshire Landed Estates in the 19th Century.* E. Yorkshire Local History Society, 1967.

E. J. D. Warrillow, *A Sociological History of the City of Stoke-upon-Trent.* Etruscan Publications, Stoke-on-Trent, 1960.

Rev. F. Watkins, *A letter to His Grace the Archbishop of York on the State of Education in the Church Schools of Yorks.* Bell & Daldry, 1860.

S. Webb, *London Education.* Longmans, Green, 1904.

F. Whellan, *History, Topography and Directory of the County Palatine of Durham,* 2nd Edition. C. Thwaites, Durham, 1894.

C. W. Whitaker, *Enfield*. G. Bell, 1911.

B. D. White, *A History of the Corporation of Liverpool 1835–1914*. Liverpool U.P., 1951.

R. J. Whiteman (ed.), *Hexton: a Parish Survey*, 1936.

E. R. Wickham, *Church and People in An Industrial City*. Lutterworth Press, 1957.

R. Wood, *West Hartlepool: The Rise and Development of a Victorian New Town*. W. Hartlepool Corporation, 1967.

Directories and Gazetteers

M. *Billing's Directory and Gazetteer of Plymouth*. M. Billing's Steam Press Office, Livery Street, Birmingham, 1887.

E. Boswell, *The Civil Division of the County of Dorset, Methodically Digested and Arranged*. Weston, Simmonds & Sydenham, Dorchester, 1833.

Bulmer's History, Topography and Directory of N. Yorkshire. T. Bulmer, Ashton-on-Ribble, 1890.

Directory of City of Lincoln, 1897. F. J. W. Ruddock, Lincoln, 1897.

Directory: The Picture of Plymouth: being a Correct Guide to the Public Establishments, Charitable Institutions, Amusements and Remarkable Objects in towns of Plymouth, etc. Rees & Curtis, Plymouth, 1812.

C. Richard, Bishop of Winchester, *Conspectus of the Diocese of Winchester*. John Bowyer, Nichols & Sons, 1854.

Eyre Brothers' Post Office Plymouth and Devonport District Directory. Eyre Bros., 1888.

J. Hatfield—*History, Gazetteer and Directory of the County of Huntingdon, Comprising a General Survey of the County. Subscriber's Copy*. J. Hatfield, Huntingdon, 1854.

Kelly's Post Office Directory—Bedfordshire, Huntingdonshire, Northamptonshire, Berkshire, Buckinghamshire and Staffordshire, 1898.
   Gloucestershire and Bristol, 1889.
   Gloucestershire, 1897.
   Northamptonshire, 1885
   Warwickshire, 1892
   Yorkshire: N. & E. Ridings with City of York, 1872.

V. C. H., *Warwickshire*, Vol. VII, 1964. *Middlesex*, Vol. II, 1962.

V. C. H., *York: E. Riding*, Vol. I: *City of Kingston-upon-Hull*. 1969.

W. White, *History, Gazetteer & Directory of Lincolnshire*. W. White, Sheffield, 1872.

White's History, Gazetteer & Directory of Warwickshire. F. White, Sheffield, 1850.

J. BOOKS RELATING TO THE LAW OF EDUCATION

L. S. Bristowe and W. I. Cook, *The Law of Charities and Mortmain being a 3rd Edition of Tudor's Charitable Trusts*. Reeves & Turner, 1889.

G. Jones, *A History of the Law of Charity 1532–1827*. C.U.P., 1969.

E. Jones and J. C. G. Sykes, *The Law of Public Education in England and Wales*, 2nd Edition. Rivingtons, 1904.

W. W. Mackenzie, *A Treatise on the Elementary Education Acts 1870–1891*. Shaw & Sons, 1892.

T. A. Organ, *The Law Relating to Schools and Teachers*. Arnold Leeds. 1900.

Owen's Education Acts Manual, 12th Edition. Charles Knight & Co., 1876.

J. Williams, *Education. A Manual of Practical Law*. Adam & Chas. Black, 1892.

Law Reports, *Chancery. Equity. Queen's Bench.*

K. BIOGRAPHIES

Anon, *Patrick Cumin, Secretary of the Education Department—a Sketch*. Hugh Rees, London, n.d.

A. H. D. Acland, *Memoir and Letters of Rt. Hon. Sir Thomas Dyke Acland*. Printed for private circulation, 1902.

J. P. Alderson, *Mr. Asquith*. Methuen, 1905.

A. O. Allen, *John Allen and His Friends*. Hodder & Stoughton, 1922.

B. M. Allen, *Sir Robert Morant. A Great Public Servant*. Macmillan, 1934.

W. Allen, *Life of William Allen, with Selections from his Correspondence*. Vol. 1. Charles Gilpin, 1846.

M. H. Allies, *Thomas William Allies*. Burns & Oates, 1907.

J. Amery, *Joseph Chamberlain and the Tariff Reform Campaign, 1901–3. The Life of Joseph Chamberlain*, Vol. 5. Macmillan, 1969.

W. H. G. Armytage, *A. J. Mundella 1825–1897. The Liberal Background to the Labour Movement*. Ernest Benn, 1951.

Lady Frances Balfour, *The Life of George, 4th Earl of Aberdeen*. Hodder & Stoughton, 1923.

Lady Frances Balfour, *A Memoir of Lord Balfour of Burleigh, K.T.* Hodder & Stoughton, 1925.

G. K. A. Bell, *Randall Davidson, Archbishop of Canterbury*. O.U.P., 1935.

A. C. Benson, *The Life of Edward White Benson*, Vol. 2. Macmillan, 1899.

F. G. Bettany, *Stewart Headlam: A Biography*. John Murray, 1926.

C. Bibby, *T. H. Huxley, Scientist, Humanist and Educator*. Watts, 1959.

G. E. Buckle (ed.), *The Letters of Queen Victoria* (3rd Series). Vol. II, *1891–1895* (1931), Vol. III *1896–1901* (1932). John Murray.

G. E. Buckle and W. F. Moneypenny, *Life of Disraeli*, Vol. 5, *1868–1876*. John Murray, 1920.

Rev. the Hon. W. E. Bowen, *Edward Bowen. A Memoir*. Longmans, Green, 1902.

R. Blake, *The Unknown Prime Minister. The Life and Times of Andrew Bonar Law, 1858–1923*. Eyre & Spottiswoode, 1955.

R. Blake, *Disraeli*. Eyre & Spottiswoode, 1966.

J. Benwick, *An Octogenarian's Reminiscences*. J. Nichols, 1902.

A. Briggs, *Victorian People*. Penguin 1955.

J. E. Carpenter, *The Life and Work of Mary Carpenter*. Macmillan, 1881.

Lord David Cecil, *Lord M.* Constable, 1954.

Lady Gwendoline Cecil, *Life of Robert, Marquis of Salisbury*. Vol. II *1868–1880* (1921), Vol. III *1880–1886* (1931). Hodder & Stoughton.

E. K. Chambers, *Matthew Arnold. A Study*. O.U.P., 1947.

Viscount Chilston, *Chief Whip. The Political Life and Times of Aretas Akers-Douglas, 1st Viscount Chilston*. Routledge & Kegan Paul, 1961.

Viscount Chilston, *W. H. Smith*. Routledge & Kegan Paul, 1965.

G. Christian (ed.), *James Hawker's Journal. A Victorian Poacher*. O.U.P. 1961.

E. Churton (ed.), *Memoir of Joshua Watson*, Vol. I., J. H. & Jas. Porter, Oxford, 1861.

W. F. Connell, *The Educational Thought and Influence of Matthew Arnold*. Routledge & Kegan Paul, 1950.

A. W. W. Dale, *The Life of R. W. Dale of Birmingham*. Hodder & Stoughton, 1899.

R. E. Davies (ed.), *John Scott Lidgett, A Symposium*. The Epworth Press, 1957.

R. T. Davidson and W. Benham, *Life of Archbishop Campbell Tait*. 2 Vols. Macmillan, 1891.

L. E. Denison (ed.), *Fifty Years at East Brent. The Letters of George Anthony Denison 1845–1896, Archdeacon of Taunton*. John Murray, 1902.

H. C. Duffin, *Thomas Hardy. A Study of the Wessex Novels*. Manchester U.P., 1962.

Mrs. E. Dugdale (ed.), *Chapters of Autobiography by Arthur James, 1st Earl of Balfour*. Cassell, 1930.

Blanche E. C. Dugdale, *Arthur James Balfour, 1st Earl of Balfour*, Vol. I. Hutchinson, 1936.

J. Dunbar, *The Early Victorian Woman. Some Aspects of Her Life 1837–1857*. Harrap, 1953.

E. L. and O. P. Edmonds, *I Was There. The Memoirs of H. S. Tremenheere*. Shakespeare Head Press, Eton, Windsor, 1965.

T. H. S. Escott, *Personal Forces of the Period*. Hurst & Blackett, 1898.

W. Evans and W. Claridge, *James Hirst Hollowell and The Movement for Civic Control in Education*. The Northern Counties Education League, Manchester, 1911.

Sir A. Fitzroy, *Memoirs* (2 Volumes). Geo. H. Doran, New York, 1925.

E. M. Forster, *Marianne Thornton 1797–1887. A Domestic Biography*. Edward Arnold, 1956.

R. Fulford, *Samuel Whitbread 1764–1815. A Study in Opposition*. Macmillan, 1967.

A. G. Gardiner, *John Benn and the Progressive Movement*. Ernest Benn, 1925.

R. and E. Garnett, *The Life of W. J. Fox, Public Teacher and Social Reformer 1786–1864*. John Lane, 1910.

A. E. Gathorne-Hardy (ed.), *Gathorne Hardy, 1st Earl of Cranbrook. A Memoir*. 2 Vols. Longmans, Green, 1910.

E. Graham, *The Harrow Life of Hy. Montagu Butler D.D., 1860–1885*. Longmans, Green, 1920.

A. S. T. Griffith-Boscawen, *Fourteen Years in Parliament, 1892–1906.* John Murray, 1907.

Lady V. Hicks Beach, *Life of Sir Michael Hicks Beach.* Macmillan, 1932.

P. Guedalla, *The Queen and Mr. Gladstone,* Hodder & Stoughton, 1933.

F. W. Hirst, *Early Life and Letters of John Morley,* Vol. 1. Macmillan & Co., 1927.

L. T. Hobhouse and J. L. Hammond, *Lord Hobhouse. A Memoir.* Arnold, 1905.

B. O. Holland, C.B., *The Life of Spencer Compton, 8th Duke of Devonshire,* 2 Vols. Longmans, Green, 1911.

M. Holroyd, *Lytton Strachey,* Vol. 1. *The Unknown Years 1880–1910.* Heinemann, 1967.

R. H. Haddon, *Reminiscences of William Rogers, Rector of St. Betelph Bishopsgate.* Kegan Paul, Trench, 1888.

T. Hughes, *James Fraser: 2nd Bishop of Manchester. A Memoir.* Macmillan, 1887.

W. H. Hutton, *Robert Gregory 1819–1911.* Longmans, Green, 1912.

L. Huxley, *The Life and Letters of T. H. Huxley.* Macmillan, 1900.

W. Jeans, *Parliamentary Reminiscences.* Chapman & Hall, 1912.

A. W. Jephson, *My Work in London.* Pitman, 1910.

W. D. Jones, *Lord Derby and Victorian Conservatism.* Blackwell, Oxford, 1956.

A. V. Judges (ed.), *Pioneers of English Education.* Faber & Faber, 1952.

G. W. Kekewich, *The Education Department and After.* Constable, 1920.

E. and T. Kelly (eds.), *A Schoolmaster's Notebook. Being an Account of a 19th Century Experiment in Social Welfare by David Winstanley of Manchester, Schoolmaster.* Chetham Society, Manchester, 1957.

H. Leach, *The Duke of Devonshire: A Personal and Political Biography.* Methuen, 1904.

R. E. Leader (ed.), *Life and Letters of John Arthur Roebuck, P.C., Q.C., M.P.* Arnold, 1897.

J. Scott Lidgett, *Reminiscences.* The Epworth Press, London, 1928.

A. L. Lilley, *Sir Joshua Fitch.* Arnold, 1906.

H. W. Lucy, *A Diary of the Unionist Parliament 1895–1900.* J. W. Arrowsmith, Bristol, 1901.

H. W. Lucy, *The Balfourian Parliament 1900–1905.* Hodder & Stoughton, 1906.

H. W. Lucy, *Memories of Eight Parliaments.* Heinemann, 1908.

H. W. Lucy, *Men and Manner in Parliament.* T. Fisher Unwin, 1919.

A. Mansbridge, *Margaret McMillan, Prophet and Pioneer. Her Life and Work.* J. M. Dent, 1932.

A. Mansbridge, *Edward Stuart Talbot and Charles Gore: Witnesses to and Interpretation of the Christian Faith in Church and State.* J. M. Dent, 1935.

Sir P. Magnus, *Educational Aims and Efforts 1880–1910.* Longmans, Green, 1910.

A. P. Martin, *Life and Letters of the Rt. Hon. Robert Lowe, Viscount Sherbrooke,* Vol. 2. Longmans, Green, 1893.

H. McLachlan, *Records of a Family 1800–1933. Pioneers in Education, Social Service and Liberal Religion.* Manchester U.P., 1935.

V. A. McClelland, *Cardinal Manning—His Public Life and Influence 1865–1892.* O.U.P., 1962.

A. McCormack, *Cardinal Vaughan.* Burns & Oates, 1966.

J. Morley, *The Life of William Ewart Gladstone.* Vol. I, *1809–1872* (1905), Vol. II, *1872–1898* (1907). Macmillan.

C. F. New, *The Life of Henry Brougham to 1830.* O.U.P., 1961.

Sir J. Otter, *Life of Nathaniel Woodard,* Lane, 1925.

Earl of Oxford & Asquith, K.C., *Memories and Reflections 1852–1927,* Vol. I. Cassell, 1928.

C. B. Patterson, *Angela Burdett-Coutts and the Victorians.* John Murray, 1953.

W. Plomer (ed.), *Kilvert's Diary: Selections from the Diary of the Rev. Francis Kilvert. 1871–1874,* Vol. 2, *1874–1879,* Vol. 3. Jonathan Cape, 1960.

H. M. Pollard, *Pioneers of Popular Education 1760–1850.* John Murray, 1956.

A. Ponsonby, *Henry Ponsonby—Queen Victoria's late Secretary: His Life from His Letters by his Son, Lord Ponsonby of Shulbrede.* Macmillan, 1942.

R. Postgate, *The Life of George Lansbury.* Longmans, Green, 1951.

G. L. Prestige, *The Life of Charles Gore, a Great Englishman.* Heinemann, 1935.

D. Read, *Cobden and Bright. A Victorian Political Partnership.* Arnold, 1967.

C. E. B. Reed, *Memoir of Sir Charles Reed.* Macmillan, 1883.

S. J. Reid, *Lord John Russell.* Sampson, Low, Marston, 1895.

T. Weymss Reid, *Life of the Rt. Hon. William E. Forster,* 2 Vols. Chapman & Hall, 1888.

B. and P. Russell (eds), *The Amberley Papers,* Vol. 2. George Allen & Unwin, (1966 edn).

John, Earl Russell, *Recollections and Suggestions 1812–1873.* Longmans, Green, 1875.

E. G. Sandford (ed.), *Memoirs of Archbishop Temple,* Vol. I, *by Seven Friends.* Macmillan, 1906.

J. Sherman, *Memoir of William Allen, F.R.S.* Charles Gilpin, London, 1851.

F. Smith, *Life and Work of Sir James Kay Shuttleworth.* John Murray, 1923.

J. A. Spender, *The Life of the Rt. Hon. Sir Henry Campbell-Bannerman, G.C.B.,* Vol. 2. Hodder & Stoughton, 1923.

G. Stephenson, *Edward Stuart Talbot 1884–1934.* S.P.C.K., 1936.

F. Storr (ed.), *Life and Remains of the Rev. H. Quick.* C.U.P., 1899.

J. Telford, *The Life of James Harrison Rigg, D.D. 1821–1909.* Robert Culley, 1909.

W. Temple, *Life of Bishop Percival*. Macmillan, 1921.

G. Wallas, *The Life of Francis Place 1771–1854*. George Allen & Unwin, 1918 edn.

G. Wallas, *Men and Ideas*. George Allen & Unwin, 1940.

S. Walpole, *The Life of Lord John Russell*. Longmans, Green, 1889.

J. T. Ward, *Sir James Graham*. Macmillan, 1967.

B. Webb (ed. B. Drake and M. Cole), *Our Partnership*. Longmans Green, 1948.

L. GENERAL

Anon, *The Cumulative Method of Voting: Its Nature, Operation and Effects as Exhibited in the Late School Board Elections*. Simpkin, Marshall, n.d.

F. Adams, *The Elementary School Contest*. Chapman & Hall, 1882.

J. W. Adamson, *English Education 1789–1902*. C.U.P., 1964.

D. H. Akenson, *The Irish Education Experiment. The National System of Education in the Nineteenth Century*. Routledge & Kegan Paul, 1970.

W. H. G. Armytage, *Four Hundred Years of English Education*. C.U.P., 1965.

W. H. G. Armytage, *The American Influence on English Education*. Routledge & Kegan Paul, 1967.

M. K. Ashby, *The Country School. Its Practice and Problems*. O.U.P., 1929.

H. Ausubel, *In Hard Times. Reformers Among the Late Victorians*. O.U.P., 1960.

G. Balfour, *The Educational Systems of Great Britain and Ireland*. 2nd edition. O.U.P., 1903.

G. Balfour, *Educational Administration. Two lectures delivered before the University of Birmingham, February, 1921*. O.U.P., 1921.

G. Baron and W. Taylor (eds.), *Educational Administration and the Social Sciences*. The Athlone Press of the University of London, 1969.

G. A. Beck (ed.), *The English Catholics 1850–1950*. Burns & Oates, 1950.

H. B. Binns, *A Century of Education Being the Centenary History of the British and Foreign School Society*. J. M. Dent, 1908 (to be reprinted by The Woburn Press).

L. A. Selby-Bigge, *The Board of Education*. Putnam, 1934.

C. Birchenough, *History of Elementary Education in England and Wales*. University Tutorial Press, 1925.

P. M. Blau, *Bureaucracy in Modern Society*. Random House, New York, 1965.

A. Briggs (ed.), *Chartist Studies*. Macmillan, 1959.

A. Briggs and J. Saville (eds.), *Essays in Labour History*. Macmillan, 1960.

C. K. F. Brown, *The Church's Part in Education 1833–1841 with special reference to the work of the National Society*. National Society/S.P.C.K., 1942.

H. J. Burgess, *Enterprise in Education*. National Society/S.P.C.K., 1958.

W. L. Burn, *The Age of Equipoise*. George Allen & Unwin, 1964.

S. Buxton, *Overpressure and Elementary Education*. Swan & Sonnenschein, 1885.

O. Chadwick, *The Victorian Church*, Part I. Adam & Charles Black, 1966.

S. G. Checkland, *The Rise of Industrial Society in England 1815–1885*. Longmans, 1964.

G. Kitson Clark, *The Making of Victorian England*. Methuen, 1962.

F. Clarke, *Education and Social Change*. Sheldon Press, 1940.

J. B. Conacher, *The Aberdeen Coalition 1852–1855: A Study in Mid-Nineteenth-Century Party Politics*. C.U.P., 1968.

J. Corlett, *A Survey of the Financial Aspects of Elementary Education*. P. S. King, 1929.

Baroness Burdett Coutts, *The Group System and Its Results Briefly Stated in a letter to the Rt. Rev. Frederick Temple, Lord Bishop of Exeter*. John Murray, 1875.

M. Cowling, *1867, Disraeli, Gladstone and Revolution. The Passing of the Second Reform Bill*. C.U.P., 1967.

Sir H. Craik, *The State in its Relation to Education*. 1st edition. Macmillan, 1882.

M. Cruickshank, *Church and State in English Education 1870 to the Present Day*. Macmillan, 1963.

S. J. Curtis, *History of Education in Great Britain*, 6th edition. U.T.P., 1965.

D.C.L., *The Education Craze and Its Results. School Boards, Their Extravagance and Inefficiency*. Harrison & Sons, 1878.

E. Eaglesham, *From School Board to Local Authority*. Routledge & Kegan Paul, 1956.

F. Engels (translated by W. O. Henderson & W. H. Chaloner), *The Condition of the Working Class in England*. Blackwell, Oxford, 1958.

T. H. S. Escott, *Social Transformations of the Victorian Age. A Survey of Court and Country*. Seeley, 1897.

H. O. Evennett, *The Catholic Schools of England and Wales*. C.U.P., 1944.

J. J. Findlay, *The Children of England. A Contribution to Social History and to Education*. Methuen, 1923.

J. J. Findlay, *The Foundations of Education*, Vol. 2. *The Practice of Education*. University of London Press, 1927.

J. C. Gill, *The Ten Hours Parson: Christian Social Action in the 1830s*. S.P.C.K., 1959.

P. H. J. H. Gosden, *The Development of Educational Administration in England and Wales*. Blackwell, Oxford, 1966.

R. Gregory, *Elementary Education. Some Account of its Rise and Progress in England*. National Society's Depository, 1901.

W. T. Haly, *Showing What is Done, What is Not Done, What We Can Do, What We Must Do To Educate the People*. James Ridgway, 1846.

J. L. and B. Hammond, *The Age of the Chartists 1832–1854*. Longmans, Green, 1930.

T. Hardy, *Jude the Obscure*. Macmillan, 1951 edition.

B. Heeney, *Mission to the Middle Classes: the Woodard Schools 1848–1891*. S.P.C.K., 1969.

D. M. Hill, *Participating in Local Affairs*. Pelican, 1970.

E. F. Hinder, *The Schoolmaster in the Gutter or a Plea for the Middle Class*. E. Stark, 1883.

E. J. Hobsbawm, *Labouring Men: Studies in the History of Labour*. Weidenfeld & Nicholson, 1964.

J. Hole, *The Working Classes of Leeds. An Essay on the Present State of Education in Leeds, and the Best Means of Improving It*. Simpkin, Marshall, 1863, reprinted The Woburn Press.

Rev. H. W. Holland, *Proposed National Arrangements for Primary Education*. Longmans, Green, 1870.

H. Holman, *English National Education. A Sketch of the Rise of Public Elementary Schools in England*. Blackie, 1898.

K. S. Inglis, *Churches and the Working Classes in Victorian England*. Routledge & Kegan Paul, 1963.

H. C. Jennings, *The Political Theory of State-Supported Elementary Education in England, 1750–1833*. Lancaster Press, Lancaster Pa., 1928.

M. G. Jones, *The Charity School Movement. A Study of Eighteenth Century Puritanism in Action*. Frank Cass, 1964.

M. B. Katz, *The Irony of Early School Reform: Educational Innovation in Mid-Nineteenth Century Massachusetts*. Harvard University Press, 1968.

J. Kay-Shuttleworth, *Four Periods of Public Education as Reviewed in 1832, 1839, 1846, 1862*. Longman, Green, Longman & Roberts, 1862.

S. S. Laurie, *Occasional Addresses on Education Subjects*. C.U.P., 1888.

W. R. Lawson, *John Bull & His Sons. A Book for Parents, Ratepayers and Men of Business*. William Blackwood, Edinburgh, 1908.

J. G. Legge, *The Rising Tide*, Blackwell, Oxford, 1929.

H. M. Lynd, *England in the Eighteen-Eighties: Towards a Social Basis for Freedom*. C.U.P., 1945.

S. Maccoby, *English Radicalism 1832–1852*, 1935; *English Radicalism 1853–1886*, 1938. George Allen & Unwin, 1938.

T. J. Macnamara, *Schoolmaster Sketches*. Cassell, 1896.

Cardinal Manning, *National Education*. Burns & Oates, 1890.

M. F. Mathews, *Methodism and the Education of the People, 1791–1851*. Epworth Press, 1949.

A. M. McBriar, *Fabian Socialism and English Politics, 1884–1918*. C.U.P., 1962.

G. E. Mingay, *English Landed Society in the Eighteenth Century*. Routledge & Kegan Paul, 1963.

J. E. G. de Montmorency, *National Education and National Life*. Swan Sonnenschein, 1906.

T. More, *The Education Brief on Behalf of Voluntary Schools*. Church Extension Association, 1890.

C. Morley, *Studies in Board Schools*. Smith, Elder, 1897.

J. Morley, *The Struggle for National Education*. Chapman & Hall, London, 1873.

J. Murphy, *The Religious Problem in English Education*. Liverpool U.P., 1959.

P. W. Musgrave, *Society and Education in England since 1800,* Methuen, 1968.

W. F. Neff, *Victorian Working Woman. An Historical and Literary Study of Women in British Industries and Professions 1832–1850.* Frank Cass, 1966.

D. Owen, *English Philanthropy 1660–1960.* O.U.P., 1965.

M. J. Quinlan, *Victorian Prelude: A History of English Manners 1700–1830.* Columbia University Press, New York, 1941.

W. J. Reader, *Professional Men. The Rise of the Professional Classes in Nineteenth Century England.* Weidenfeld & Nicholson, 1966.

J. H. Rigg, *National Education: In Its Social Conditions and Aspects, and Public Elementary School Education, English and Foreign.* Strahan, 1873.

B. P. Roberts (ed.), *Education in the Nineteenth Century.* C.U.P., 1901.

R. Robson (ed.), *Ideas and Institutions of Victorian Britain. Essays in Honour of George Kitson Clark.* G. Bell, 1967.

D. Rubenstein, *School Attendance in London 1870–1916: A Social History.* University of Hull Press, 1968.

J. Runciman, *Schools and Scholars.* Chatto & Windus, 1887.

K. de Schweinitz, *England's Road to Social Security.* A. S. Barnes, New York, 1943.

R. J. W. Sellick, *The New Education: The English Background 1870–1914.* Isaac Pitman, 1968.

Nassau W. Senior, *Suggestions on Popular Education.* John Murray, 1861.

H. Silver, *The Concept of Popular Education.* MacGibbon & Kee, 1965.

B. Simon, *Studies in the History of Education 1780–1870.* Lawrence & Wishart, 1960.

B. Simon, *Education and the Labour Movement 1870–1920.* Lawrence & Wishart, 1965.

W. O. Lester Smith, *Education.* Pelican, 1962.

W. O. Lester Smith, *Government of Education.* Pelican, 1965.

W. A. L. Stewart and W. P. McCann, *The Educational Innovators 1750–1890.* Macmillan, 1967.

M. Sturt, *The Education of the People: A History of Primary Education in England and Wales in the Nineteenth Century.* Routledge & Kegan Paul, 1967.

J. C. Tarver, *Some Observations of a Foster Parent.* Constable, 1897.

R. H. Tawney, *The Radical Tradition* (R. Hinder, ed.). Pelican, 1966.

F. Temple, *Oxford Essays: contributed by Members of the University.* John W. Porter, 1856.

B. M. Thompson, *Professional Solidarity Among the Teachers of England.* Columbia U.P., 1927.

E. P. Thompson, *The Making of the English Working Class.* Gollancz, 1963.

F. Thompson, *Lark Rise to Candleford: A Trilogy.* O.U.P., 1954.

J. Thompson, *Forty-Four Years of the Education Question 1870–1914.* Sherratt & Hughes, 1914.

A. Tropp, *The School Teachers: The Growth of the Teaching Profession in England and Wales from 1800 to the Present Day.* Heinemann, 1957.

J. R. Vincent, *Pollbooks: How Victorians Voted.* C.U.P., 1967.

H. Ward, *Notes for the Study of English Education from 1860–1902.* Bell, 1929.

G. M. Young (ed.), *Early Victorian England*, Vol. I. *1830–1865.* O.U.P., 1934.

Index